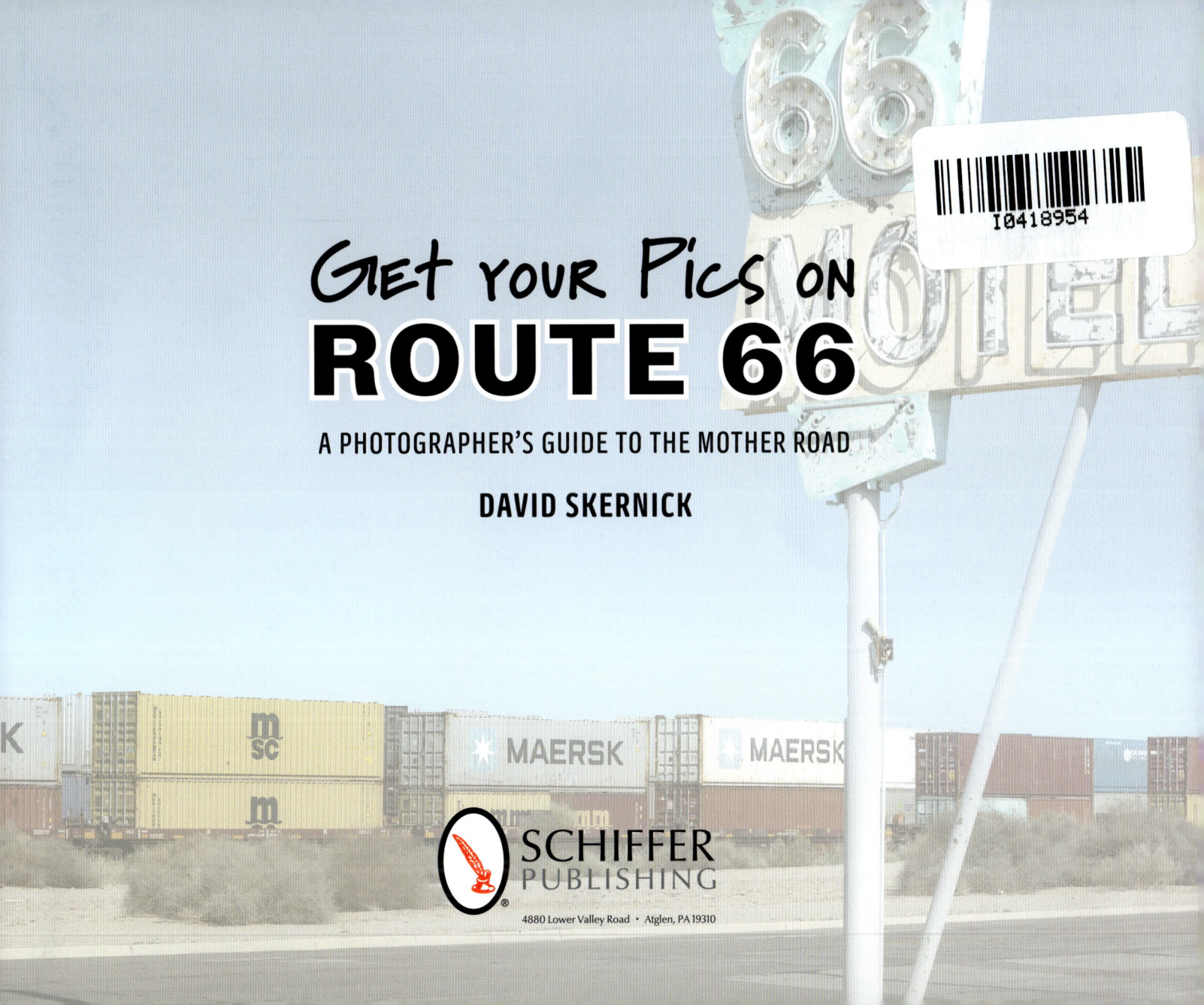

Get your Pics on
ROUTE 66

A PHOTOGRAPHER'S GUIDE TO THE MOTHER ROAD

DAVID SKERNICK

SCHIFFER
PUBLISHING

4880 Lower Valley Road • Atglen, PA 19310

Other Schiffer Books by the Author:
Back Roads of the Southwest, ISBN 978-0-7643-5858-6
Back Roads of the Midwest, ISBN 978-0-7643-6483-9
Back Roads of Southern California, ISBN 978-0-7643-5763-3
How Did You Get That Shot? A Photographer's Journal from America's Back Roads, ISBN 978-0-7643-5728-2
Easy Astrophotography: Shooting the Night Sky, ISBN 978-0-7643-6684-0

Edited by Ian Robertson
Designed by Kate North
Cover design by Kate North
Type set in Marydale Bold/Quicksand Book

ISBN: 978-0-7643-7099-1
Printed in China

10 9 8 7 6 5 4 3 2 1

MIX
Paper | Supporting responsible forestry
FSC® C104723

Published by Schiffer Publishing, Ltd.
4880 Lower Valley Road
Atglen, PA 19310
Phone: (610) 593-1777; Fax: (610) 593-2002
Email: info@schifferbooks.com
Web: www.schifferbooks.com

For our complete selection of fine books on this and related subjects, please visit our website at www.schifferbooks.com. You may also write for a free catalog.

Schiffer Publishing's titles are available at special discounts for bulk purchases for sales promotions or premiums. Special editions, including personalized covers, corporate imprints, and excerpts, can be created in large quantities for special needs. For more information, contact the publisher.

For Barbara and Becky, I hope we will all be together again at the end of the road.

The spirit of Route 66 is in the details: every scratch on a fender, every curl of paint on a weathered billboard, every blade of grass growing up through a cracked street.

—John Lasseter

If you ever plan to motor west
Travel my way,
Take the highway that's the best.
Get your kicks on Route 66.
—Song written by Bobby Troup, recorded by Nat King Cole in 1946

CONTENTS

Introduction

Some people see a sign that says "5-mile hike" as a calling. They are undaunted and might even look forward to longer treks. Some of them don't even take a camera. These are generally the same people who like broccoli. Me? I like to sit on my couch and eat cookies. The couch I like best is the front seat of my Ford F150 truck. When I'm driving "Bob," I feel like I'm sitting on my favorite couch as America rolls by. The only thing that is better is stopping to photograph something special, or to purchase a unique (nonbroccoli) treat to munch on along the way.

If the above rings true with you, especially if you love taking pictures, a road trip along Route 66 may be the perfect getaway. Consider me your guide and photo guy. There have been dozens of books written about Route 66. It is a popular iconic American subject. I used several of them, including *EZ 66* by Jerry McClanahan and an app called Ultimate Route 66 Guide, to help keep track of all the twists and turns. I needed to drive the entire route and all the alignments to pare it down so you can do the trip effortlessly and photograph the sights along the way. In other words, mine is a guide to the photo road trip. I'll give you the town names or stretches of road where we photographed; all you need to do is stay close to Interstates 40, 44, and 55 and look for the signs and landmarks mentioned. I'll guide you to some of the wildlife refuges and state and national parks along the way as well, because who doesn't love to photograph nature and animals? This book will keep you on the pavement and help you find the best of the "Mother Road" within 500 feet of your car, truck, or motorcycle. Walking around and hiking is always an option. You will find plenty of places to stretch your legs.

Route 66 was one of the original US highways. Established on November 11, 1926, the highway became one of the most famous roads in America. Commonly known as the "Mother Road," "Main Street of America," "America's Highway, "the Will Rogers Highway," and simply "Route 66," it was recognized in popular culture by a hit song, the *Route 66* television show in the 1960s, and of course the *Cars* movie in 2006. The original road began in Chicago, Illinois, and wound through Missouri, Kansas, Oklahoma, Texas, New Mexico, and Arizona, finally ending in Los Angeles, California. It went through major cities such as St. Louis, Tulsa, Albuquerque, and Flagstaff, as well as small towns such as Galena, Cuba, Oatman, Tucumcari, and Amboy. There are still some good-sized stretches of the old road, and all kinds of

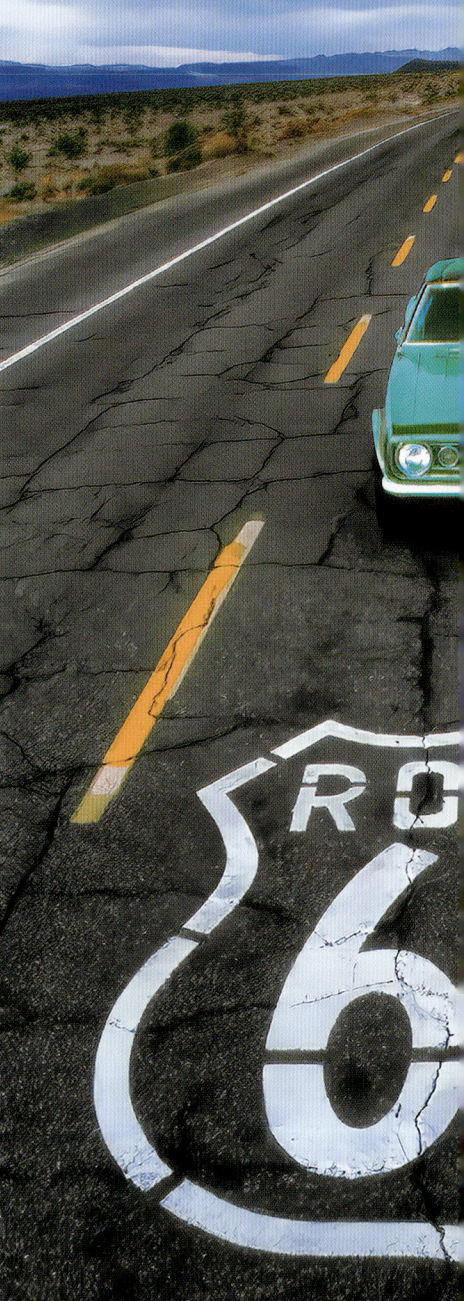

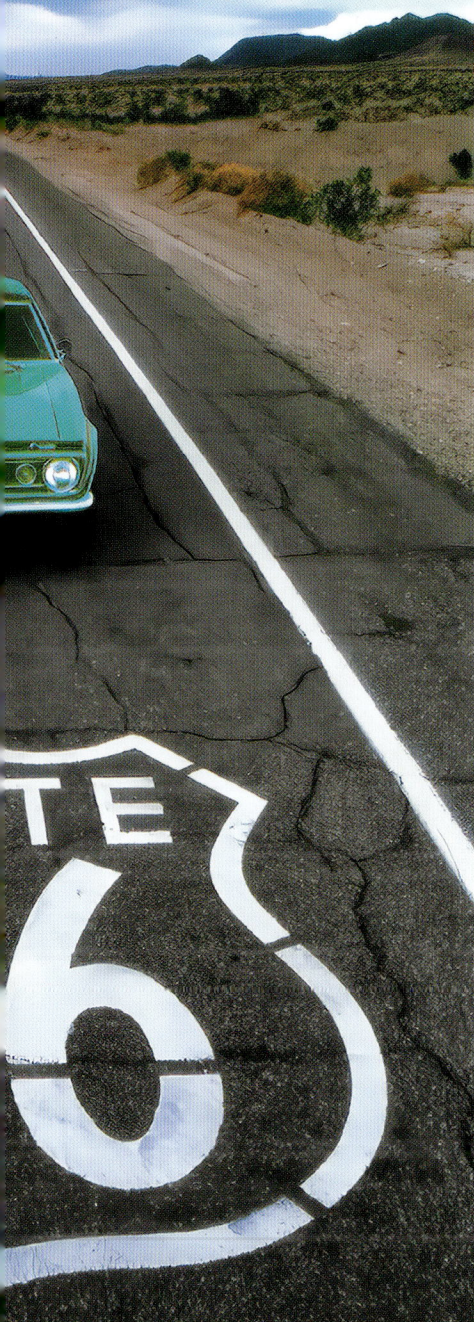

original and refurbished businesses along the way. We are going to drive it the other way—that is, from Los Angeles to Chicago.

The easiest way to follow the road is to, um, follow the road. There are signs everywhere, starting in Santa Monica. Again, I'm not talking about uncovering every mile and brick of the original high-way, instead keeping to it when it is easy to do. Interstate 40 through California, Arizona, New Mexico, and Texas and into Oklahoma replaced much of the road in those states. Keep your eyes open. There are countless exits clearly marked with the "Historic Route 66" sign. Get off at these exits, and you will be on well-paved roads that follow a large percentage of the old route through many towns full of the cool stuff I'll show you in this book. You will have to spend some time on the in-terstate in these states. In Arizona there is a long, 140-mile stretch of the Mother Road. Starting in Oklahoma, you can keep to Route 66 with very little or no freeway driving at all for about 400 miles. This is the longest continuous stretch of Route 66, although the actual highway numbers may vary. In Oklahoma City, Interstate 44 replaces the 40 as the closest freeway. You can continue to follow Route 66 easily through Missouri. At St. Louis, our accom-panying freeway becomes Interstate 55

all the way to Chicago, but again, you can pretty much keep to Route 66 if you follow the signs, apps, and this book.

There are many places where you can try different "alignments" of the old route. Our road changed course over the years to accommodate towns, businesses, and so on. Most are clearly marked. I will men-tion and suggest that you try some of these alternate roads. Be aware that some of the landmarks will change or actually move. Many are sold and traded to different people or towns. For example, the Gemini Giant was removed from his launchpad in Wilmington, Illinois, but I have been assured that he will show up back in Wilmington in his new spot soon.

I have included some of my most talented students' work alongside my own. They see things differently and look for completely unique things to photograph. Including their work will give you tons of ideas so you can find your own way to see and capture Route 66 with your own cameras.

I have met folks on the great road from all over the world. It would seem that the one thing we all agree on is that Route 66 is incredible. I dedicate this book to all of us—to world peace! Let's all get together on Route 66, take some photos, eat ice cream and cheeseburgers, and just have a good time!

◄ 1966 Camaro on Route 66 near Amboy, California
Gayle Pepper

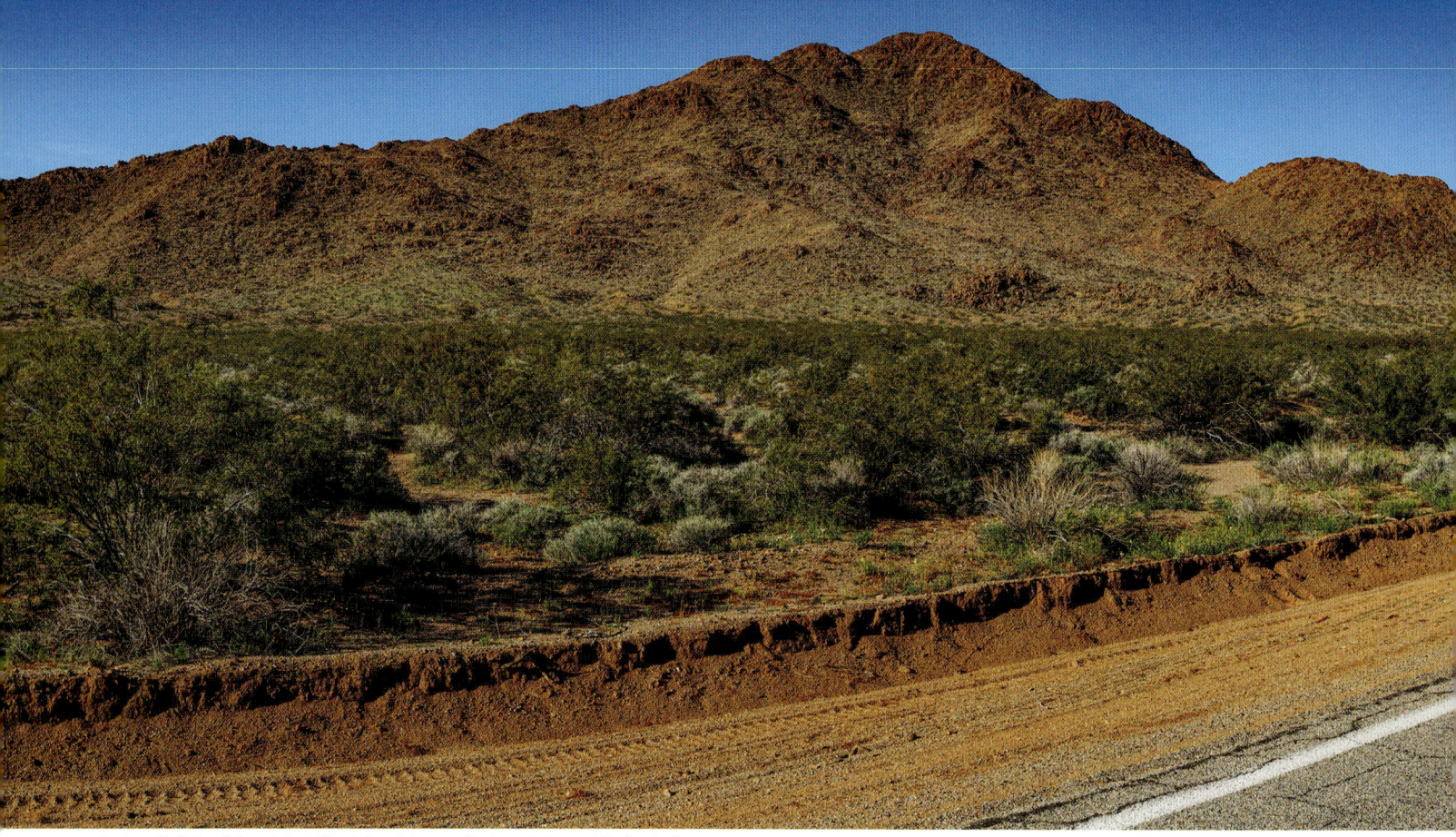

Route 66 (Goffs Road) through the California Desert, between Newburry Springs and Needles, looking west

How to Use This Book

I'm writing this book as if you are riding along next to me. I'll show you the sights and help you get the best photos you can. I'll share photo tips about the art of composition and camera settings and technique. No special equipment is needed. Whatever you like to shoot will be fine. If you are a "serious" photographer, you will have tips on f/stops, shutter speeds, ISO, lens use, and so on along the way. You have access to all of our settings in the appendix, as you always do with my books. If you are a more casual photographer, with maybe a phone for a camera, I will help you compose your photos to make a chosen statement and a better photograph. In either case, I will just sort of be there with you, sharing ideas and trying to help.

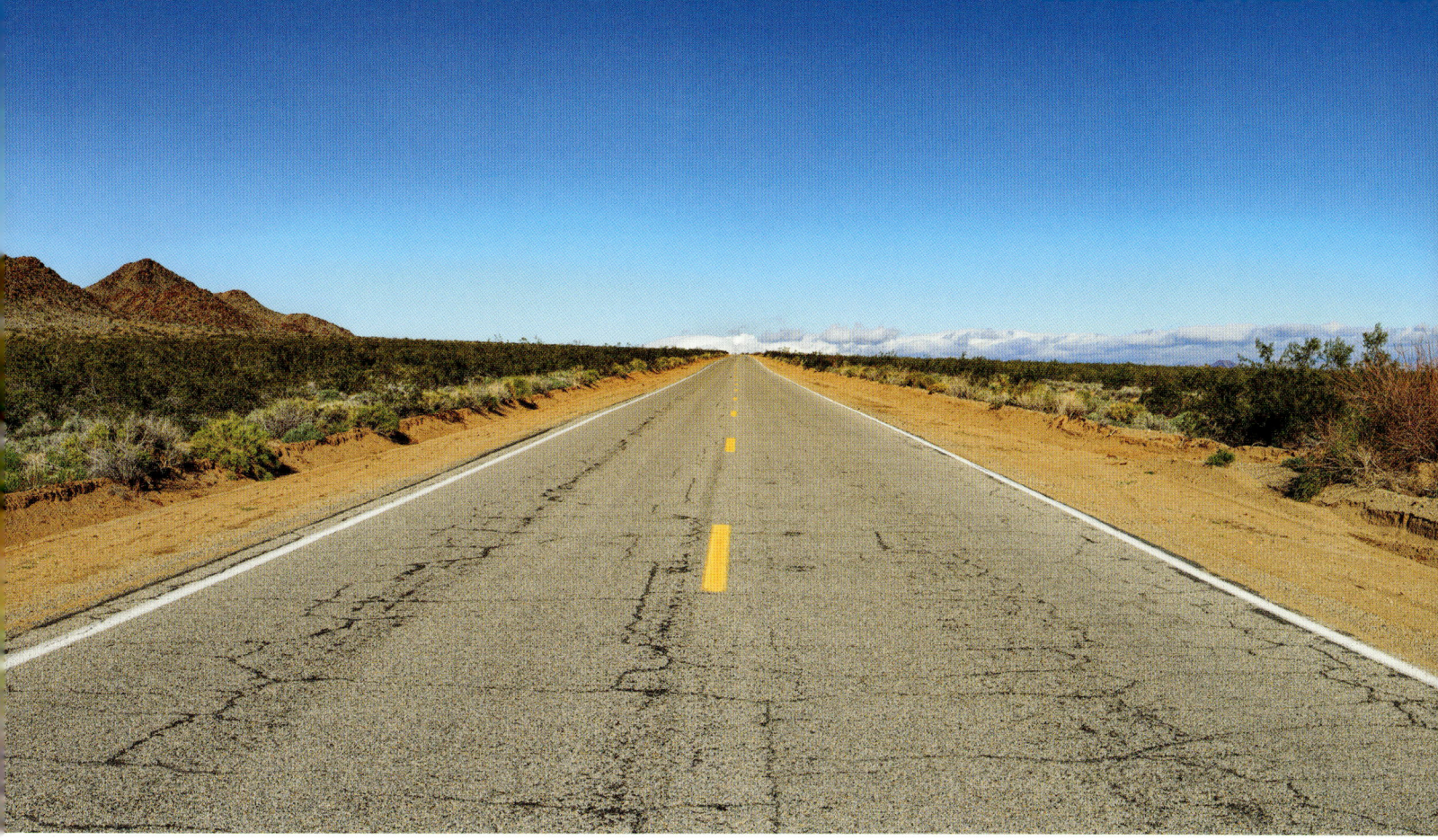

Use this book as a guide to the things my students and I found to photograph. The page headings will tell you where each photo was taken. You can just follow the photos and look for the sites. If you read all the tips, maybe you will get more ideas about how to best render your own personal images. You should also look at the credit lines. I picked very particular students to contribute to this book. Each photographer has a specific and unique eye. You might find that you like the way Becky or Barbara sees, or maybe someone whose name doesn't begin with a "B." The most important thing is to stay on the route and keep your eyes open! Route 66 is a treasure trove of cool stuff to photograph.

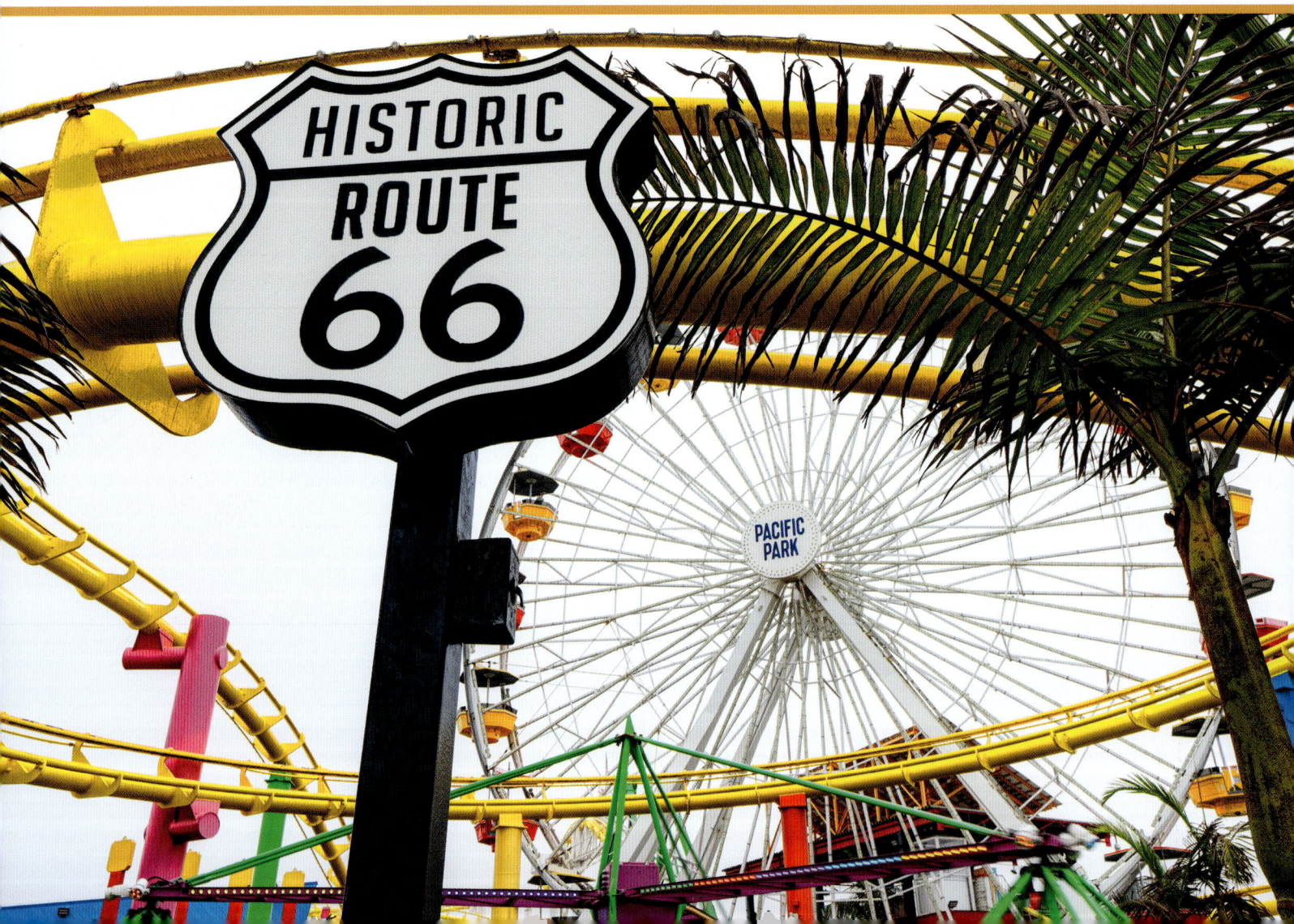

This book starts in Santa Monica, California, and ends in Chicago, Illinois. Pretty much all the other Route 66 books start in the east and head west.

They always say that you should just read them backward if you want to go the other way. Okay—same for us, but here is why I recommend the west-to-east itinerary.

Every good photographer knows that if you are shooting with any camera from the cheapest point and shoot to an 8 × 10 view camera, it is best to keep the sun at your back. The light is always better that way. So, if you are going to drive close to 2,500 miles looking for photographic opportunities, wouldn't you want the sun at your back?

If you drive with me, you can sleep in a little every day, have a yummy breakfast at one of the terrific diners along the way, and have good light in front of you until sunset.

At Oklahoma City our route heads north. Go outside and face north and south just about any time of the day. Which has better light? The northern sky almost never includes the sun, but the southern sky often does. Photographing toward north is always better than south.

I suggest early spring or late fall for your trip. Better light and better weather. Summer can be insanely hot in the desert, and you might get heavy snow along the northern route in the winter. As you'll see in this book, I once had snow in Arizona in February! Route 66 close to Halloween is always fun. The decorations are fantastic!

One last thing before we roll out on Route 66 together. I don't like power lines and poles in my photos. It's a choice. If you don't mind them and accept them as part of the modern scene, or as an enhancement to your composition, great! My students and I sometimes leave them in for just those reasons. I believe that our art is to photograph what we see, not always exactly what is there.

The first step is to try to find an angle where you can hide lines, poles, and anything else that you feel detracts from your subject. Often I find that in doing that practice, I will find a better angle of view for my composition than I may have found without being forced to walk around. The last line of defense is postprocessing. In Photoshop, I use a combination of content aware fill, the clone stamp, the remove tool, and the spot-healing brush to remove lines, poles, and anything else that I can't avoid and feel detracts from my composition. Again, this is an artistic decision. There is no right or wrong here. Approach each image independently.

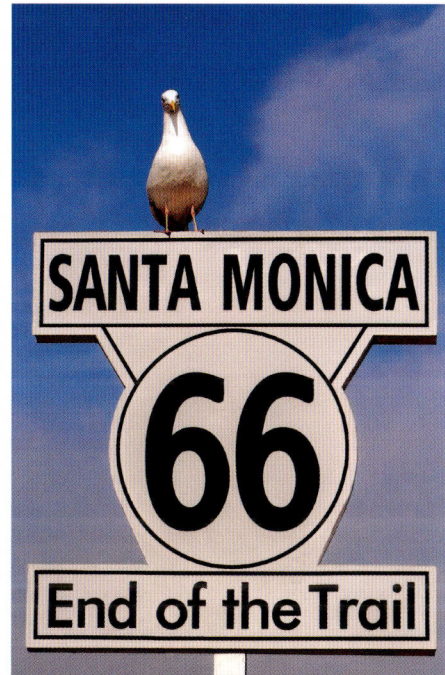

Santa Monica Pier, California   *Anne Schlueter*

◄ Santa Monica Pier, Los Angeles, California, the western terminus of Route 66 and the starting point for our trip
David Skernick

Los Angeles, Highland Park, and Pasadena, California

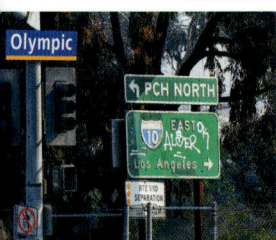

Alternate western terminus
David Skernick

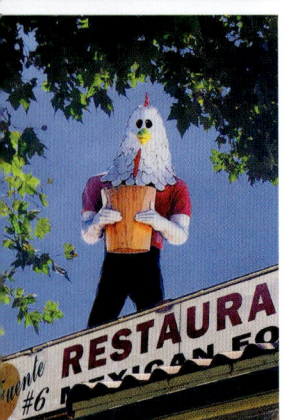

Chicken Boy, Highland Park, California
David Skernick

Although most people agree that the Santa Monica Pier in California is the official western terminus of Route 66, some still say that the original end of the road is in Los Angeles, at the corner of Olympic and Lincoln. Today there is no sign or mention of Route 66 at that location. Nothing to see here, folks.

Chicken Boy is our first real Route 66 icon. At 22 feet tall, the fiberglass statue towers over the businesses in this small neighborhood. It has graced several locations along Route 66 since the '60s and is now on a rooftop just north of downtown Los Angeles at 66 Figueroa Street. Arnold Schwarzenegger recognized Chicken Boy with the Governor's Historic Preservation Award in 2010.

I used my iPhone to take Chicken Boy's picture. It's a busy area, and I found it easier to get the low angle through the trees with my phone. Any camera can create a one-of-a-kind fine-art photograph. Of course, sometimes we just want to capture a memory. I was excited to spot Chicken Boy and am happy to have the photo to share the find.

It took eighteen months to construct the Colorado Street Bridge in Pasadena, California. Construction was completed in 1913. It connected Pasadena to Los Angeles and became part of Route 66 from 1926 to 1940. The bridge has been known as "suicide bridge," since more than one hundred people have jumped to their deaths into the Arroyo Seco below. A number of spirits are still said to wander the bridge and the Arroyo to this day.

Closed after the Loma Prieta earthquake in 1989, the bridge was reopened in 1993 and can be enjoyed with all of its original ornate detail. A suicide prevention rail was also added.

When Jackie and I went out in search of photos of this grand old bridge, we found traffic and private property. These are the usual challenges of photographing in cities. We found a few spots to shoot some nice abstracts and details, then found the Desiderio Neighborhood Park. Here we finally discovered some angles where Jackie could use the wide-angle lens she wanted to use to show the size and breadth of the 150-foot arches that define this magnificent bridge.

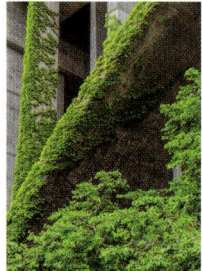
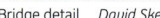

Bridge detail   *David Skernick*

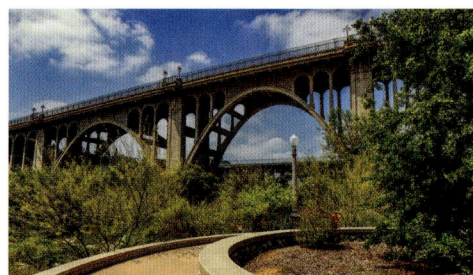

Colorado Street Bridge, Pasadena, California   *Jackie Rosenthal*

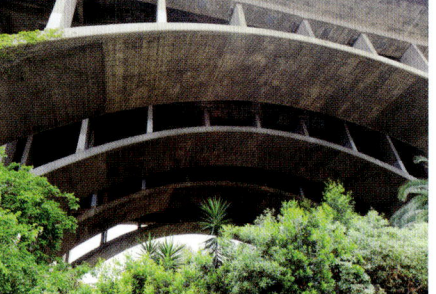

Colorado Street Bridge, Pasadena, California   *Jackie Rosenthal*

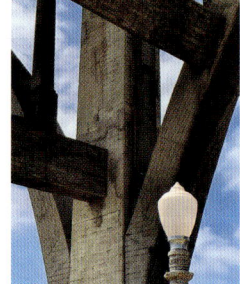

Bridge detail   *Jackie Rosenthal*

Rancho Cucamonga and Rialto, California

As you drive east from Los Angeles, the city will seem to just go on and on. You will actually be going through a series of smaller cities and towns, but over the years they have all sort of melded together.

Strip malls, fast food, and other businesses roll endlessly by on Foothill Blvd. (Route 66) as you navigate your way toward the desert and the rest of the Mother Road. Keep your eyes open and you will see many Route 66 signs and the occasional photo op!

The two stops pictured on the right were our favorites the day we drove this part of the road. There were some others, but these were the ones that had me screech Bob the Truck to a stop. The Historic Cucamonga Service Station was under renovation at that time so we skipped it.

The Lantern sign was taken with my phone. It was one of those times when I needed to be too close to the traffic to get the angle I wanted, so the phone was easier, faster, and safer.

This is the first of two Wigwam Motels you will see as you motor east on Route 66. The other, in Holbrook, Arizona, comes up later in this book. These are working motels where you can book a tepee for the night!

Pepper took this beautiful detail photo and processed it with a warmer tone. It's your shot—the compositional and processing decisions are yours to make. I took a huge double pano. Kathi chose her phone to create her pano of the Wigwam Motel room interior. It was amazingly roomy in there, but the phone was a good choice, as it so often is!

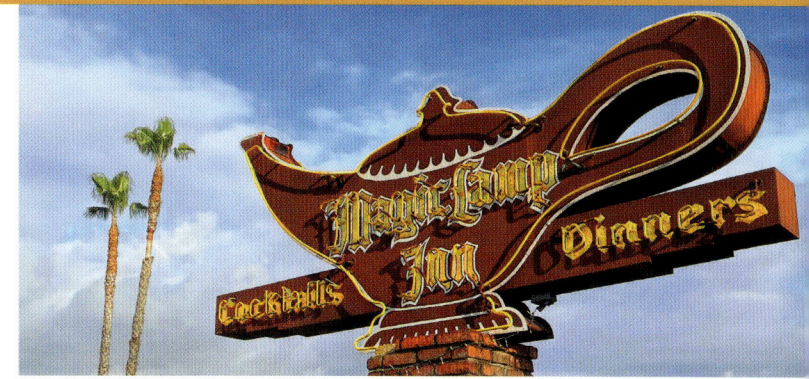

Magic Lamp Inn, Rancho Cucamonga, California · David Skernick

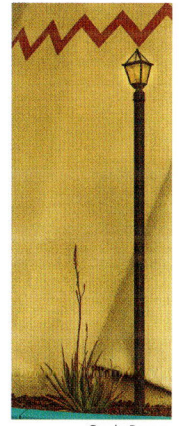

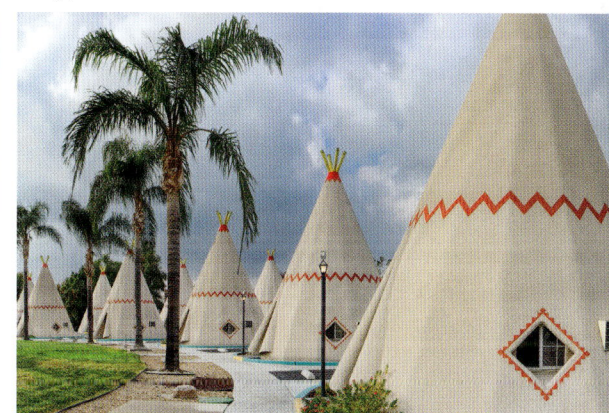

Gayle Pepper · Wigwam Motel, Rialto, California · David Skernick

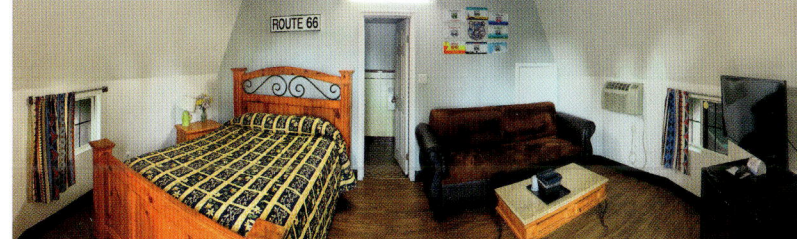

Wigwam Motel interior, Rialto, California ▶
Kathi Mangel

Victorville and Oro Grande, California

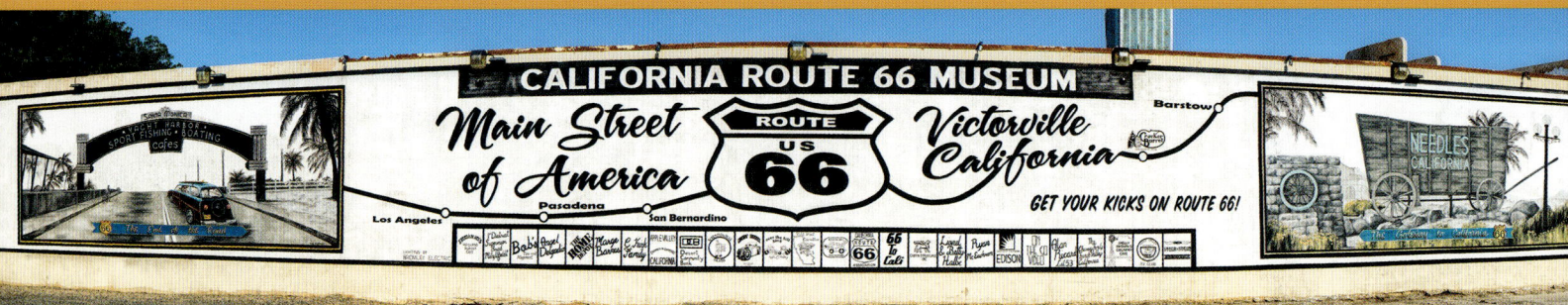

California Route 66 Museum mural, Victorville, California

David Skernick

Look for the National Old Trails Highway (Route 66) in Victorville, California. There is a Route 66 Museum, and I found this cool mural. Murals are natural panoramic subjects, but you can photograph them with wide-angle lenses or create your own composition by isolating different areas with normal or telephoto lenses.

The focal length of a lens determines what kind of lens you have. Very generally, 50mm is what you see with your own eye. Something 4 feet away looks like it is 4 feet away. A 50mm lens has always been considered a "normal" lens for that reason. Lower focal lengths, such as 28mm or 18mm, give you a wider angle of view and make the objects and scenes in your shot appear farther away. Conversely, lenses with focal lengths above 50mm, such as 100mm, 135mm, or 300mm, are telephoto lenses. They appear to bring your subject closer or allow you to isolate a small area of your total scene. Zoom lenses have variable focal lengths and therefore provide amazing versatility. They offer you the most-efficient and least expensive lens options.

"Prime" or "fixed" lenses have only one focal length and are therefore sharper than zooms. They are typically "faster" as well. This means they open to wider apertures, such as f/4.0, f/2.8, or even f/1.4. This increases the light coming into the camera, so you can use a faster shutter speed.

You can stay on Route 66 all the way from Victorville to Barstow, California. The photo below was taken along the way as I entered the town of Oro Grande. I have heard that the Cross-Eyed Cow Pizza, shown here, makes an incredible pizza. I was there too early to find out for myself, but the early-morning hour provided the perfect light for this photo. Sometimes you have to make painful choices.

Cross-eyed cow, Oro Grande, California ▶
David Skernick

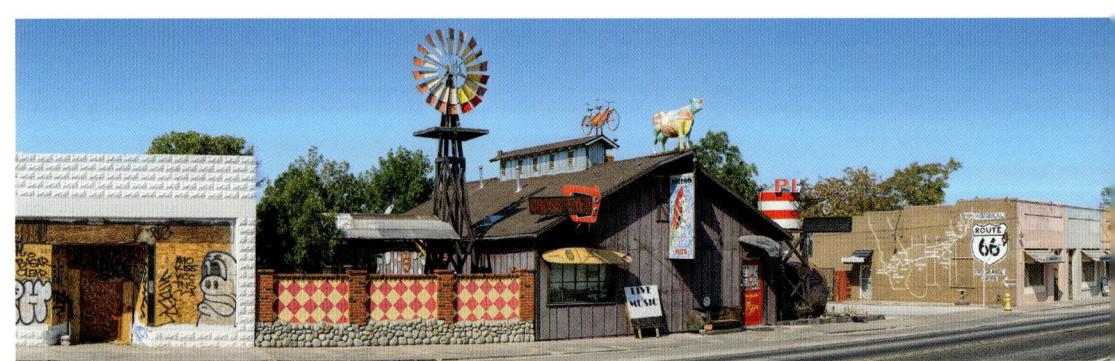

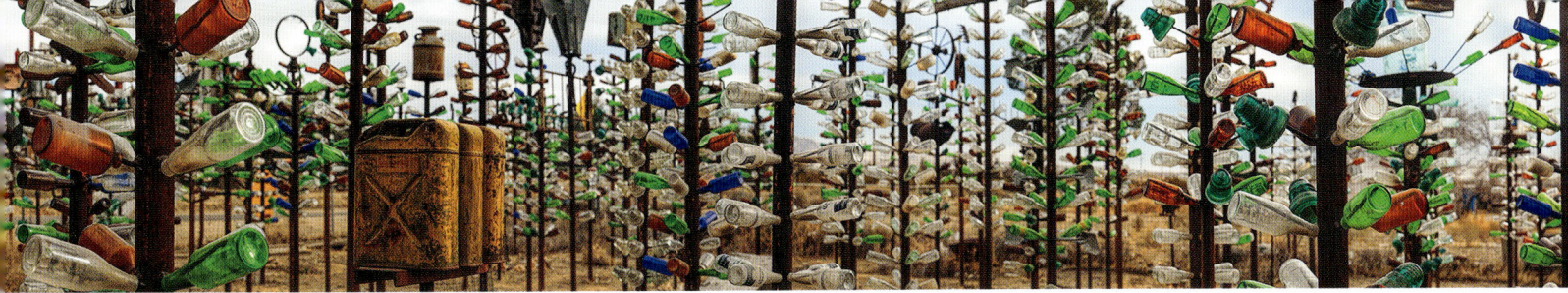

Elmer's Bottle Ranch, Oro Grande, California

David Skernick

Elmer Long had a passion. He collected bottles. He found them in the desert, in abandoned houses, in the streets, and so on. Trained as a welder, Elmer was a scrap metal artist, as well as a collector. He created over two hundred bottle trees out of scrap metal and bottles. The "ranch" covers about 2 acres and is free to the public. I was fortunate to meet Elmer a few years before his death in June 2019. He told me the love of bottles started with his father, who had always collected them for as long as Elmer could remember. The ranch is still open. Elmer's family keeps it up and running. Roadside attractions are one of the things that make Route 66 special. Even though we just got started, this is one of my favorites.

I chose to photograph Elmer's Bottle Ranch with a panoramic photo. As a photographer, I was trained in the art of seeing things through the confined dimensions of a 35mm piece of film, approximately 3:2, slightly wider than tall. I have worked within these boundaries, but it never felt quite right. I found myself secretly envious of painters, who could select any size of canvas on which to create art. When I found panoramic photography, I realized I had discovered my unrestrained canvas. Panoramic photographs are carefully crafted from multiple photographs that are combined to form one large image. With panoramas, I can photograph without traditional framing limitations. I feel that panoramas are best able to convey what you would have seen had you been standing there beside me when I took the picture. This is exactly the way I want you to feel when looking at this and many of my photos.

Kathi saw Elmer's Bottle Ranch as an opportunity to shoot details. She used slightly longer lenses (a 105mm and a 135mm) to isolate specific bottles. Note how conscious she was of the direction of light and how much that raises the quality of her images.

You always want to "fill the frame." What I mean is, use your entire viewfinder to describe your composition. The open sky enhances this composition. It was a good choice to include it.

The bottles lean to the right. It is best to have them on the left, where they have room to point. This is called looking space or nose room.

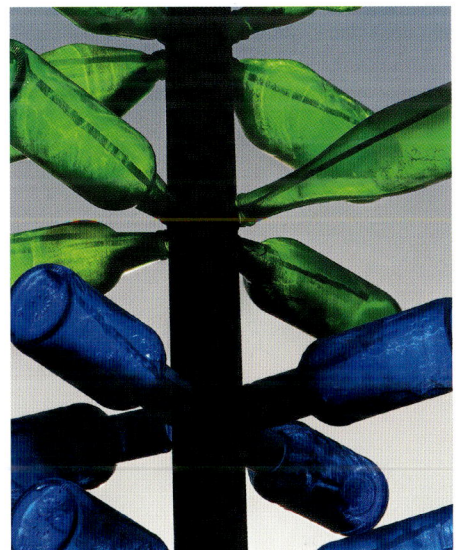

◄ Bottle tree detail
Kathi Mangel

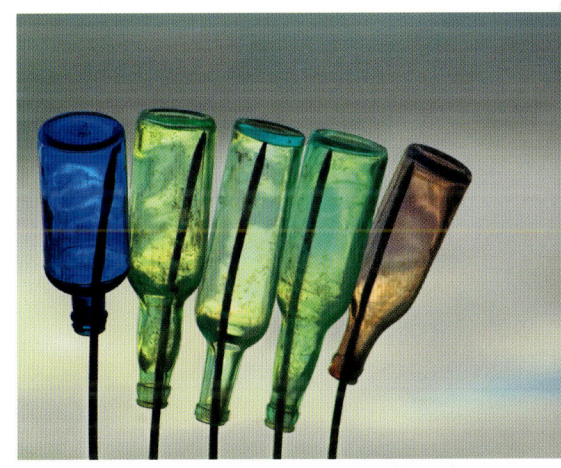

Bottles   Kathi Mangel

Newberry Springs and Amboy, California

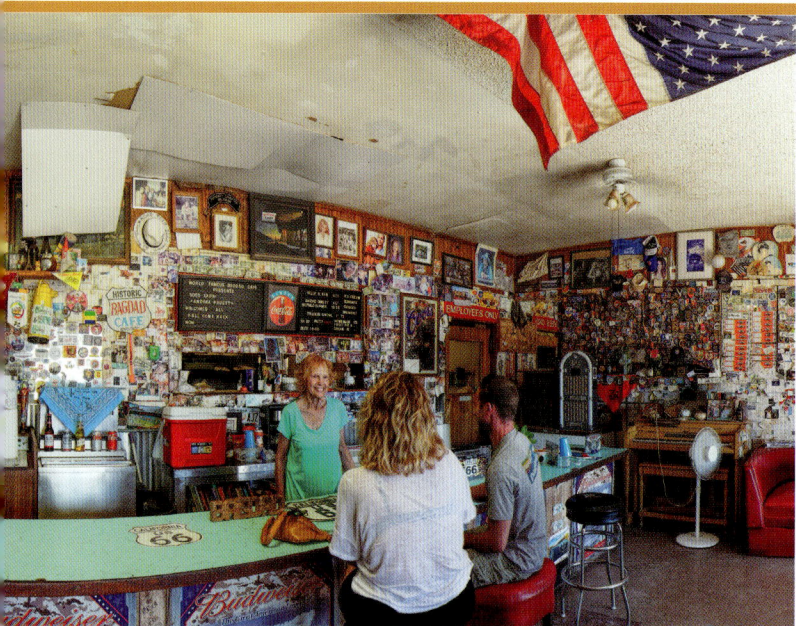

Andrea at the Bagdad Cafe, Newberry Springs, California

David Skernick

Interior shots on Route 66 are a great way to tell the story of the Mother Road. They are uniformly inviting and cluttered with souvenirs and memorabilia.

This is the Bagdad Cafe in Newberry Springs, California. It is one of the iconic destinations along the Mother Road.

Andrea has owned the café for almost thirty years. The couple sitting at the counter are from France. People come from all over the world to follow Route 66. I sent this photo to Andrea, and it is now included as just one more thing for tourists and Route 66 enthusiasts to look at on the wall as they enjoy a cheeseburger and a soda.

Becky took great pains to keep her photo of Roy's Cafe in Amboy level to offset that cluttered look that all Route 66 interiors seem to share. It is best to use a sturdy tripod to pull that off. Most cameras have a menu setting that will show you a grid in your viewfinder. That will help you level a shot like this, or the one above. Many cameras have levels that can be accessed through their menus. There are also small levels made to attach to your camera on the hot shoe. That's the place where an auxiliary flash would attach.

Crooked photos, unless intentional, look wrong from the start. Often you will need to "square" yourself to your scene, which means being lined up in front and at the same height. You can't always do that. Sometimes you want to be on an angle, or you are looking up or down. In those cases, choose the vertical or horizontal axis and make it straight. Becky squared herself to her subject, but in my photo above I chose to shoot from an angle, so I made the vertical axis straight.

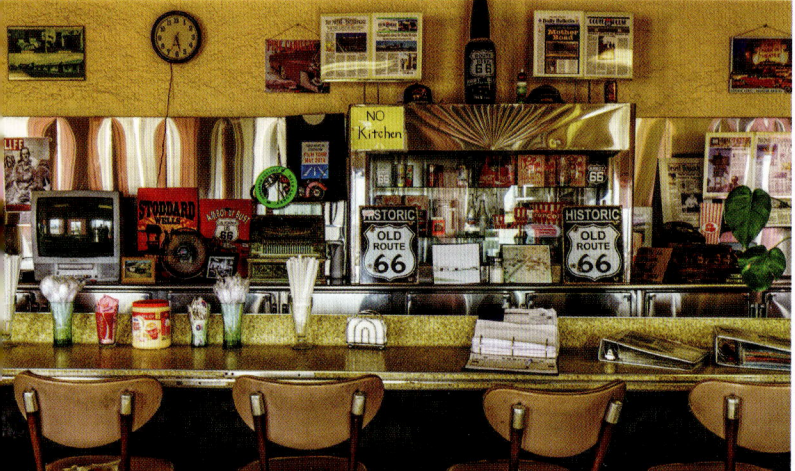

◄ Roy's Café, Amboy, California
Becky Waters

Roy Crowl opened Roy's in 1938 as a gas and service station along US 66 in Amboy, California. Back then, Route 66 was the primary road between Chicago and Los Angeles. If you were headed east or west, you were on the Mother Road. Crowl and his son-in-law Herman "Buster" Burris added the café, a repair garage, and the auto court. By the '50s, when the town's population was around seven hundred, the Roy's complex employed seventy people. In 1972, Interstate 40 opened and bypassed the small town of Amboy. All the businesses failed almost overnight. There are plans for restoration that have included a Kickstarter campaign to restore the sign. The entire town of Amboy was listed for sale on eBay. The highest bid was $995,900, but the listed value was $1.9 million.

I have photographed Roy's many times. This photo was taken from across the street. That angle allows you to see the San Bernardino Mountains in the background.

Overcast can be wonderful light because it is not directional. Being able to shoot in all directions is a fantastic advantage when you are on the road and can't wait around or come back for the best time. I also liked the stormy weather this day because it made the little cabins look like safe havens. In truth, they will need quite a bit of work to be habitable again.

Roy's Motel, Amboy, California ▶
David Skernick

Becky took this wonderful photo at night from down the road to the left. By including the edge of the café, she made the houses look even safer and more inviting. Always remember that your photos tell the story you want to tell, not always the actual circumstances. In other words, photos *do* lie, or at least they can. Try to make your statement obvious by making conscious decisions about everything that impacts your image.

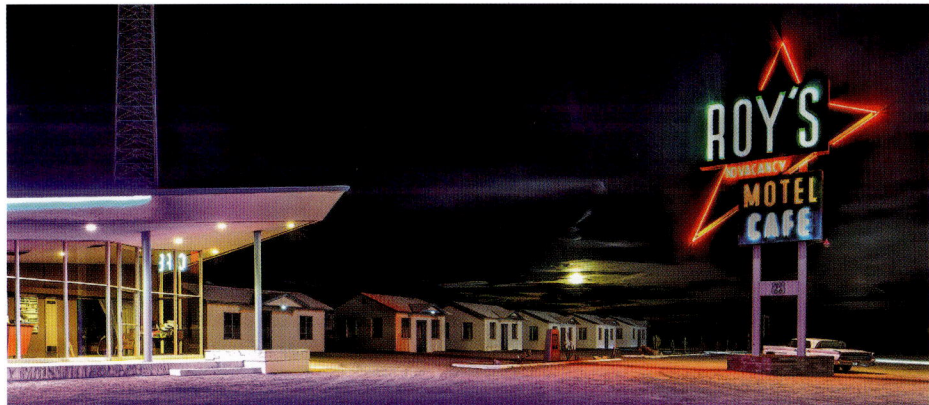
Roy's Motel at Night, Amboy, California   *Becky Waters*

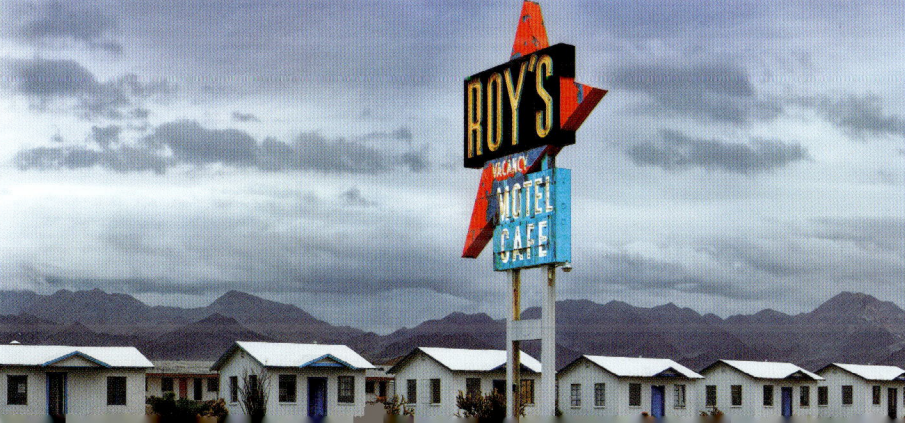

Needles, California

Needles, California, is the last town you will find along Route 66 heading east before crossing into Arizona. The town was formed when the Southern Pacific Railroad, Atlantic and Pacific Railroad, and Santa Fe Railroad all joined together to form the 35th Parallel Transcontinental Railroad in 1883. The railroad workers made Needles their home.

Route 66 rolls right through Needles. There are many murals, old buildings, and signs of the old road. I was happy to find this one with trains going by behind it. I thought they both helped tell the story of the town and filled out the composition nicely. Sometimes no clouds is the perfect sky. Look for the subject and angle that works with the background and sky you have.

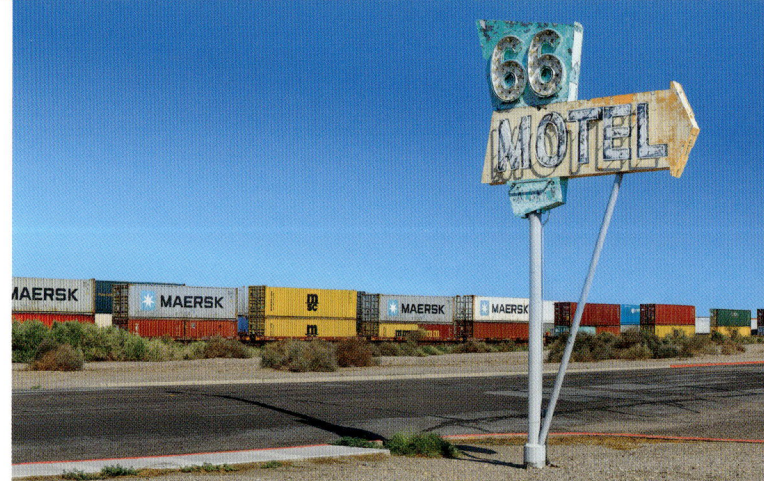

66 Motel, Needles, California   *David Skernick*

Good food in Needles! The pizza here is tasty, and check out the Wagon Wheel Restaurant for a great meal! The skillet pot roast is incredible. My waitress was right. She said, "It's all about the sautéed mushrooms."

The woman walking the dog happened by as I was taking this panorama. I think she makes the shot! I liked the sign on the theater, but without her, the dog, and that fantastic shadow, the blank wall might have overwhelmed my composition. I wanted to include the building so I could also include those terrific clouds just that way. The luck of someone walking her dog made it all come together.

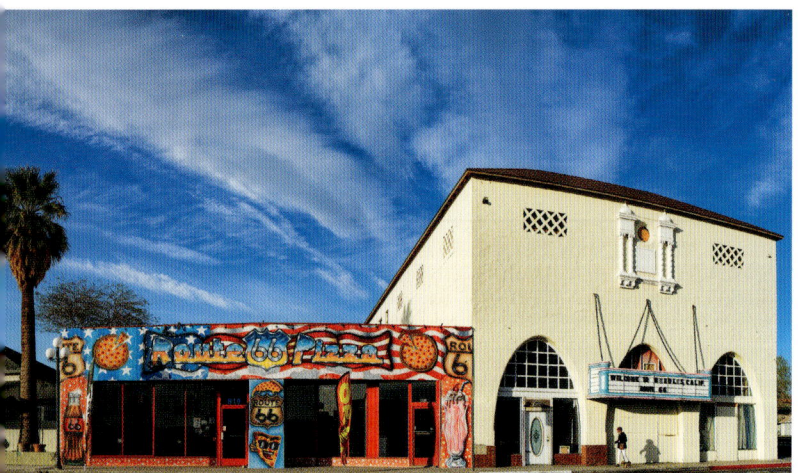

Route 66 Pizza and Theater, Needles, California   *David Skernick*

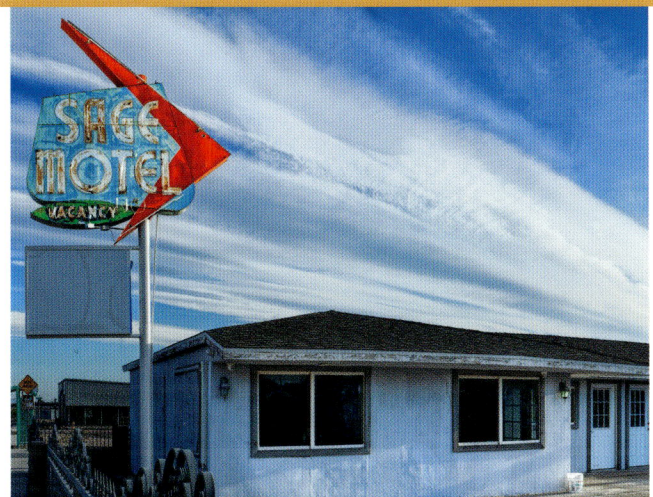

Sage Motel, Needles, California

David Skernick

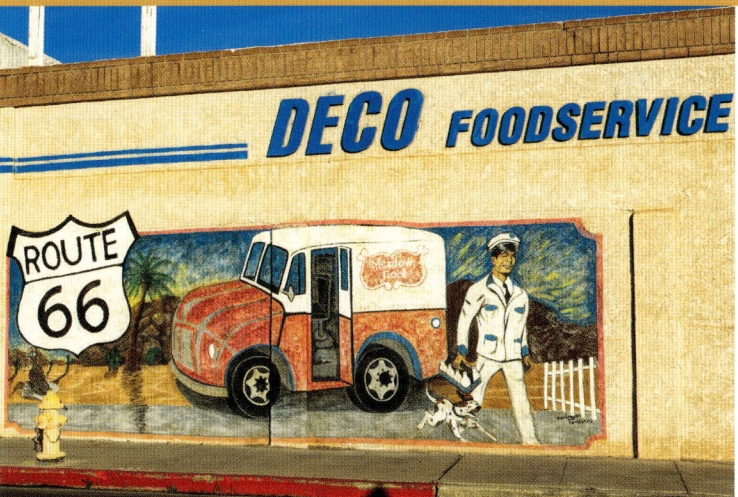

Mural at Deco Foodservice, Needles, California

David Skernick

There are many murals around Needles. These were just a few that caught my eye and were in the right light when I was there. The Sage Motel is closed, but there was a truck there, maybe doing repairs. So many Route 66 businesses are being refurbished and brought back. It is wonderful to see the old road becoming new again. It's almost as good as shooting the old, weathered stuff!

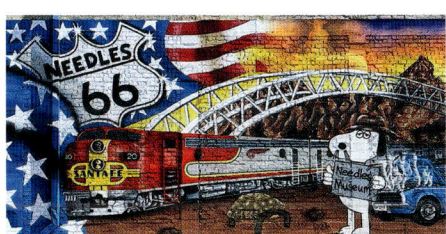

Route 66 Museum mural, Needles, California

David Skernick

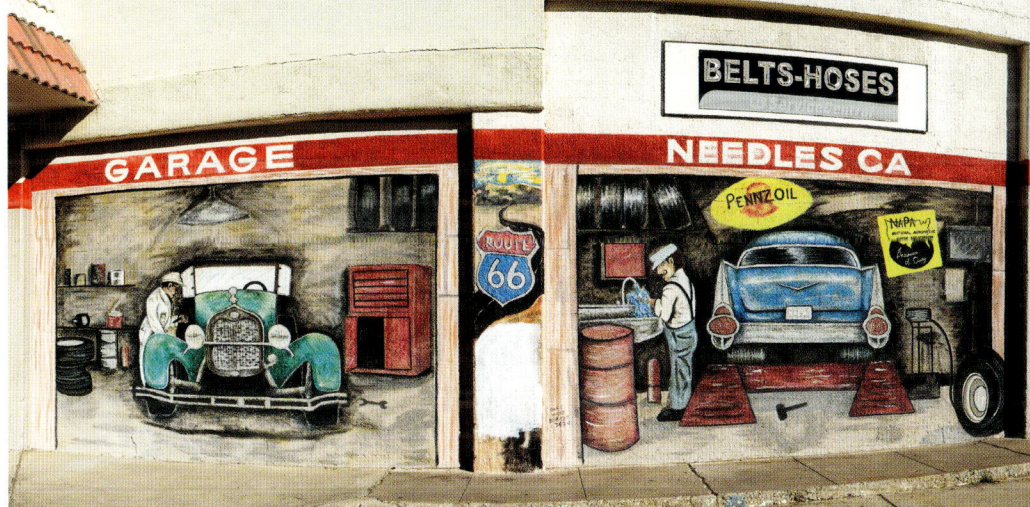

Garage mural, Needles, California

David Skernick

Havasu National Wildlife Refuge, Arizona

Topock Marsh is an inlet covering 4,000 acres within the Havasu National Wildlife Refuge. It is just east of Needles, California. Get off Interstate 40 when you see the historical 66 sign pointing you toward Oatman, Arizona, and you will find it. The marsh represents more than 40 percent of what remains of the backwaters of the Colorado River. It is populated by songbirds, waterbirds, migratory waterfowl, and other wildlife. I came across this snowy egret convention in the spring.

Snowy egrets, Topock Marsh, Arizona

David Skernick

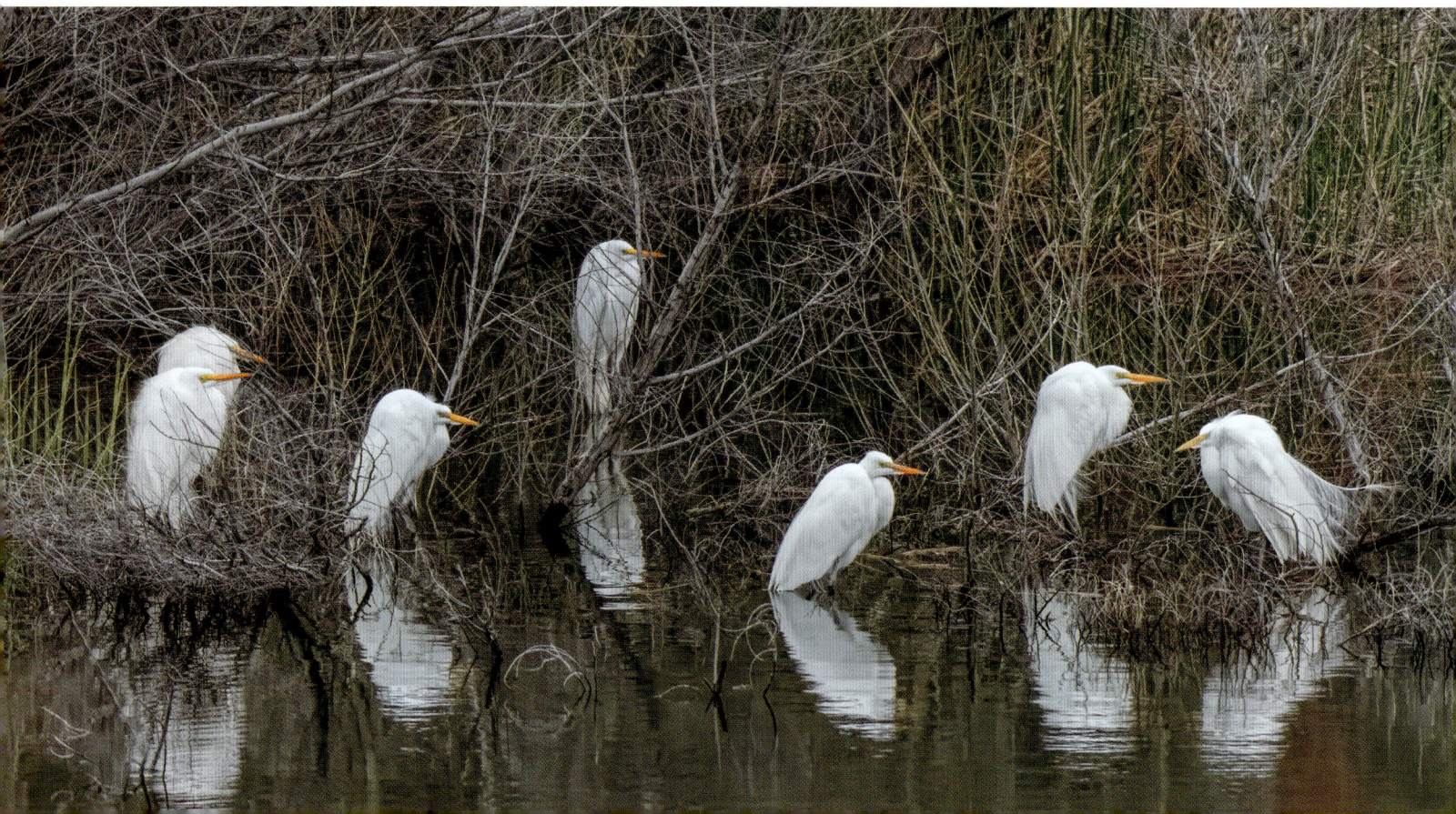

When I photograph birds, I use a long lens and a fast shutter speed. I won't even try to capture a photo at less than 1/2000. They move fast and are—well—twitchy.

Birds are constantly grooming themselves. For the shot on the facing page, I waited patiently for ten or fifteen minutes to get all the beaks showing at the same time.

Using the continuous setting so that you can shoot multiple photos per second might help you capture that perfect moment. You should shoot in short bursts. Be intentional with your timing and just use the bursts to give you a better chance of getting exactly what you want. I saw the lizard in the bird's mouth on the left but concentrated on getting all three birds in the shot as separated as possible. I counted on the burst to capture a good angle on the poor lizard.

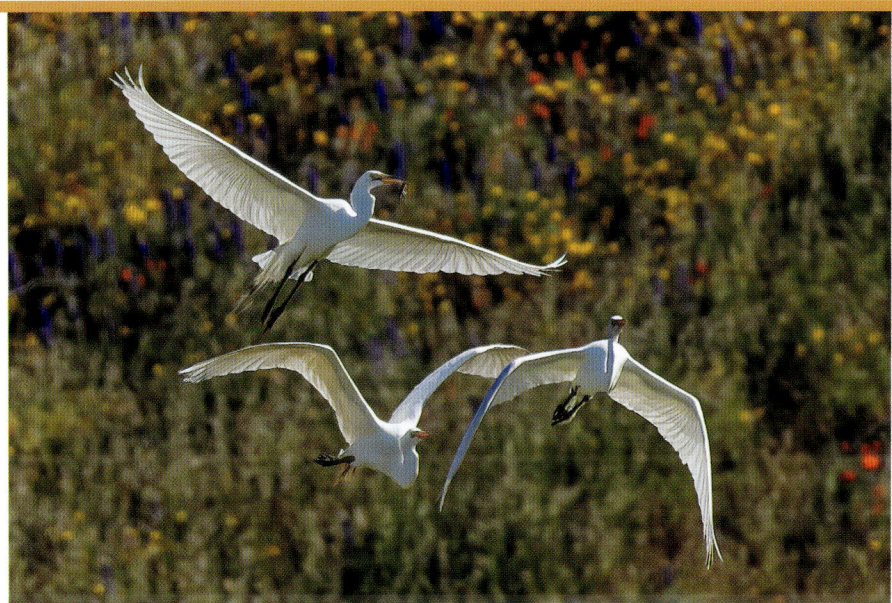

Egrets in flight

David Skernick

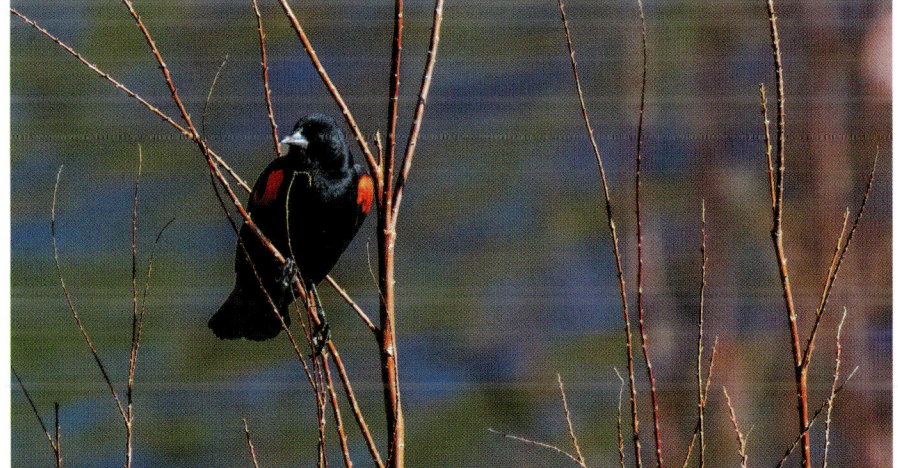

When shooting a single bird, try to shoot as they come to a position. If you wait, they might move, and you will miss that perfect moment. They move fast—like I said, "twitchy"—so you might get a blur even at a fast speed.

Try to catch light in their eye. That's actually called a "catch light." Be patient and wait for them to turn into the light. Last, birds have a translucent nictitating membrane, sometimes called a "third eyelid." This membrane closes or blinks across the eye from front to back. Be patient to get a shot when the eye is clear.

◄ Red-winged blackbird
David Skernick

16

Trains on Route 66

Trains are a special part of the Route 66 experience. The road runs alongside much of the Transcontinental Railroad. You can expect to see trains often as you enjoy the Main Street of America.

This train was parked, so it was easy to get up close with a wide-angle lens and show both the size and the length of the beautiful engine. The panorama helped me include the entire train. At the back of the book, check out the appendix to find all the camera and lens choices, as well as the settings used for each photo. Also listed are how many levels and exactly how many photos make up each of the panoramic photos. The image on the right was made with twenty-four separate photos taken across two levels. That is two rows of twelve photos each.

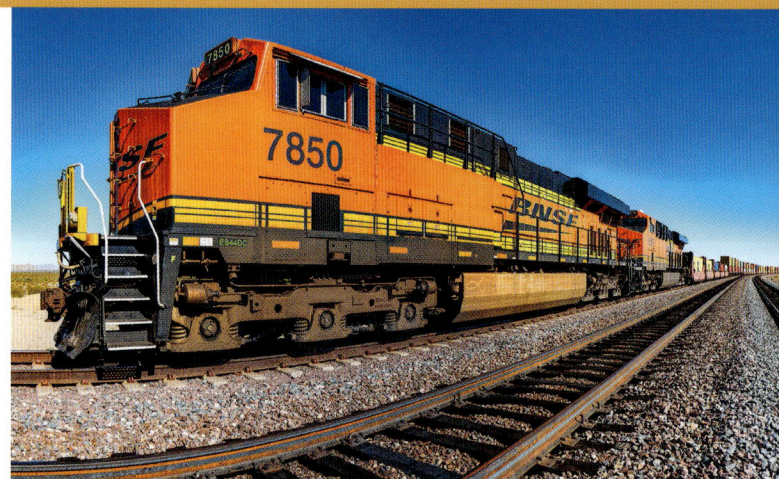

BNSF Railroad, California/Arizona border

David Skernick

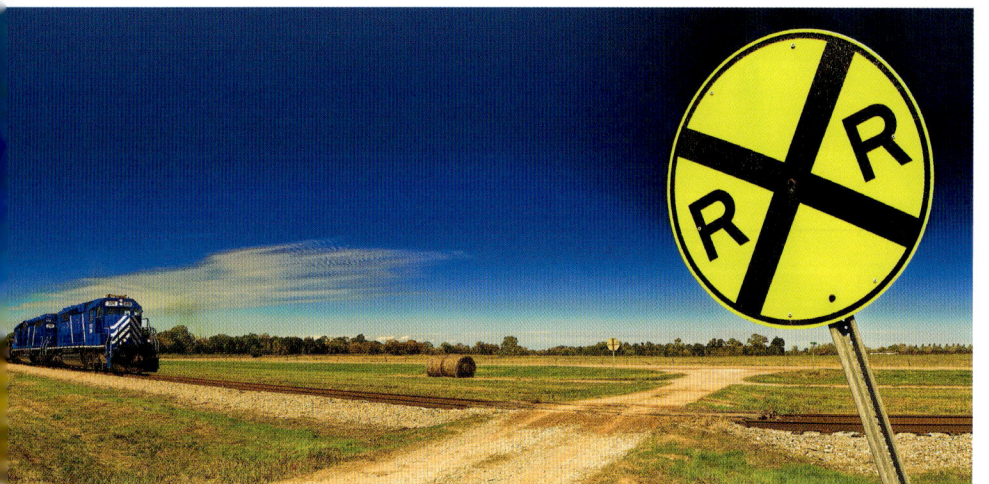

Train in Oklahoma

David Skernick

There are as many ways to depict trains as there are trains themselves. Here I waited for just the moment when the sign would appear huge and the train would look small.

Look for trains in every state as you travel Route 66. If you find a perfect spot for a shot, it might be worth waiting for a train to come along. They seem to come often. Make sure the tracks look used. Lots of rust and grasses growing up and around the rails may be a sign that you are waiting for a train that will never come.

Oatman, Arizona

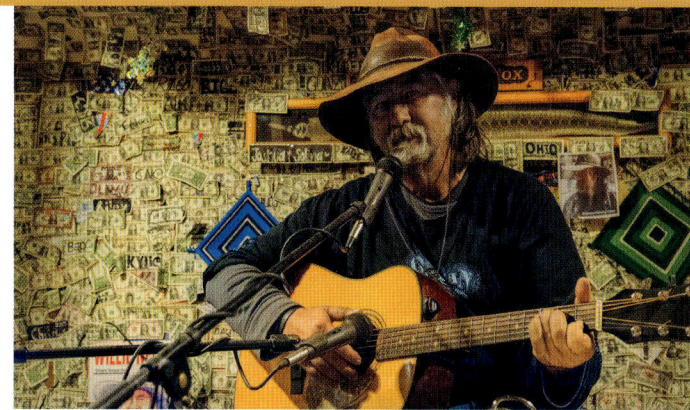

Once upon a time, in the 1860s, a gold-bearing ore shoot was discovered in a prominent quartz vein outcrop near what became Oatman, Arizona. The mining town is in the Black Mountains of Mohave County, Arizona. Driving up to the town at 2,710 feet on winding roads gives you a taste of how isolated the town once was. Today it is a tourist attraction, but it is still a place of history. In the summer there are Wild West shows and scores of people wandering the old streets and in the buildings. Even in the off-season, you won't have Oatman to yourself, but it will be quieter!

You should find it well worth your time to visit Oatman. Whatever the season, it is an interesting old town with some good photo opportunities. Founded in 1906, it is the only genuine Old West town along the Mother Road.

Singing cowboy, Oatman Hotel *Kathi Mangel*

The best food we found was at the Oatman Hotel. Check it out. It is full of interesting exhibits about the town's history. Kathi set her ISO to 25600 to get a shutter speed fast enough to keep the musician from blurring. Flash would not have looked as natural. Yes, that is cash on the wall of the restaurant inside the Oatman Hotel. There must be thousands of dollars, euros, pesos, and so on pasted on those walls! Judy found a spot where she could fill her frame with different bills from all over the world.

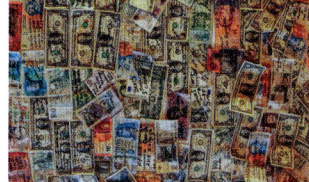

Oatman Hotel in Oatman, Arizona, sign
David Skernick

Cash Wall *Judy Nussenblatt*

The one constant in Oatman is the wild burros. They are the descendants of those used by the miners of the past, who then abandoned them when they left town.

Today, Oatman donkeys roam the city streets freely and head to the Black Mountains to graze and sleep at night. Although it is illegal to feed them, they remain forever hopeful and will walk right up to you. They can be found on the roads leading up to and away from Oatman, as well as walking around Main Street in town.

Interaction between animals is always a way to get a special shot of wildlife. Wait for it and you might get lucky.

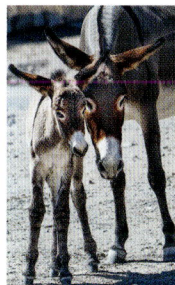
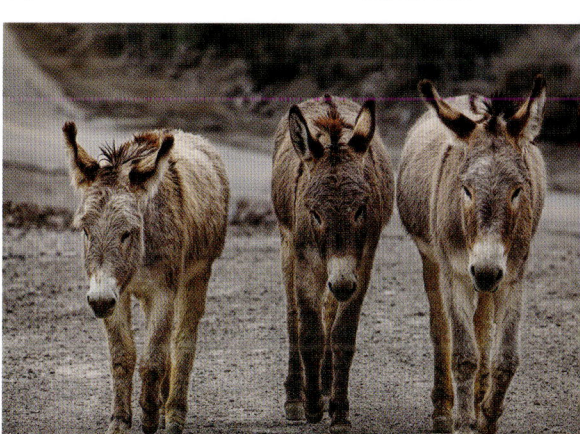

Wild burros, Oatman, Arizona
David Skernick

Wild burros, Oatman, Arizona ▶
Monica Bayless

Oatman to Kingman, Arizona

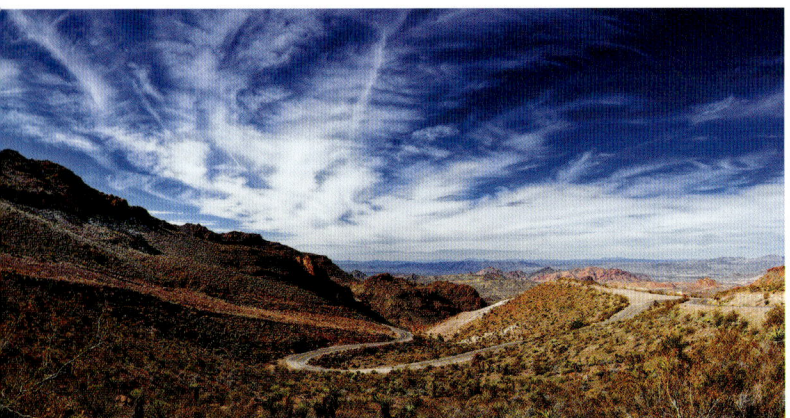

Sitgreaves Pass, Arizona

David Skernick

In western Arizona, for about 140 miles from Topock to Ash Fork, you can drive the original Mother Road on two-lane highway uninterrupted by interstate freeways. Coming from the west, Oatman was our first stop along that stretch of road.

This is Sitgreaves Pass. It is Route 66 between Oatman and Kingman, Arizona. Also known as the Oatman Highway, this mountain pass is approximately 50 miles long and 3,586 feet high at its highest point. It's a narrow, winding road that can be a little scary even now with four-wheel drive. Bob the Truck is a Ford F-150 and seemed a little too big as I drove into some of the tight switchbacks near the summit. I can only imagine navigating this ride in the 1920s and '30s with the cars and trucks of that time.

Teddy bear cholla, or jumping cholla, is native to northwestern Mexico and the southwestern United States. As a photographer, I like this cactus because it catches and seems to radiate light. It is great to shoot front or backlit because of this. I found this grove growing along the Oatman-to-Kingman stretch of Route 66 early in the morning in pretty light.

Be careful around this cactus! They call it "jumping" because it seems to leap out and attach to anything or anyone that comes close. It can be very hard and painful to remove. Yep, I speak from personal experience.

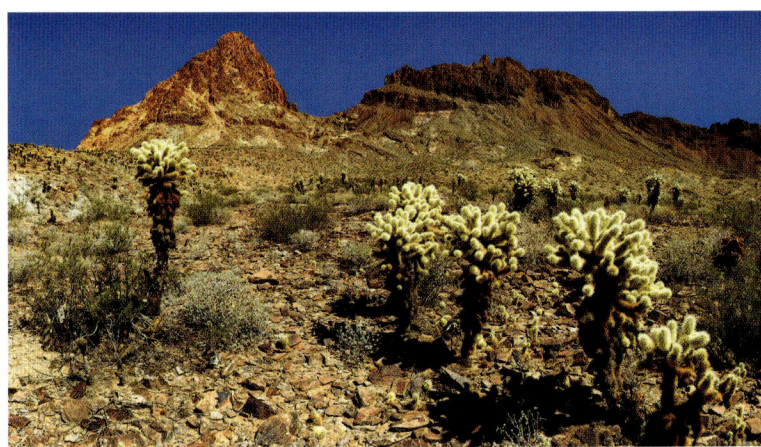

Teddy Bear Cholla, Oatman Road, Arizona

David Skernick

Cool Springs Station, Kingman, Arizona

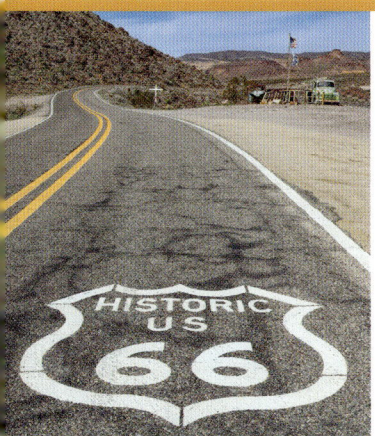

Route 66, Cool Springs Station, Arizona *Carol Zulman*

Cool Springs Station is a good place to stop before Kingman to pick up a cold drink and have a conversation with one of the many Route 66 experts along the way. These friendly folks always seem happy to talk and pose for photos. They have great stories and new information about the old road.

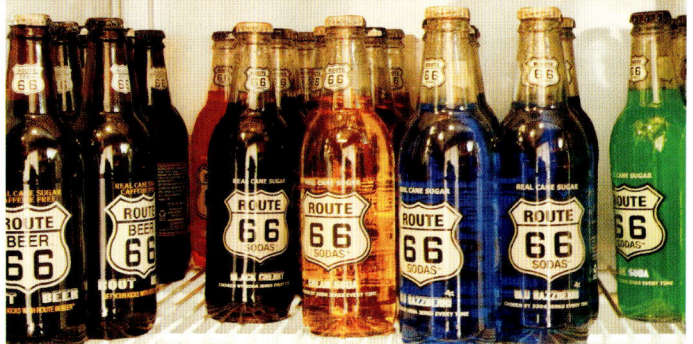

Cool Springs Station, Arizona *Judy Nussenblatt*

The old Route 66 road signs are gone. They have all been taken by souvenir hunters. These painted signs are nice and will last longer. Carol included Cool Springs Station up on the right of this wide-angle road shot, while Judy grabbed a cool drink and shot with a more "normal" lens. Notice how differently the two lenses render their scenes.

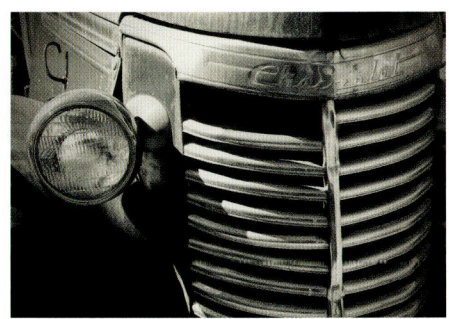

Chevy Grill *Susan Vizuary*

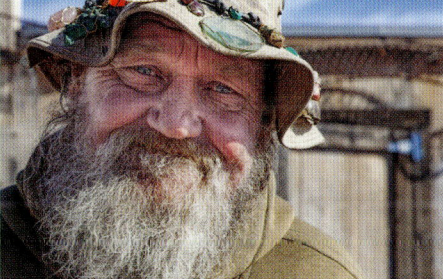

Cool Springs Station *Monica Bayless*

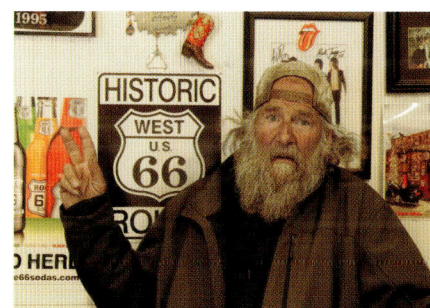

Cool Springs Station *Judy Nussenblatt*

Above you can see three different types of portraits. I call Susan's grill a portrait because I believe that she has rendered an image that portrays personality by isolating that particular detail of the car, and by choosing to process her photo in black and white. There is no doubt that both Monica and Judy portrayed personality by consciously choosing background, focus, and timing. When photographing a person or animal, the exact moment you choose to shoot is critical, whether you are using an $8,000 DSLR or an old phone. If you are good, you might just catch someone in the act of being themselves.

Kingman, Arizona

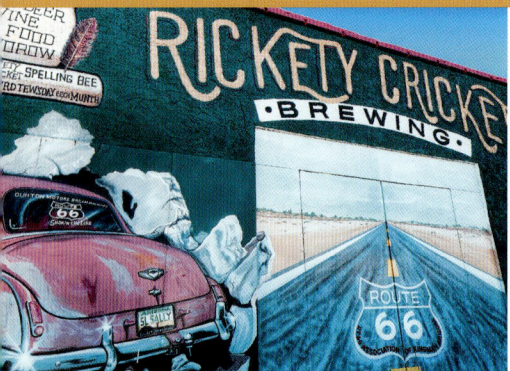

Barbara Balik

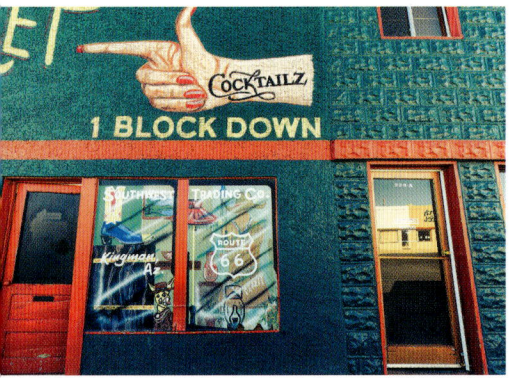

Rickety Cricket, North Beale Road,
Kingman, Arizona   Barbara Balik

Kingman, Arizona, is a good place to stop, enjoy the Route 66 experience, and get a room for the night. Although Kingman is a fairly large city, you can stay on Route 66 and go through just a small part of it, avoiding the traffic and congestion that comes with any city. Stay close to Andy Devine Avenue (Route 66). There are lots of motels and Route 66 attractions both on and just off that road.

Take the fork onto North Beale Road. It runs parallel to Route 66 for a couple of blocks. Look for a huge "Welcome to Kingman" sign. You'll see some great Route 66 stuff to photograph. Note that even though walls are flat, Barbara needed to use f/11 to ensure constant focus, since she is about 5 foot 2 and these walls are around 15 feet tall. Looking up is the same as looking out. You need to increase your depth of field to keep everything in focus.

Shooting signs at night is easy. Just expose for the sign. That means if there is a ton of black sky, your camera may overexpose the photo trying to light the sky. As long as you fill the frame with your subject, as Susan did here, you won't have any problem at all. Susan chose an angular composition. Everything you do should be intentional. If you prefer a straighter shot, take it. Just do it on purpose, and it will never be "wrong."

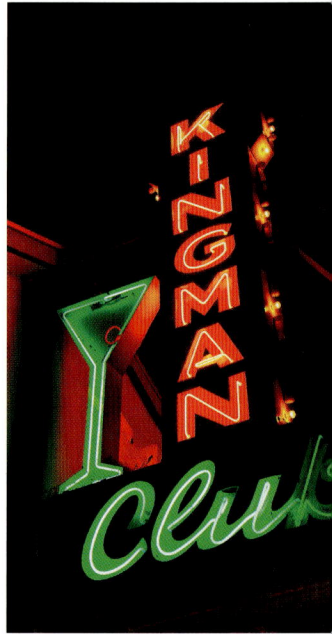

Kingman Club, Kingman, Arizona   Susan Vizuary

Primp My Pet is on Route 66 in Kingman. The composition is super-tight to hide the other buildings in the background. I wanted this, and only this, in my shot. Try to find just the right angle to isolate what you want.

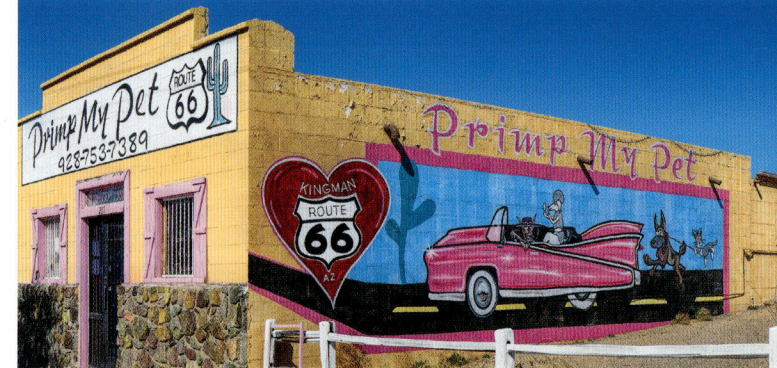

Primp My Pet, Kingman, Arizona ▶
David Skernick

21

Not only is Mr. D's the best hamburger in town, it is also a terrific place to take a night photograph! The full moon? Well, yeah, a photographer should always pay attention to the phases of the moon when you are traveling. I like the app "Sun n Moon." It is one of those no-brainer free apps that works every time. If you are more serious about astrophotography, I suggest the "Photo Pills" app.

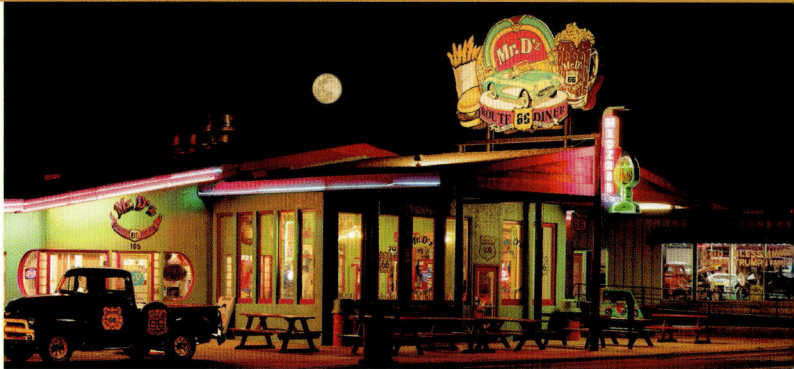

Mr. D's, Kingman, Arizona

David Skernick

Now, speaking of the moon. It was really there—right where you see it in this shot. However, the exposure for the moon would be different than the exposure for the building. To avoid the moon blurring, your shutter speed needs to be at least 1/60 (for a moon, this relatively small in your photo), but preferably 1/80–1/125. You can increase your ISO if you need to make your shutter speed faster. Even though the shutter speed may suggest otherwise, always use a tripod and be sure to use a self-timer, mirror lockup, exposure delay mode (Nikon), and a cable release to eliminate any camera movement from the shot, especially if using a long lens. The smallest vibrations can have a huge impact on sharpness.

My shutter speed for Mr. D's was 1/20. That would have blurred the moon into a football shape and overexposed the moon to the point of losing all detail. The only solution was to take two photos: one exposed for the moon and one exposed for the rest of the shot. Then I had to put them together in postprocessing. This is pretty advanced stuff. If you want to

pursue it, Schiffer Publishing has published another book that I wrote with my friend Brian Valente. That book will give you exact step-by-step recipes for all kinds of night (astro) photography and postprocessing. *Easy Astrophotography* is available online, or at your local bookstore. Sorry for the commercial.

Consider these two photographs of the same sign. It is obvious that Susan and Judy visited Kingman at two different times, during two different seasons. I've heard students deciding on which of my workshops to attend say things like, "I've been there already, so I want to go somewhere else." I get it. You have limited time to travel and want to spend your time seeing new things. As a photographer, I argue that returning to a location, especially a favorite one, in a different season is always worth doing and is often like seeing it as new all over again. Notice how leaving the power lines gives you a feeling of cold wind sweeping past the sign.

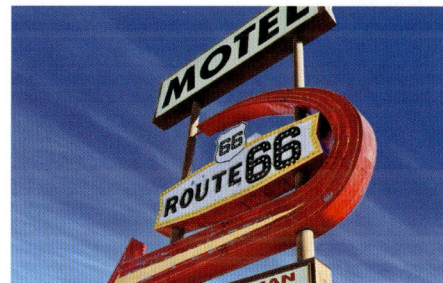

Motel Route 66, Kingman, Arizona

Susan Vizuary

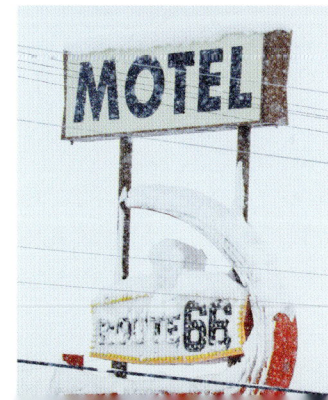

Winter ▶
Judy Nussenblatt

22

Giganticus Headicus, Kingman, Arizona

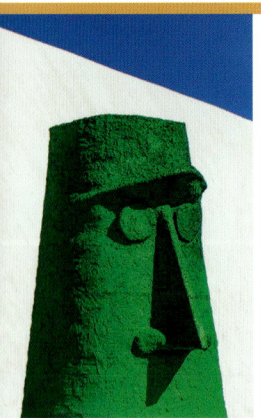

Headicus detail
Gayle Pepper

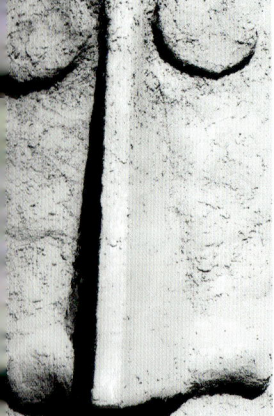

Headicus close-up
Gayle Pepper

About 25 miles east of Kingman, look for "Giganticus Headicus" on your left. It is a giant, tiki-style head created in 2004 by Gregg Arnold. This is another one of my favorite Route 66 icons.

I took a wide double panorama, including the 14-foot head on the "snow trip," while at another time Pepper shot two very creative versions. By using the building and sky as elements, rather than just as backgrounds, she brought out the lines of the statue and rendered it more as a piece of art than just a funny big head. In black and white and further isolated, it takes on a whole new look. Pepper said she was going for a midcentury modern look. I love people who can look at something like Giganticus Headicus and think of midcentury modern art. I think she achieved her goal.

Everywhere you go on Route 66, there are old cars and trucks. Susan used an 18mm lens and got super close to distort the truck and nail this shot!

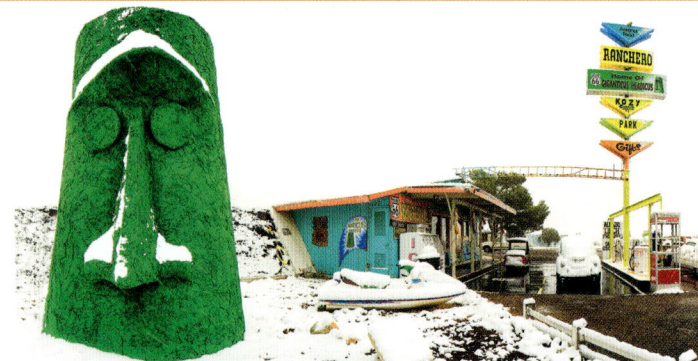

Giganticus Headicus, Kingman, Arizona
David Skernick

One of the times I drove past Giganticus Headicus, I had my dog, Dudley, with me. Yeah, I had to stop for a photo. I chose my phone and a low angle to get an awkward, silly view and to accentuate my pup's head. Putting his ears back was Dudley's idea. I love it when a model knows how to pose.

The story you choose to tell is always your own. Art, whether it be drawing, sculpting, photography, or any other, is the only place in life where you can get exactly what you want. Make your statement unique and personal, even if it's just funny!

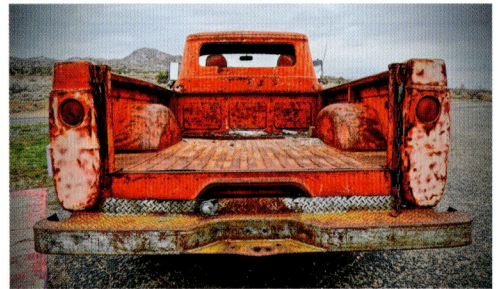

Old truck
Susan Vizuary

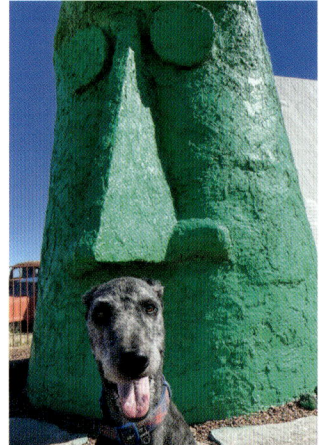

Dudley
David Skernick

Kingman to Seligman, Arizona

As you head east out of Kingman on old Route 66, the next big town you will come to is Seligman. Along the way, there will be several places worth a stop. Some of them are on the following pages. Keep looking around as you drive. Although I have driven Route 66 many times, my books are not in any way meant to be exhaustive depictions of everything that is along any road, but collections of photographs of what I (and in this book, my students) have found that impressed us at that particular time in that particular light. I hope you will find many things that we may have missed or passed up, or that look different to you when you drive down the Mother Road. Send me some photos! I'd love to see what you find!

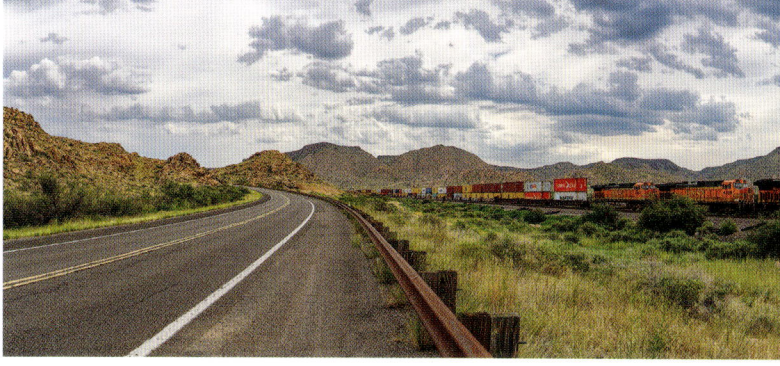

Route 66 east of Kingman, Arizona *David Skernick*

The season or time of day that you come across something you might want to photograph will always change the way that thing appears. Now add to that the weather, the light, and the mood you are in, and the picture changes even more. And after all that, there might be a train! Every time I drive this stretch of Route 66, it looks different. You can see that each photo was taken from a slightly different location, but they are within a quarter mile of each other.

The photo on the right was taken just before a big snowstorm. I loved the ominous storm clouds. I chose to include a lot of the road to put you right into the scene. The train was a gift. The panorama above was taken on one of my more recent rides along America's Highway. This time I set up the shot and waited for a train to come along. On Route 66, you seldom have to wait a long time for a train. This time I wanted the train to a be a subject in my composition instead of just a lucky element

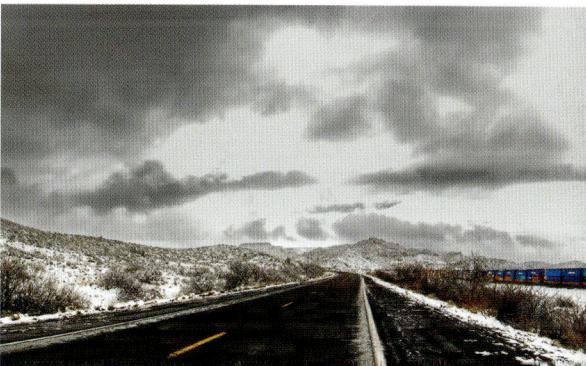

Same road, different day *David Skernick*

We had snow one year in February! It was so rare that it closed the entire area. Roads got plowed eventually, and we headed out to capture some really unusual scenes for that region.

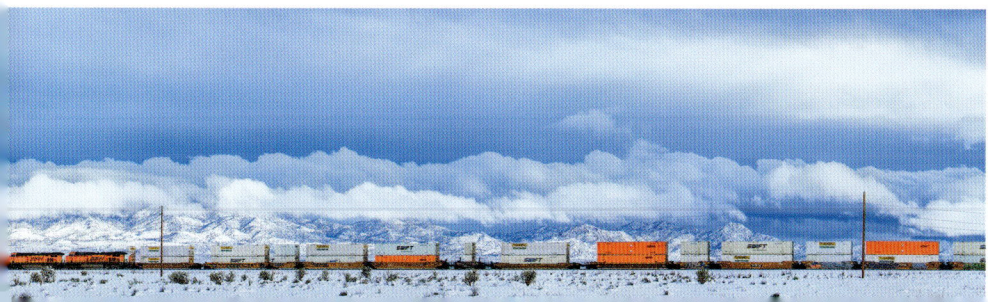

◄ BNSF Railroad with the Peacock Mountains, Arizona
David Skernick

Hackberry, Arizona

A little farther down the road you will come to Hackberry. There you will find a general store that is pure Route 66. They are happy to have photographers inside and out. I always ask first. It's just polite, and a good habit to get into. Sometimes the answer is no, but here we were welcome. They even let us bring our tripods into the store.

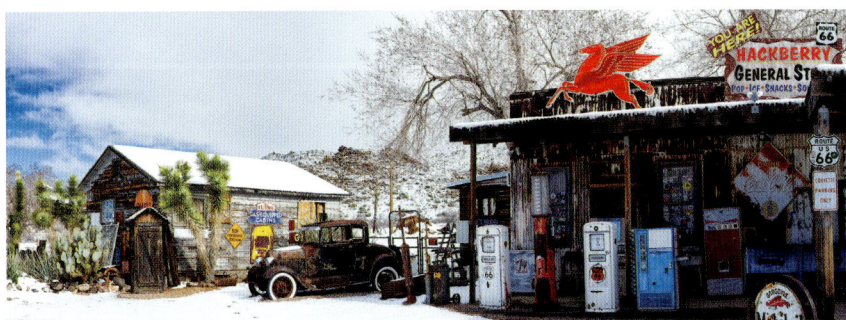

Hackberry General Store, Arizona   *David Skernick*

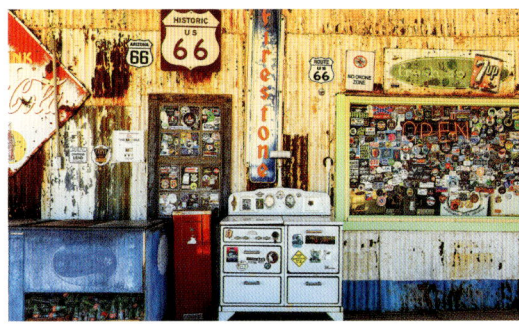

Hackberry wall   *Barbara Balik*

It is always interesting to see how different photographers approach the same scene. The five photos on this page were captured by four photographers. Look at how in one shot (*below*), the car is more the prime subject, and in the other the wall and outhouse get your attention first. Then there is Barbara going after a wall (*upper right*) and Monica spotting the bottles and icicles. There isn't one way to shoot any subject. There isn't even a "best" way, although we often prefer one way to another. Never feel like it's all been done until you have done it your way.

Hackberry car   *Susan Vizuary*

Hackberry outhouse   *Monica Bayless*

Frozen bottles   *Monica Bayless*

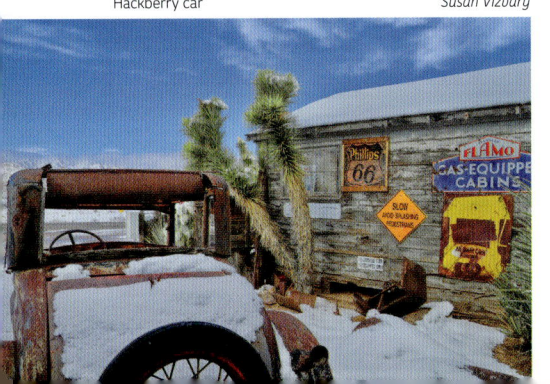

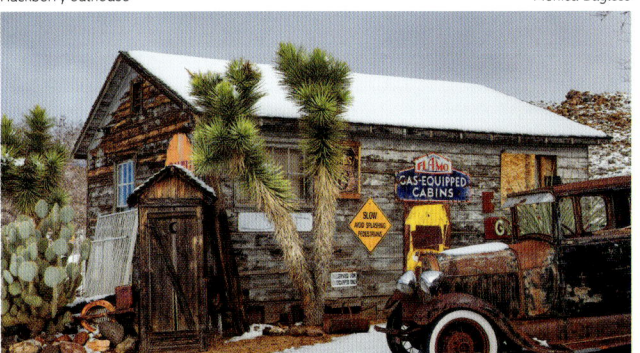

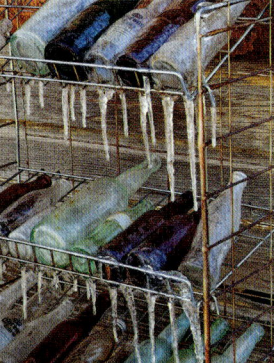

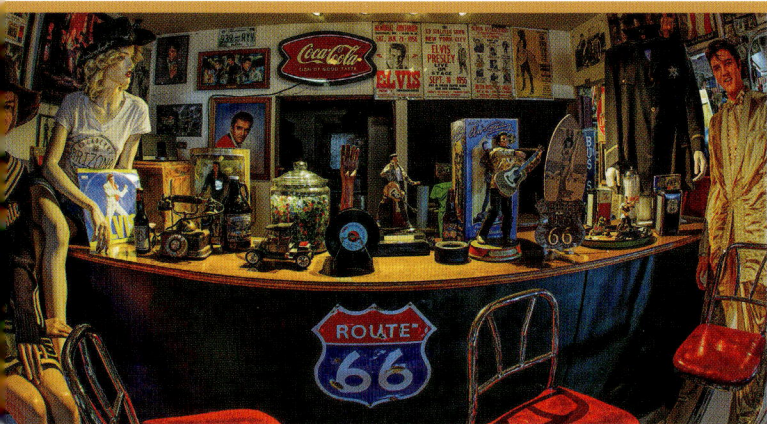

Hackberry General Store interior, Hackberry, Arizona   *Gayle Pepper*

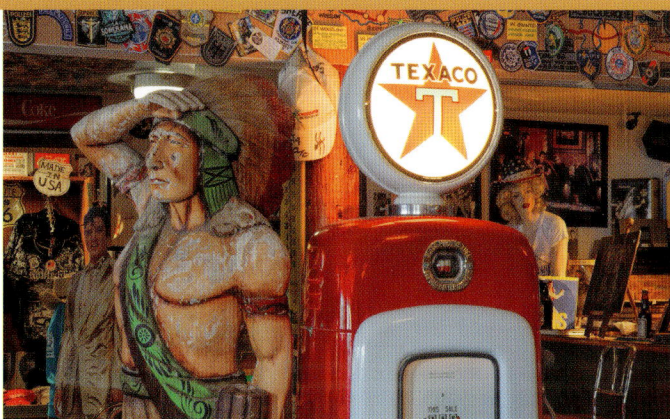

Hackberry General Store interior   *Carol Zulman*

All these photos were taken inside the Hackberry General Store. Tripods were used at all times. Do not even consider shooting your DSLR or mirrorless camera inside without flash or a tripod unless you want to boost your ISO way up and have an image full of noise. The exception to this comes with some of the new phones. They have very fast lenses and are small and light enough to be held steady. It was nice of the people running the store to allow us to come in with tripods. We were careful not to knock anything over or trip anyone.

A tripod gives you the freedom to use slow speeds to gather more light in a low-light situation. They also make you slow down and consider your composition more completely and carefully. To a serious photographer, a tripod is one of the most important tools you have. You should have a good, sturdy tripod. I believe the definition of a good tripod is one that is too heavy and too expensive—sorry.

Hackberry General Store interior   *Kathi Mangel*   Whoop Ass   *Judy Nussenblatt*   License plates   *Susan Vizuary*

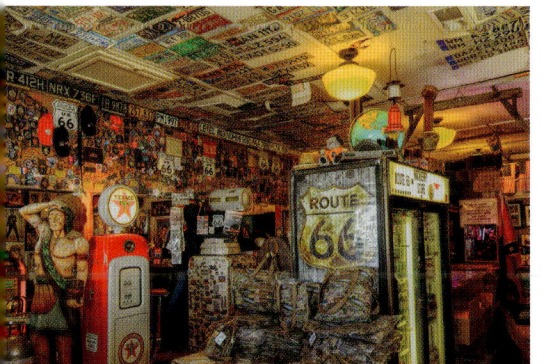

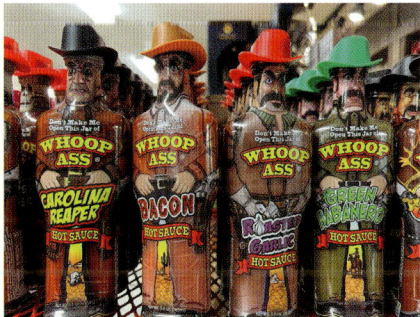

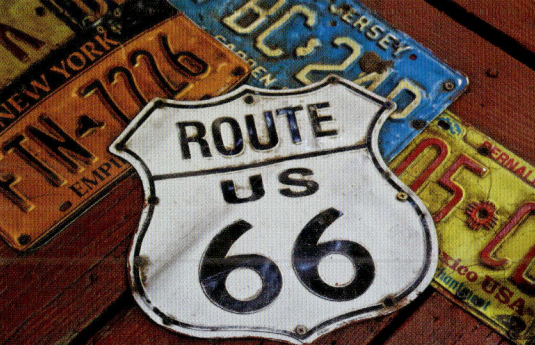

Valentine, Arizona

Valentine (about 30 miles east of Kingman) is the home of "Keepers of the Wild," a nonprofit animal sanctuary. They have rescued animals from unfortunate situations. Many were in the entertainment world. These animals cannot return to the wild. Some of them spent their lives in small cages, in some cases too small for the poor creature to even turn around. My love for animals is such that I sometimes think that I know what they are feeling. Walking around this beautifully kept small zoo, I believe I saw grateful, happy faces.

A long lens (200mm or better) and a fast shutter speed are the two most important things when photographing wildlife. I use lenses as long as 500mm. A zoo is still wildlife, although there are fences keeping you at a distance, rather than good sense. For animals, I keep my shutter speed at a minimum of 1/1000 (1/2000 for birds). Whatever I have to accept as an ISO is okay with me. I'd rather have noise than blur—it is just that simple. Keep in mind that whether the animal is in motion or not, you are excited and more likely to shake your camera. Here I also used a wide aperture. At f/5.6 when I was close to the fence and the subject was farther back, the fence seemed to disappear entirely as a result of that low depth of field. If there is a highlight or glare on the fence, or if the fence is too thick, this won't work. If a highlight is your problem, try moving so you can shoot into your own shadow. Topaz software works great to help improve sharpness and remove noise.

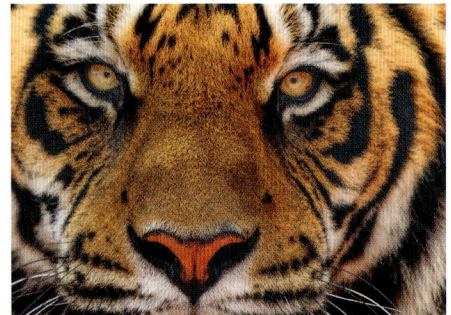

Tiger, Keepers of the Wild *David Skernick*

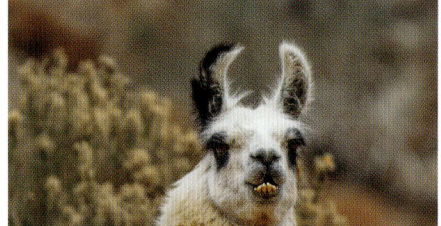

Lion, Keepers of the Wild, Valentine, Arizona *David Skernick*

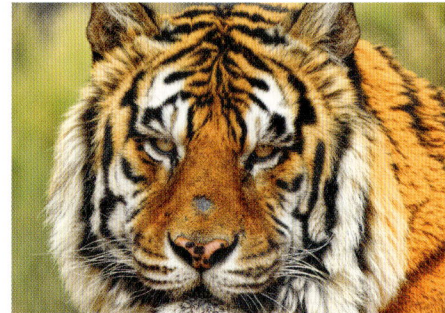

Tiger, Keepers of the Wild *David Skernick*

Black leopard, Keepers of the Wild *David Skernick*

Llama, Keepers of the Wild *David Skernick*

Capybara, Keepers of the Wild *David Skernick*

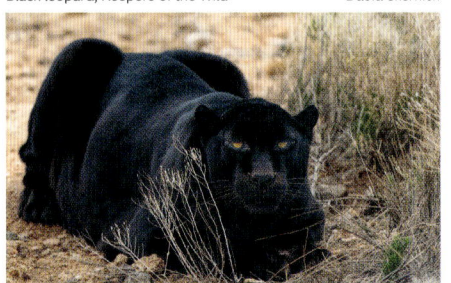

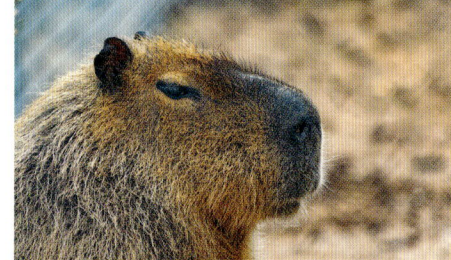

Truxton and Peach Springs, Arizona

The little town of Truxton, Arizona, was founded in 1951. Route 66 was only twenty-five years old at the time. The town is named for Truxton Beale (1856–1936), an American diplomat. Today, there are very few people who call Truxton home. It is another casualty of Interstate 40. I had passed this sign several times and thought about photographing it each time. Sometimes you just have to wait for inspiration. The light and clouds on this day came together to give me exactly what I didn't know I had been waiting for.

There is another small town before you get to Seligman. The town of Peach Springs is a great place to stop for a bite to eat, or gas, and maybe by the publishing of this book, an electric charging station as well. Peach Springs is the tribal headquarters for the Hualapai Indian Reservation.

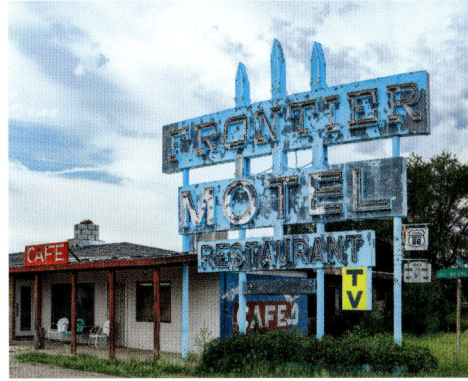

Frontier Motel, Truxton, Arizona   *David Skernick*

Just up the road, and still to be considered Peach Springs, you will come across the Grand Canyon Caverns Grotto. This is Route 66 gold. I gotta say, I love this dinosaur. It's *huge!* You'll need a super-wide-angle lens to capture this fellow unless you shoot a panorama! At least an 18mm lens or wider. This guy hangs out at the motel up the road from the actual caverns.

There is a road to the left of the dinosaur that loads down to the caverns. There's a gift shop down there too. Caves and caverns are not impossible to photograph. You either need a tripod for slow exposures or a flash. Unfortunately, either one is hard to use in cramped places and can be obnoxious to other visitors. I recommend you do as I did: Enjoy the tour and trust your memory for a change.

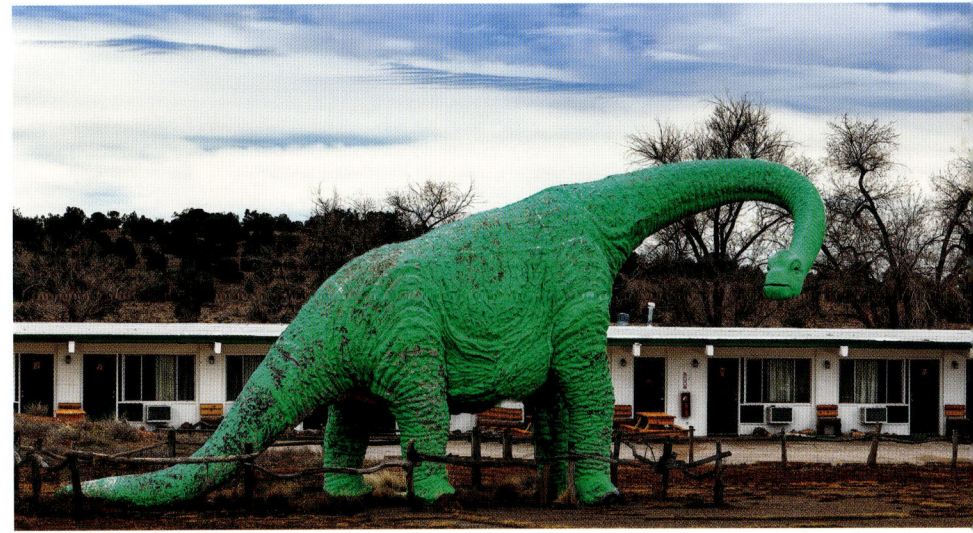

Grand Canyon Caverns Grotto, Peach Springs, Arizona   *David Skernick*

Seligman, Arizona

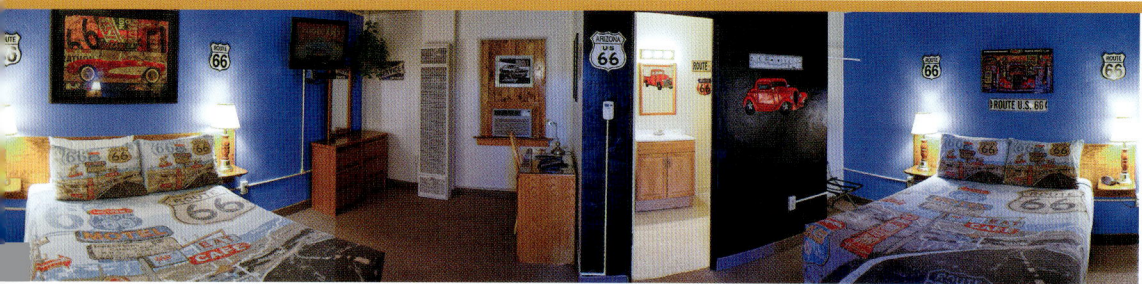

Historic Route 66 Motel interior, Seligman, Arizona   *David Skernick*

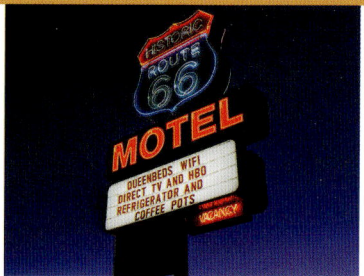

Motel sign   *Gayle Pepper*

Seligman calls itself the birthplace of Route 66. They earned that right because the residents of Seligman (notably Angel Delgadillo) convinced the state of Arizona to dedicate Route 66 as a historic highway. It is a wonderful place to photograph America's Highway.

I drive through every chance I get and spent three days there with a group. We never ran out of things to shoot.
There are many great choices of places to stay in Seligman. We chose the Historic Route 66 Motel. This was my room!

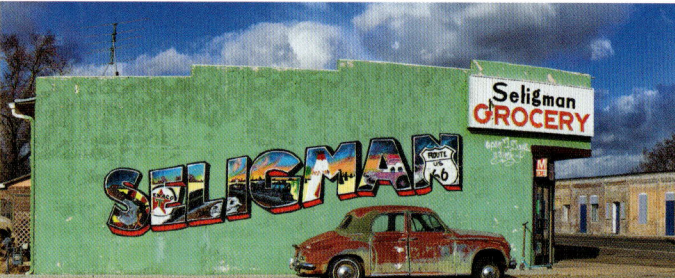

Seligman Grocery   *David Skernick*
Clayton   *Judy Nussenblatt*

Delgadillo's Snow Cap Drive-In, Seligman, Arizona   *David Skernick*

Above left is the grocery store where we picked up provisions. Clayton was working that day. He shared with me that he was named after the star of *The Lone Ranger*, Clayton Moore. Judy chose black and white for her portrait of Clayton. He was happy to pose for this picture.

Delgadillo's Snow Cap Drive-In is a historic roadside attraction in Seligman. Built in 1953, the drive-in is all about great food and having fun. I had the "cheeseburger with cheese." "Dead chicken" was another menu choice. The staff happily posed for this phone pano.

Details, details. Sometimes the best way to photograph an area like this, which is so overwhelmingly full of opportunities, is to look for the small shots. Look for details that tell the story of what you see. They are like short stories. Sometimes you don't need the whole novel.

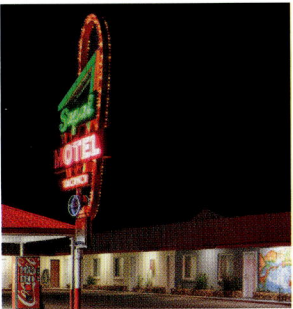

Supal Motel, Seligman, Arizona
David Skernick

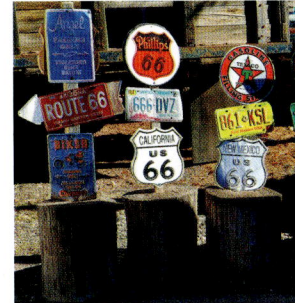

Signs, Seligman, Arizona   *Susan Vizuary*

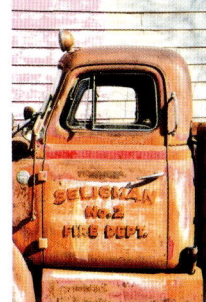
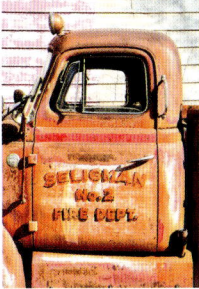

Truck, Seligman, Arizona
Susan Vizuary

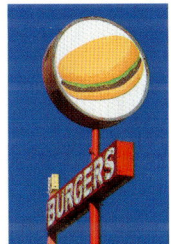

Burgers   *David Skernick*

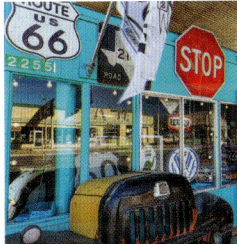
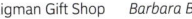

Seligman Gift Shop   *Barbara Balik*

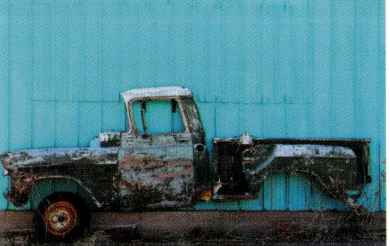

Wall detail, Seligman, Arizona   *Judy Nussenblatt*

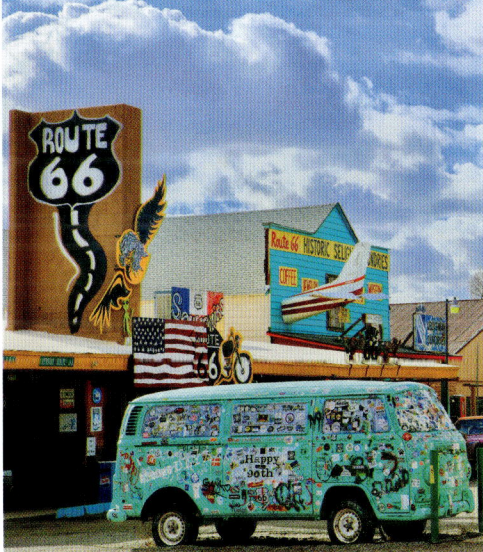

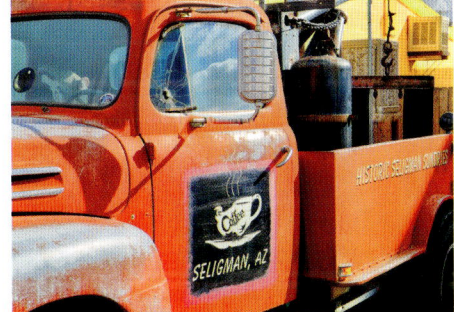

Historic Seligman Sundries truck   *Susan Vizuary*

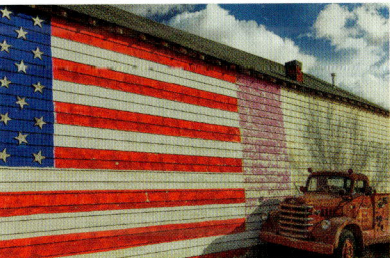
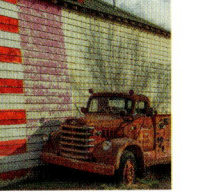

Flag mural, Seligman, Arizona   *Gayle Pepper*

VW bus, Seligman, Arizona   *Susan Vizuary*

Seligman, Arizona

The Roadkill Cafe is a must-stop for great food and a hilarious menu.

Below is Grandma Betty. She is the baker at the Roadkill Cafe. I would move to Seligman for her pies alone. I grabbed this with my phone while waiting for my breakfast burrito (also worth the move).

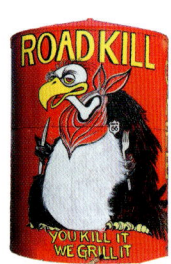

Judy Nussenblatt

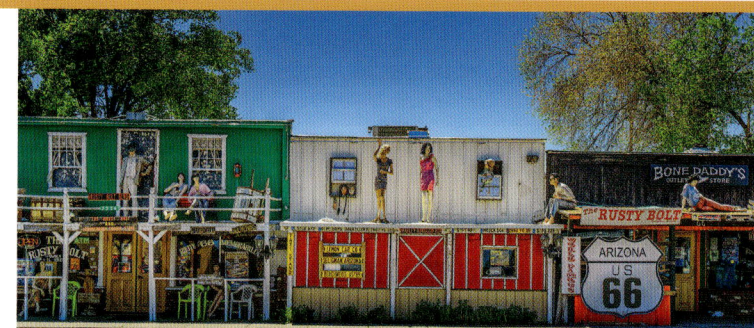

Main Street, Seligman, Arizona

Becky Waters

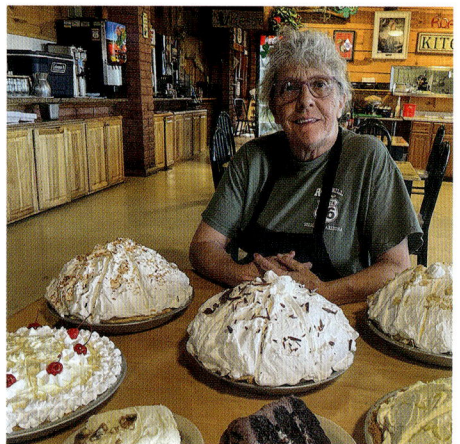

Grandma Betty, Roadkill Cafe

David Skernick

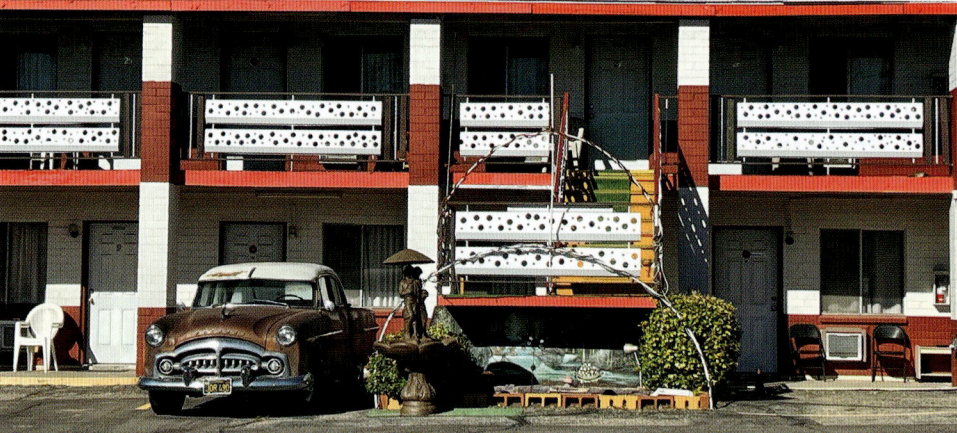

Motel, Seligman, Arizona

Judy Nussenblatt

Most people don't shoot panoramic images. Their photos are the usual 2:3 ratio we all know and love, but sometimes it works to crop your photos into a shape that helps define your composition. You may have noticed that many of the photos in this book have been cropped to shapes that just make better compositions. If you want to make a standard print, be sure to crop to a standard print shape, such as 8 × 10, 5 × 7, or 11 × 14. These are very specific shapes. Don't worry about the size (in inches or pixels). Keep the full resolution and just save your file into different cropped shapes. If you use "save as" or "save as a copy," you will still retain your original in case you want something different later.

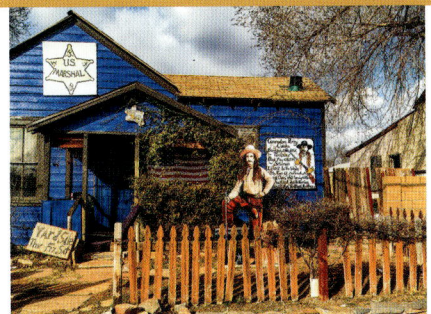

House, Seligman, Arizona   *Barbara Balik*

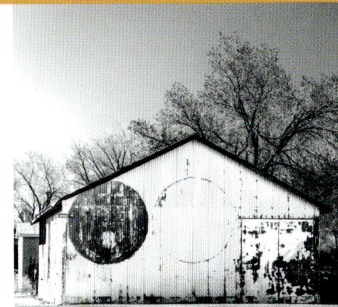

Garage, Seligman, Arizona   *Gayle Pepper*

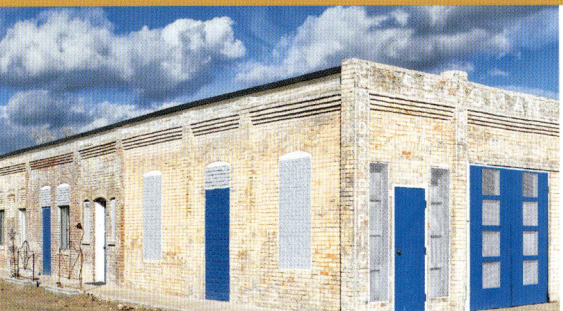

Old post office, Seligman, Arizona   *David Skernick*

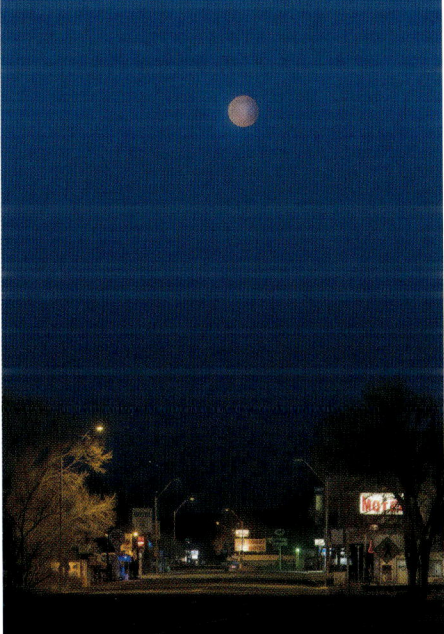

Blue-moon eclipse (2018),   *David Skernick*
Route 66, Seligman, Arizona

It was fantastic to have so much time with some of my most talented students in Seligman. In the last few pages, you have seen many of their photos from that trip. Having time to wander around the town gave us the chance to find other buildings that were off the main road, some of which are shown on this page.

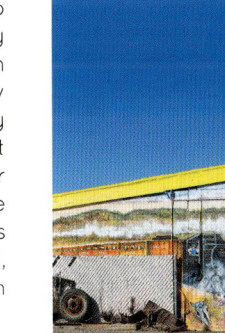

Copper Cart, Seligman, Arizona   *David Skernick*

Of course, time is relative. I took the photo on the left on another trip, when I was staying in Seligman for just one night while on my way to another location. My timing happened to coincide with the blue-moon eclipse on January 31, 2018. I checked my "Photo Pills" app (a must for astrophotography) and found the perfect location at the edge of town, aiming right down the middle of Seligman on Route 66. It was 5:00 a.m. and freezing, but I got the shot!

Seligman to Ash Fork, Arizona

As you head east out of Seligman on old Route 66, you will go through a desolate desert landscape and end up in Ash Fork. After that, you'll have to get back on Interstate 40 for a while. Look for Burma Shave signs along the way. A couple of miles east of Seligman, you will cross a bridge over railroad tracks. This is a photo opportunity no matter what time you get there. There is plenty of room on either side of the bridge to park safely. There is even a road to get down to the tracks under the bridge. I like the views from the top better.

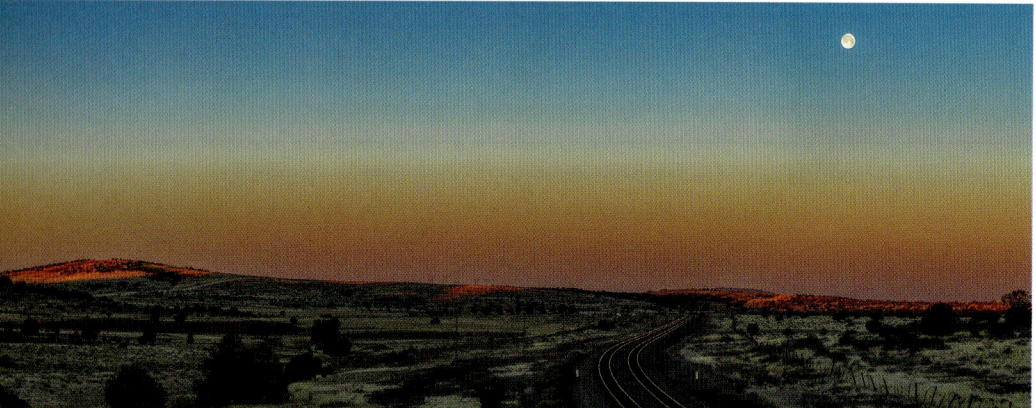

Train tracks between Seligman and Ash Fork, Arizona, looking west

David Skernick

I shot both of these at sunrise. Do your homework and know when sunrise, sunset, moonrise, and moonset will be. Know the phases of the moon as well. I used "Sun and Moon" again as I did in Kingman. I chose a day when moonset was just after sunrise. Looking west, I had the beautiful light from the sun coming up behind me and the setting moon in front. Your exposure can be constant here because there is plenty of light to use a shutter speed fast enough to stop the movement of the moon. A train would have been nice, but I think the shot works without one.

Just before that, I used a slow shutter speed on the other side of the bridge, facing east a little before the sun rose. A shutter speed of 1/8 blurred the train just a little. I wanted it to still look like a train but to show the motion as well. Too slow a shutter speed would abstract the train more than I wanted, and too fast a speed would make the motion less obvious.

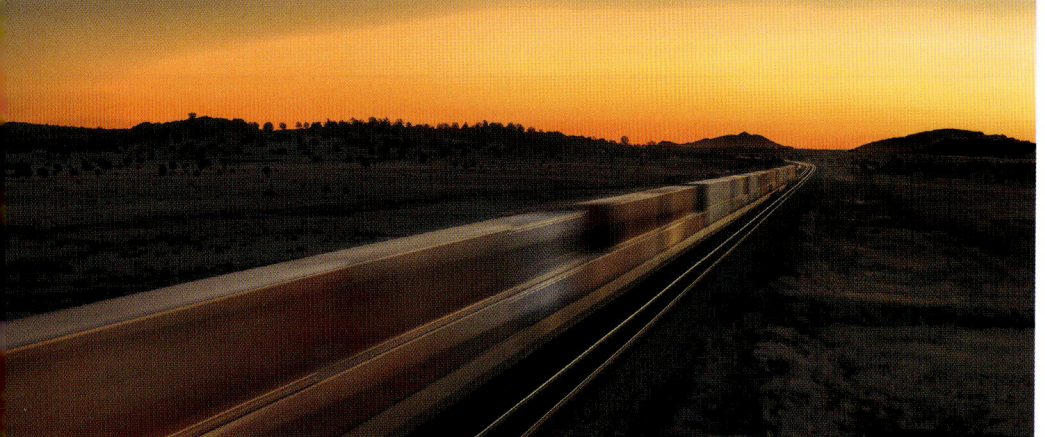

◄ Train tracks between Seligman and Ash Fork, Arizona, looking east
David Skernick

I came across these fellas on different trips along this same stretch of Route 66. There were no fences or branding that I could see, so I think they might be wild. Either way, they were beautiful. Don't get hung up on what you might be seeing—just get the shot! I went for a long lens and a fast shutter speed. I stayed close to my truck so they wouldn't notice me as much. If you walk toward a wild animal, it might run away. Then again, they might come over to say hello. Either way, it may change the photo you saw when you pulled over. I spent awhile just leaning against Bob the Truck for cover and stability and took lots of pics.

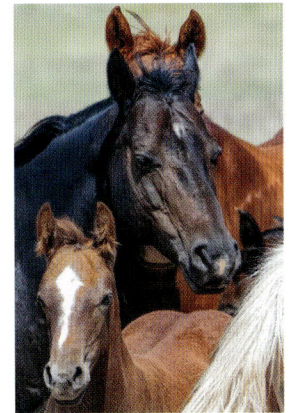
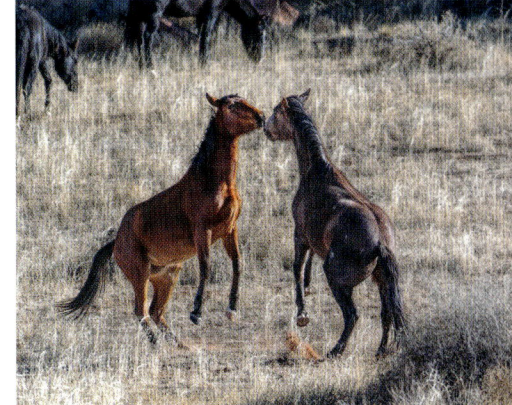

Curious colt *David Skernick* Wild horses along Route 66, Arizona *David Skernick*

Ash Fork, Arizona

There is a Route 66 museum in Ash Fork and a few interesting signs and buildings, and of course there are trains. We stopped to photograph the old Alpine Motel, and this guy showed up in his '58 Chevy. He had albums of old Route 66 snapshots in his car and would have talked to us all day long about his life living on the Mother Road. Nice guy!

He drove by several times blasting Beach Boys from his car and waving at us as he passed by. Pepper got this great shot, complete with the dice hanging from his rearview mirror when he stopped right in front of the photo she was setting up of the motel. Try to be prepared for change so you can react fast and capture a lucky moment.

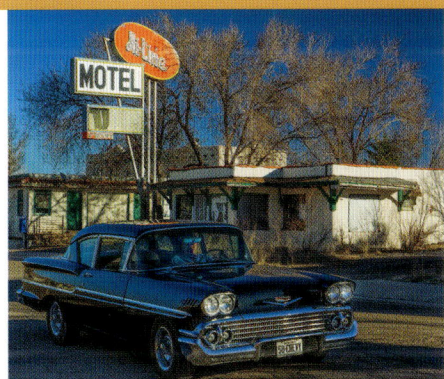

'58 Chevy and Alpine Motel, Ash Fork, Arizona *Gayle Pepper*

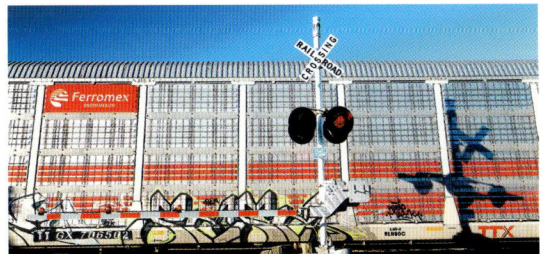
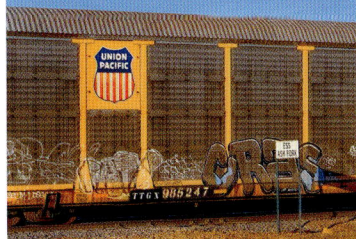

Train crossing, Ash Fork, Arizona *Barbara Balik*

Union Pacific train car, Ash Fork, Arizona *Gayle Pepper*

Both Pepper and Barbara used fast speeds to stop the motion of the trains. You always have a choice when shooting motion to stop blur or pan it. A pan is when you move with the motion and shoot at a slow speed to blur the background.

Williams, Arizona

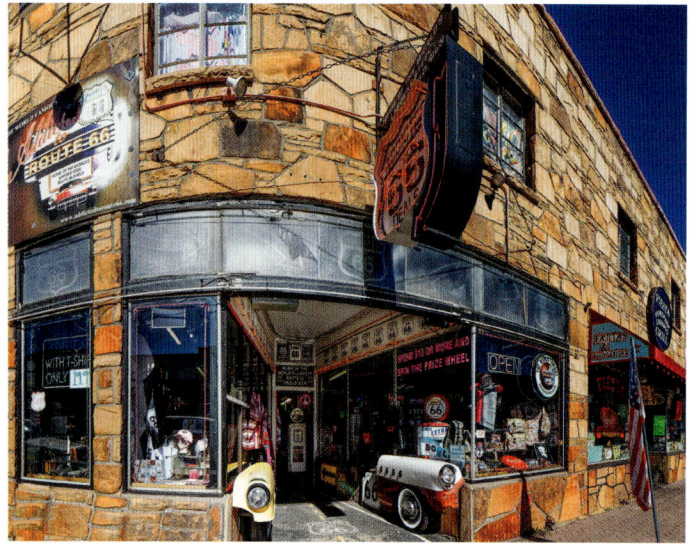

Addicted to Route 66, Williams, Arizona

David Skernick

Not all panos are shaped like bumper stickers. The above image is made up of two rows of photos with eleven shots in each row. The squarish shape was the result.

There are many towns in Arizona that love the Route 66 tradition. Count Williams, Arizona, as one of them. Leave I-40 when you see the Historic 66 sign at Williams, and you will find yourself on a long road full of motels, restaurants, and shops all dedicated to the Main Street of America. Make sure you ask permission to photograph; we were told "no" at a few locations. At the Addicted to Route 66 store, Chris not only welcomed us in but even posed for us.

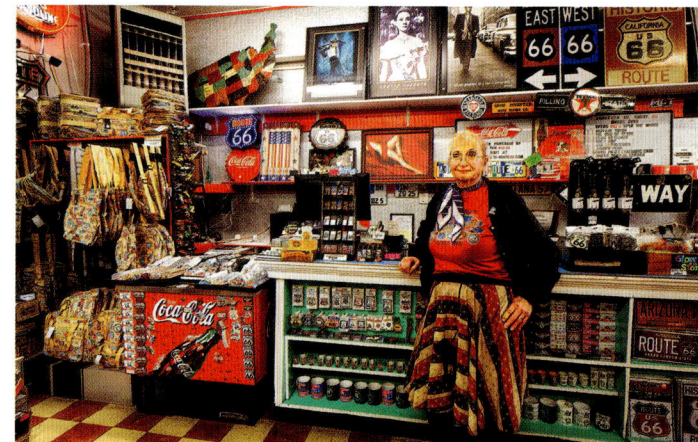

Chris

Barbara Balik

Interior and Elvis

David Skernick

Miniature cars

Susan Vizuary

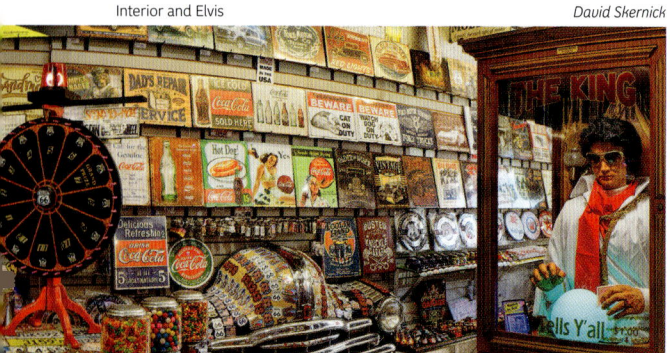

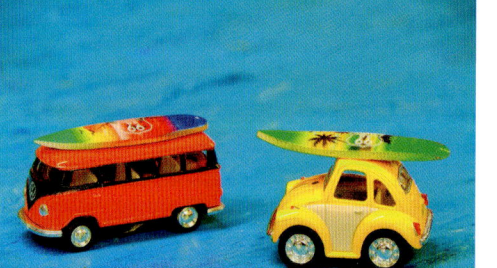

Susan set this little shot up on the counter and used the available light in the store. She used a macro lens to get close to these tiny toy cars.

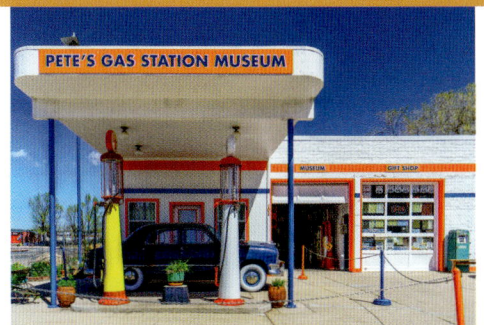

Pete's Gas Station Museum, Williams, Arizona *Becky Waters*

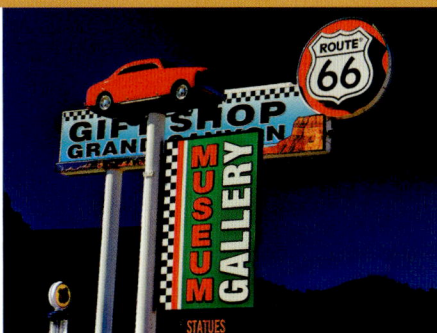

Signs, Williams, Arizona *Gayle Pepper*

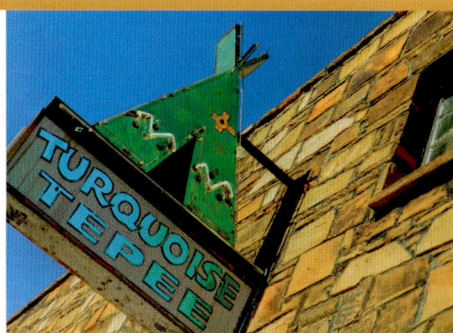

Turquoise Tepee detail, Williams, Arizona *Gayle Pepper*

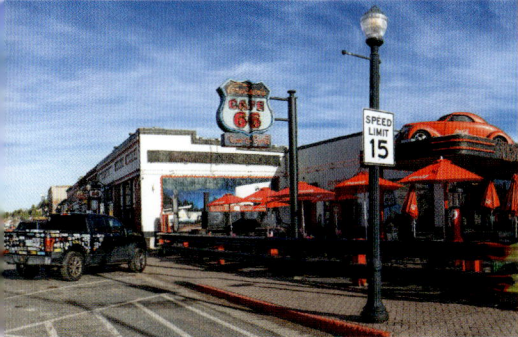

Cafe 66 and Main Street, Williams, Arizona *David Skernick*

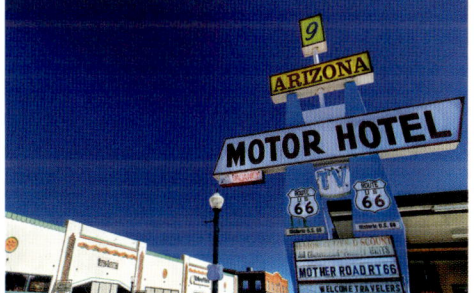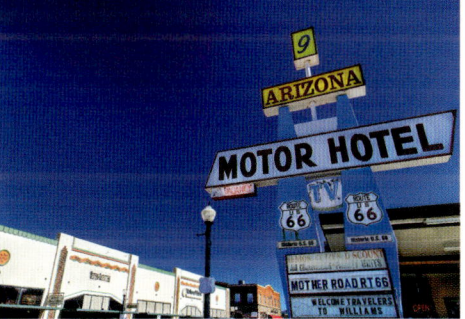

Arizona Motor Hotel, Williams, Arizona *Barbara Balik*

Do you want people in your photos? That is entirely your choice. It's one thing to take a shot of a friend or family member to show scale, or whom you travel with, or what a great time you are having together; it's another to include people you don't know. My personal choice is generally not to include people I don't know unless they are intrinsic to the story I'm telling. Try titling your shot before you finalize your composition. If my title is "Crowds Flock to Route 66," I better have some people in my shot.

A person or animal in any photo instantly becomes your subject. We are simply wired to pay more attention to living things. Williams is a busy town. A lot of people come there to experience America's Highway. Many techniques exist to make the crowds disappear, or at least not to appear in your photo. You could slow your shutter speed way down with a neutral-density filter and blur them out of existence, but we found easier ways to deal with the problem.

Becky waited for her shot (*above*) to clear of people, while Barbara and Pepper found angles where the people walking by would not show. On another trip, I shot early, before the crowds showed up on Main Street, but snuck Bob the Truck in so you would know whom I was with.

Grand Canyon National Park, Arizona

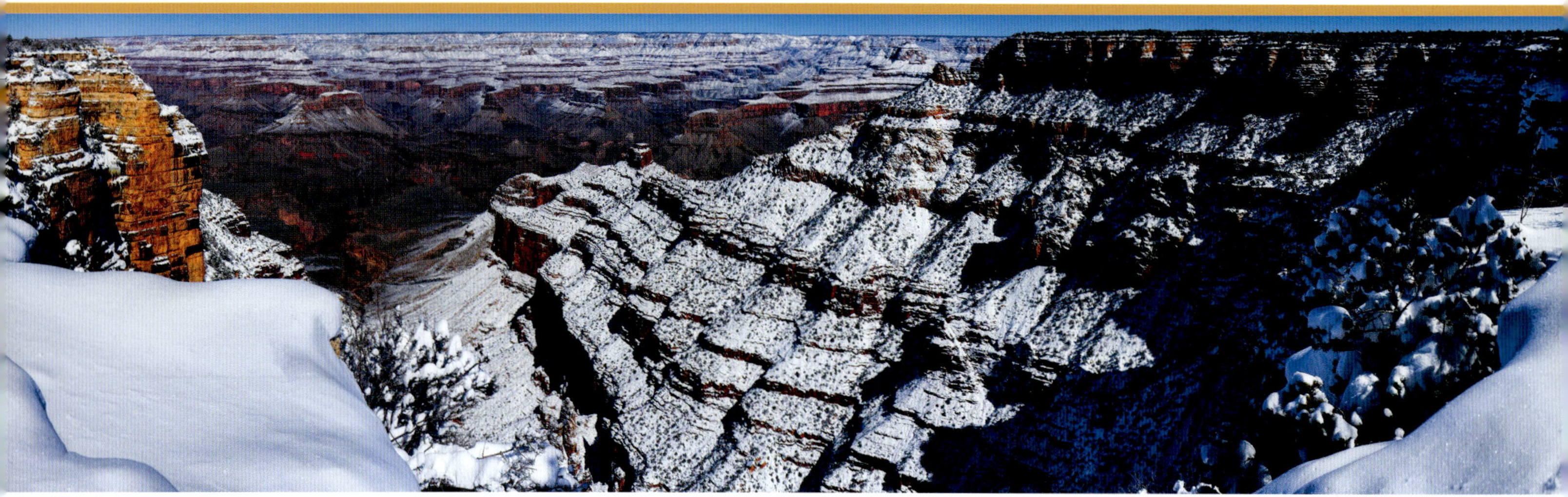

Pipe Creek, South Rim, Grand Canyon, Arizona

Desert View, South Rim, Grand Canyon, Arizona

David Skernick

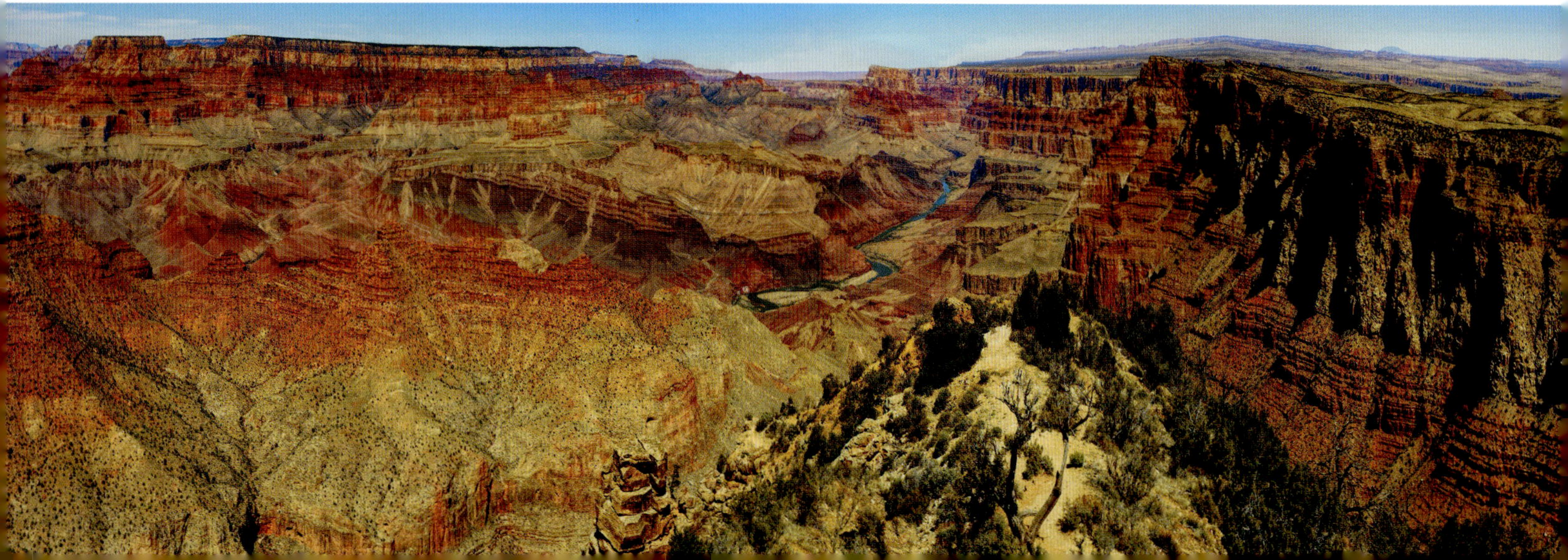

David Skernick

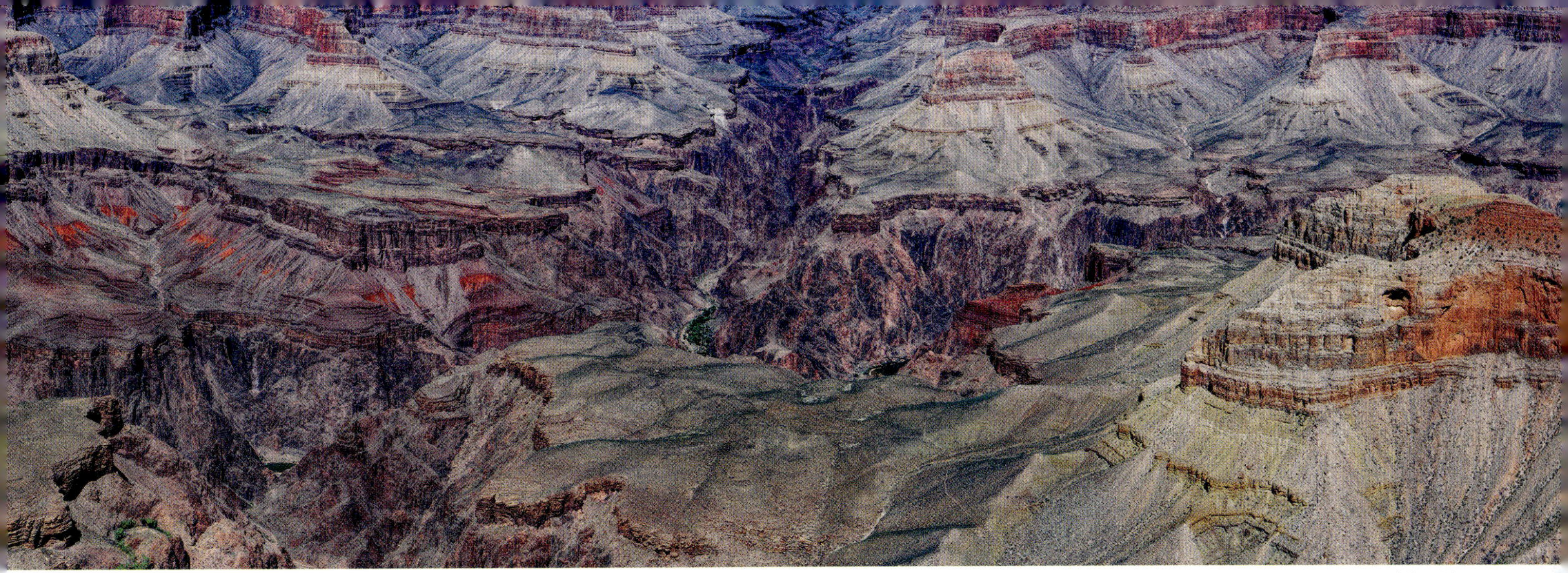

Yavapai Point, South Rim, Grand Canyon, Arizona

David Skernick

Grand Canyon National Park is not on Route 66. The South Rim of the canyon is about 50 miles north of Williams, Arizona, on Highway 64. I told you I would keep you on the Mother Road and not take you off-road or out of your way, but hey! This is the Grand Canyon! If you have the time, it really is worth the short detour.

All these photos were taken from the South Rim. The North Rim is certainly worth your time as well, but you have to drive all the way around the canyon to get there. It would change your trip significantly. For the South Rim, you will need to add only a couple of days to your planned itinerary. Be sure to make reservations for each night you will be near the canyon. There are always lots and lots of people visiting this national park.

Bring every lens you have. This is a photographer's paradise. Wide angle is great if you have consistent light. Telephoto lenses will allow you to shoot details of the canyon. Be on the lookout for interesting birds, deer, foxes, and other wildlife. Anything is possible in a national park.

My best advice is to take every turnout and hike every trail that will give you different views of the canyon. As you can see, all the views are different and always worth a photo or two. Just watch your depth of field. F/11 should work most of the time if the front element in your shot is at least 20 feet away from you.

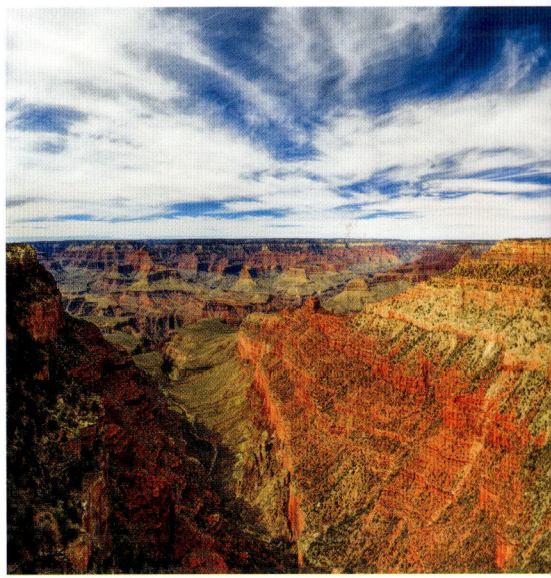

Near Mather Point, South Rim, Grand Canyon, Arizona

David Skernick

Flagstaff, Arizona

Watch the signs on Interstate 40 and you will see the exit into Flagstaff, Arizona, clearly marked with the Historical Route 66 sign. There is plenty to photograph in Flagstaff. But wait! You might want to switch to an east-to-west route in Flagstaff. Most of the things you'll want to photograph are on the north side of the street. It is easier to stop when your location is on your right. I drive all the way to the last Flagstaff exit (easternmost, exit 204, Walnut Canyon) and then drive 66 back (westbound). At the end, I get back on I-40 and head east toward Winslow, Arizona. Yes, it seems a little strange to do it that way, but it is much easier and safer to stop and photograph. It adds only a few miles. Your trip on the Mother Road is not about getting anywhere, but about being somewhere. Leave enough time to enjoy the ride, or maybe you can do it in sections at different times, or even in different seasons.

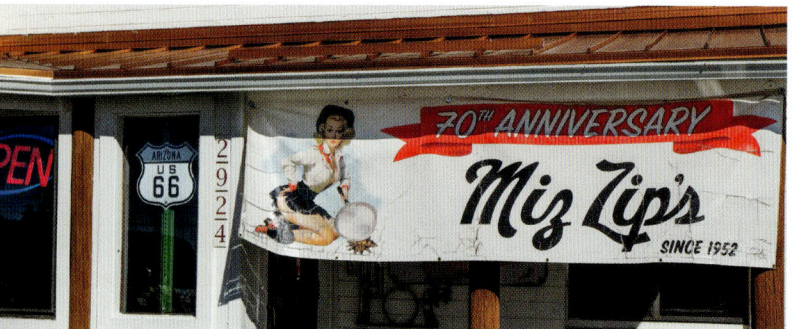

Miz Zips, Flagstaff, Arizona   *David Skernick*

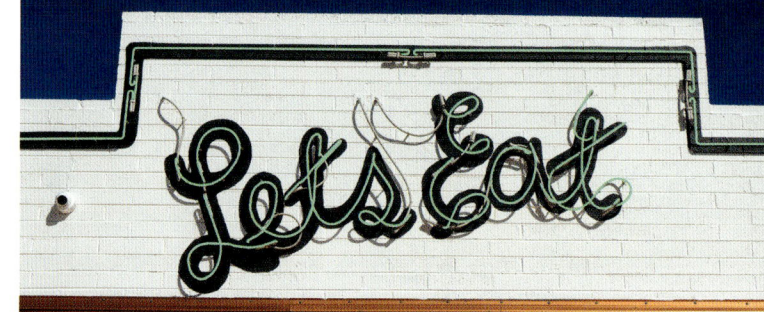

Let's Eat   *David Skernick*

I feel as if these locations really speak to what Flagstaff must have been like in the '50s, '60s, and '70s on America's Highway. Use a telephoto lens to isolate small areas and signs. I like to limit my photos to just the one subject I want to depict. Longer lenses help me do that.

Whispering Winds Motel, Flagstaff, Arizona   *David Skernick*

Whispering Winds sign   *David Skernick*

66 Motel, Flagstaff, Arizona   *David Skernick*

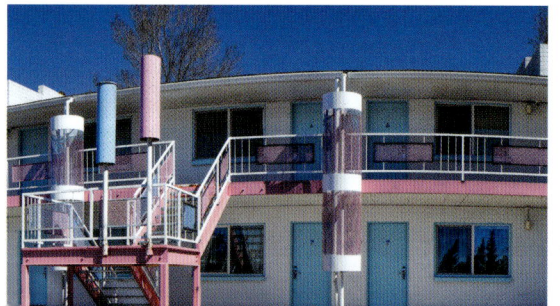

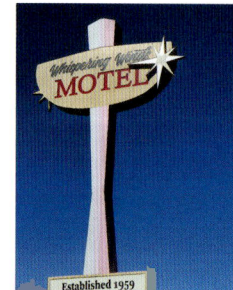

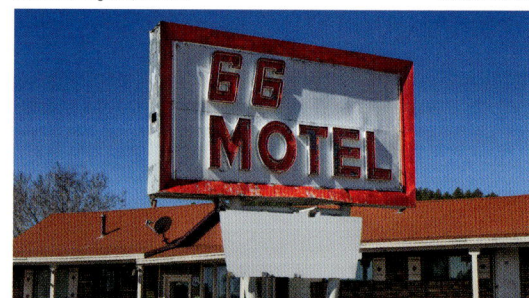

Flagstaff has grown into a true metropolis over the years. Drive carefully and watch the traffic. The Mother Road is still there, although it might feel a little like it is hiding in the corners. Keep a sharp eye and you may find all sorts of relics from the past, and perhaps a few new ones.

The Hotel Monte Vista at 100 North San Francisco Street, just off Route 66, opened on January 1, 1927. Zane Grey was just one of the big investors in the project. Hollywood celebrities are said to have stayed here often. Part of the movie *Casablanca* was filmed at the Monte Vista.

There have been many ghost sightings at this hotel. Some have reported seeing the "Phantom Bell Boy," who is said to knock on your door in the middle of the night to talk to you.

I stood back and used a telephoto (135mm) lens to create my panoramic photo without getting any other buildings or other extraneous elements in my shot.

Becky found this mural, and I spotted the painted wall of the Salsa Brava Restaurant. I admit that my find doesn't scream Route 66, but we are looking for things we want to photograph, and it's a great place to stop for lunch!

Hotel Monte Vista, Flagstaff, Arizona   *David Skernick*

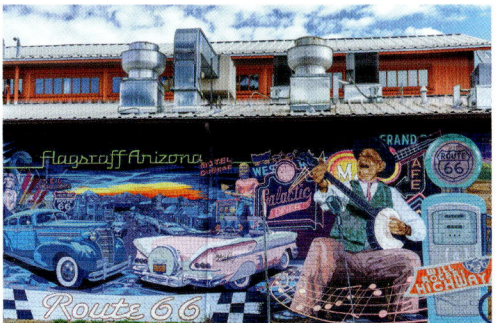

Mural, Flagstaff, Arizona   *Becky Waters*

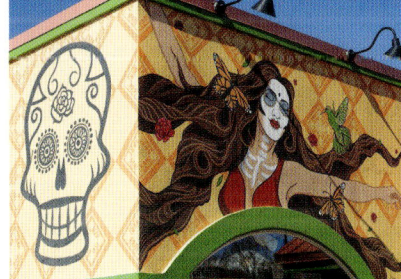

Salsa Brava Restaurant, Flagstaff, Arizona   *David Skernick*

Interstate 40, Arizona

In Arizona, you will have to spend some time on the interstate. The I-40 replaced all of Route 66. Every town and city is worth visiting. In between you will find a few random exits marked with the historical sign as well. There is even a deer farm and a meteor crater. Keep your eyes open and you might find exits worth checking out that are not marked as part of the old road.

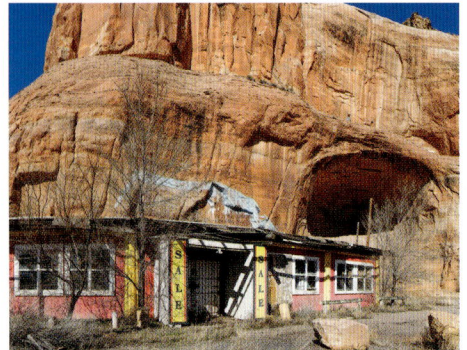

Ganado, Arizona   *David Skernick*

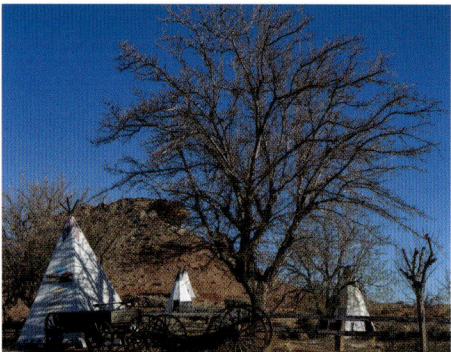

Geronimo   *David Skernick*

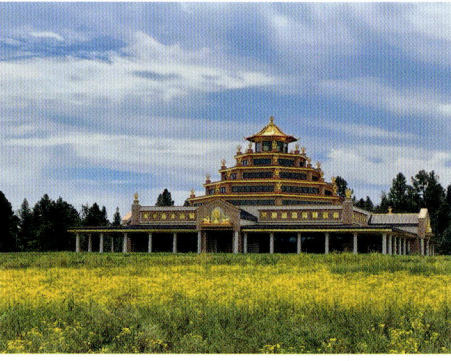

Kadampa Temple for World Peace, Williams, Arizona   *David Skernick*

In Ganado, Arizona, there are a whole bunch of places to buy Navajo art and food. I found this older, abandoned stand that seemed to be getting reclaimed by the surrounding rocks.

Take the Geronimo exit and you will find tepees and petrified wood, as well as food and souvenirs.

The Kadampa Temple for World Peace is near Williams. I whipped out my phone. The clouds were perfectly spaced around the building. I knew I might not get the DSLR set up in time to catch them.

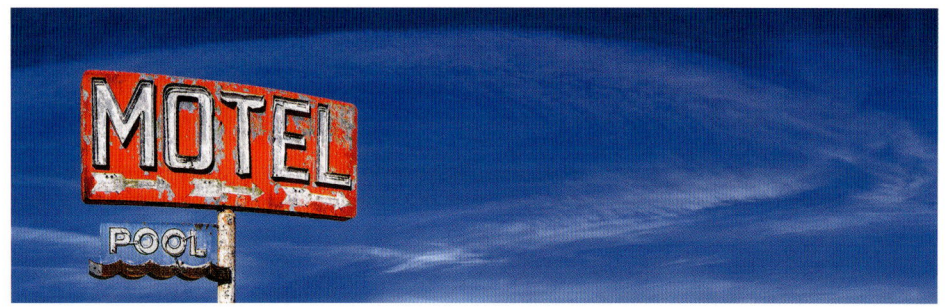

Motel sign along I-40, Arizona   *David Skernick*

This motel sign is on the side of the highway west of Kingman. I thought that looping cloud made the extra negative space work.

Relative sizes are always fun to play with. The dinosaur was huge, but not really bigger than the building. It looks like the idea of clean restrooms infuriates him! Be deliberate about where you stand in relation to all the elements in your photo. Pepper's arrow on the far right (*below*) is another great example of size distortion. Size matters!

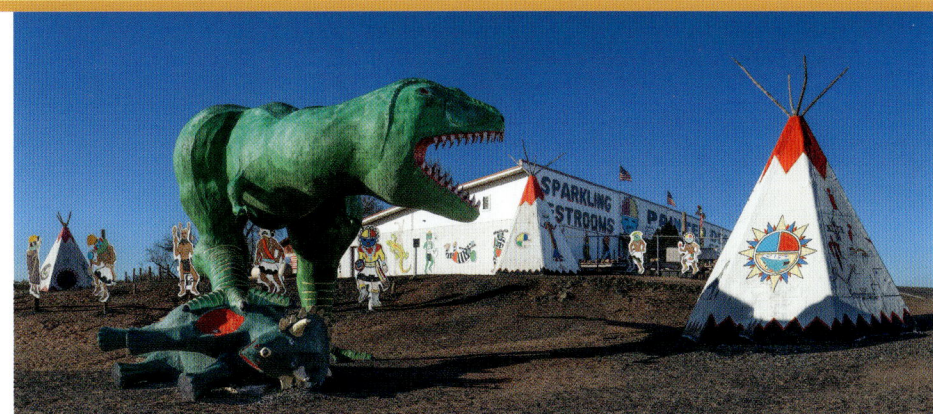

The Painted Desert Indian Center, Sun Valley, Arizona   *David Skernick*

There are a couple of ghost town trading posts east of Flagstaff. Check them out if you have time. Our favorite stop was the Twin Arrows Trading Post (*below*). The business was another Interstate 40 casualty. People just don't stop as often if they have to exit off a freeway. So much of Route 66 business was adversely affected by our need to get there faster. Take your time and you will see so much more. In the shot on the left, I stood back to get both whole arrows. Pepper got close to highlight only one arrow, and Becky went off to shoot the old building. My favorite thing about leading groups is how every participant sees things differently.

The last time I drove by there was only one arrow. The rule "Take only pictures" is not always followed. For me, it is one of the reasons that I love photography. It's like being a kid and always getting "yes" to the question "Can I have that?"

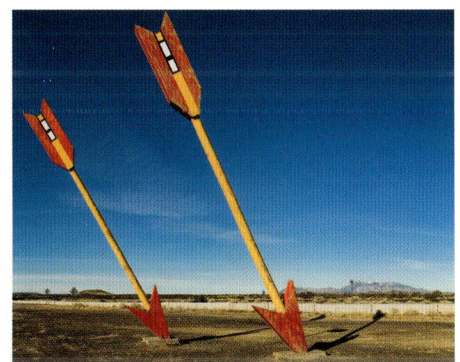

Twin Arrows Trading Post, I-40, Arizona   *David Skernick*

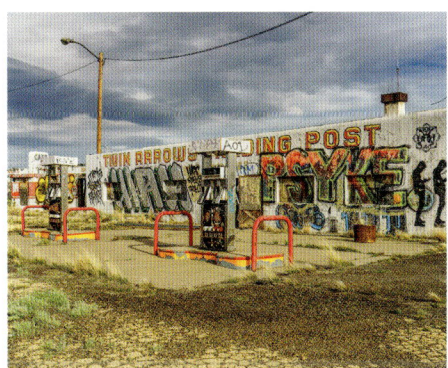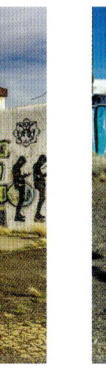

Trading post   *Becky Waters*

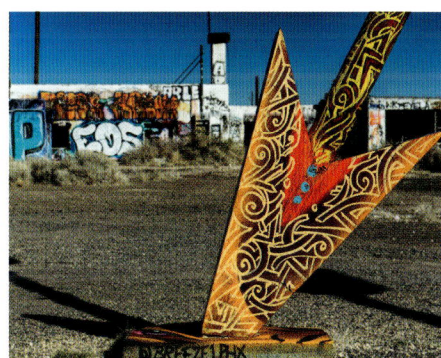

Single Arrow   *Gayle Pepper*

Winslow, Arizona

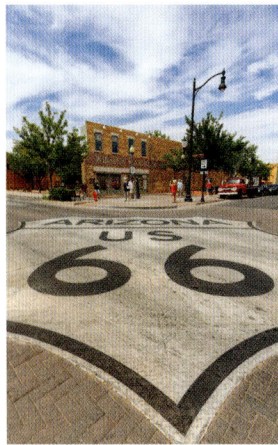

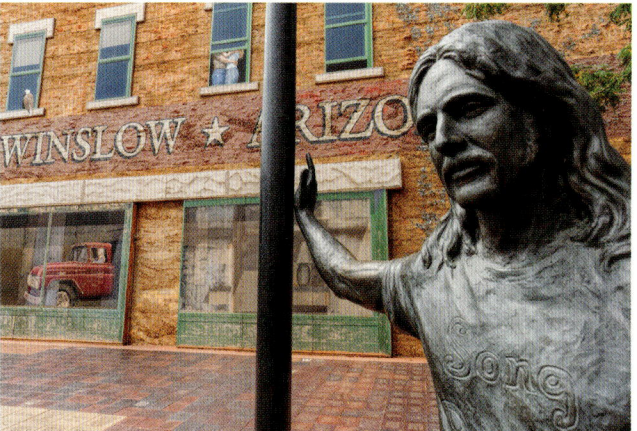

You will want to stop in Winslow, Arizona, even if you are not an Eagles fan! There are excellent motels and souvenirs. I found a couple of photo ops as well. I used an extreme wide angle (16mm) to get the huge amount of content and depth of field on the town square. One of the properties of wide-angle lenses is tons of focus. We talk about depth of field a lot. It simply means "stuff in focus." What is in focus along with your subject will either enhance or detract from that subject. To control depth of field is to control the story you want to tell.

Route 66, Winslow, Arizona *David Skernick*   Standing on the corner of Winslow, Arizona   *David Skernick*

A couple of pages ago, I wrote that people and animals will always get your attention in a photograph. They will automatically become your subject, whether that was your intention or not. Did you notice my new friend Blas and his old friend Buffalo on the far left of my shot? They may be small, but it doesn't matter. In this case, I was happy to include the owner of Earl's in my picture, and I can never refuse a dog!

Letters and numbers will also become important in your composition. If there is something to be read, it will be read. Try to recall what you saw first. Was it the man and the dog, "Earl's Motor Court," or the Route 66 sign? Make sure that people, animals, and words are not taking over your statement. I wanted all those things to be important in this photo, but they would have been whether I liked it or not.

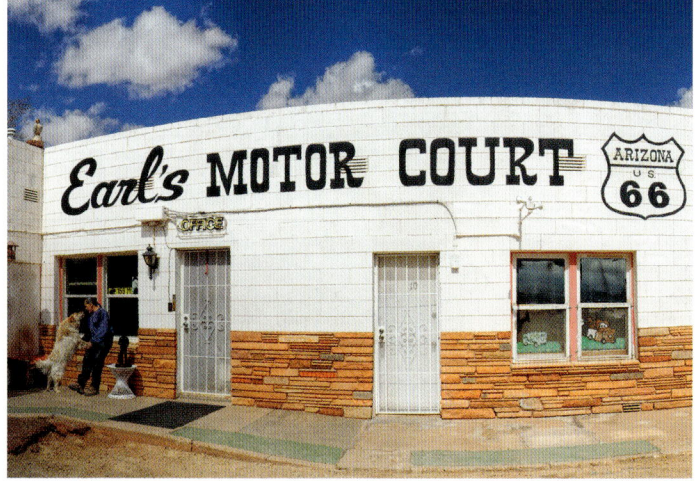

Blas and Buffalo at Earl's Motor Court, Winslow, Arizona   *David Skernick*

Joseph City and Holbrook, Arizona

Joseph City, Arizona, is home to the famous Jackrabbit Trading Post and billboard. Once there were jackrabbit signs covering 1,000 miles along Route 66. Look for the few remaining signs showing the little rabbit and the distance back to this point.

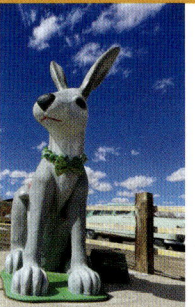

Rabbit   *David Skernick*

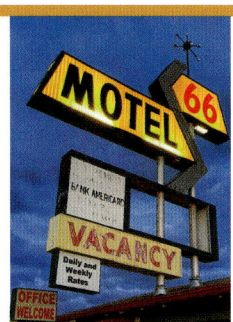

Motel 66 Holbrook   *David Skernick*

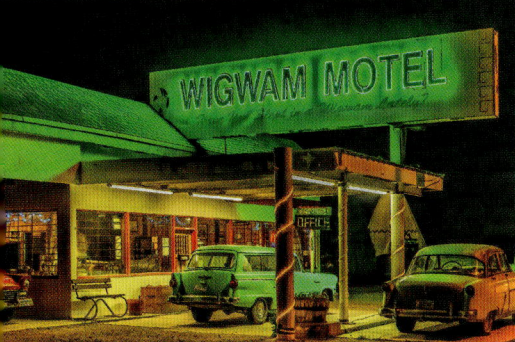

Wigwam at night, Holbrook, Arizona   *Becky Waters*

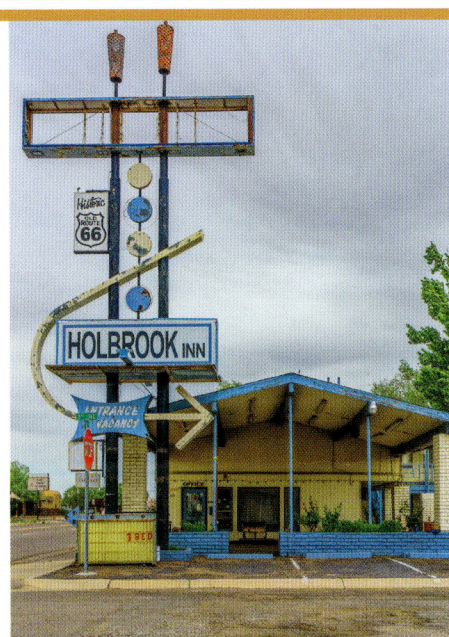

Holbrook Inn, Holbrook, Arizona   *Becky Waters*

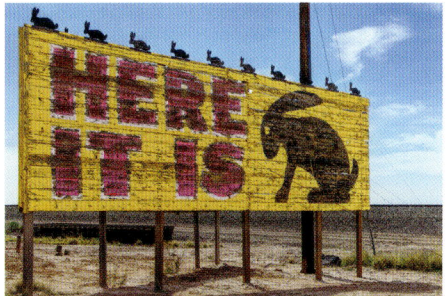

Jackrabbit sign, Joseph City, Arizona   *Becky Waters*

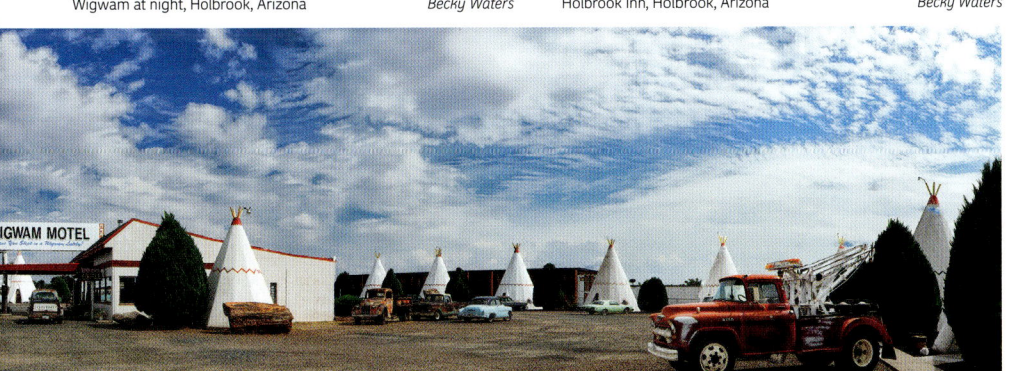

Wigwam Motel, Holbrook, Arizona   *David Skernick*

In Holbrook, Arizona, you'll find another of the two Wigwam Motels along Route 66. The other one was in San Bernardino, California. Look how different these two compositions of the same subject are. You will find many old buildings and signs in Holbrook, and yes, you can sleep in a wigwam!

Petrified Forest National Park, Arizona

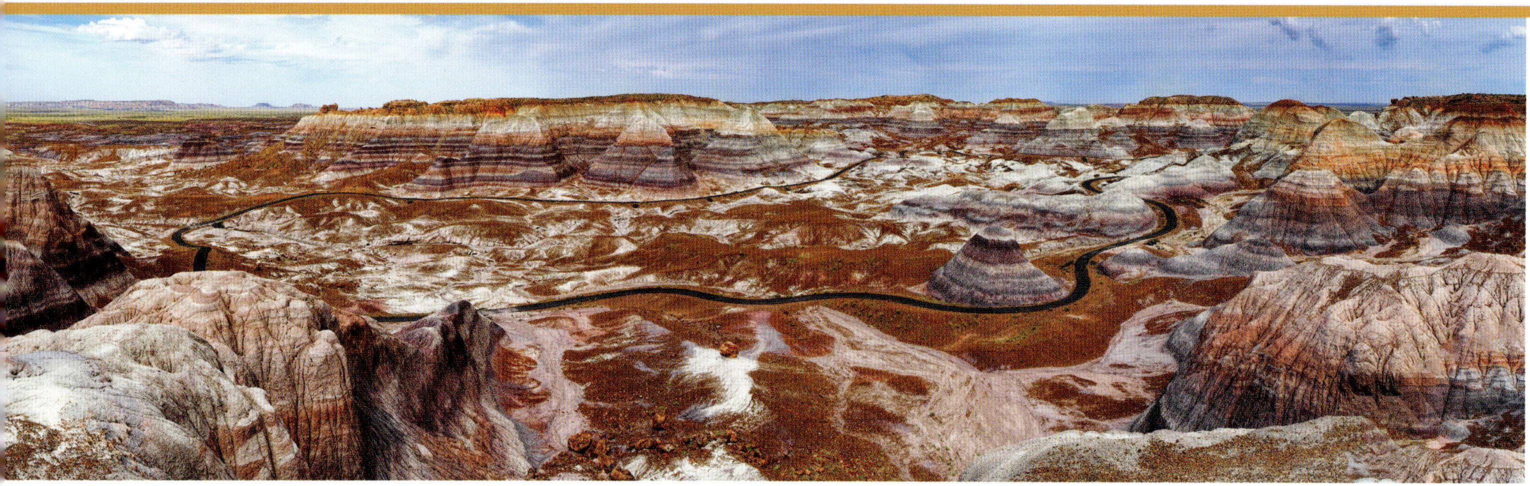

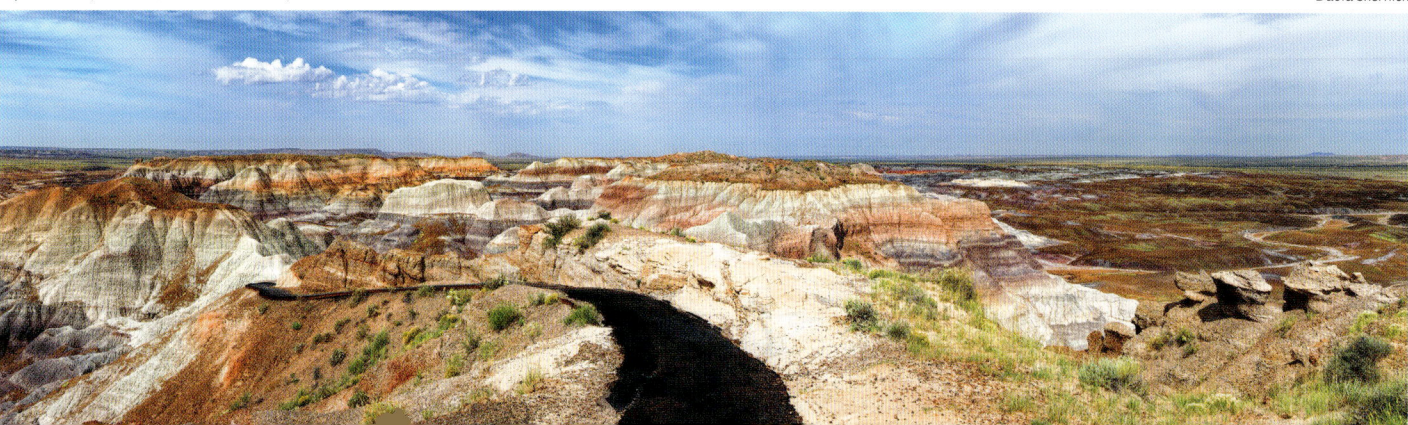

Blue Mesa Trail, Petrified Forest National Park, Arizona

David Skernick

The stretch of Route 66 that fell within the borders of Petrified Forest National Park was open from 1926 to 1958. Eventually the Mother Road was moved north, closer to what is now Interstate 40. Take Highway 180 to loop through the park and return to I-40 up the road. No worries—you won't miss anything special. Petrified Forest National Park includes dramatic landscapes and rock formations, as well as fantastic hiking trails. It is a nice change from the urban landscape of Route 66. Fossils found within the park have been traced to the Triassic Period (252–201 million years ago).

Top of the trail, Petrified Forest National Park, Arizona

David Skernick

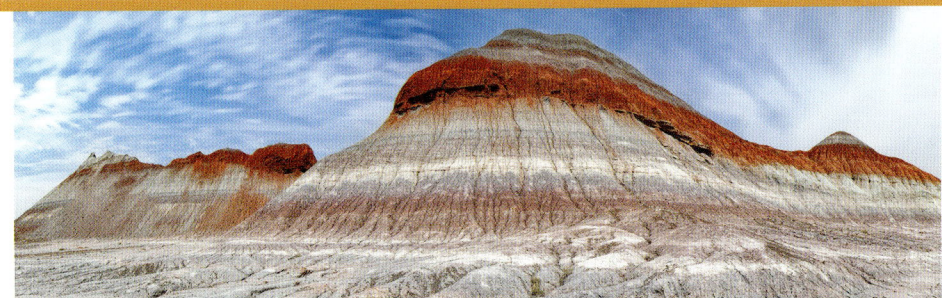

The Tepees, Petrified Forest National Park, Arizona

David Skernick

I could not decide between color and black and white for this photo. One of the great advantages of digital photography is that you can easily render both versions in postprocessing. Where does your eye go in these two photos? Do you notice the cracks, texture, and lines more in the black-and-white version? Does your eye move to the reds first in the color version?

This photo (*below*) was taken just outside the national park boundary. The Painted Desert covers 7,500 square miles. Petrified Forest National Park encompasses about 1,500 square miles within that desert. There is more petrified wood in the Painted Desert and Petrified Forest National Park than anywhere else in the world.

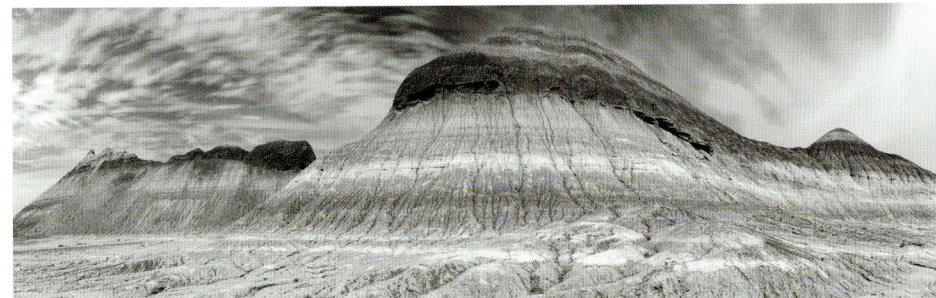

The Tepees, black and white

David Skernick

Chinde Point, the Painted Desert, Arizona

David Skernick

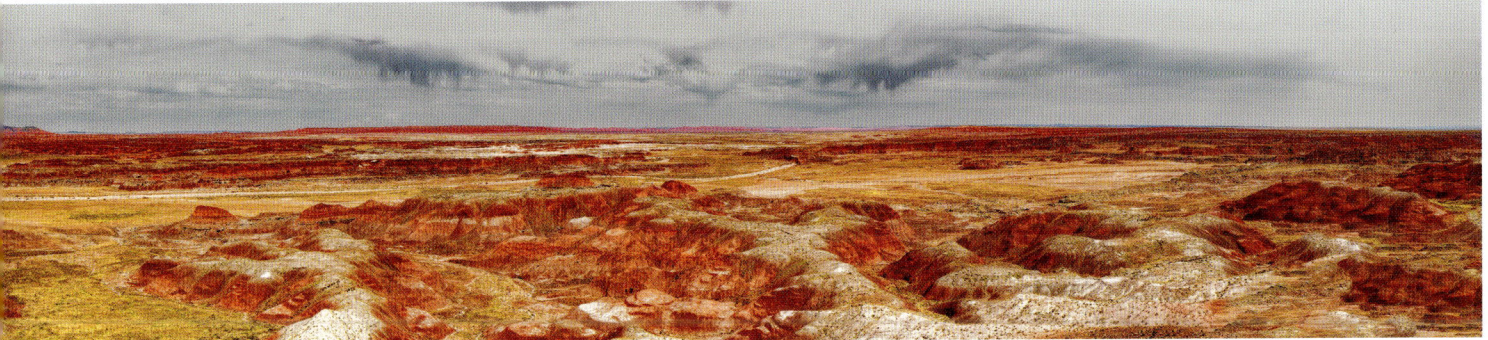

Whiting Brothers

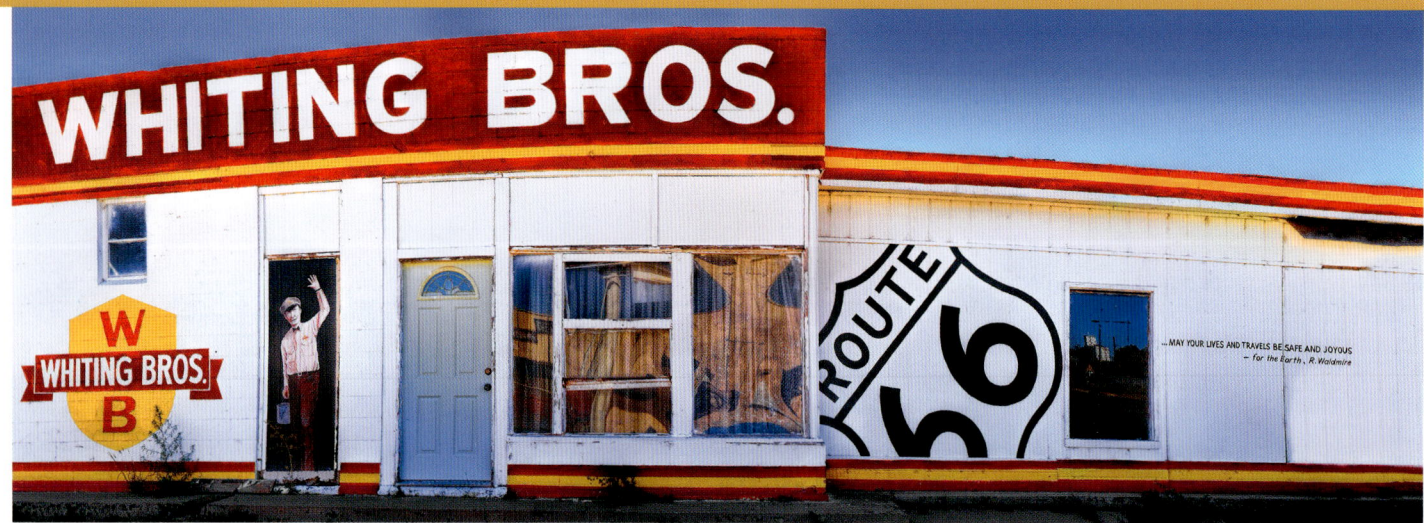

Whiting Bros. mural, Tucumcari, New Mexico

David Skernick

Whiting Bros. signs and remnants of their old buildings can be seen occasionally along Route 66. I did a little research and found that during the same year that Route 66 began to be built, the four Whiting brothers started building a chain of gas stations and motels in the Southwest that would eventually cover Route 66 from Lenwood, California, to Shamrock, Texas. They built over a hundred stations. Thirty-two could be found along Route 66. They were as common to see as Stuckey's, Burma-Shave signs, and Indian Joe's Trading Posts.

The Arab oil embargo in 1973 and the expansion of the interstate highways led to the Whiting brothers selling off their businesses a little bit at a time, until there was almost nothing left. Today, except for one remaining Whiting Brothers station in Moriarty, New Mexico (*next page*), and a few buildings that have been utilized for other businesses' purposes, all that is left of the Whiting empire are its fading yellow and orange signs and crumbling buildings. Soon these too will most likely disappear, ending another chapter of Route 66 history.

I found this rare motel sign in Continental Divide, New Mexico. I shot with a long lens to isolate the sign. I liked the way that long patch of sky repeated the shape of the sign. Always be on the lookout for that type of good fortune. It can sometimes be the difference between a snapshot and a photograph.

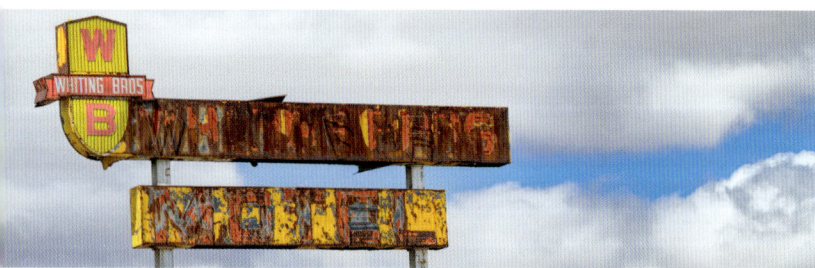

◀ Whiting Bros. Motel sign, Continental Divide, New Mexico
David Skernick

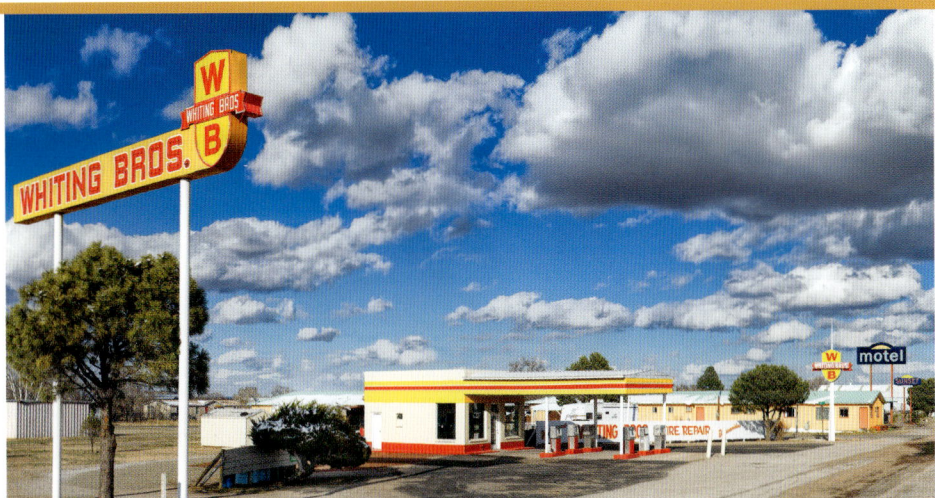

Whiting Bros. Gas Station, Moriarty, New Mexico

David Skernick

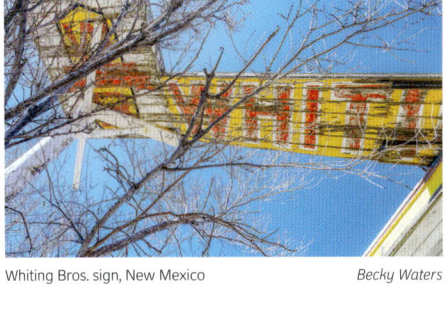

Whiting Bros. sign, New Mexico

Becky Waters

Above is the last standing Whiting Brothers gas station. It may not be a working business, but the people of Moriarty, New Mexico, keep it pristine for all who travel Route 66 to enjoy.

Becky took the shot above in San Fidel, New Mexico. Look how the angle she chose makes it look like an airplane wing. Shooting through the branches added to that fiction as well. Every choice you make, including angle and what you include or don't include in your photo, helps tell a story. Be intentional about the story you tell.

On the left are the front and back of a single sign I found in Casa Blanca, New Mexico. The far-left shot was taken in beautiful morning light. I wanted only the sign and that great cloud in the photo. I walked close to the sign and pointed my camera up. When I returned along the same route that evening, the sky had clouded over. I shot from the other side and included the road and poles to show location and tell more of that part of the story.

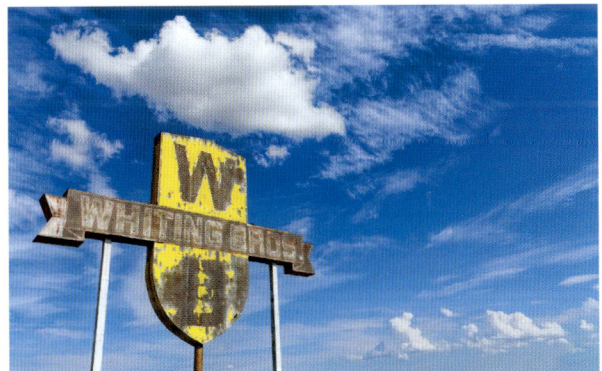

Whiting Bros. sign, Blanco, New Mexico

David Skernick

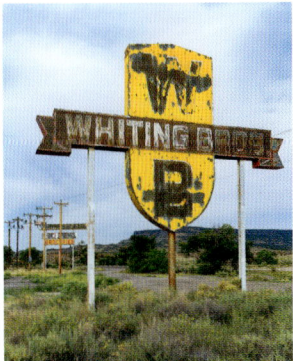

Opposite direction

David Skernick

Gallup, Continental Divide, and Milan, New Mexico

Exit the I-40 into Gallup, New Mexico. You will find cool signs, good food, and nice places to spend the night. Watch the signs and you can stay on Route 66 east of Gallup. You will be on several New Mexico highways, but they follow old Route 66. Watch the signs carefully.

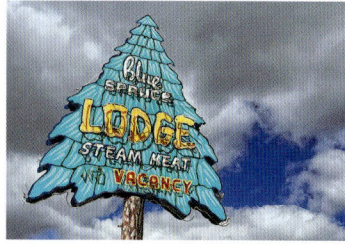

Blue Spruce sign, Gallup, New Mexico *David Skernick*

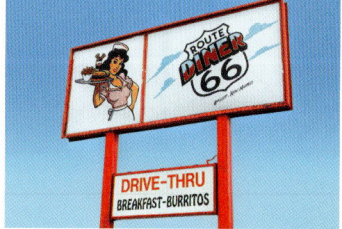

Route 66 Diner, Gallup, New Mexico *David Skernick*

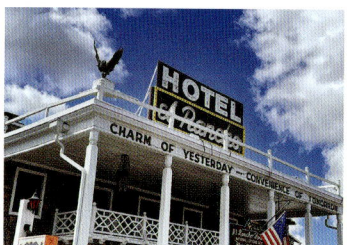

Hotel El Rancho, Gallup, New Mexico *David Skernick*

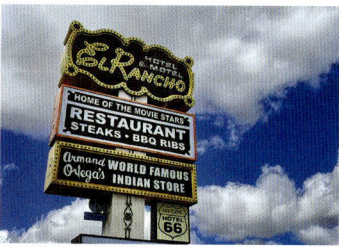

Hotel El Rancho sign, Gallup, New Mexico *David Skernick*

The Blue Spruce is closed, but the Hotel El Rancho is going strong and is a great place to stay. The Route 66 Diner is open and will be glad to see you! If you

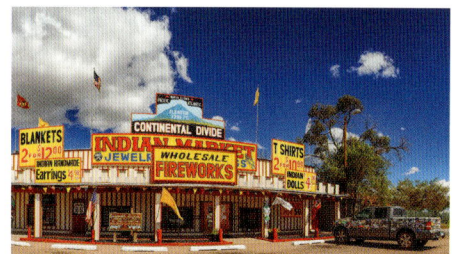

Indian Market, Continental Divide, New Mexico *David Skernick*

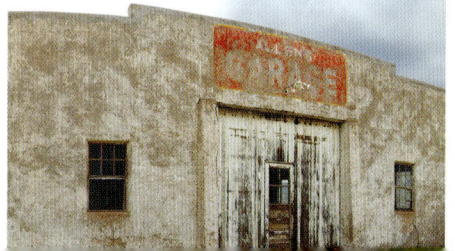

◄ Allen's Garage, Milan, New Mexico *David Skernick*

are wondering, I did use the drive-thru and I did get a breakfast burrito. So good! I found the old garage on the bottom left in Milan, New Mexico, on old Route 66 between Gallup and Grants. I liked the way that all the windows looked different from this angle. I cut the shot close on both sides because I wanted you only to look "out" from those windows.

You want to use your composition to force those who look at your photos to see what you saw when you discovered your image.

I actually avoided an old car parked next to the building. A couple of my students would think that a terrible oversight. I like shooting old cars too, and they are plentiful along the Highway of America, but this time I thought they detracted from my composition.

There is no need to include elements just because they are there. Always consider whether they add or detract from your subject. If the backup singers drown out the lead singer, it isn't harmony—it's just noise.

On the other hand, in the above left photo taken in Continental Divide, I included Bob 3 in the parking lot. Am I just sentimental? Maybe, but I thought a truckful of stickers in a parking lot of a market with all those signs was not a distraction, but rather a natural addition to the scene. It's okay if you disagree. I am only trying to give you an idea of what goes through my head when I'm taking my own photos. There's no right and wrong here; it's art! My intent is always to help you make your statement as clearly as possible.

The Acoma Indian Reservation and San Fidel, New Mexico

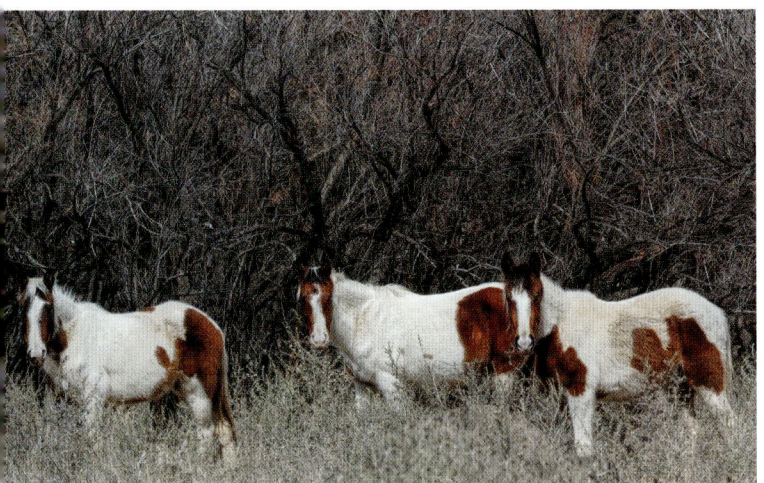

Horses on the Acoma Indian Reservation, New Mexico   *David Skernick*

You have to get back on the 40, but you'll see anothe Historic 66 sign at exit 117. NM 124 (Route 66) winds along a beautiful canyon, past old signs and buildings, within the Acoma Indian Reservation. The reservation towns are closed to the public, but it is a pretty stretch of road.

I found these sweet horses in the canyon. The white hair against the darker trees may have created an exposure problem. My camera meter might have been fooled into overexposing the horses while trying to expose the dark content.

Check the "Preview" options in a DSLR or mirrorless camera. Make sure your replay is set to show "clipping." These are some-times called "flashies" or "highlights." The white areas of your photo will flash where the whites are so bright that they will lose detail. If you are looking at a histogram, you would see the peaks start to crawl up the right side of the box.

The solution is to use your exposure compensation (the plus/minus thing) to underexpose your photo just under flashing (1/3 stop). This may seem complicated, but if you expose every shot you take this way, you will have the most detail possible to work with in postprocessing.

Finding a frame for your subject is always a good idea. Here the fence, flowers, trees, and road all serve that function. The flowers were there in the fall. I took this photo in September. I drove by in March and the flowers were gone. When you see something worth shooting, never put it off. Even waiting to shoot "on the way back" can be a mistake, unless the light is all wrong when you are there the first time. Often you forget to stop or don't see that thing you wanted to shoot when you are coming from the opposite direction, or you return at a different date. Carpe diem!

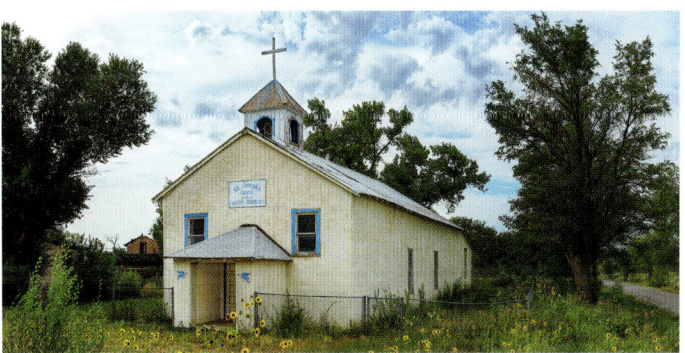

St. Joseph's Church, San Fidel, New Mexico   *David Skernick*

50

Albuquerque, New Mexico

Albuquerque, New Mexico, is a big city! Be prepared for traffic and congestion. Route 66 follows Central Avenue through the city. You will see many signs, murals, and old motels that are part of Mother Road history. Many of the old buildings have been repurposed. Watch out for private property. The photos on these pages were taken quickly. We jumped out of our cars and snapped quickly with our cameras, and often just our phones. You will be dodging traffic and will find yourselves in neighborhoods where you need to be aware of your surroundings. We enjoyed ourselves and found the hunt and snacks well worth the effort.

The photos on these pages are in no particular order. I just put them together like a puzzle to give you an idea of what we found. I have spent time driving through Albuquerque several times, in different seasons and times of day. Each time I seem to find something new that I want to save as a photo. Try to take the time to drive Central Avenue (Route 66) in both directions. You will see more that way. Look for a sneak group shot in Anne's photo of Lindy's Diner. Sometimes we can't resist hamming it up!

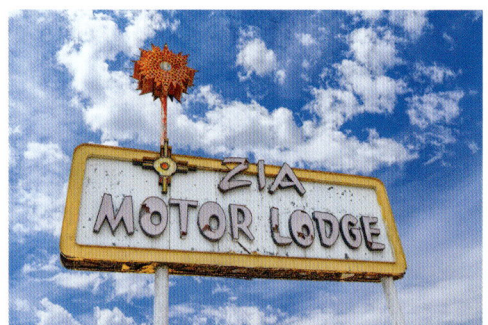
Zia Motor Lodge sign, Albuquerque, New Mexico *David Skernick*

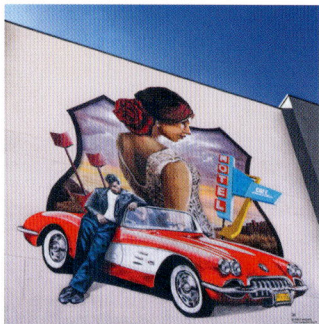
Paths 1 mural, Albuquerque, New Mexico
Becky Waters

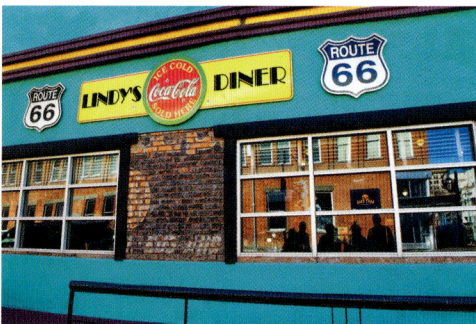
Lindy's Diner and Alburquerque group shot *Anne Schlueter*

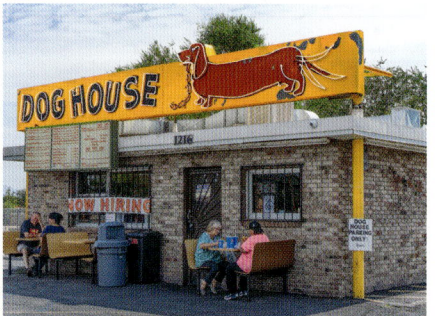
Dog House, Albuquerque, New Mexico *David Skernick*

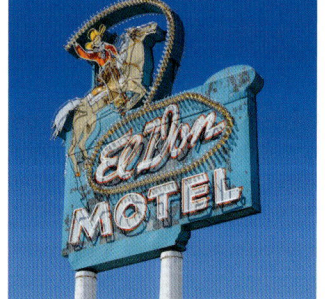
El Don Motel sign, Albuquerque *David Skernick*

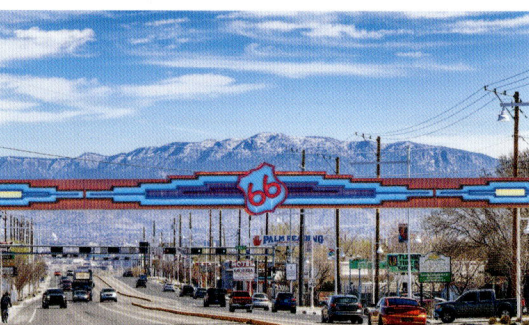
Central Avenue, Albuquerque, New Mexico, looking west *David Skernick*

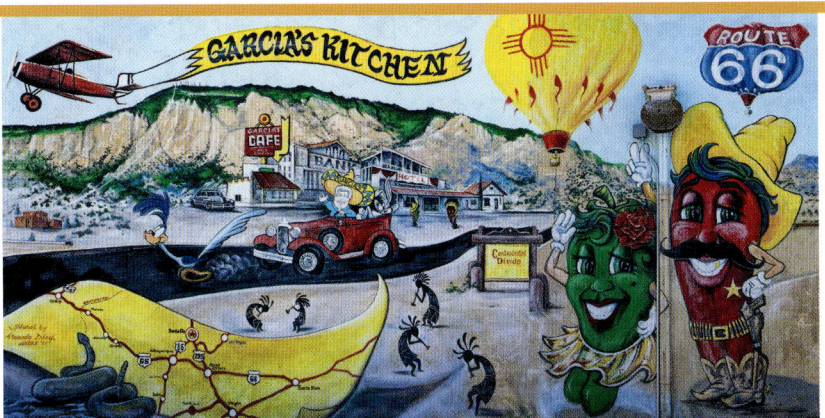

Garcia's Kitchen, Albuquerque, New Mexico

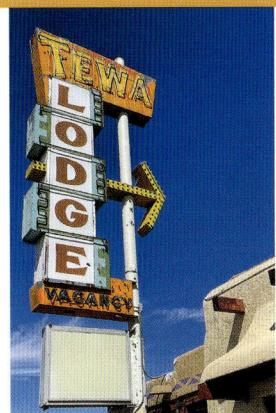

Tewa Lodge, Albuquerque *David Skernick*

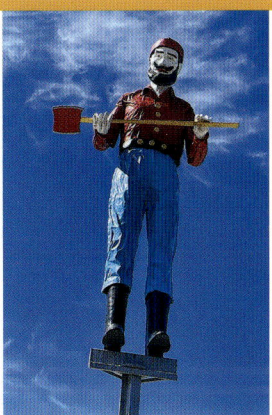

Paul Bunyan, Albuquerque, New Mexico
David Skernick

When photographing signs, try to be aware and deliberate about what else you include in your pictures. Look how important clouds, or the lack of clouds, are to these photos, some of which were taken on different days, in different seasons. Change your angle and be patient to get the clouds where you want them to be in your composition. If there are no clouds at all, find the best light you can, and use the sky as a negative space. It should create a pleasing shape to go with your subject, rather than overwhelming it. Use angle and timing to make even your simple sign images more interesting and appealing.

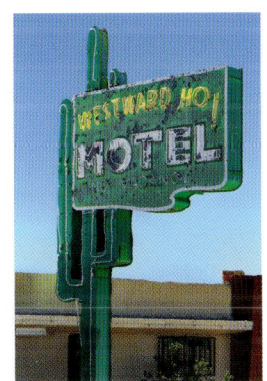

Westward Ho Motel *David Skernick*

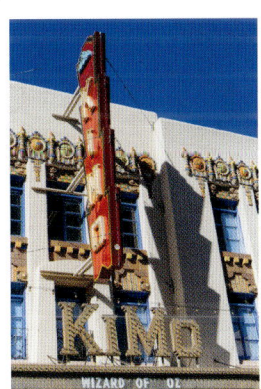

Kimo Palace Theater *David Skernick*

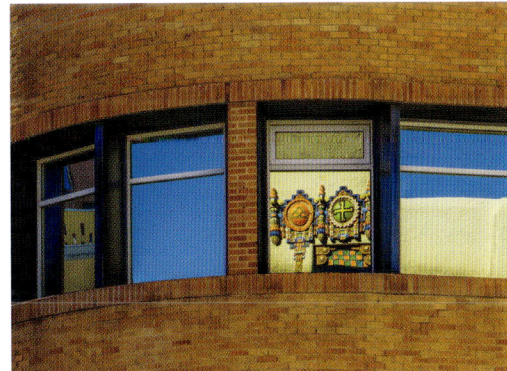

Kimo Palace Theater, Albuquerque, reflection *Becky Waters*

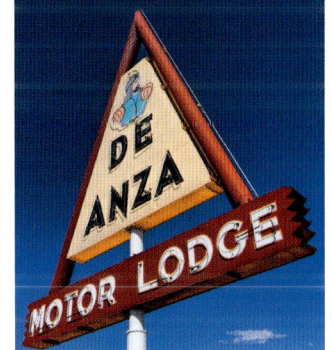

De Anza Motor Lodge, Albuquerque
David Skernick

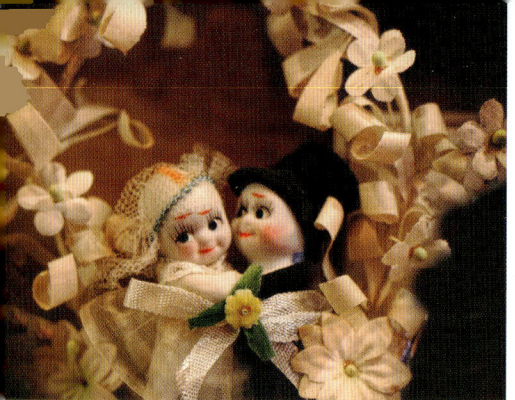
Tinkertown wedding — *Gayle Pepper*

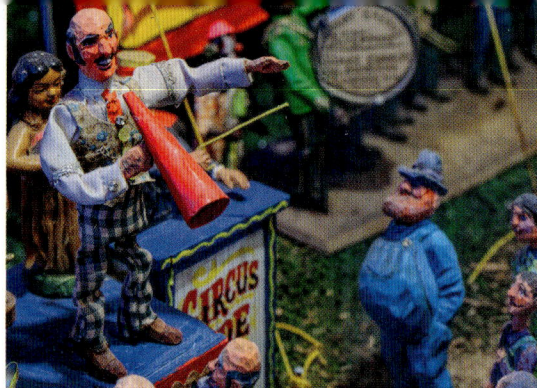
Tinkertown barker — *David Skernick*

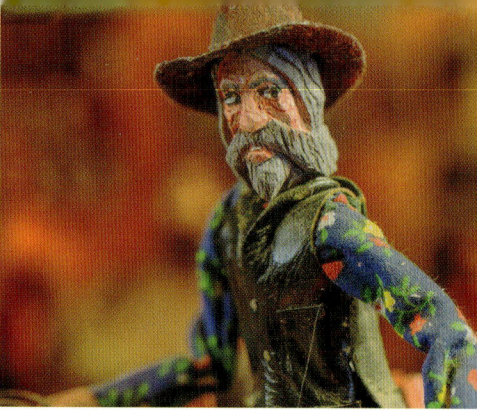
Tinkertown cowboy — *Gayle Pepper*

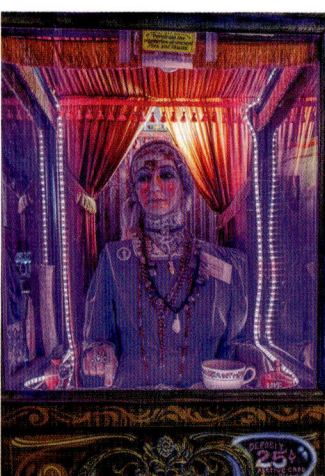
Tinkertown gypsy — *Becky Waters*

Just east of Albuquerque, take exit 175 off the I-40 to 14 North and head up the Turquoise Trail to Sandia Park. This treat is off Route 66, but just by a few miles. It is worth your time! Look for signs to Tinkertown. Ron Ward and his wife, Carla, traveled the country, painting carousels for carnivals. When they retired, Ron started carving little figures and scenes, as well as making some phenomenal paintings. Adding an astounding collection of all sorts of memorabilia from fairs, carnivals, and circuses, the couple put together a museum called "Tinkertown." I don't have the words to tell you how amazing this place is, but luckily, as it turns out, I have some photos! These were taken in the museum. Some with phone cameras, some with DSLRs and mirrorless cameras on tripods. Set your white balance to auto, say hi to Carla for me, and just have a great time!

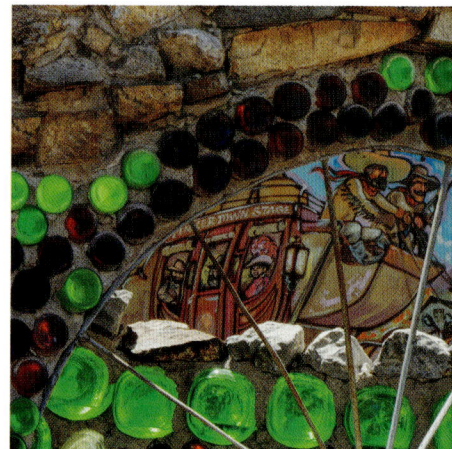
Tinkertown bottles — *Diane Waldron*

Tinkertown drum — *Anne Schlueter*

Tinkertown clowns — *David Skernick*

Tinkertown tickets — *David Skernick*

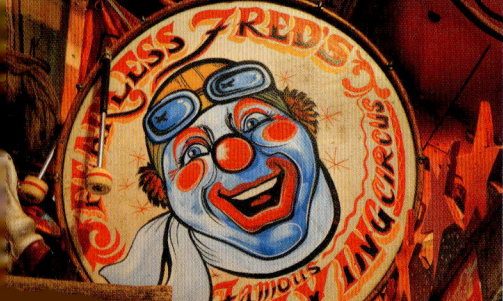

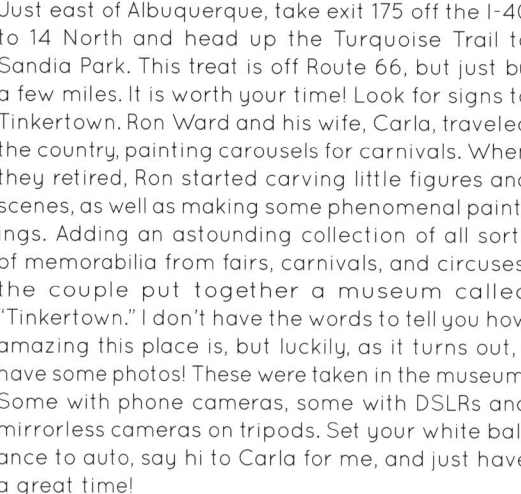

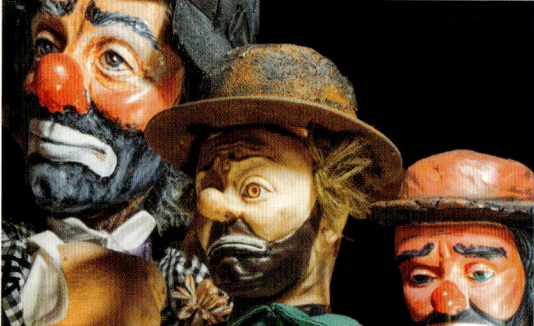

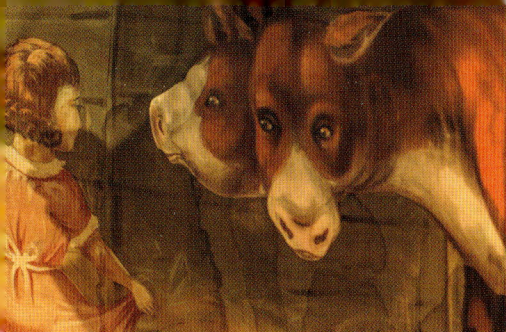

Tinkertown cows *Gayle Pepper*

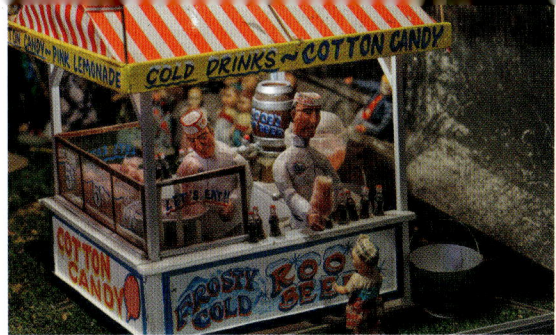

Tinkertown treats *David Skernick*

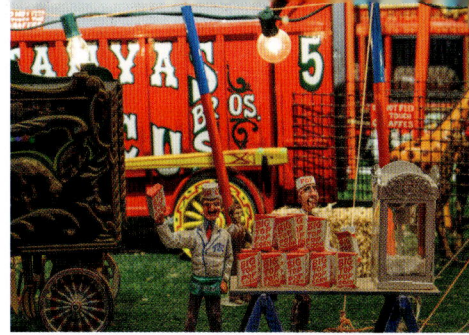

Tinkertown circus *David Skernick*

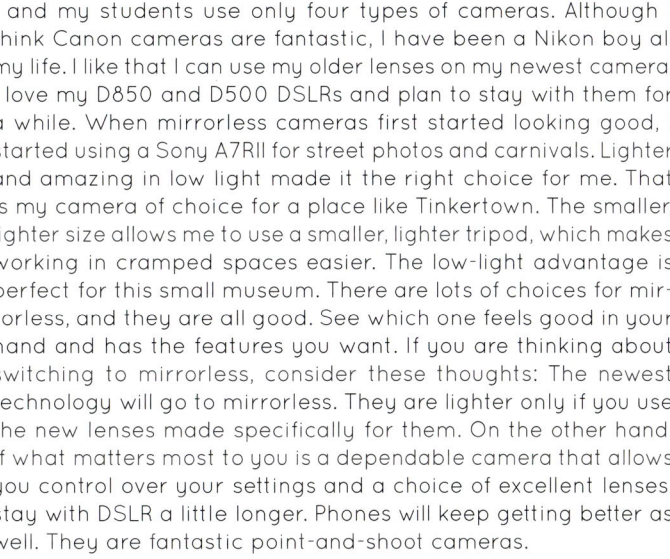

If you have checked the appendix, you might have noticed that I and my students use only four types of cameras. Although I think Canon cameras are fantastic, I have been a Nikon boy all my life. I like that I can use my older lenses on my newest camera. I love my D850 and D500 DSLRs and plan to stay with them for a while. When mirrorless cameras first started looking good, I started using a Sony A7RII for street photos and carnivals. Lighter and amazing in low light made it the right choice for me. That is my camera of choice for a place like Tinkertown. The smaller, lighter size allows me to use a smaller, lighter tripod, which makes working in cramped spaces easier. The low-light advantage is perfect for this small museum. There are lots of choices for mirrorless, and they are all good. See which one feels good in your hand and has the features you want. If you are thinking about switching to mirrorless, consider these thoughts: The newest technology will go to mirrorless. They are lighter only if you use the new lenses made specifically for them. On the other hand, if what matters most to you is a dependable camera that allows you control over your settings and a choice of excellent lenses, stay with DSLR a little longer. Phones will keep getting better as well. They are fantastic point-and-shoot cameras.

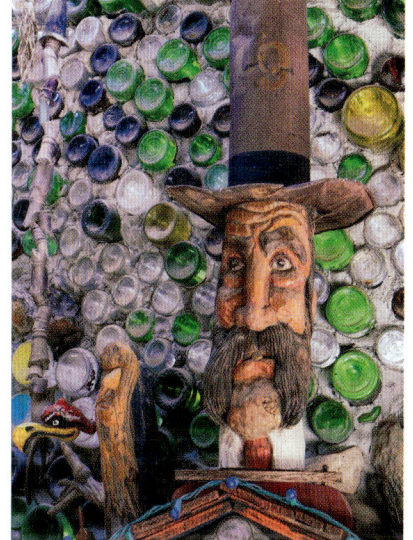

Tinkertown pioneer *Becky Waters*

Tinkertown speaker *Anne Schlueter*

Tinkertown painting *Becky Waters*

Tinkertown porch *Diane Waldron*

Tinkertown wagon *Anne Schlueter*

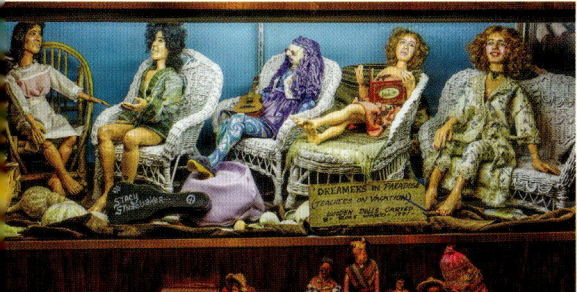

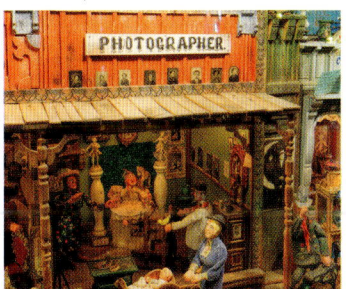

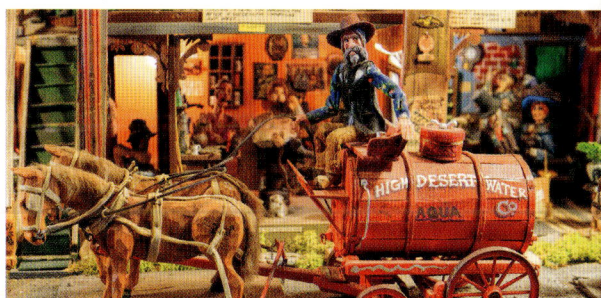

Edgewood, New Mexico

From I-40, take exit 176 onto New Mexico Highway 333 and you will be on Route 66 again. Just past mile 4, turn your music off and drive exactly 45 miles per hour. If you listen very carefully, you will hear "America the Beautiful" coming up from your tires on the pavement. You gotta love Route 66! It's been a long time since this was created, and it is hard to hear all but the last six notes or so clearly, but it's there!

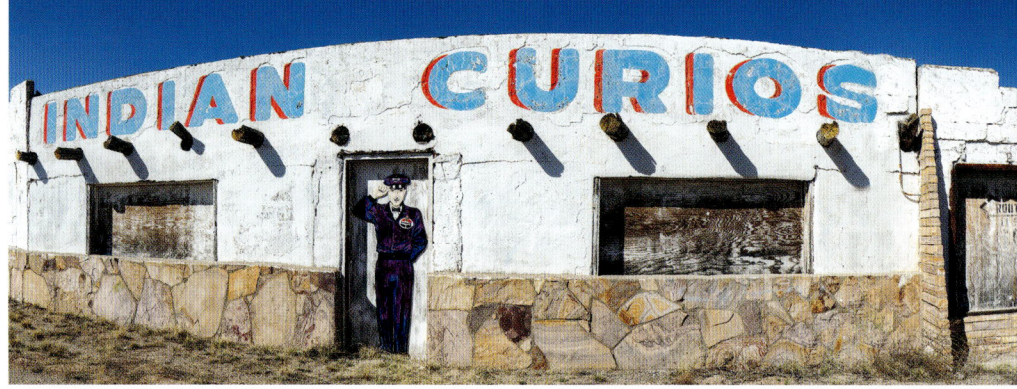

Indian Curios, Edgewood, New Mexico

David Skernick

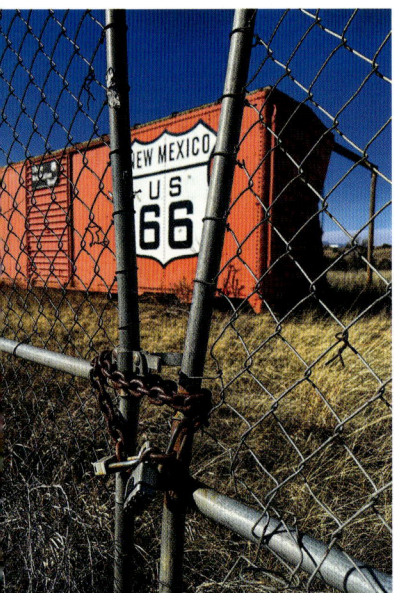

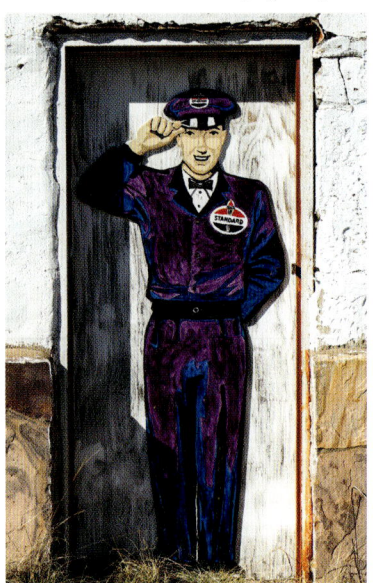

On Route 66, look to your left and you will see this old shop in Edgewood. The saluting gas station attendant looks like he has been repainted recently. The 66 sign, on the other hand, is faded almost out of existence. The Mother Road is like that. The old and new mixed together. We do that too. Sometimes you will enhance in Photoshop, but sometimes you don't have to, and sometimes you don't want to. No advice here—just one of those observations I think are worth noting. To the left of the old Curio shop, there is this cool train car behind this very serious-looking lock and chain. Several photographers tried to find a way to get around the fence issue and failed. The train car was too big and close to the fence to be shot without the links showing up and distracting from the subject. Pepper solved the problem by making the fence and chain part of her story. You know that old saying "If you can't beat 'em, join 'em?" Sometimes that will be the only way you can make a shot work. "Love the one you're with" works too.

Train car and fence, Edgewood, New Mexico
Gayle Pepper

Standard Oil Man, Edgewood

Diane Waldron

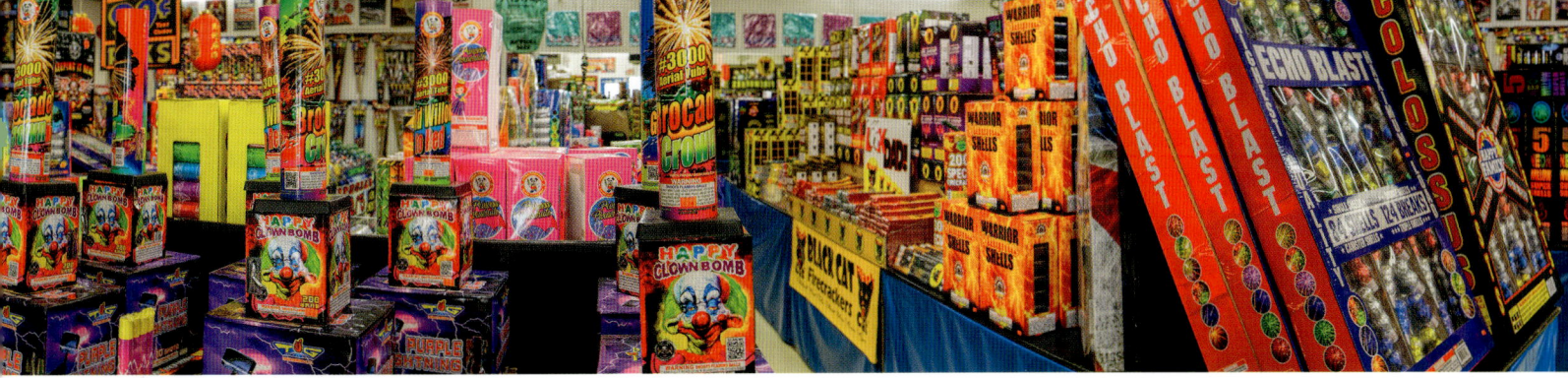

Fireworks World interior, Moriarty, New Mexico

David Skernick

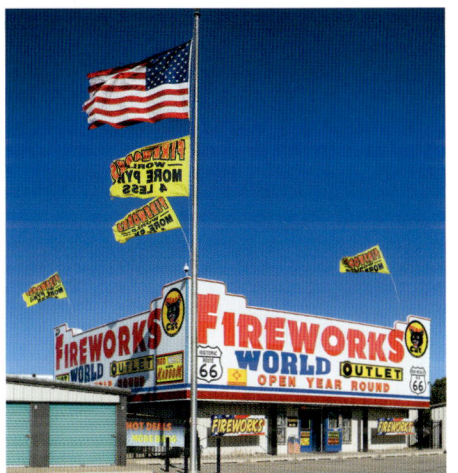

Fireworks World, Moriarty, New Mexico *David Skernick*

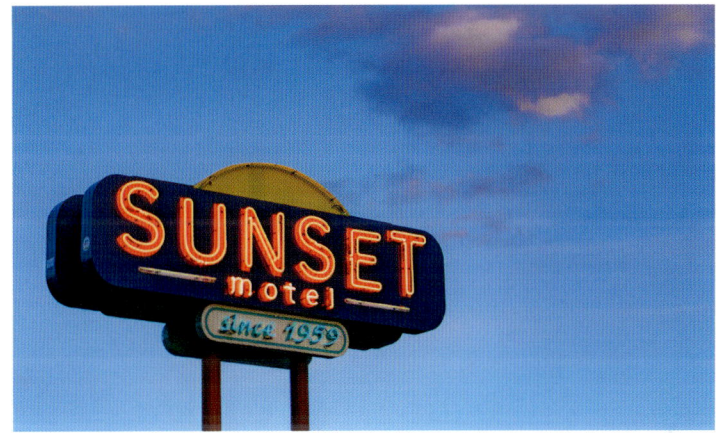

Sunset Motel sign, Moriarty, New Mexico *David Skernick*

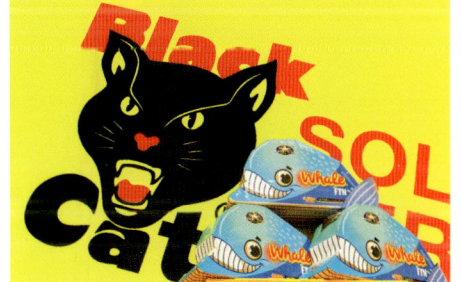

Black Cat sign, Moriarty, New Mexico *Anne Schlueter*

Moriarty, New Mexico, is home to the last Whiting Brothers gas station. It was shown on an earlier page, along with Whiting Brothers signs and the story behind the business. We found this fantastic fireworks outlet there too. Anthony let us in to photograph the bright, colorful boxes and displays. The wind was up that day, as you can see. I used a fast shutter speed to capture the Stars and Stripes in midwave. There was nothing I could do about the other flags waving the wrong way to be read. It's okay, though, because this is a photo of an interesting building. The flags are just a frame for the most important sign—the one on the building itself. I stayed at the Sunset Motel on another trip along Route 66. It's a perfect motel. Great beds, clean rooms, hot showers, Wi-Fi, and lots of TV channels. What else do you need? The owner, Mike, made me feel totally welcome. I shot his sign for him at sunset!

Santa Rosa, New Mexico

Santa Rosa, New Mexico, became a transportation hub in 1930, when the original Route 66 alignment went right through the small town. Back then, the road turned here toward Santa Fe. In 1937 the east–west alignment went through Albuquerque instead, but Santa Rosa remained on the route. By the way, I followed the route through Santa Fe and found no proof at all of the Mother Road, other than small signs letting me know I was on track. Santa Rosa is full of Route 66 buildings and signs and is home to a wonderful car museum.

In the early years of Route 66, many towns didn't want the car exhaust and commotion of the road in their towns. Later on, they saw the profits that came with the route, and sought re-alignments that would bring the potential business closer. There were physical logistics that also caused the route to be realigned.

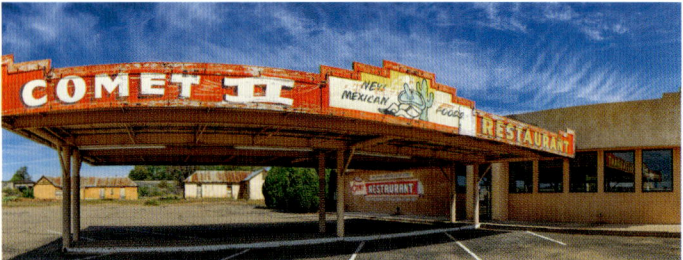

Comet II Restaurant, Santa Rosa, New Mexico   *David Skernick*

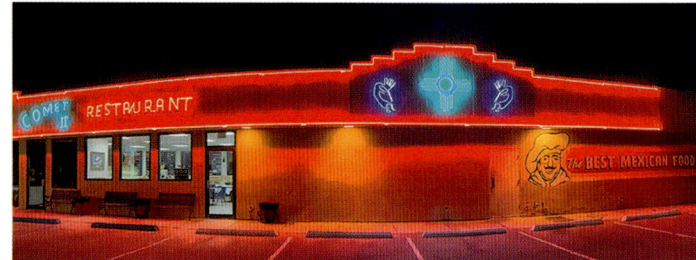

Comet II Restaurant, night, Santa Rosa, New Mexico   *David Skernick*

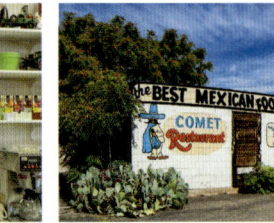

Jonny at the Comet II *David Skernick*

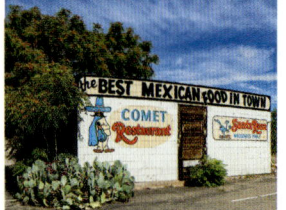

Comet II Restaurant sign *David Skernick*

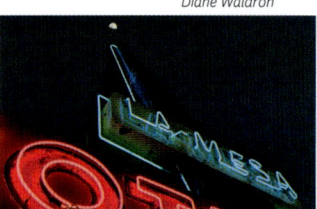

Pie Man
Diane Waldron

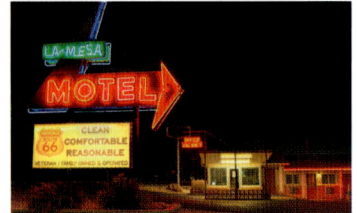

La Mesa Motel, Santa Rosa, New Mexico
Anne Schlueter

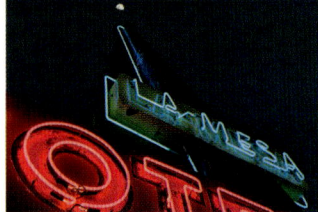

La Mesa sign and moon   *David Skernick*

This is where we ate, and this is where we slept. Yeah, we ate at a couple of other places, such as Chico's and Mr. Bee's—both were fantastic—but the Comet II was special because ninety-year-old Jonny Jr. cooked our meals himself and treated us like part of the Martinez family. The restaurant was started in 1927 and is still owned and run by the same family. It was also a really cool place to photograph in all kinds of light.

We stayed here at the La Mesa Motel. It is the perfect Route 66 motel! Clean, updated, and totally comfortable rooms and beds. The owners are there in case you need anything anytime, and then, there's that sign! If something is worth photographing, it is probably worth photographing more than once, from different angles and in different light. It's called investigating your subject. Spend the time. Set a goal, such as five photos, to challenge yourself.

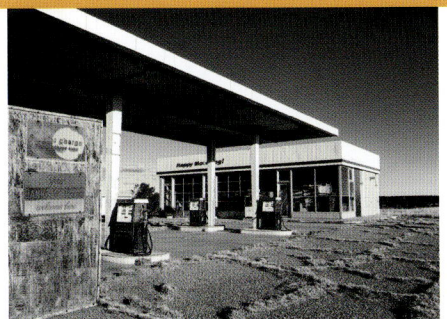

Old gas station, Santa Rosa, New Mexico   *Diane Waldron*

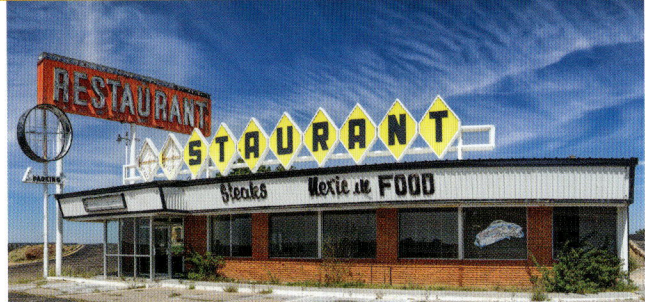

Closed restaurant, Santa Rosa, New Mexico   *David Skernick*

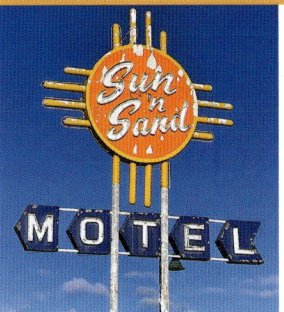

Sun 'n Sand sign   *David Skernick*

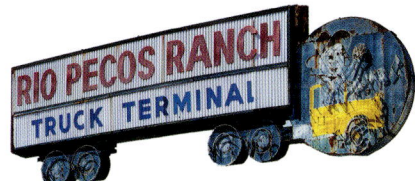

Rio Pecos Ranch, Santa Rosa, New Mexico   *David Skernick*

There is a lot to see and photograph around Santa Rosa, New Mexico. Diane's photo (*above left*) was taken close to our motel. Blue Lake (*right*) is down the street, closer to town.

The Blue Hole is one of seven lakes in Santa Rosa that are connected underground. This one is 81 feet deep and a constant 62 degrees Fahrenheit. It is along the 1937 Route 66 alignment. Because I had clouds that resembled the shape of the lake, I chose to use a wide-angle lens and took a huge double panorama. I used a 35mm lens and shot two rows of nine photos each to achieve this image. You could get a similar visual effect using an ultrawide lens, such as an 18mm, or even a fish-eye lens, but there would be distortion. Fish-eyes are typically wider than 15mm and can be as wide as 3mm. These expensive,

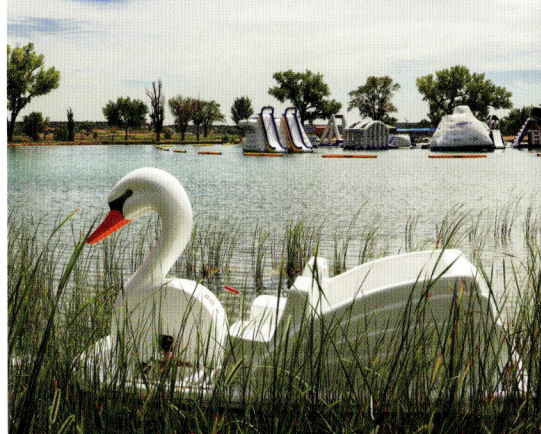

Blue Lake, Santa Rosa, New Mexico   *David Skernick*

unique lenses may render a round picture. "Flat-field fish-eyes" are more common and less expensive and distort less.

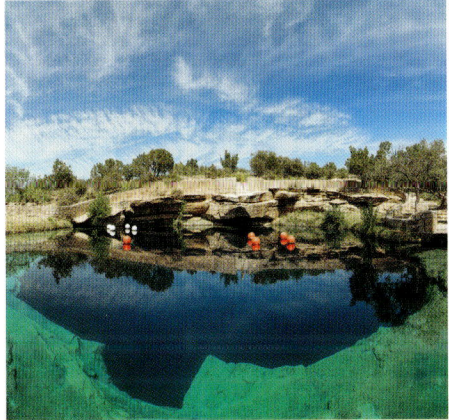

The Blue Hole, Santa Rosa, New Mexico   *David Skernick*

Route 66 Auto Museum, Santa Rosa, New Mexico

The Route 66 Auto Museum in Santa Rosa is a new business that celebrates the old road and makes it interesting for a new generation. Owners Anna and Bozo welcomed us in with our tripods to photograph their amazing collection. We could have spent days there. I had to tear my students away! If you are into cars, this stop is a must.

White balance is a setting in your camera that allows white to look white in different types of light. In sunlight, white would look blue; in tungsten (lightbulbs), white would be yellow orange. In the fluorescent light of this and most other museums and businesses, white would be a kind of greenish purple. Keep that white balance (WB) on Auto, and all will be well! If you are shooting RAW, you can adjust the white balance during processing.

The photos on this page show the museum as a museum. They show you what is there in only a general sense. You will see in those images on the facing page how true artists choose to use this opportunity. Each photo, although taken in the museum, tells only the story of shape, color, and line. These are captures of what was seen, more than simply what was there. If I sound proud, I think you will see why.

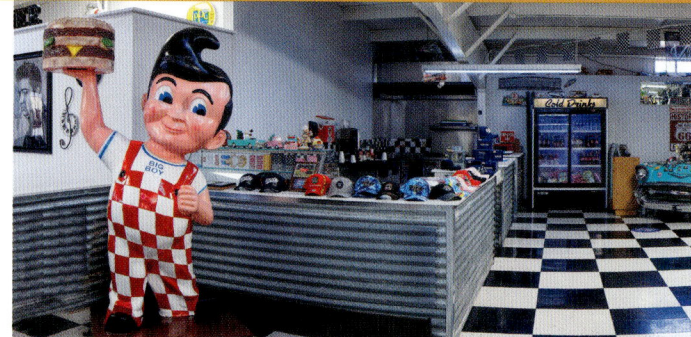

Big Boy, Route 66 Auto Museum, Santa Rosa, New Mexico
David Skernick

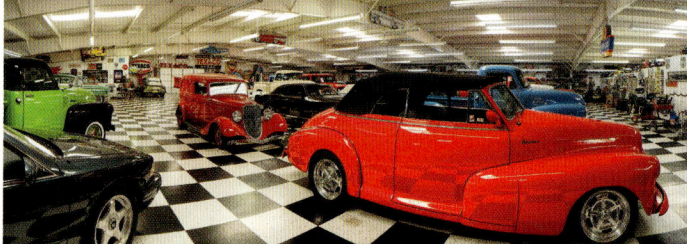

Route 66 Auto Museum, Santa Rosa, New Mexico
David Skernick

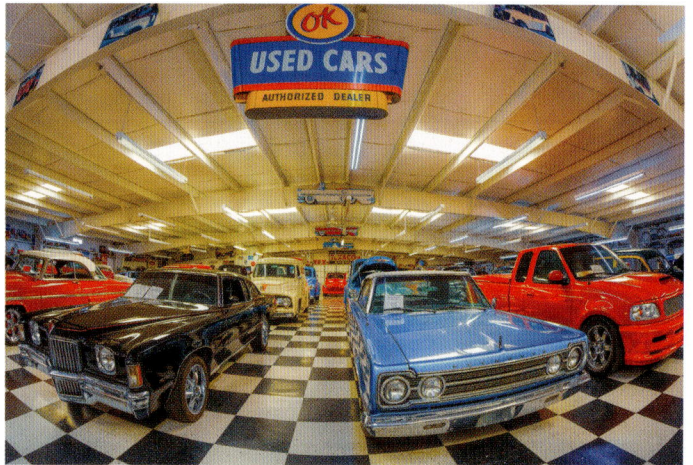

Even in general photos like these, it is important to define your subject. Have you ever seen a movie that didn't have a starring role? Your composition or statement needs to clearly define what you choose to be your subject. Big Boy (*above*) takes over my shot simply because he depicts a human being. We have talked about how people always get your attention first. The red car in the lower photo gets your attention because it is big, red, and in front. Can you look at Pepper's photo without reading "OK Used Cars"? I bet you can't. You do it every time, even though you already know what it says. You are the director of your own photographs. Be sure you pick the "star."

◄ Route 66 Auto Museum
Gayle Pepper

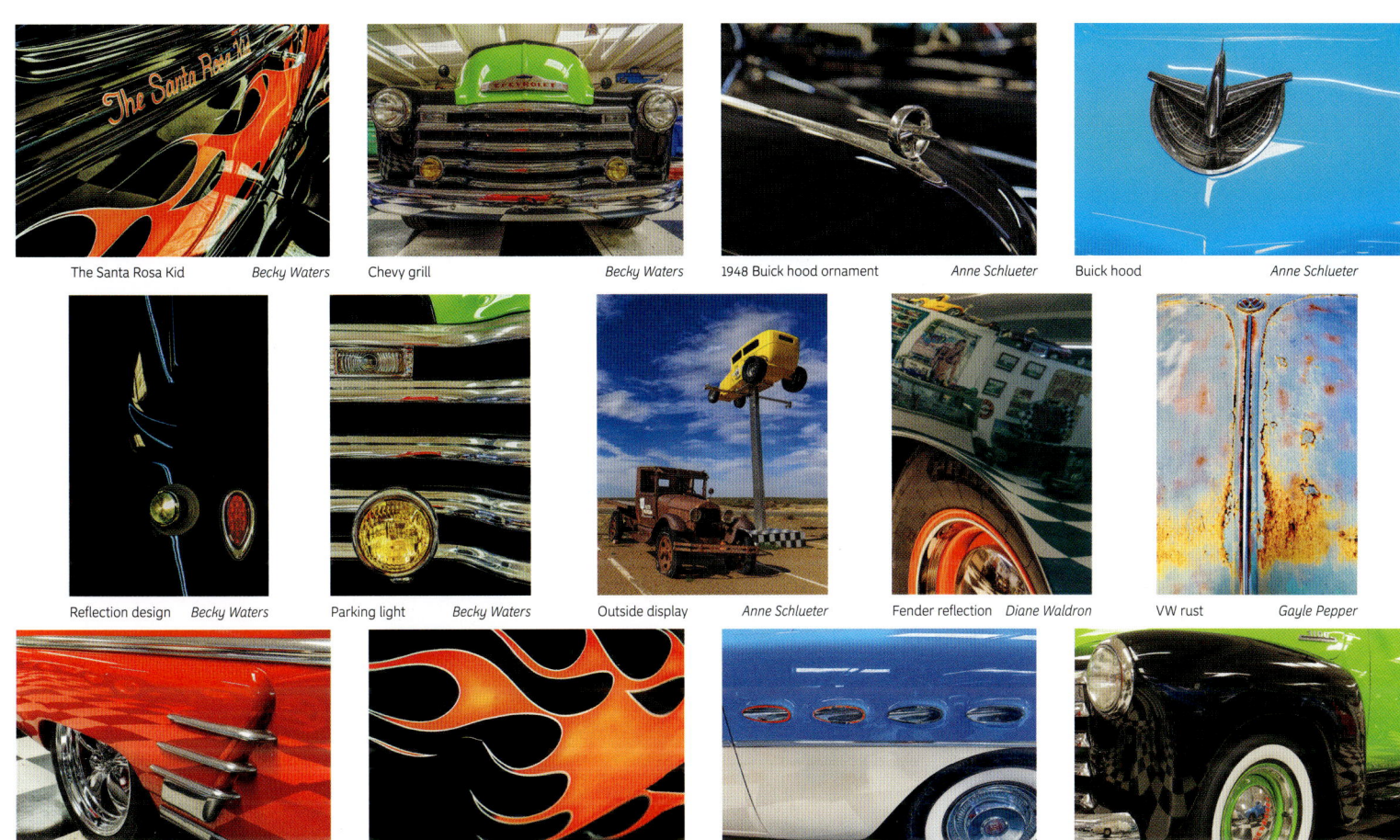

The Santa Rosa Kid — *Becky Waters* Chevy grill — *Becky Waters* 1948 Buick hood ornament — *Anne Schlueter* Buick hood — *Anne Schlueter*

Reflection design — *Becky Waters* Parking light — *Becky Waters* Outside display — *Anne Schlueter* Fender reflection — *Diane Waldron* VW rust — *Gayle Pepper*

Mercury Monterey — *Anne Schlueter* Flames — *Gayle Pepper* Buick Century — *Gayle Pepper* Chevrolet 3100 — *Diane Waldron*

The day we visited the museum, the wind was blowing like crazy in Santa Rosa. This can happen in New Mexico, or anywhere with lots of open space. On this day the gusts were as high as 70 miles per hour. Not only is that way too uncomfortable to be out and about, but the debris in the air might damage your camera or lens. Museums are great places to take refuge from extreme weather. Look how my students took advantage of that opportunity. I am showing only their work here, because frankly, they are better at this kind of photography than I am. Anne took the middle shot before we left. The clouds were moving fast, and she waited for just the right moment to take her photo. Timing is always a huge part of photographic composition.

Santa Rosa and Puerto de Luna, New Mexico

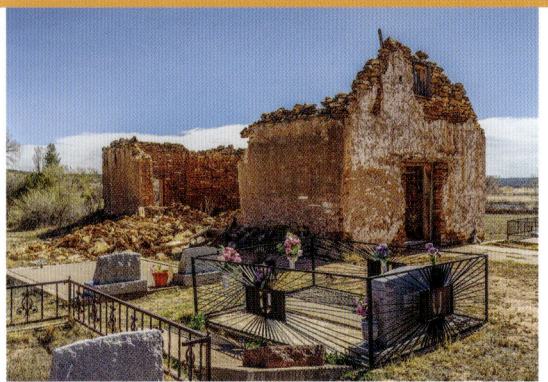

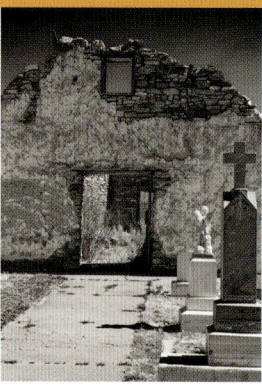 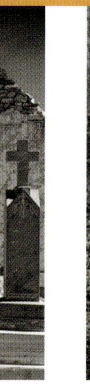

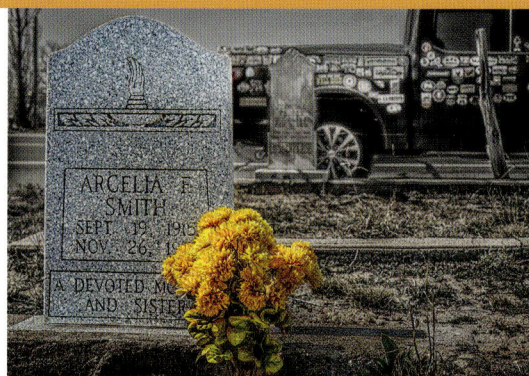

Santa Rosa de Lima Chapel and Cemetery, Santa Rosa, New Mexico *Becky Waters*   Santa Rosa de Lima   *David Skernick*   Santa Rosa de Lima Chapel and Cemetery   *Becky Waters*

Take 3rd Street off Route 66 in Santa Rosa and look for the Santa Rosa de Lima Chapel and Cemetery. It's a wonderful place to take some interesting photos. The road becomes Route 91 out of town. It leads to the small town of Puerto de Luna and the little church on the right. The morning light is perfect. This will take you about 10 miles off Route 66. This ride and coffee, and a breakfast sandwich at Mr. Bee's, is a terrific way to spend the early hours of one day.

Sometimes in this book I'll give you a choice between black and white and color but include both versions. On this page and the next, Becky and I made the choices for you. When do you want black and white? Black and white forces the viewer to see line, form, and content without the distraction of color. It also has an "old" connotation.

Look at all these photos. Color, black and white, and a mixture of the two. All were chosen intentionally to create very different compositions. How do you react to them? Do you think the choices made help or hinder the compositions?

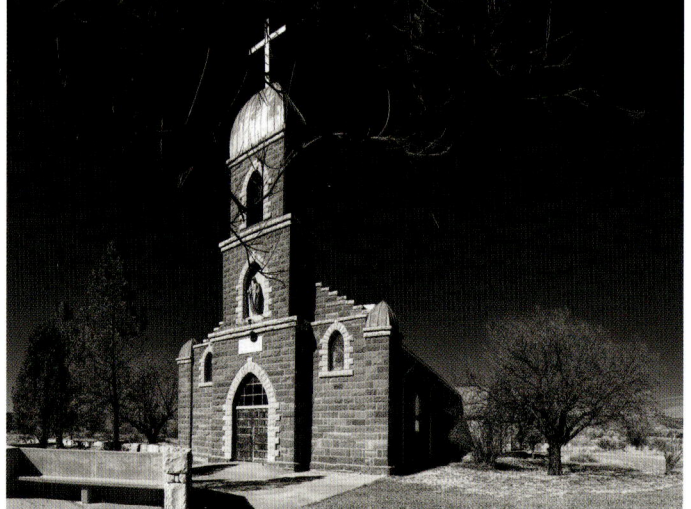

Puerto de Luna Church (1882), New Mexico   *David Skernick*

Cuervo, New Mexico

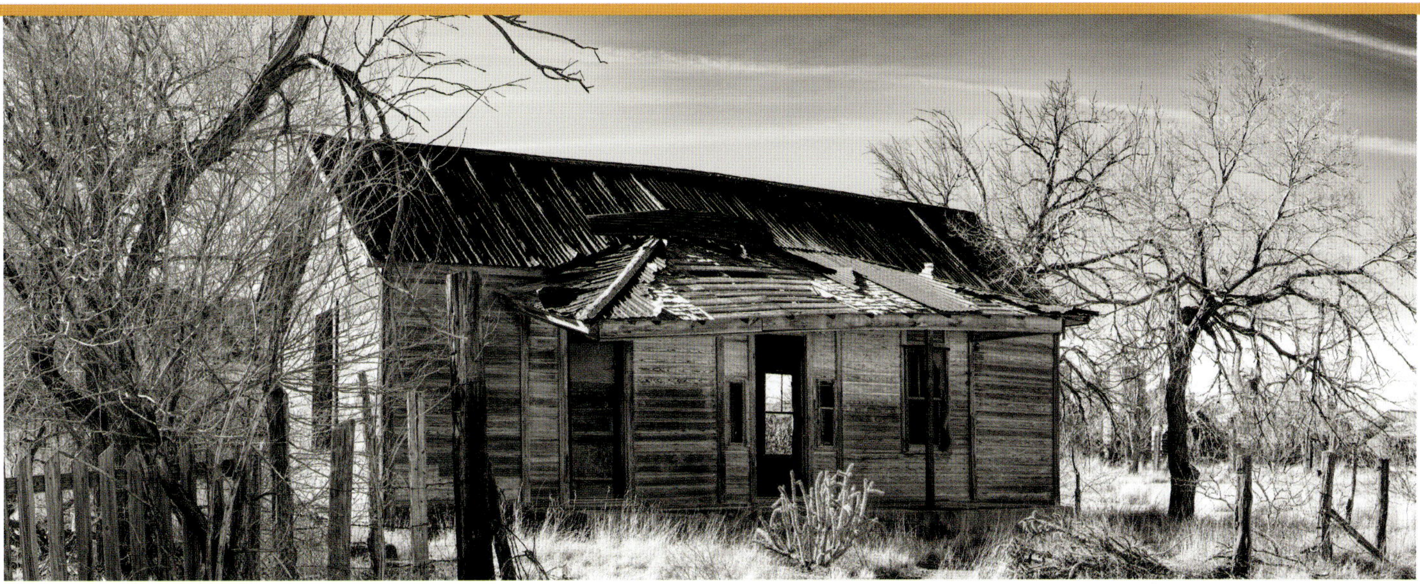

![House, Cuervo, New Mexico]

House, Cuervo, New Mexico

David Skernick

The first exit off Interstate 40, east of Santa Rosa, is Cuervo. Take that exit and head to the north frontage road and you will find this small ghost town. Founded in 1901, Cuervo has lots of buildings, abandoned cars, and dirt roads. In other words, it is a photographer's candy store!

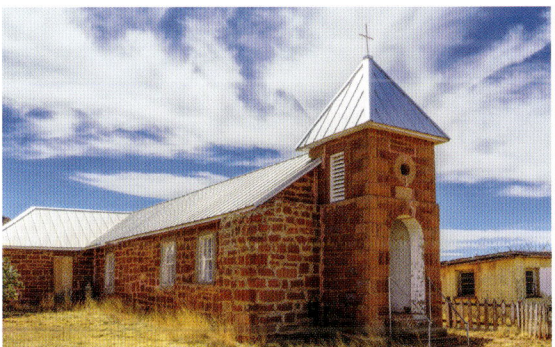

Church, Cuervo, New Mexico

Becky Waters

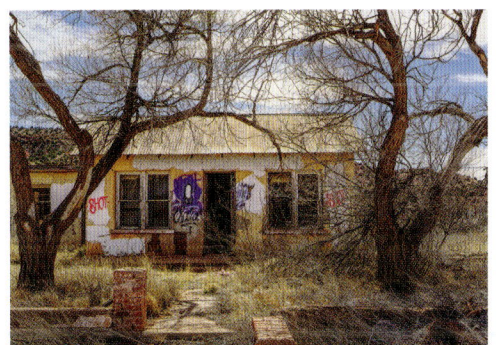

Graffiti, Cuervo, New Mexico

Becky Waters

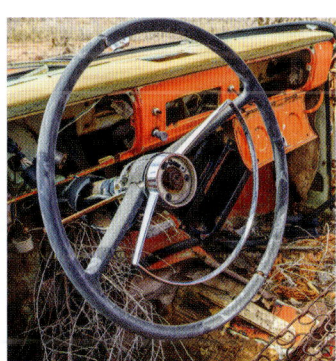

Car, Cuervo, New Mexico

Becky Waters

Tucumcari, New Mexico

Coming from the west on Interstate 40, take the first Tucumcari exit. Stay on Route 66 all the way until the road leads you back onto the freeway at the other end of town. Then come back and get a room. You are going to want to spend at least a day or two photographing Tucumcari. If you look very closely, on the next four pages you will see Bob the Truck parked in front of just one of my favorite places to stay. There are lots of excellent motels and restaurants in town.

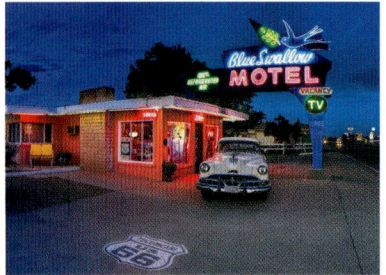

Blue Swallow Motel, Tucumcari, New Mexico
David Skernick

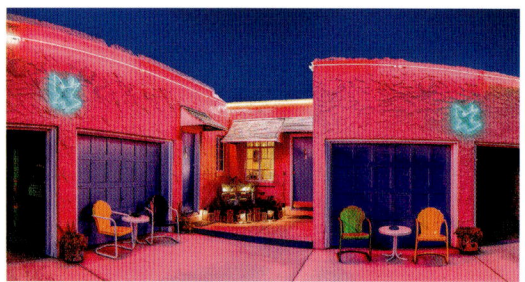

Courtyard
David Skernick

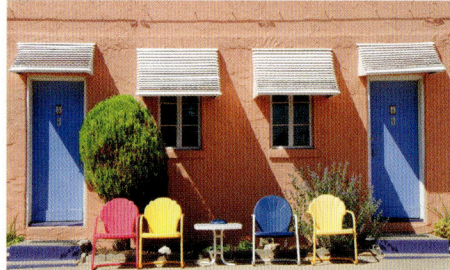

Porch
Judy Nussenblatt

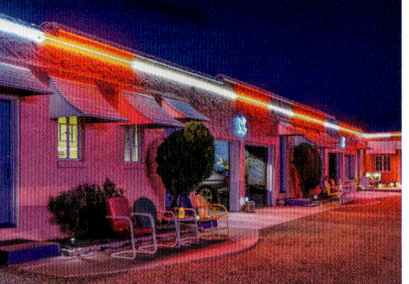

Motel rooms
Becky Waters

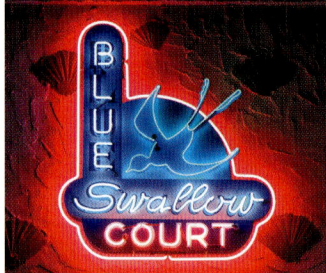

Neon sign
Becky Waters

The Blue Swallow Motel is a famous Route 66 attraction. You can stay here! We photographed it in every kind of light. Look how differently each person in our group chose their compositions. For neon, stay on aperture priority (A) (AV), choose your f/stop for depth of field, and let your camera set the shutter speed. Low ISO (100 or 200) and use your tripod!

You will want to stop at Tepee Curios for souvenirs, and a photo or two. I shot at night and included the building and sign. Susan focused on just the sign at sunset. Sunset is a terrific time to shoot neon signs, since you get the sky colors as well as the neon lights. You need to choose your shot in advance. You may have time to get only one or two images at that magic time.

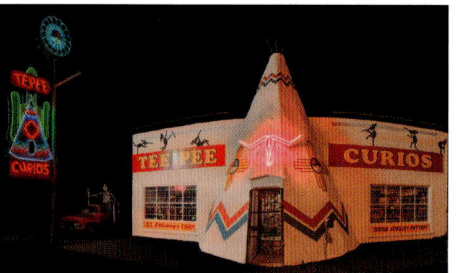

Tepee Curios, Tucumcari, New Mexico
David Skernick

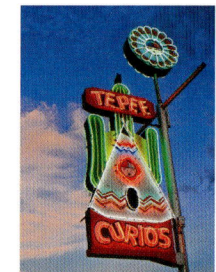

Tepee sign
Susan Vizuary

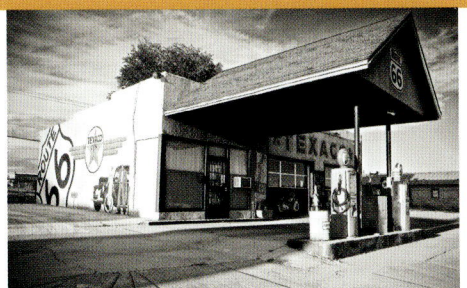
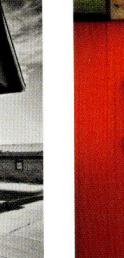

Texaco station, Tucumcari, New Mexico *Susan Vizuary*

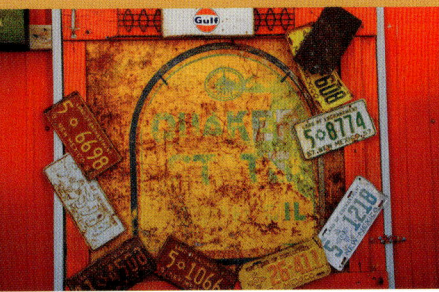

Tucumcari Gas Station wall *Susan Vizuary*

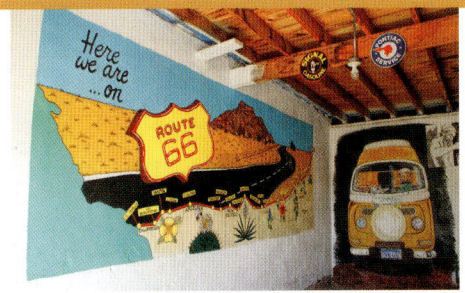

Blue Swallow Garage *Judy Nussenblatt*

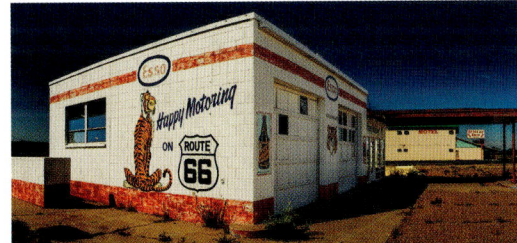

Esso station, Tucumcari, New Mexico *David Skernick*

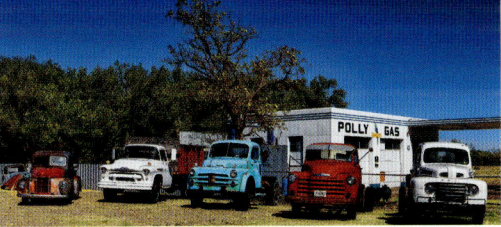

Polly Gas, Tucumcari, New Mexico *David Skernick*

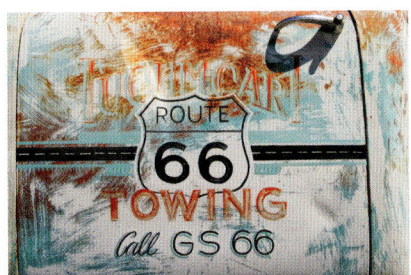
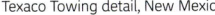

Texaco Towing detail, New Mexico *Judy Nussenblatt*

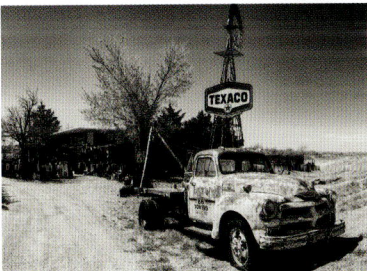

Texaco tow truck, Tucumcari, New Mexico *David Skernick*

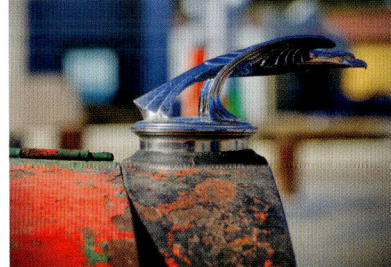

Hood ornament, Tucumcari, New Mexico *Susan Vizuary*

Gas stations are a huge part of America's Highway. No surprise there! Some are photography gold. Look for murals, details, and old cars and trucks. A couple of these were processed in black and white. There is a connotation of age in black and white. It almost feels like you took a time machine back to an earlier time, when Route 66 was the only route.

Tucumcari, New Mexico

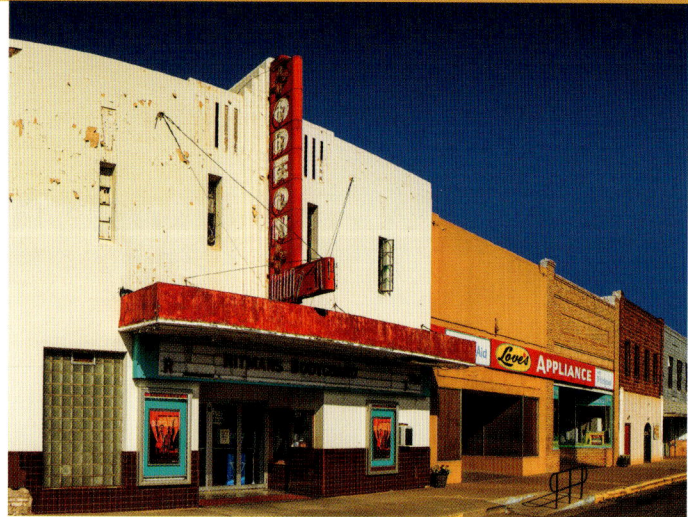

Odeon Theater, Tucumcari, New Mexico

David Skernick

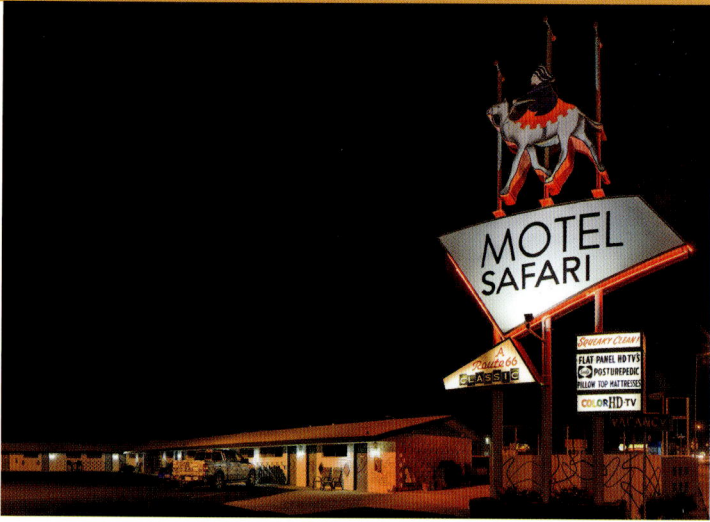

Motel Safari, Tucumcari, New Mexico

David Skernick

While in Tucumcari, be sure to look around the rest of the town. There is some cool architecture and a fantastic dinosaur museum. The old Paradise Motel at the west end of town was still standing the last time I was there, but it always feels like it won't be for long. As with so many places like this, watch out for broken glass and so on.

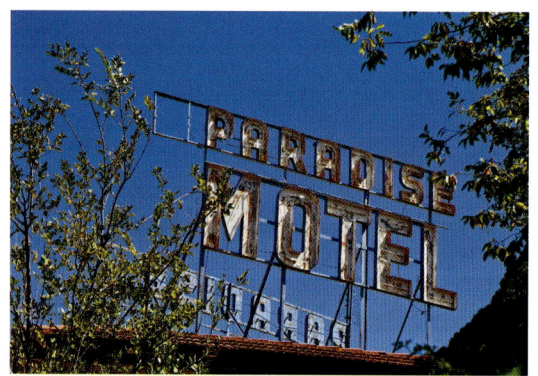

Paradise Motel sign, Tucumcari, New Mexico

Susan Vizuary

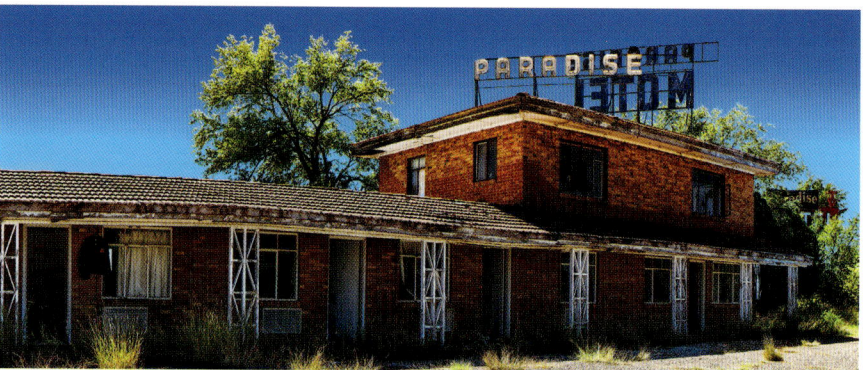

Paradise Motel, Tucumcari, New Mexico

David Skernick

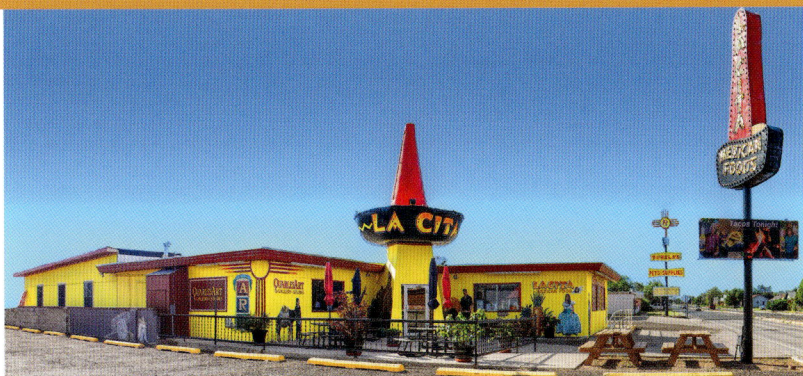

La Cita, Tucumcari, New Mexico (2022) *David Skernick*

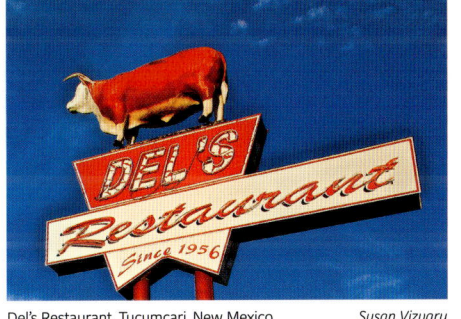

La Cita, Tucumcari, New Mexico (2016) *Becky Waters*

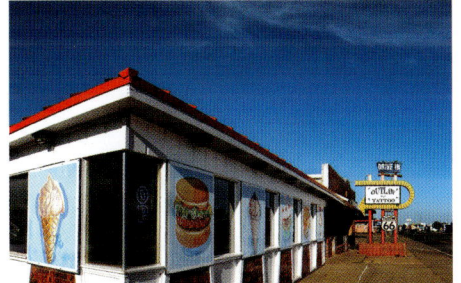

Deli, Tucumcari, New Mexico *David Skernick*

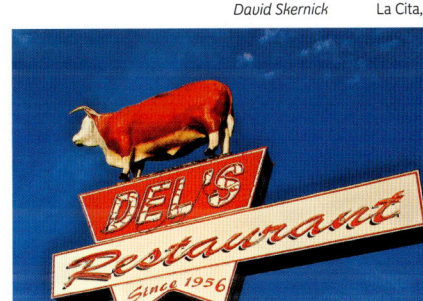

Del's Restaurant, Tucumcari, New Mexico *Susan Vizuary*

La Cita, the Deli, and Del's Restaurant all are open for business as I write this book. I have eaten at all three and recommend that you enjoy their food, as well as their architecture. Note that on Becky's trip, La Cita was a different color. I wonder what color it will be when you find it!

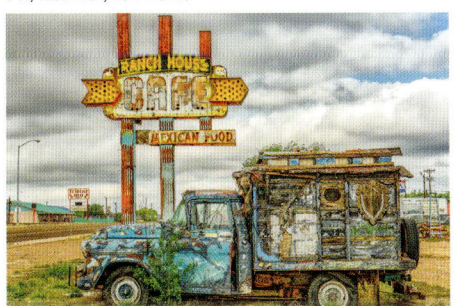

Ranch House Cafe, Tucumcari, New Mexico *Becky Waters*

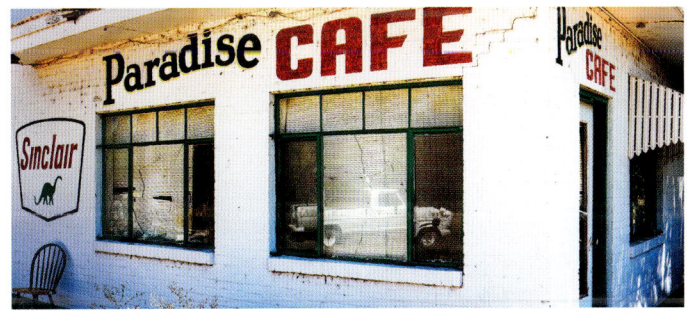

Paradise Cafe, Tucumcari, New Mexico *David Skernick*

Ute Lake State Park, New Mexico

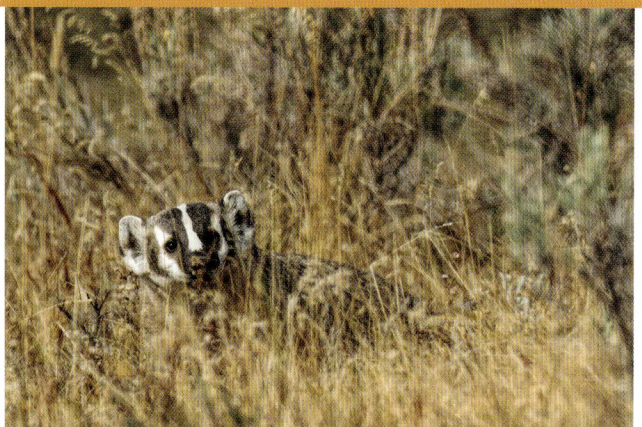

Badger, Ute Lake State Park, New Mexico *David Skernick*

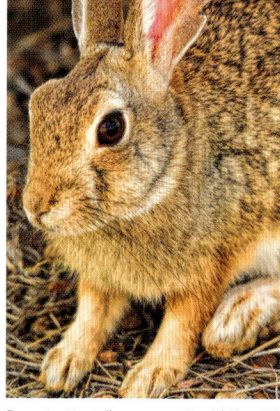

Desert cottontail *David Skernick*

Just before you reach the New Mexico / Texas border, look for Ute Lake State Park. It is a huge reservoir full of fish and wildlife. The lake itself is one of the longest in the state, at almost 13 miles. It is part of the Canadian River, which you will cross later on in Oklahoma along Route 66.

Always be prepared for wildlife. I almost tripped over this little rabbit while walking back to my truck after taking the landscape photo below.

I had a 35mm lens on my camera at the time. A lens that wide would make the little animal look tiny and lost in any composition, even though I was super close.

Lucky for me, I had a second camera over my shoulder with a telephoto lens. Why? Because I was in a place where I might find birds and other wildlife. Ask me how many shots I missed before learning this valuable lesson! May my experience (screw-ups) help you!

With the long lens, I needed to back up from the rabbit to (at least) 13 feet to focus. Always know the closest focal point of your lenses. I was fortunate to have a patient subject.

The badger was a similar story. I was actually looking for waterbirds but was exited to spot that little guy watching me from the high grasses.

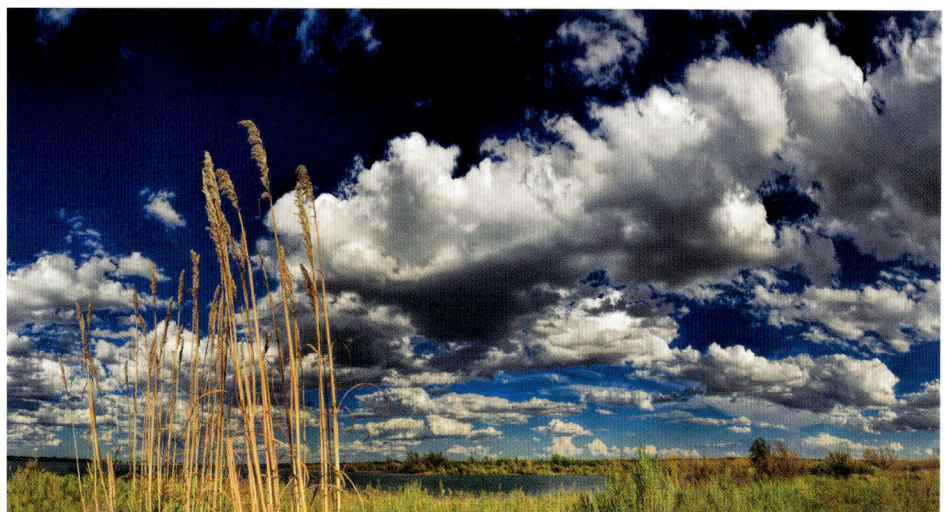

Reeds and clouds, Ute Lake State Park, New Mexico *David Skernick*

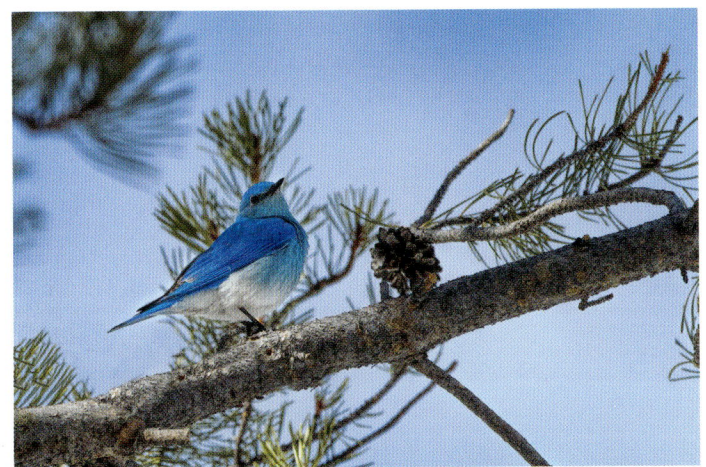

Mountain bluebird, Ute Lake State Park, New Mexico

David Skernick

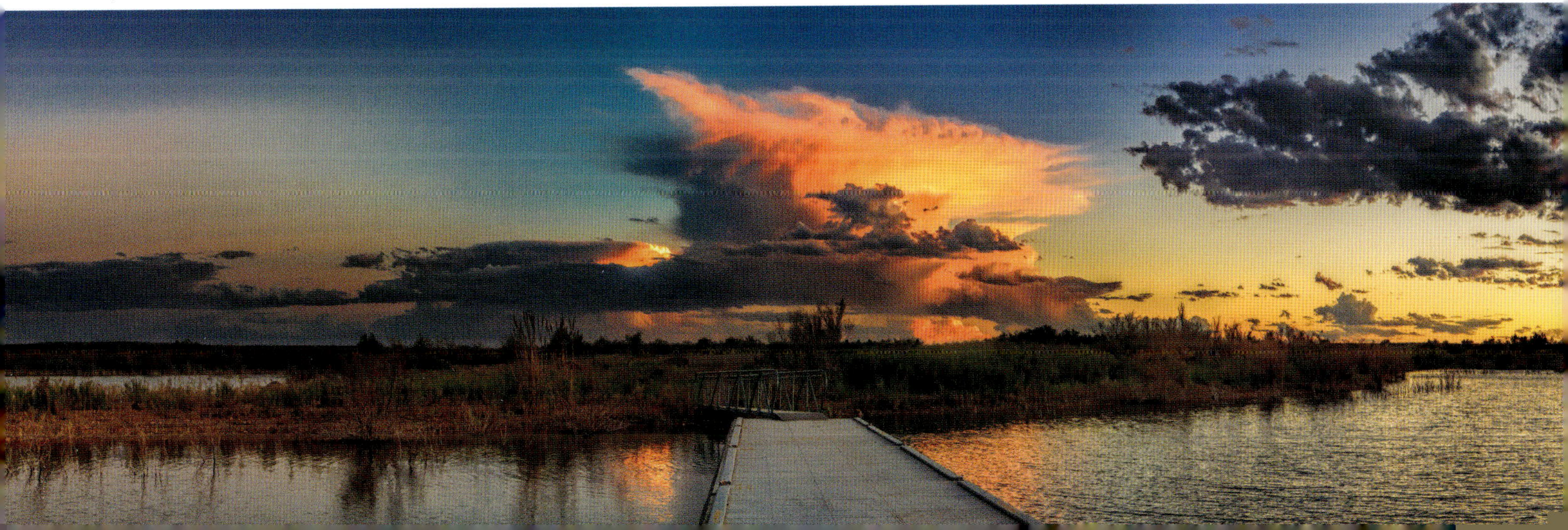

Sunset, Ute Lake State Park, New Mexico

I was driving through the park when I saw this little bird land in a tree I was about to pass. I braked gently so as not to scare the little fella. I rolled down my window as I reached for my camera. You might have figured out that I let go of the wheel to make these two moves. Busted. As I rolled to a stop, I leaned out and grabbed this quick shot of a species of bird I've been trying to get a good shot of for years. Be as prepared as you can. There is just no way I could have captured this photo if my camera and long lens hadn't been within my reach. Even if you are not chasing photographs, keep binoculars or a little telescope handy to look for small birds and wildlife.

I like to use piers as leading lines from the shore out to a body of water. On this day the sunset was behind the land, so I had to shoot the opposite way. I like the way the composition turned out. There will always be things out of our control. We have to learn to "punt."

David Skernick

Adrian and Vega, Texas

Route 66 crosses the Texas Panhandle at the north end of the state. You can find great photo opportunities in the small towns along the way. If you want to be on the old road, follow the frontage roads along I-40 and exit often. Adrian, Texas, is the exact midpoint of the Mother Road between Los Angeles and Chicago. I was only half finished with my sticker map of the route on the doors of Bob the Truck. See the completed map at the end of the book. I had a good lunch and got my midpoint sticker at the diner across the street. Try Rooster's Mexican Restaurant in Vega too. The burritos are incredible!

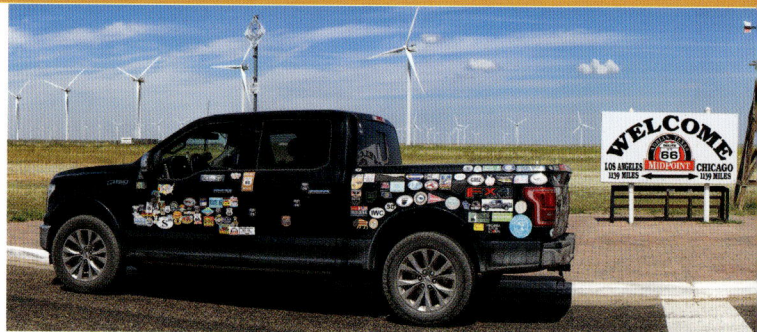

Bob the Truck at the midpoint, Adrian, Texas

David Skernick

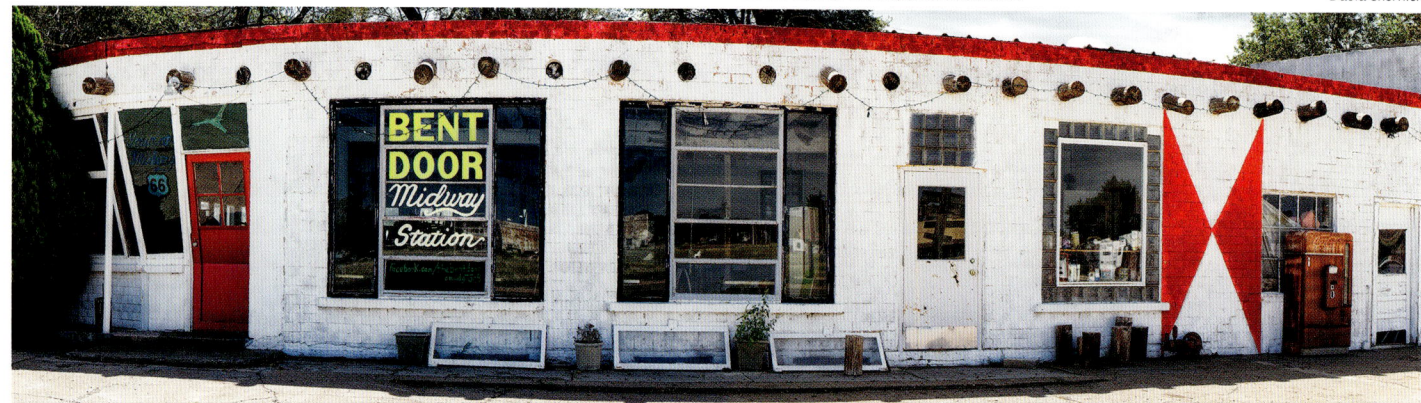

The Bent Door Station, Adrian, Texas
Red truck, Adrian, Texas

David Skernick

Rooster's Mexican Restaurant, Vega, Texas

David Skernick
David Skernick

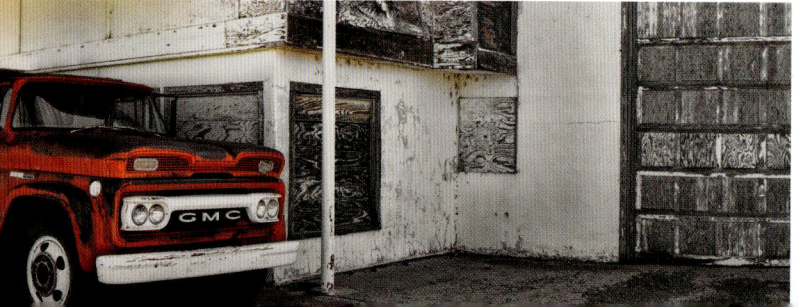

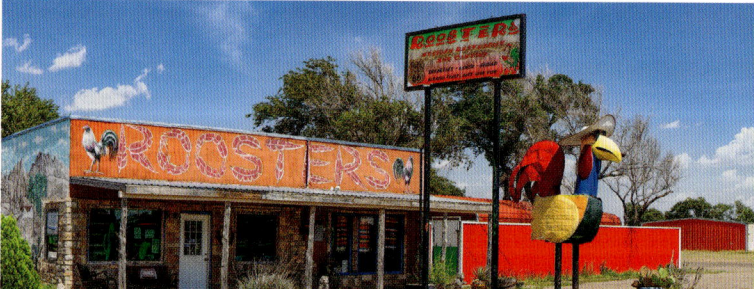

Almost Amarillo, Almost Route 66, Texas

Just west of Amarillo, along I-40, you will come across the Cadillac Ranch (*below*), a public art installation and sculpture. Created in 1974 by Chip Lord, Hudson Marquez, and Doug Michels, it has become part of the Route 66 culture, as has the Slug Bug Ranch, up the road in Conway. But have they? That depends on whom you talk to. The purists say that these are not part of the route, but just attractions near it. Since our reason for traveling the road is to find things worthy of photographs, I included them as just that. The Big Texan is a steak house found along Interstate 40. Great steaks and a fun place. Route 66? Maybe.

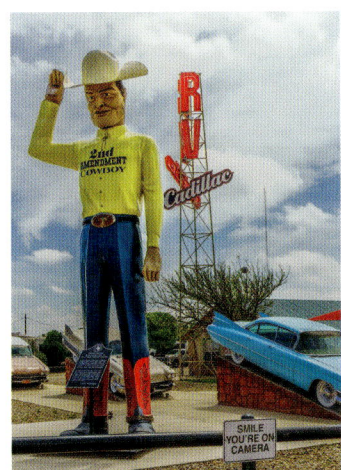

Second Amendment Cowboy, I-40, Texas
Becky Waters

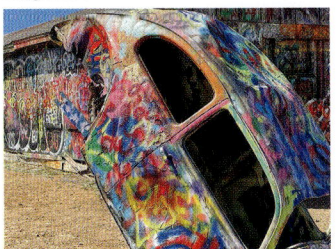

Slug Bug Ranch, Conway, Texas   *David Skernick*

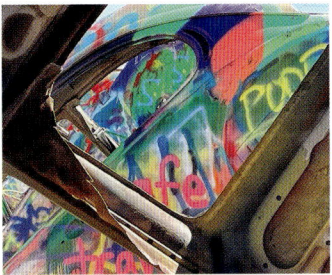

Slug Bug detail   *David Skernick*

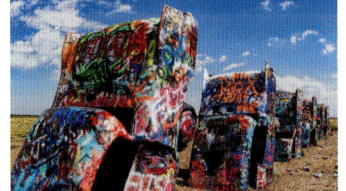

Cadillac Ranch, I-40, Texas   *David Skernick*

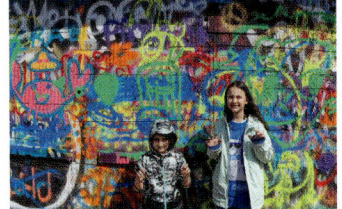

Kids at the Slug Bug Ranch, Conway, Texas
David Skernick

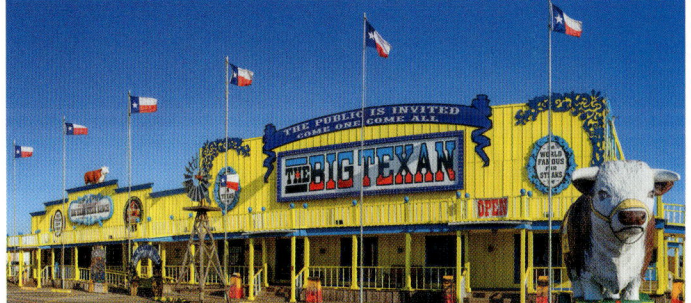

The Big Texan, I-40, Texas   *David Skernick*

Repeating forms often make for great photos. At the Cadillac Ranch, I tried to take advantage of that and shot the row of cars. The Slug Bug Ranch has a more difficult background. I found a more pleasing composition by zeroing in on a single bug and using the barn as a background. I took a second shot through the windows, and then I got lucky. A friendly family showed up. The two kids were happy to pose with their paint-stained hands. Both Cadillac and the Slug Bug Ranches sell spray paint and invite people to add to the art.

In all cases, I had to face in a given direction because it was early in the day, and the light was much better in one direction than the other. Becky was lucky when she shot the giant cowboy (*above*) to have been there at the right time to shoot from the perfect angle.

Amarillo, Texas

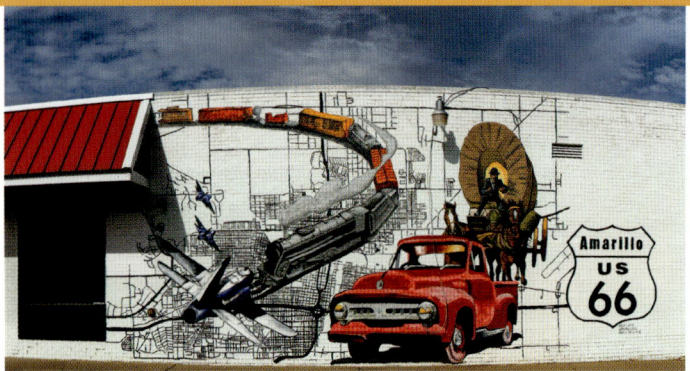

Mural on 6th and Virginia, Amarillo, Texas *David Skernick*

Route 66 follows 6th Street in Amarillo, Texas. There is a small stretch of that street that holds to the Mother Road tradition. Here you can find murals, antique stores, and cafés that honor the Route 66 culture. Hide and Seek Treasures has some unusual Route 66 antiques.

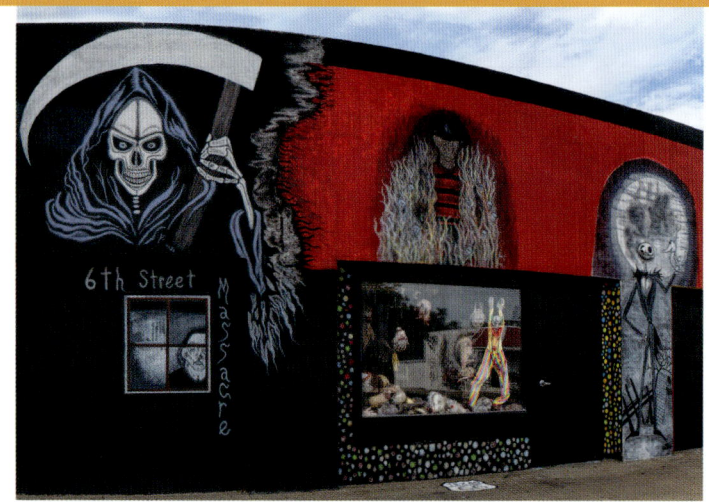

6th Street Massacre, Amarillo, Texas *David Skernick*

Interior of Hide and Seek Treasures *David Skernick*

Hide and Seek Treasures, Amarillo, Texas *David Skernick*

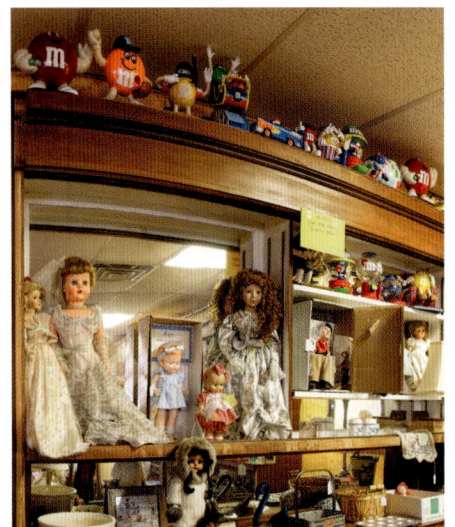

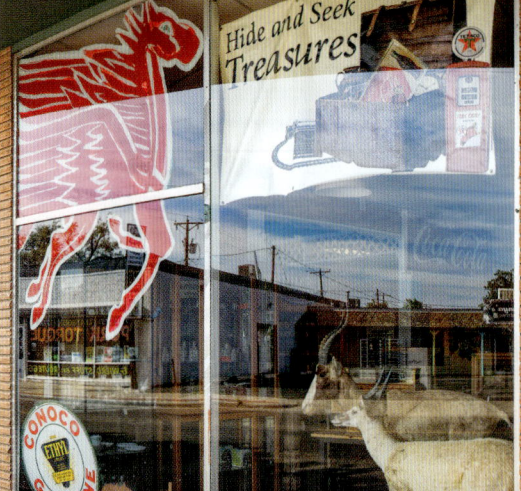

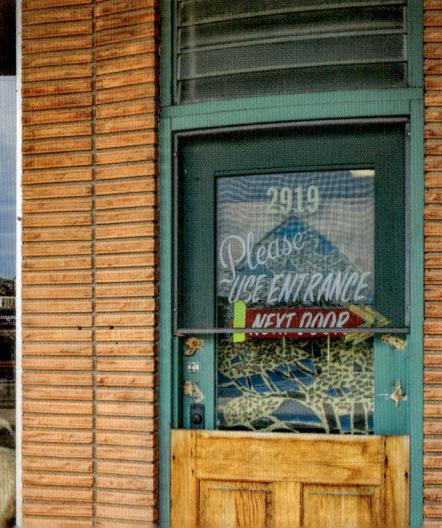

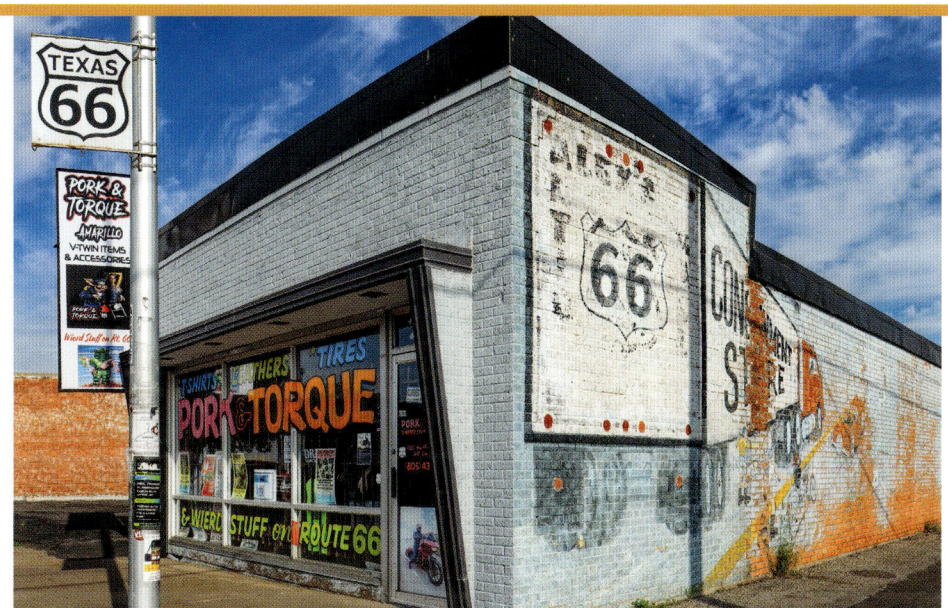

Pork and Torque, Amarillo, Texas

David Skernick

How do you not stop to look at a business called "Pork and Torque"? I chose to shoot from the corner, both to include the faded mural on the side of the building and to accentuate the word "torque" by literally torquing the angle of the photo. Sometimes you can reinforce a statement simply by shooting from a chosen angle.

I met Dmingo on 6th, when I came across him sitting on his bike in a perfect spot for a cool photograph. I was nervous at first to approach this scary-looking guy (yeah, I'm old and small), but once I spoke to him, we became fast friends. He even removed his kerchief so I could take a second shot showing his face. I like both versions. Do you?

My new friend Dmingo is an amazing airbrush artist. He is committed to the promotion of art and artists in Amarillo, Texas.

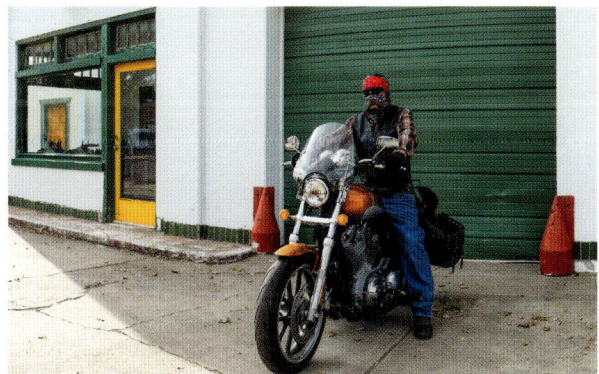

Dmingo Arte, Amarillo, Texas

David Skernick

Dmingo unmasked, Amarillo, Texas

David Skernick

Conway and Groom, Texas

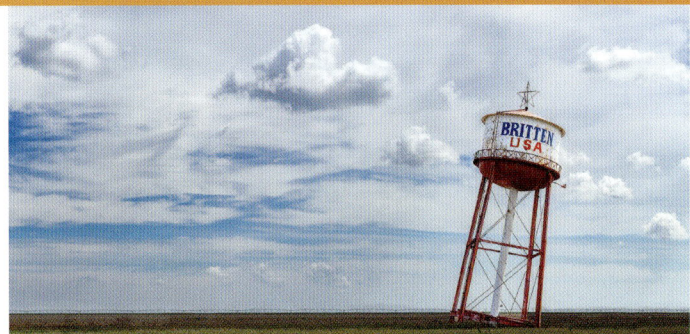

Britten USA, Groom, Texas — *David Skernick*

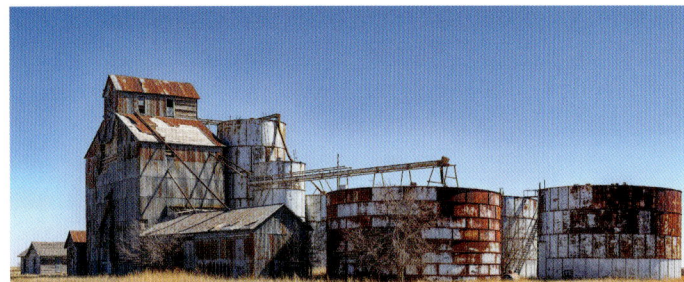

Grain storage, Groom, Texas — *David Skernick*

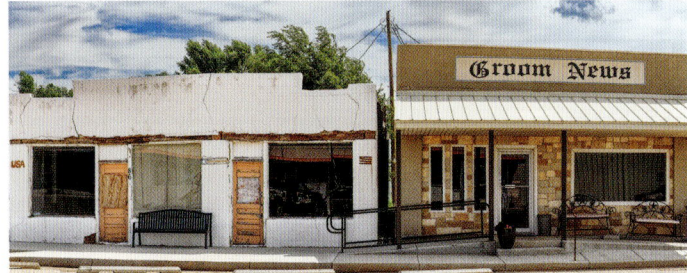

The Groom News, Groom, Texas — *David Skernick*

Ralph Britten bought, towed, and tilted this water tower directly over his truck stop alongside Route 66 near Groom, Texas. That structure burned to the ground many years ago. Back in the day, people would stop their cars and run into the truck stop to warn that the water tower was falling. Ralph would then explain that it was built that way, and offer the well-wishers coffee and food. Brilliant marketing strategy, and kind of ironic that the café burned down.

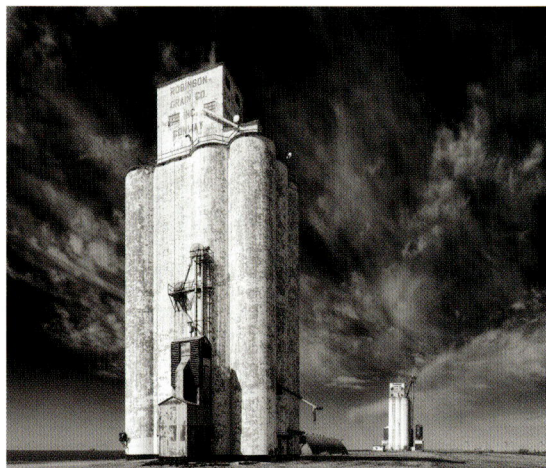

Robinson Grain, Conway, Texas — *David Skernick*

Some of the photos on this page are very simple, in that they have very little in their compositions aside from their subjects. Texas is a huge state. I think that shots like these give you that feeling of expanse that defines the way driving through Texas makes you feel. Route 66 runs through only Texas's panhandle, so you may not get the true sensation of endlessness that is the state of Texas.

McLean, Texas

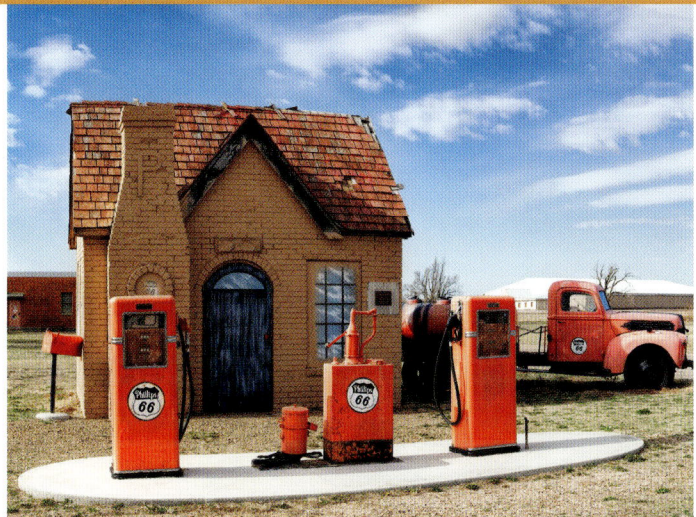

Phillips gas station (1929), McLean, Texas   *David Skernick*

This little gas station (*left*) in McLean, Texas, was the first Phillips 66 gas station in Texas and the first restored station on old Route 66. It was built in 1929.

One version of the story behind the name Phillips 66 is that it was inspired by a test drive at 66 miles per hour on a stretch of Route 66 in Oklahoma.

In cities, even small towns, there are often challenges with the elements in the background. My composition is tight here because I did not want to include houses, streets, and other buildings. I would have liked to have moved to my right and include more of the truck and the tank behind it than you see here. Too much stuff in the background made that impossible.

I have admitted that I remove the power lines and poles that I find distracting in my photos. I did so here, but I do not want to remove buildings. We all have our own set of rules. Mine seems to end at architecture. For now.

Texas is certainly not the only state where you will see horses, but there are a whole lot of them! There are endless ranches and farms, and they all seem to have horses. I am always on the lookout for any type of animal. I love them. I love photographing them too.

In the spring there are little ones. You knew that, but I want to remind you here to look for them. If you see a bunch of horses in a field, it might be worth a stop to see who is hiding out in the middle. Be patient and, like I have said before, stay close to your car so you don't spook them.

I keep a dedicated camera within reach of my driver's seat at all times when I'm on the road. My 200–500mm f/5.6 lens is attached to my D500, my ISO is high, and my f/stop is low. I am ready shoot from a distance and to stop action. If you don't have two cameras, keep a long lens on to be ready for animals. Landscapes will wait for you to set up your other lenses and settings.

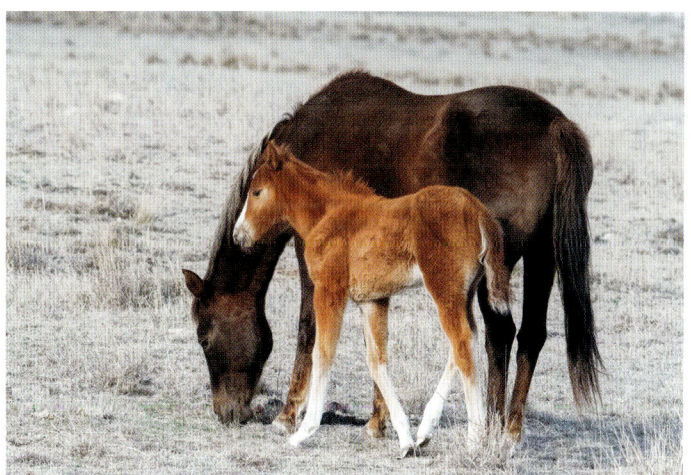

Horses near McLean, Texas   *David Skernick*

Shamrock, Texas

Shamrock is a small Texas town with a big Route 66 tradition.

The U Drop Inn is one of my favorite Route 66 destinations. I wanted to find an original way to photograph it. As I was setting up to take this shot, I got a lucky break: This guy pulled up and left his motorcycle in the perfect spot! When he looked up and saw me, he went to move his bike. I yelled over to leave it right where it was. I was grinning like a fool, because I knew he had just added the perfect prop for my composition. I am sure he thought I was nuts, but I got a better photo than I had expected.

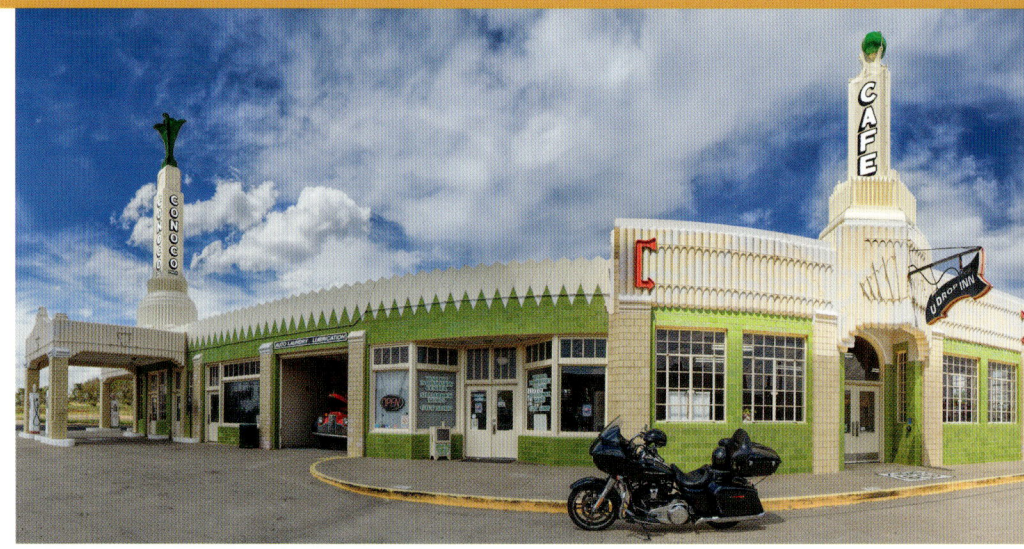

The U Drop Inn, Shamrock, Texas   *David Skernick*

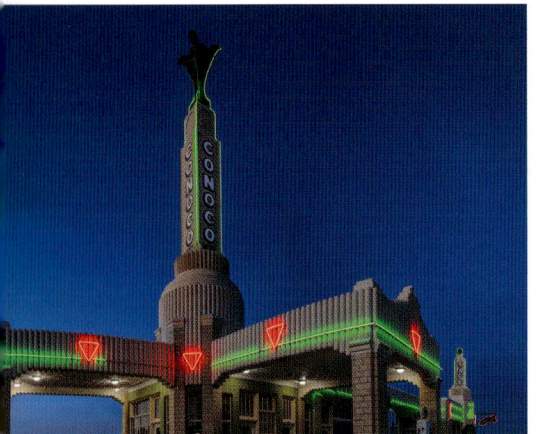

The U Drop Inn at night, Shamrock, Texas   *David Skernick*

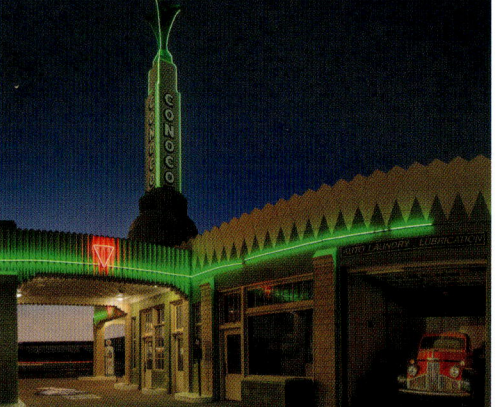

The U Drop Inn and moon, Shamrock, Texas   *David Skernick*

On another trip I had time to stay over and photograph the location at night. Shamrock has quite a few nice motels. I took the time to walk all around and found a couple of angles I liked. My daytime shot (*above*) was of the entire building. I liked that one enough to use it for the book cover. I wanted something different for the night shots. I looked for some detail compositions. I wanted to make the neon lights my prime subject. The moon was just luck.

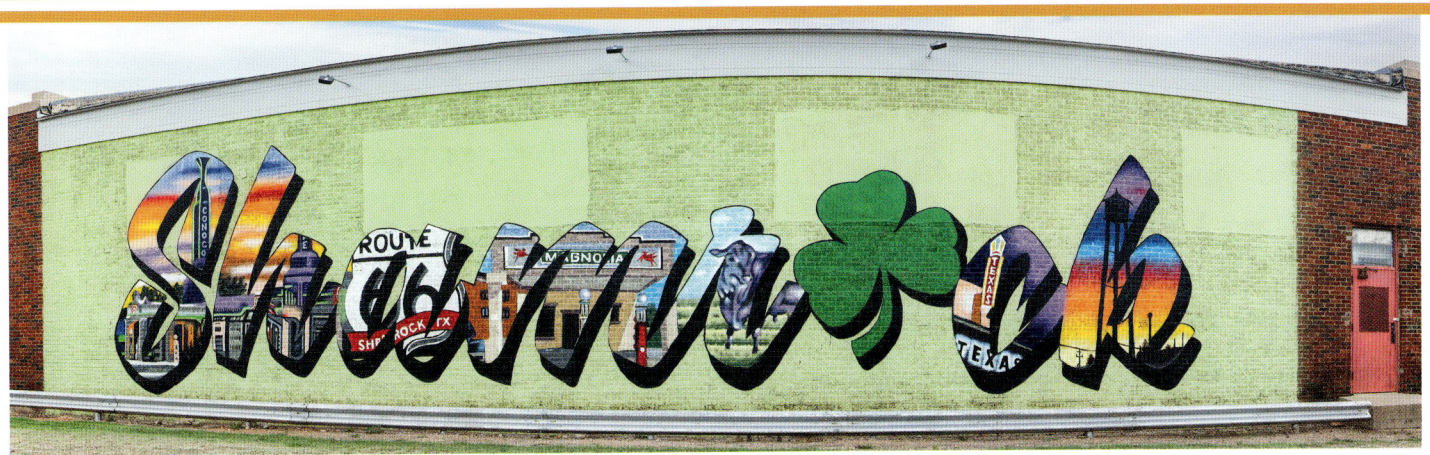

Shamrock mural

David Skernick

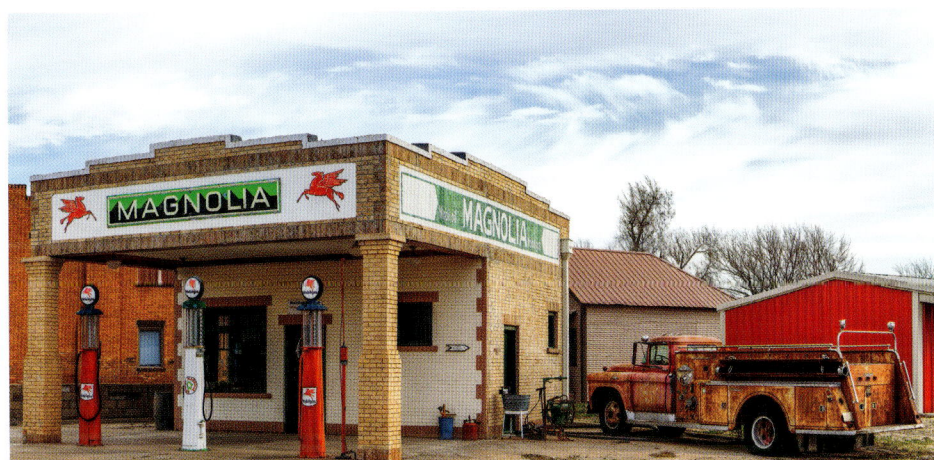

The Magnolia Gas Station (1929), Shamrock, Texas

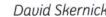
David Skernick

The Magnolia Gas Station was completed on May 18, 1929. The town of Shamrock has protected it and kept it beautiful for all to enjoy. The fire engine adds just the perfect touch to set off the building and complete the story. That is another thing to love about Route 66. So often there is an old car or truck that adds the frosting on your cake, so to speak. You may have read on the last page about how lucky I felt when a motorcycle wound up in the right place at the right time. If you look closely at that photo, you will see that there are already two trucks perfectly placed by the owner.

Tye Thompson, Shamrock, Texas

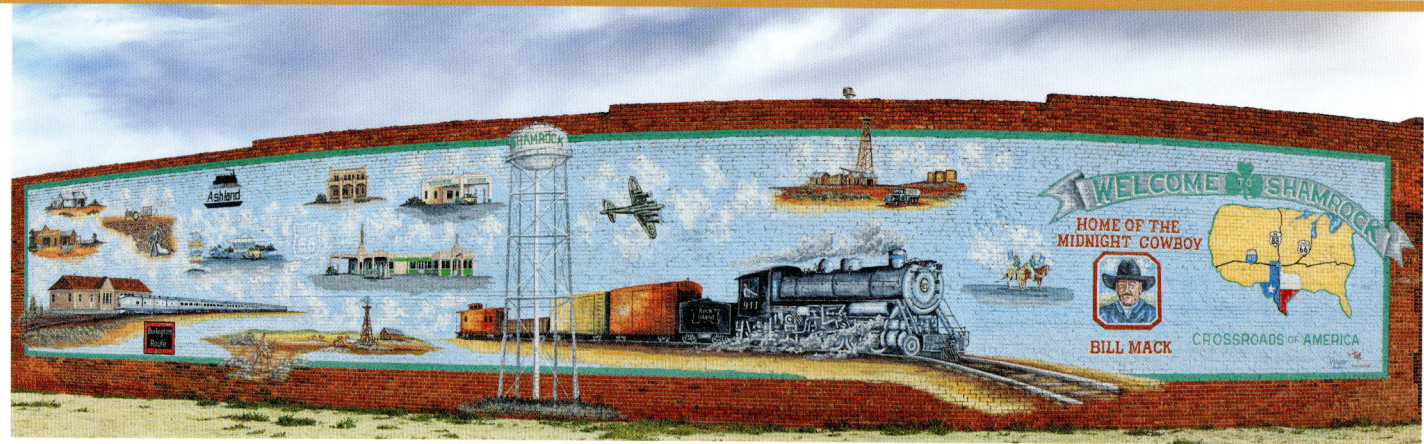

Mural on Tower Plaza by Tye, Shamrock, Texas

David Skernick

Here's a great story. I was leaving my motel in Shamrock, Texas, a while back when this guy walked up to me and started talking about the stickers on Bob. He gave me one. It says "Don't Mess with Texas." I put it on the back of the truck while we were talking. He told me he was a mural artist and that he painted a lot of murals in Shamrock. He gave me directions to some of his murals. I photographed the one above that day and was happy to have made a new friend. The Mother Road inspires all kinds of collectors and artists. I am fortunate to have befriended so many.

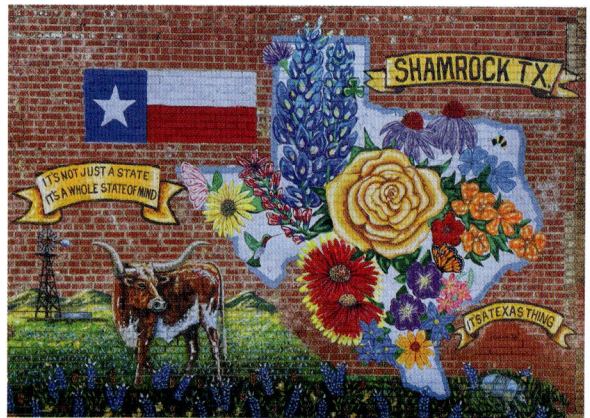

Tye's most recent painting

David Skernick

Tye Thompson

David Skernick

On my last trip to Shamrock, I went looking for Tye. I found my friend in the same motel. We had a great visit; he let me take his photo and then took me on a tour of his paintings. As we drove around town looking at paintings on walls, businesses, museums, and houses, and even on a dumpster, he told me a little bit of his history.

I'll try my best to convey this kind, interesting man's story by showing you his work and relaying what he shared with me as we drove around Shamrock in his truck.

77

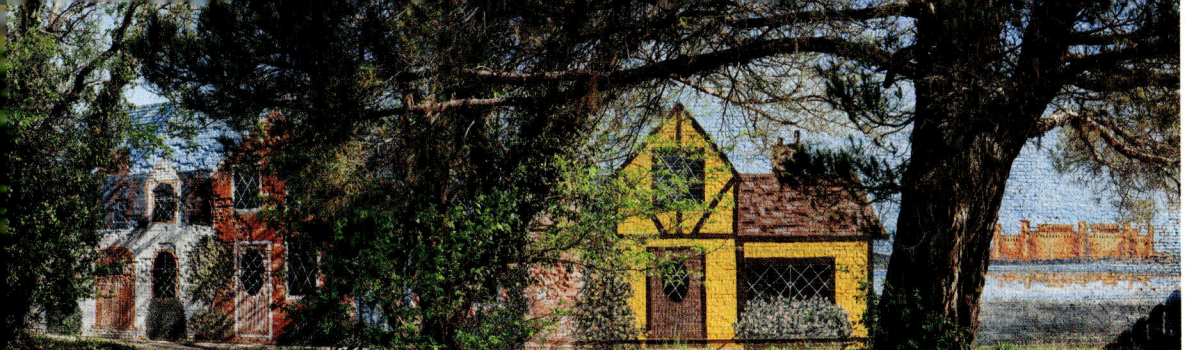

The Artist Village, painted by Tye in his twenties

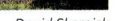
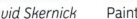
David Skernick   Painted dumpster   David Skernick

Tye Thompson was born in Amarillo, Texas, in 1952. His family moved to Shamrock when he was five years old. He rode bulls in rodeos, and he was paid to barbecue—something special for any Texan—he was a bartender and a bass player in a band, but mostly he painted. His work is literally everywhere in Shamrock, Texas. Recently, Tye had a stroke. He's getting better all the time but still can't use his dominant left hand to paint. He is working hard to overcome the problem and is planning his "best painting ever" of the town Dairy Queen as it was in its (and his) heyday. It was the hangout where Tye and his friends spent countless hours. I can't wait to see the painting. I hope you will look for it as you motor through Shamrock looking for Route 66 gold. Thanks, Tye, love your work!

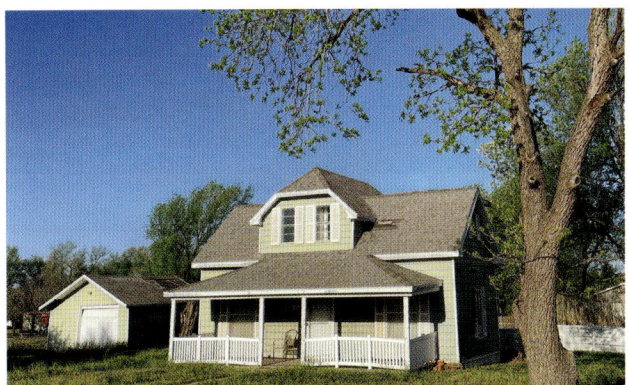

Tye's boyhood home in Shamrock   David Skernick

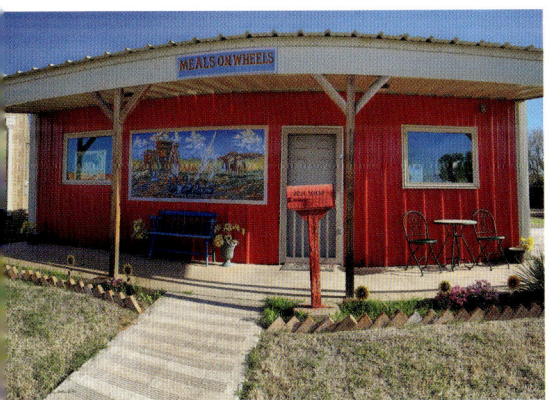

"The original Meals on Wheels"   David Skernick

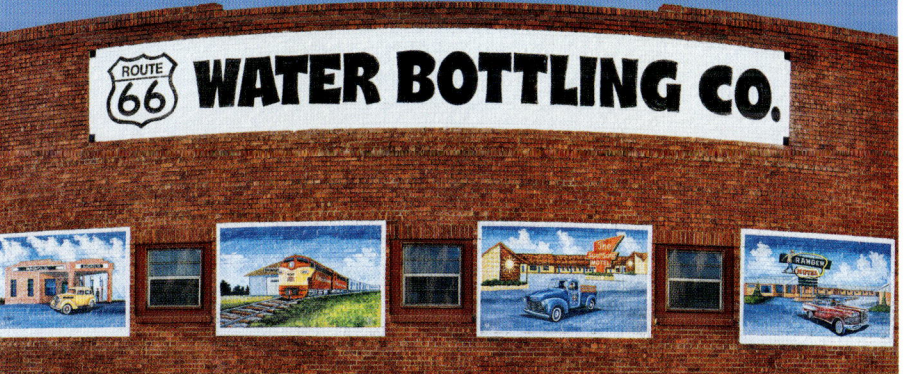

Water Bottling Company, Shamrock, Texas   David Skernick

Erick, Oklahoma

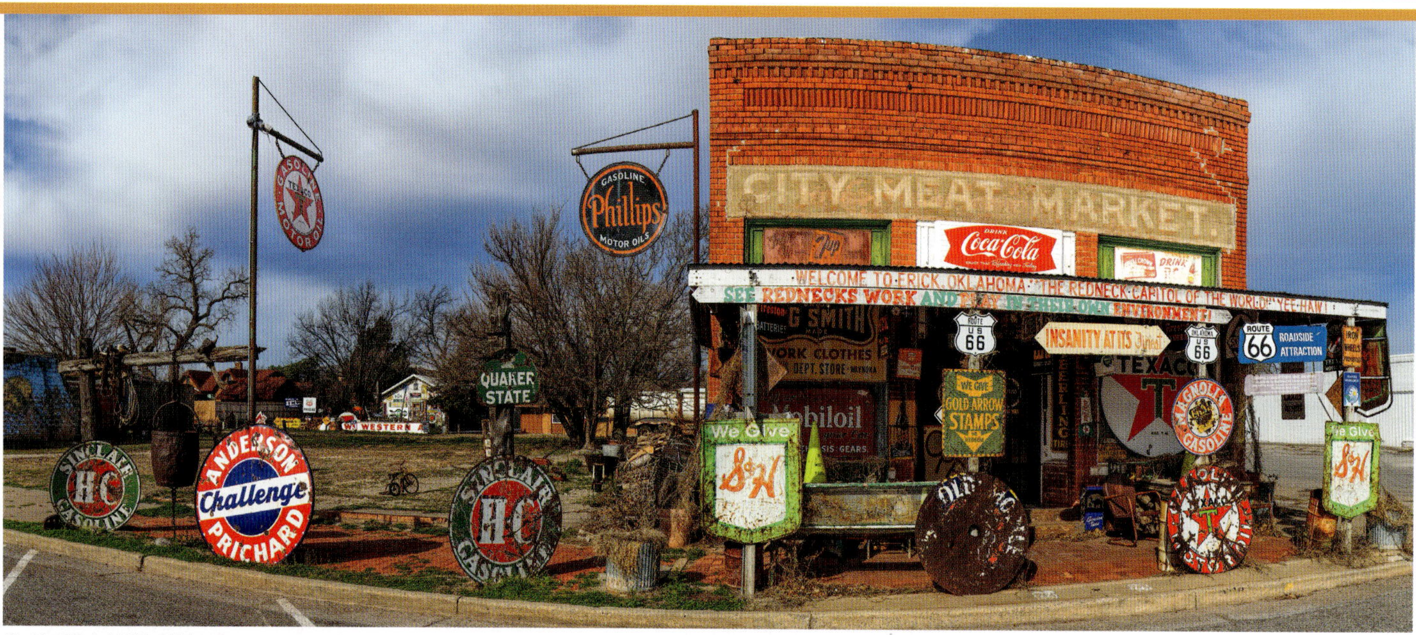

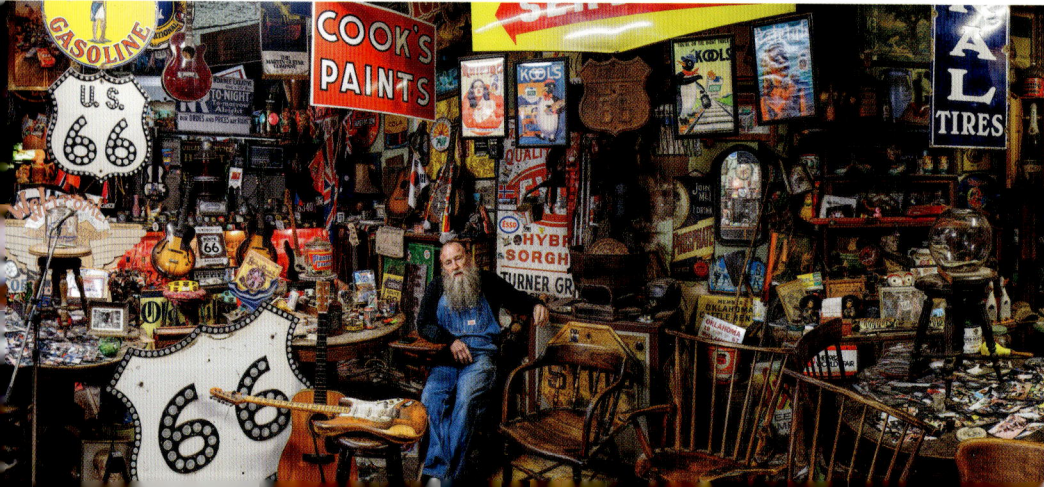

City Meat Market, Erick, Oklahoma

David Skernick

The famous Sandhills Curiosity Shop is housed in the City Meat Market building, the oldest brick building in Erick, Oklahoma. Erick was founded in 1901. The creator of the shop, Harley E. Russel III, who also performs there as a musician, lives in the house you can see in the background of the above photo. He was kind to pose for me and hold still during the long-exposure panorama on the left. The Oklahoma Route 66 Association inducted Harley, and his late wife, Annabelle, into its hall of fame.

◄ Harley and his collection
David Skernick

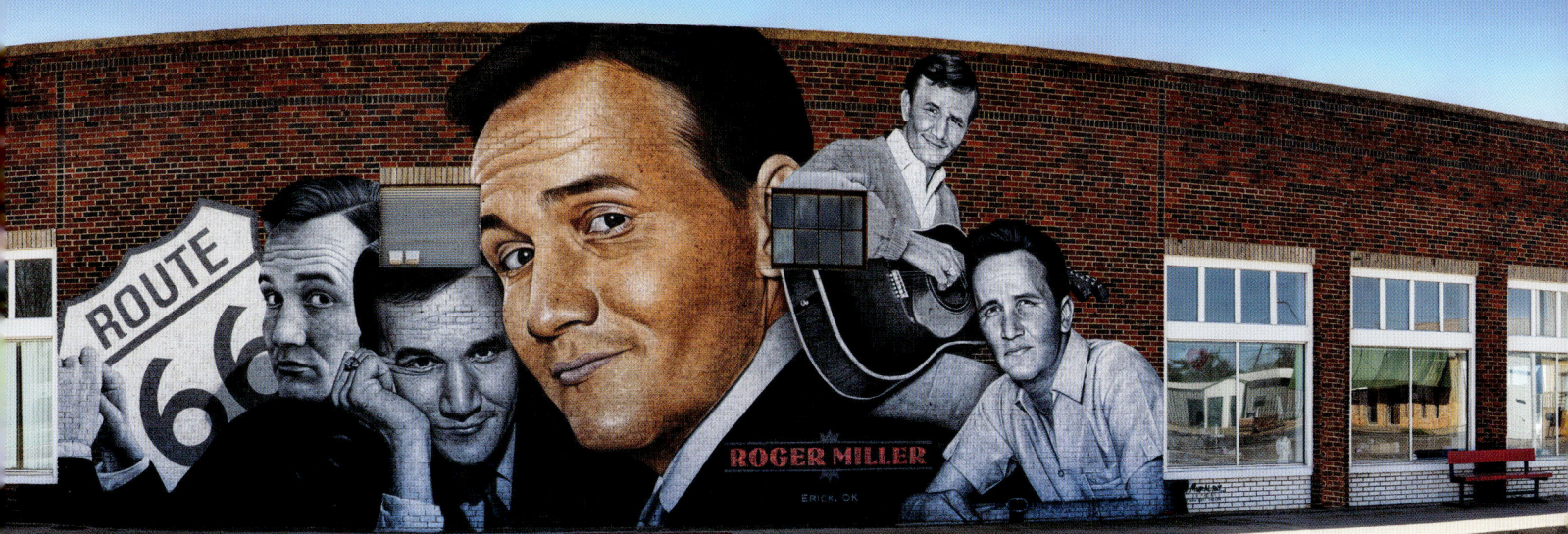

Brian Lewis's mural on Route 66 in Erick, Oklahoma

David Skernick

Oklahoma has a lot of Route 66 history and pride. They call their portion of the road the "Main Street of Native America." Be prepared to stay a while, eat some BBQ, and take a whole bunch of photos!

The West Winds Motel is barely still standing. The Kemp family who owns it would like to bring it back to life. I hope they find a way. We photographers love to shoot old falling-down buildings, but restored, this iconic Route 66 landmark would make a beautiful new addition to the old road going through Erick, Oklahoma. When I was there, Debbie Kemp came out to show me some old "check-in" cards she had found in the motel. Looking at those names was kind of eerie. The past never seems that far away on Route 66.

The West Winds Motel, Erick, Oklahoma

David Skernick

Sayre, Oklahoma

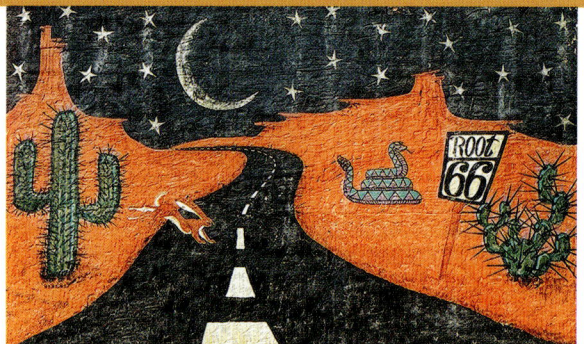

66 Lounge, Sayre, Oklahoma *David Skernick*

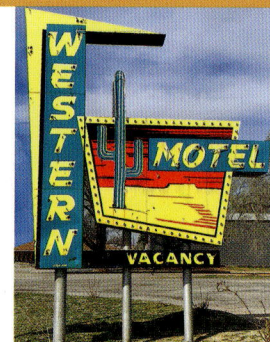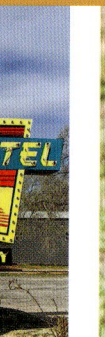

Western Motel, Sayre *David Skernick*

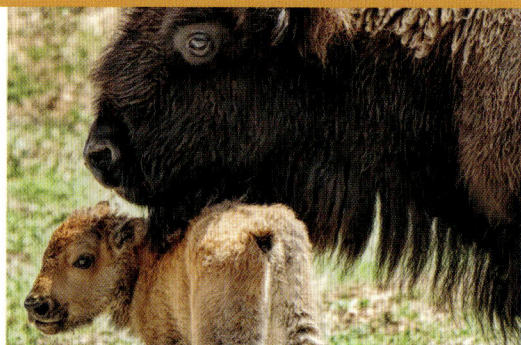

Buffalo mother and calf *David Skernick*

The Western Motel sign and the mural at the 66 Lounge are just across the street from each other in Sayre, Oklahoma. They were easy to photograph. I just filled the frame and let the content speak for itself. The old garage presented more of a challenge. What got my attention was the stark white against the perfect blue sky. The negative space was as important to me as the building. I used a wide-angle lens to create the distortion that makes that space more interesting. Conversely, when I spotted the old granary (*below*), I chose a telephoto lens to compress the buildings together to make the textures and shapes of the buildings more prominent.

While I was shooting the granary, Lester Gray came along. He has lived in Sayre for a good part of his life. He shared an interesting story with me. Up until 1936, a mistake was made because of confusion over which river was nearby. The result was that the people of Sayre thought they lived in Texas, rather than Oklahoma. The travelers for those first ten years (Route 66 opened in 1926) would have been caught up in the confusion as well.

Lester also told me about the buffalo ranch just south of town. Cross back across I-40 and take a left on CR 1210. You can't miss it!

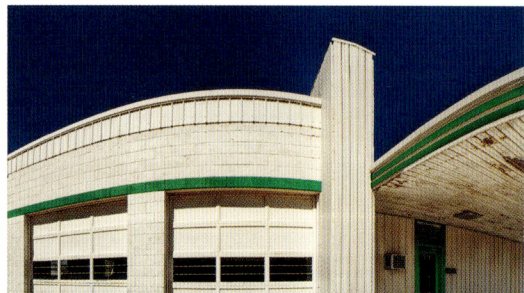

Old gas station, Sayre, Oklahoma *David Skernick*

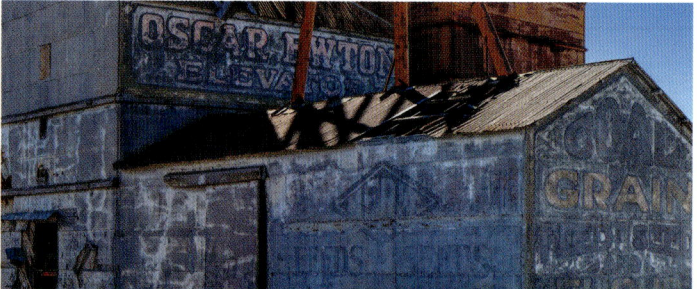

Granary, Sayre, Oklahoma *David Skernick*

National Route 66 Museum, Elk City, Oklahoma

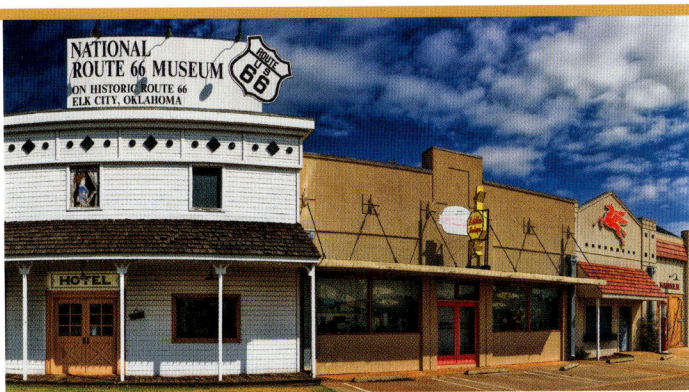

National Route 66 Museum, Elk City, Oklahoma   *David Skernick*

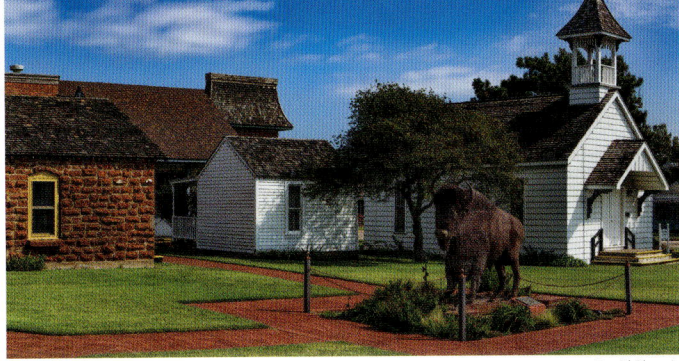

Old Town Museum, Elk City, Oklahoma   *David Skernick*

The National Route 66 Museum in Elk City, Oklahoma, has exhibits about the Mother Road and the history of the eight states that the road crosses. It also includes the National Transportation Museum, the Old Town Museum, a Farm and Ranch Museum, a Blacksmith Museum, and tons of outdoor displays worth your time and energy. They also boast the world's biggest Route 66 sign, but the people of the Motorheads Bar, Grill, and Museum in Springfield, Illinois, may have them beat (stay tuned).

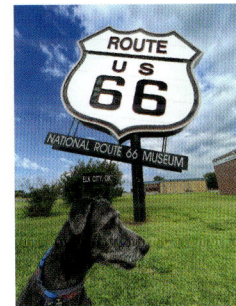

Dudley working for scale
David Skernick

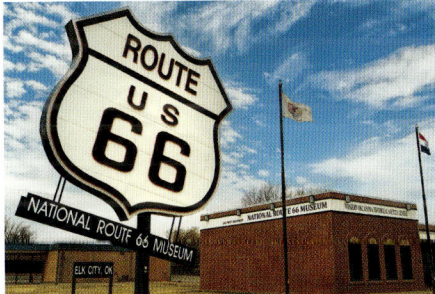

World's biggest Route 66 sign, National Route 66 Museum
David Skernick

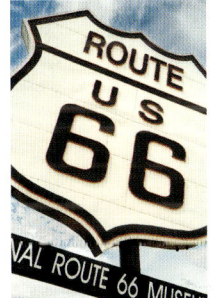

Route 66 sign   *David Skernick*

How do you show size? You can put anything with a known size in your shot to show scale. I used Dudley the Wonder Dog on one visit and the surrounding buildings another time. Note that the sign appears smaller with my pup in front than it does with the buildings behind. You can also cut the sign off. When you cut something off, you make it look bigger. Do you see what I mean? Shooting from below helped in all three cases.

Wichita Mountains Wildlife Refuge, Oklahoma

Between Elk City and Clinton, Oklahoma, you will see signs to Clinton and Foss Lakes. They are part of the Wichita Mountains Wildlife Refuge. Where there are lakes, there is wildlife. There is a larger area of the same refuge about 30 miles to the south. It's worth your time if you love to see and photograph wildlife.

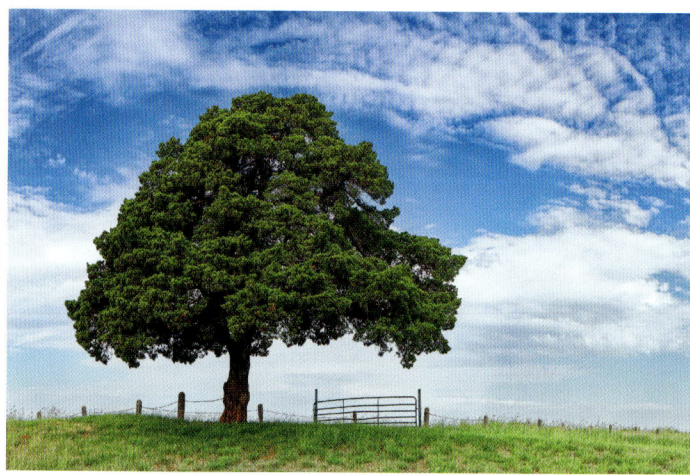
Tree at Clinton Lake, Oklahoma   *David Skernick*

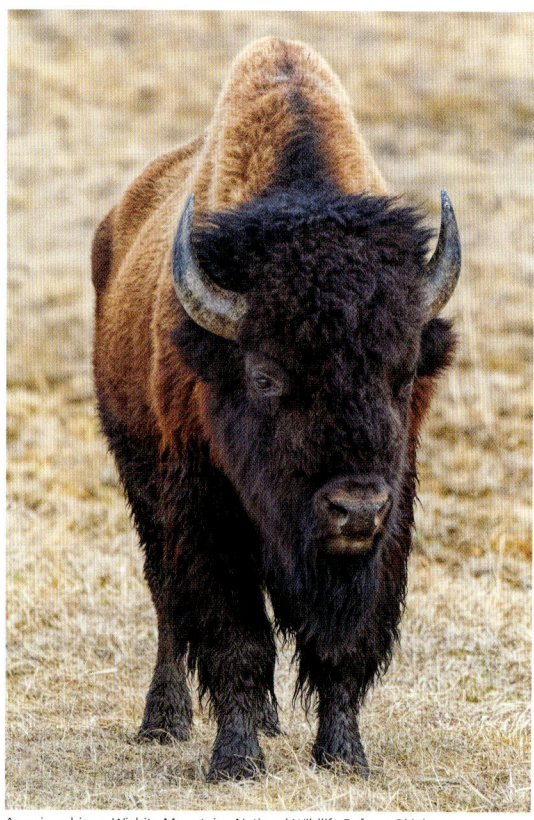
American bison, Wichita Mountains National Wildlife Refuge, Oklahoma
David Skernick

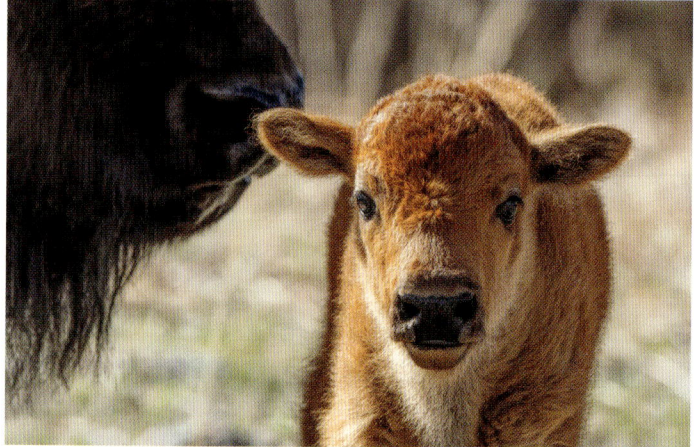
American bison calf, Wichita Mountains National Wildlife Refuge, Oklahoma   *David Skernick*

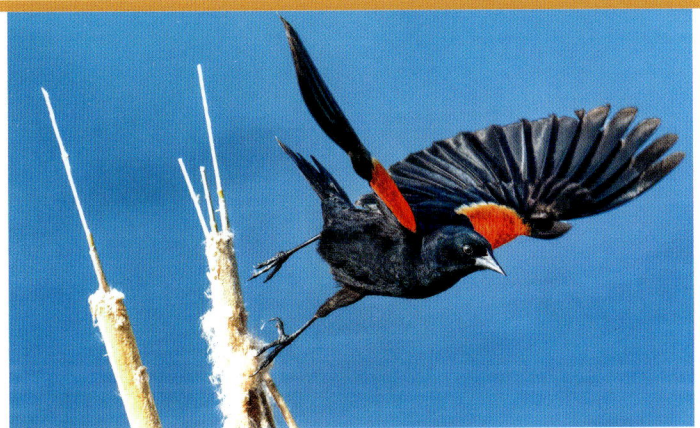

Red-winged blackbird, Oklahoma *David Skernick*

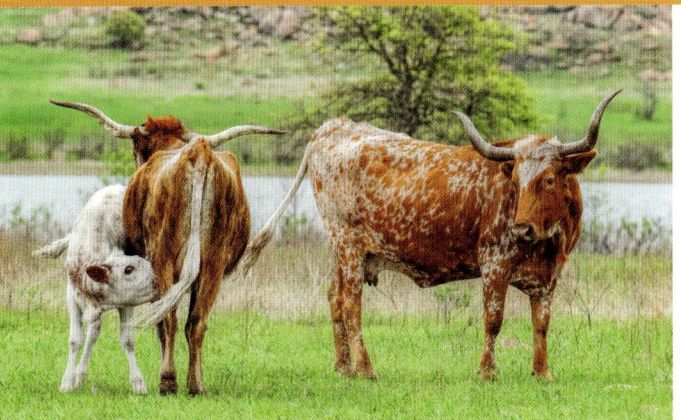

Longhorn cattle, Wichita Mountains National Wildlife Refuge, Oklahoma *David Skernick*

The Wichita Mountains Wildlife Refuge covers about 60,000 acres. It includes areas of grass prairie, granite mountains, and several freshwater lakes and streams. It's a great opportunity to get out of your car and take a hike, or to kayak through nature. I love the Route 66 towns, food, and people, but a little quiet and beauty is a nice break.

Photographing birds and other wildlife has been mentioned before. Long lenses, fast speeds, readiness, and timing. Those are the keys to any type of action photography. On this page, you see three photos that make timing the star. I watched that bird for a while. I took several shots of him sitting on those cattails. They were good photos—not great, but good. Then he took off and I got a more interesting shot. The cattle were nothing special, but again, I was patient. The moment finally came, with the calf nursing and the second adult looking in that direction. I wasn't waiting for that. You seldom know what you are waiting for, but when it happens you need to be ready. Same thing with the mother turning up behind the bison calf on the facing page. The birds on the left were pure luck. I loved the four of them walking in a row. The reflection made it even better. I was ready to shoot when the guy in front spread his wings—magic!

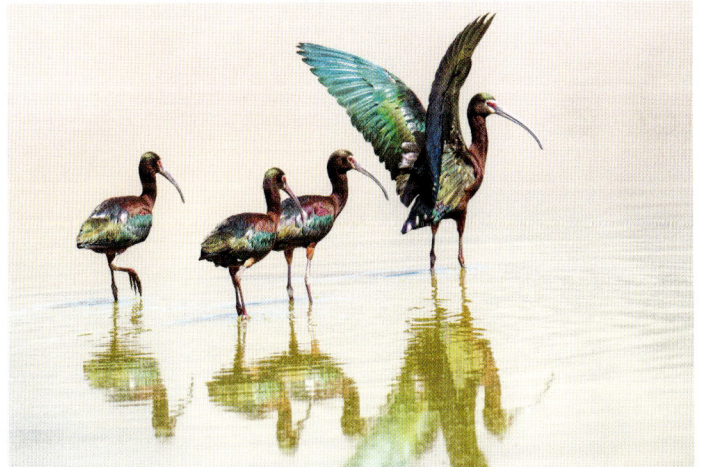

Glossy ibis, Wichita Mountains National Wildlife Refuge, Oklahoma *David Skernick*

84

Clinton, Oklahoma

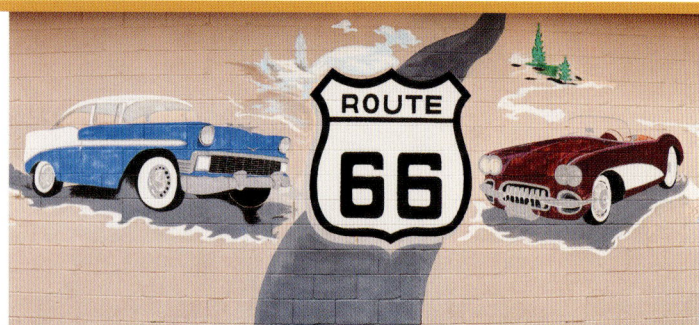

Route 66 mural, Clinton, Oklahoma *David Skernick*

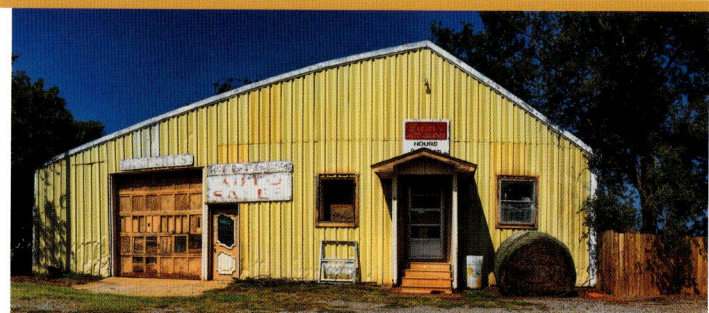

Belter's Auto Salvage, Clinton, Oklahoma *David Skernick*

In Clinton, Oklahoma, Route 66 follows Gary Avenue. Pay attention as you drive through town. You will see some terrific old remnants of America's Highway. There is also plenty of good food and places to stay.

When I spotted McLain Rogers Park (*below*), I wanted to have a pleasing scene inside the frame caused by the sign. I walked around to find this angle that included the trees and road. Down the road, still in Clinton, I spotted this interesting garage (*above*). I went for a straight-on shot to accentuate the strange shape of the building. I thought a straight shot for the mural was best as well. For the old motel sign on the right, I went for a wide lens and a low angle to accentuate the height and size of the sign.

The Route 66 Museum in Clinton, Oklahoma, is another excellent place to learn about the history of Route 66 and check out some really boss cars. Did you see how I threw in that '60s slang? It's sort of the same way I threw Bob 4 into the pano I shot (*below*) of the museum. I shot this one with my phone. Nothing is better when you are in a hurry. I was standing in the middle of the road, so I had to be fast.

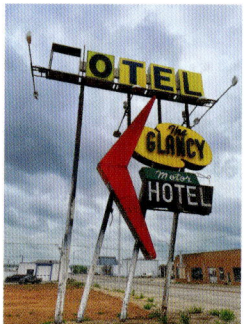

The Glancy   *David Skernick*

McLain Rogers Park, Clinton, Oklahoma   *David Skernick*

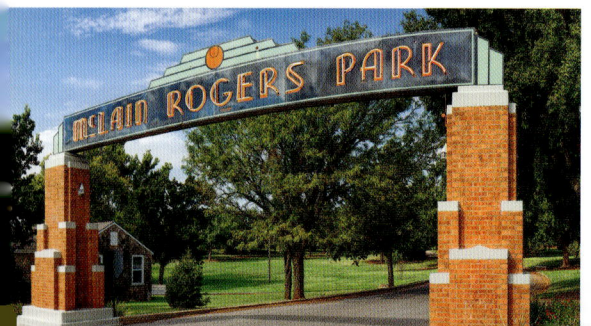

Route 66 Museum, Clinton, Oklahoma   *David Skernick*

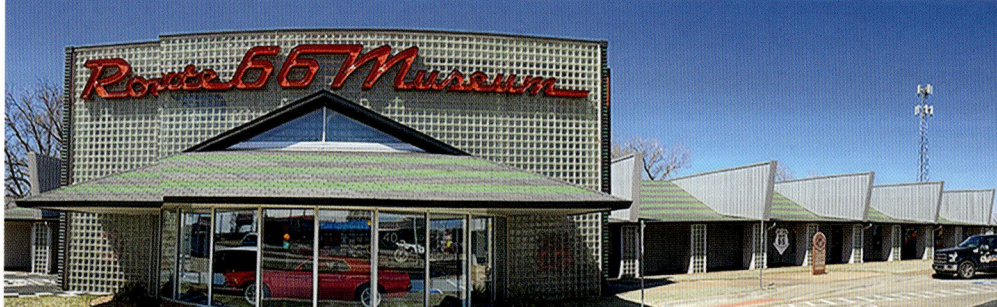

Along the freeway you'll pass the sign on the right, depicting a proud Cherokee Native American. I chose to include only the words "TRADING POST." "Boot Outlet" seemed distracting. I was not photographing an advertisement for the business. Our art is one of subtraction. We look at the whole scene and then hone down our compositions to make a personal statement. Lucille's (*below*) is visible from I-40. Get off at the next exit to be back on Route 66.

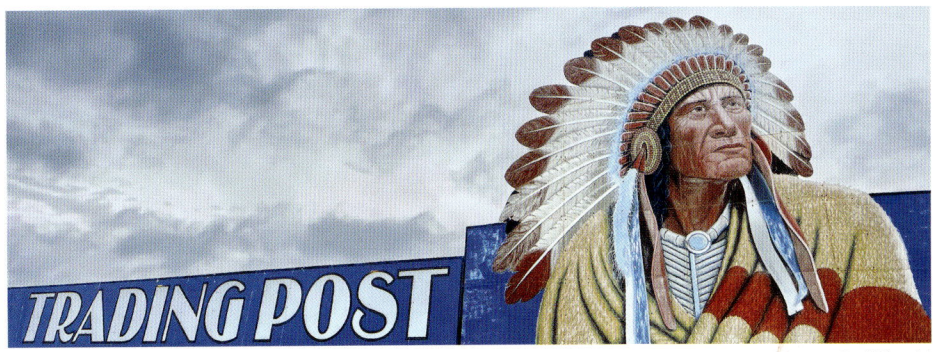

Custer City Trading Post, Oklahoma

David Skernick

Hydro, Oklahoma

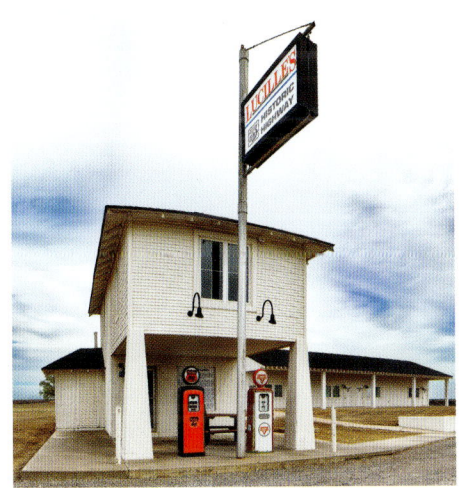

Lucille's Gas Station and Motor Court (1929), Hydro, Oklahoma
David Skernick

Lucille's Gas Station was built in 1929. Lucile and Carl Hamons bought the station and motor court in 1951. She lived there until her death in 2000.

The bridge is the old US 66 Canadian River Bridge. It took you from Canadian to Caddo Counties. Spanning 3,944.33 feet in length, it was built jointly by the state and federal governments. Construction started on August 2, 1932, and it was completed on July 1, 1933. As of the writing of this book it is being restored.

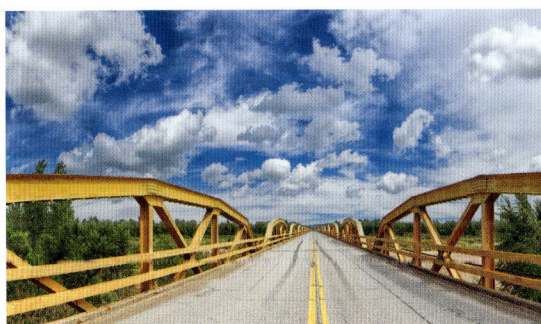

Old US 66 Canadian River Bridge, Oklahoma   *David Skernick*

Calumet and El Reno, Oklahoma

At Calumet, watch for the Historic Route 66 sign to exit Interstate 40. Take a left (north) off the exit and either go straight or turn right to take different alignments of Route 66. The one that follows Route 281 will take you over the Canadian River Bridge; the other heads into El Reno. I suggest you take the time for both.

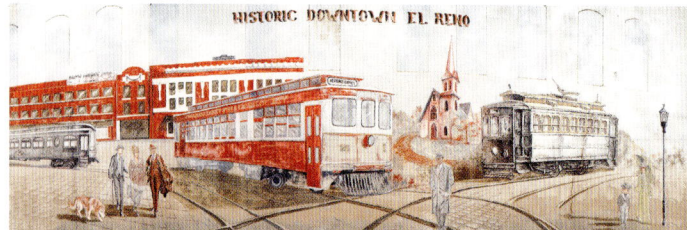
Historic El Reno mural, downtown El Reno, Oklahoma   *David Skernick*

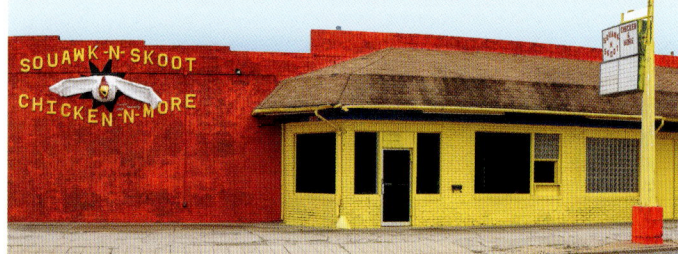
Squawk-N-Skoot, El Reno, Oklahoma   *David Skernick*

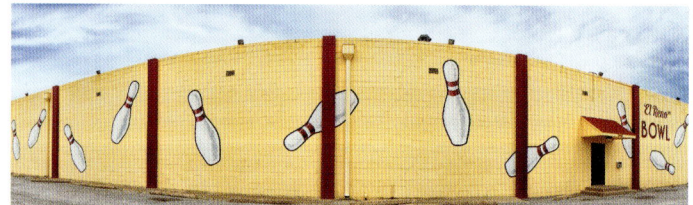
El Reno Bowl, Route 66, Oklahoma   *David Skernick*

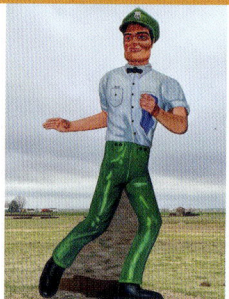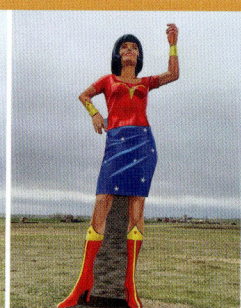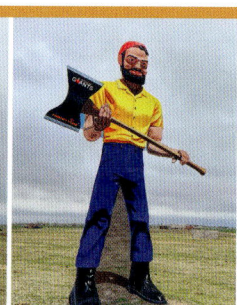
John Cerney's Muffler Men, Calumet, Oklahoma   *David Skernick*

The above tributes to the Muffler Men by John Cerney are along Route 66 in Calumet, Oklahoma. I chose to depict them this way since they are 50 feet apart. Great to drive by, but hard to photograph together. Continue along the road and you will come to El Reno. I found quite a few reasons to spend time there. Although I couldn't resist stopping to shoot this great chicken place, El Reno, Oklahoma, is the home of the Onion Burger. At least three diners on three blocks downtown will make you an unforgettable burger!

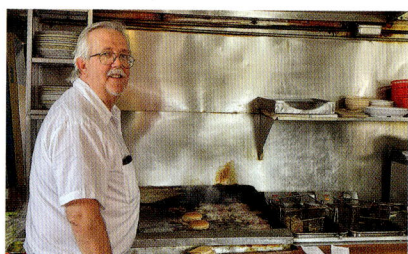
Edward at Robert's Grill, El Reno   *David Skernick*

This is Edward at Robert's Grill. That's my burger on the grill! The El Reno Bowl was closed when I went by. Great! No cars in the way. I stopped by later to photograph the interior, but I prefer this outside wall.

Yukon, Oklahoma

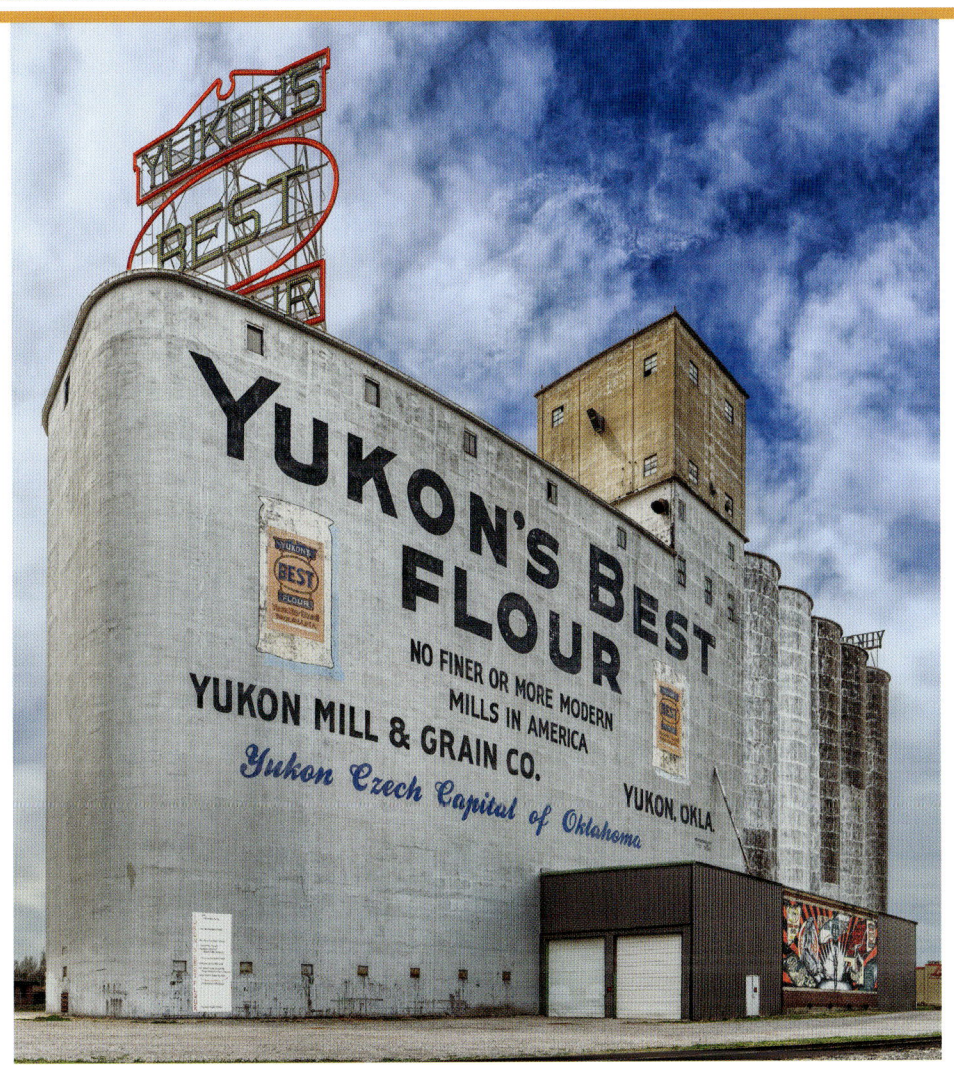

Yukon's Best Flour Mill was built in 1902. The sign on top was added in the 1940s. Also known as "the Silos," the structures of the original Yukon Mill and Grain Company, and Dobry Mills, tower over Route 66.

A developer is proposing a plan that includes a new five-story office park, apartments, two multilevel parking garages, and a hotel and convention center on Main Street.

He promises that this amazing landmark will be preserved in the plan. Let's hope that is true. This huge double pano almost shows you how big this five-story high building looks from the ground. Almost—I used it big on this page because it seemed somehow wrong to show only a small print.

Standing near it, I felt like I was on the ocean as this huge ship was passing by. I tried to convey that feeling in my photo by choosing an angle that would distort the shape a little, making the front look bigger than the back.

A train going by would have been really cool, but I am not sure those tracks are even still in use. I waited awhile. I wanted the clouds to move into a better position. No trains. If you get a shot with a train, send it to me, I would love to see it!

◀ Yukon's Best Flour Mill, Yukon, Oklahoma
  David Skernick

Oklahoma City and Edmond, Oklahoma

At Oklahoma City, our interstate companion goes from the I-40 to I-35, then I-44, but you can stay on Route 66. It's not easy, but watch the signs and you can do it. If you choose to skip the city, put Arcadia into your GPS and rejoin Route 66 there. I had friends to help me navigate, so I braved the congestion and traffic. The *Summer of '66* poster by Nick Bayer was in perfect late-afternoon light as we passed through the city.

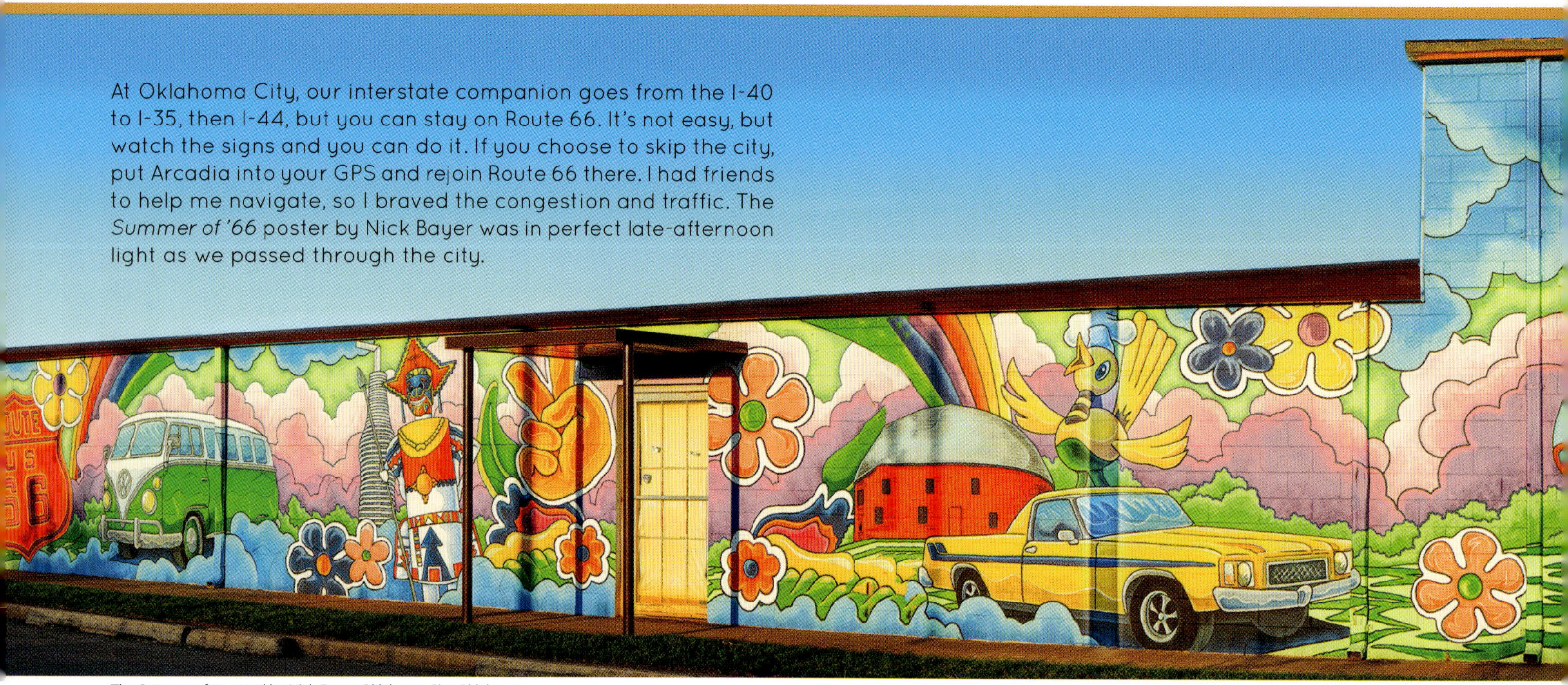

The *Summer of 66* mural by Nick Bayer, Oklahoma City, Oklahoma

The original 1926 alignment of Route 66 ran alongside Lake Overholser, on the western side of Oklahoma City. The bridge on the right was part of that road and crosses the very top of the lake. I thought it was worthy of inclusion, and I wanted to get a good shot. I walked across the bridge in both directions, looking for a road shot. Aside from having to dodge traffic, I didn't find an interesting way to make that work. There was a small park down below the bridge, so I went down there next. I walked down to the water and considered several locations where I could include the lake and the bridge but was still not inspired.

Then I saw that tree. Sometimes you see a shot before you even pull your car over. You know exactly what you want to do, and all that is left is making decisions about f/stop and shutter speed. This time I had to put in some actual legwork, but I am happy with my final composition.

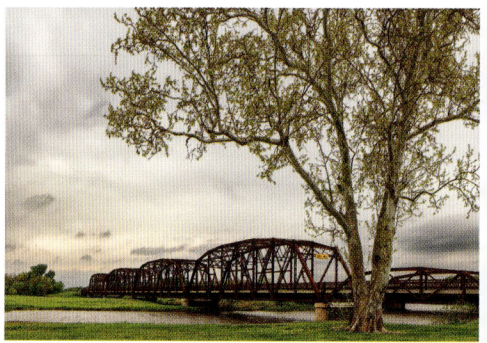

Bridge over Lake Overholser, Oklahoma City, Oklahoma   *David Skernick*

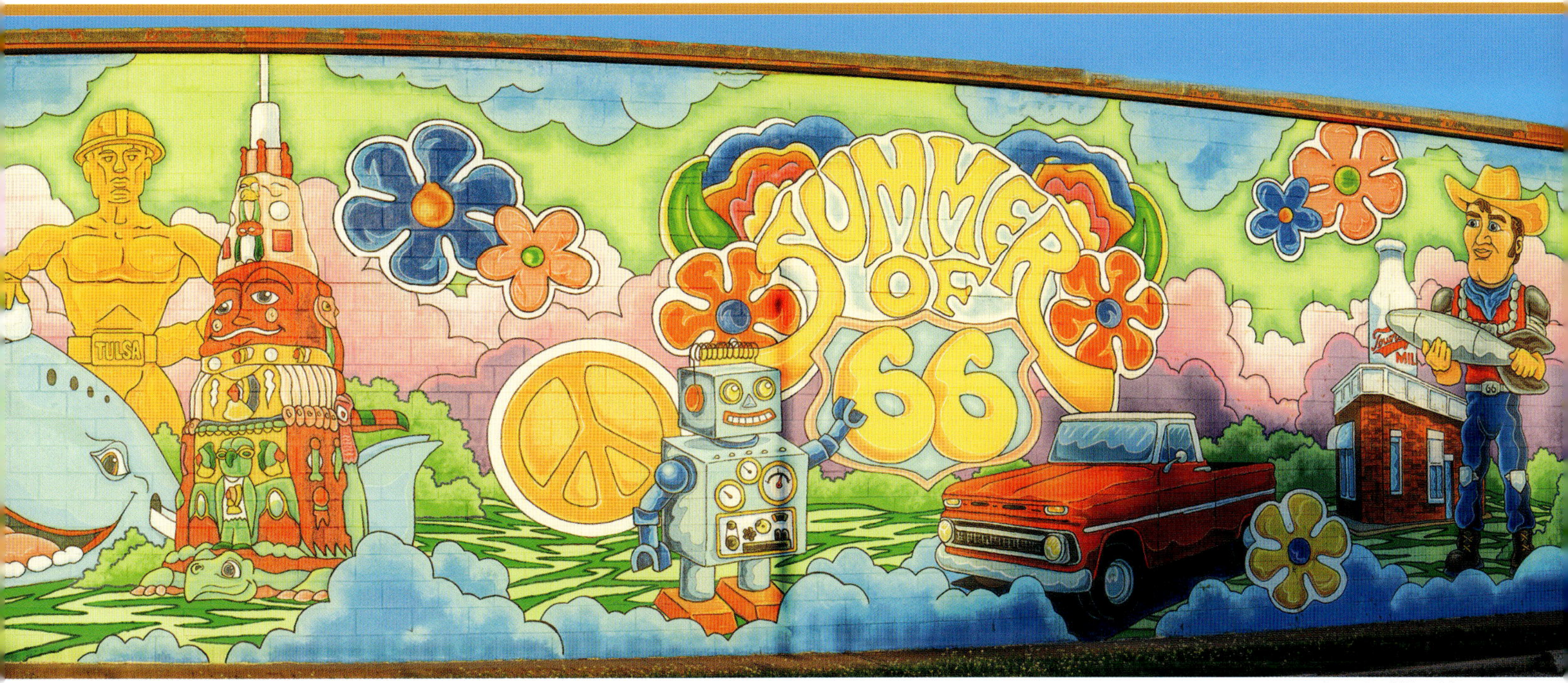

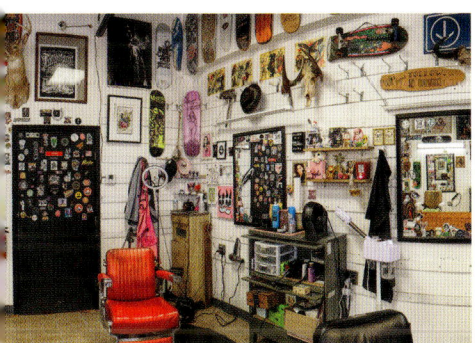

David Skernick

I found myself in need of a haircut. Being on the road is never without its small challenges. Lucky for me, Tom's Barbershop was right there on Route 66 in Edmond, Oklahoma.

When I walked into the shop, Chasity said she could take care of my shaggy hair in about twenty minutes. Give me twenty minutes to kill, and I'll look for something to photograph.

The barbershop was the perfect Route 66 location. Just look at those walls! Stickers, heads, skateboards; I asked permission and then ran out to Bob the Truck to grab a camera and tripod.

Interiors and other close quarters offer the opportunity to portray clutter and a sort of coziness at the same time. The shot on the left is a sixteen-shot double pano. The right angles could not be rendered this way without this technique. A wide angle would give you a different look. I am not saying this is better; it is just what I wanted to do. Always find a way to do it your way.

Bob's Barbershop, Edmond, Oklahoma   *David Skernick*

90

Arcadia, Oklahoma

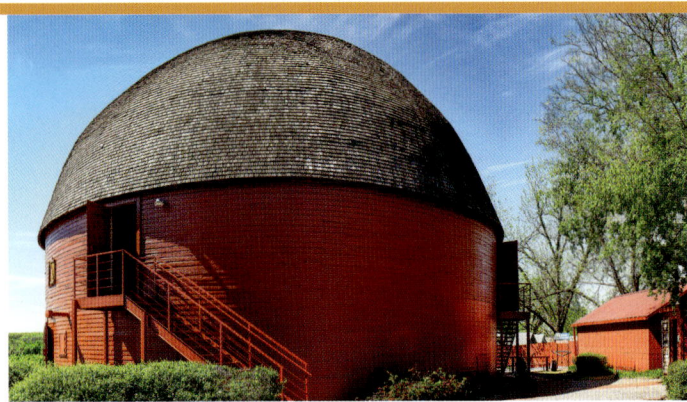

The Round Barn, Arcadia, Oklahoma   *David Skernick*

The Round Barn is a famous Route 66 attraction. There is a pretty cool museum inside and some old farm machines outside. Lots of good stuff to photograph. I found morning light to be best here to get a pleasing angle in good light.

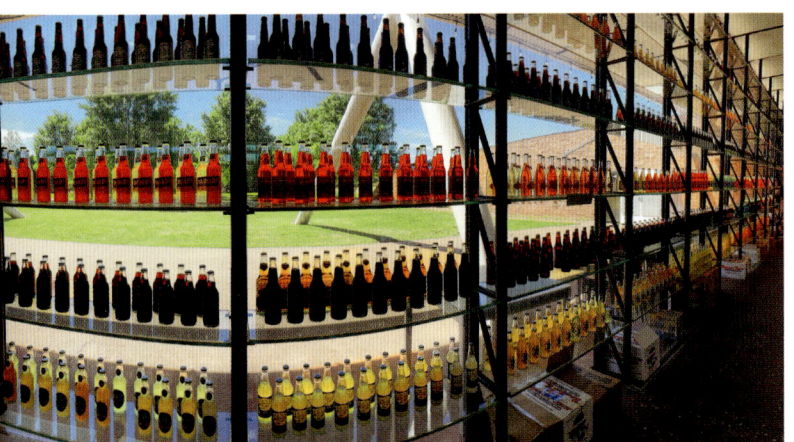

Pop's iPhone pano, Arcadia, Oklahoma   *David Skernick*

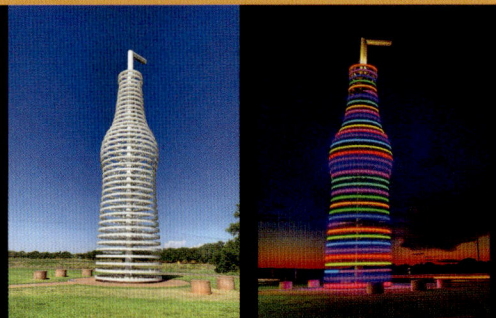

Pop's 66, Arcadia, Oklahoma   *Anne Schlueter*

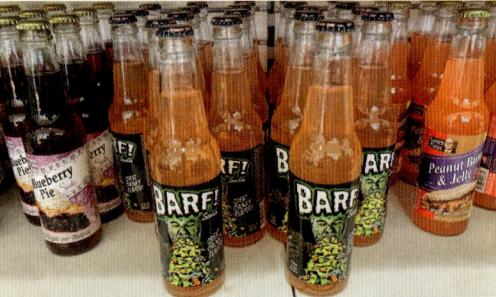

Barf   *Anne Schlueter*

If you are in the mood for a good burger and a crazy-flavored soda, you gotta stop at Pops 66 in Arcadia, Oklahoma. We shot the giant bottle coming and going that day. Anne processed her two shots as one file. This is called a "diptych," which is defined as any object with two flat plates that form a pair. You can make one in post or simply hang two photos together. The sunset shot was taken in aperture priority mode ("A" or "AV," depending on your camera). She lowered her ISO to get a slower shutter speed to blur the passing car lights. Pops 66 boasts over six hundred tasty flavors. If you are courageous and curious, how about an ice-cold bottle of Barf?

Luther and Warwick, Oklahoma

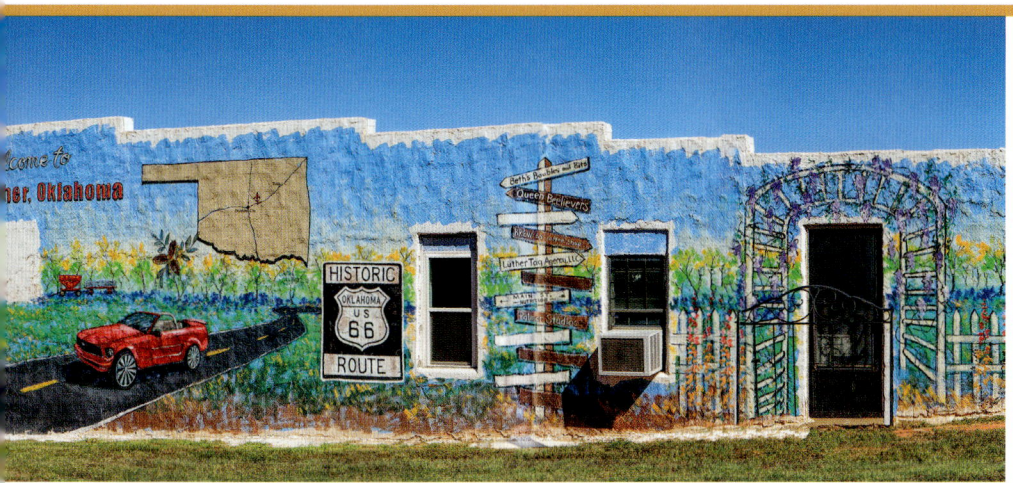

Welcome to Luther, Oklahoma

David Skernick

This mural is in Luther, Oklahoma. I took a pano! There was a phone pole in front that I removed in postprocessing, using the clone stamp. If you plan on doing that, find an angle that will place the object somewhere easy to replicate. I was able to move so the pole could be to the left of the door. The lines in the fence post on the right were easy to copy. I left the air conditioner on purpose. I like it but didn't like the pole. Your shot, your choice.

In Warwick, Oklahoma, at the Seaba Station, I used a simple trick to get rid of unwanted elements. There were lots of newer buildings around this hundred-year-old gas station. I just cropped in really tight in postprocessing to hide them and allowed the old station to stand alone.

I had to back up into the road a little to get the sides of the building straight, I wanted to accentuate the boxiness of the building, so it was important to me to get all the lines parallel. This is called "squaring to your subject" and is achieved by centering yourself in front of your subject. I then backed up until the vertical lines appeared straight.

To the left of the station, there is a small museum and gift shop. Jerry had all kinds of interesting stories to impart as I bought a cool new T-shirt to add to my collection.

Around the back, you can find an original rock restroom. It is very old and no longer in use. I checked it out, considered a photo, but decided I really did not need to document an old bathroom. To each his own.

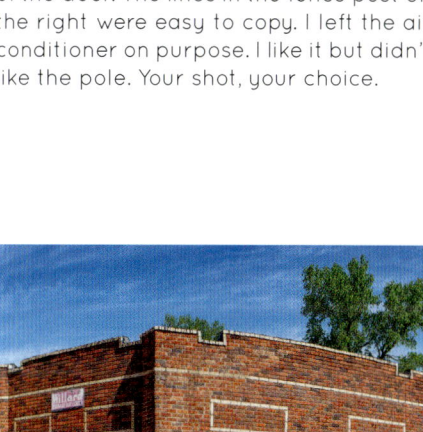

The Seaba Station, Warwick, Oklahoma

David Skernick

Chandler, Oklahoma

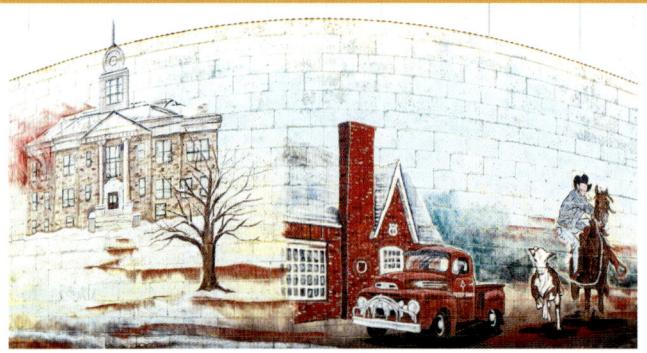

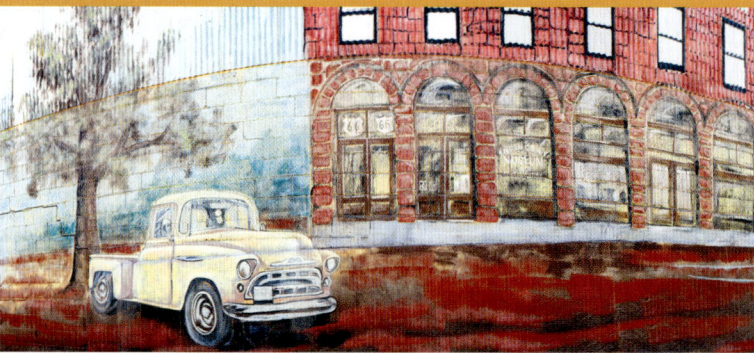

Lincoln County mural, Chandler, Oklahoma

David Skernick

Sometimes two shots are better than one to describe a subject. Here are two different details of a huge mural, the exterior and interior of an attraction, and daytime and nighttime at the Lincoln Motel. I thought one photo worked to describe the little Phillips 66 gas station. I always try to spend plenty of time on something worth photographing. Coming back at a different time, or even a different season, is a treat. Edit carefully before showing your work. Variations and more information can be interesting, but redundancy is boring.

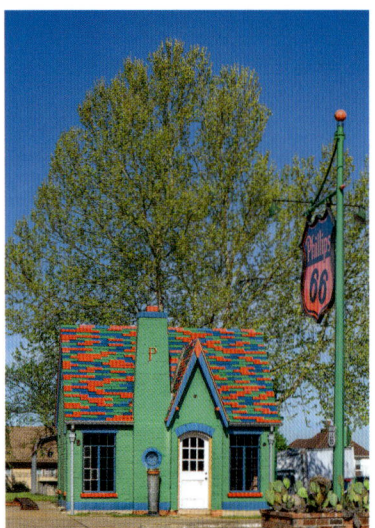

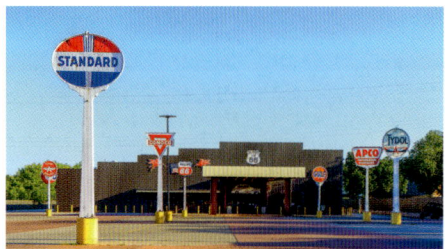

Parking lot, Route 66 Family Fun Center, Chandler, Oklahoma
Becky Waters

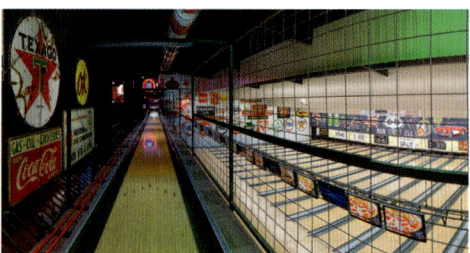

101 Foot Bowling Lane, Route 66 Family Fun Center   *David Skernick*

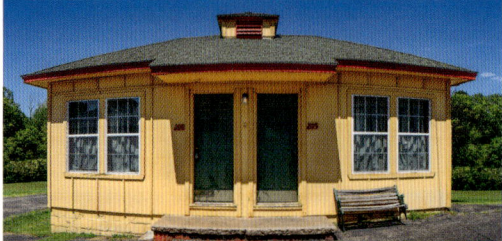

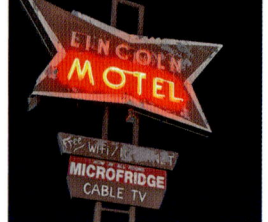

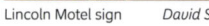

1930 Phillips 66 station   *David Skernick*   Lincoln Motel rooms, Chandler, Oklahoma   *David Skernick*   Lincoln Motel sign   *David Skernick*

Stroud and Bristow, Oklahoma

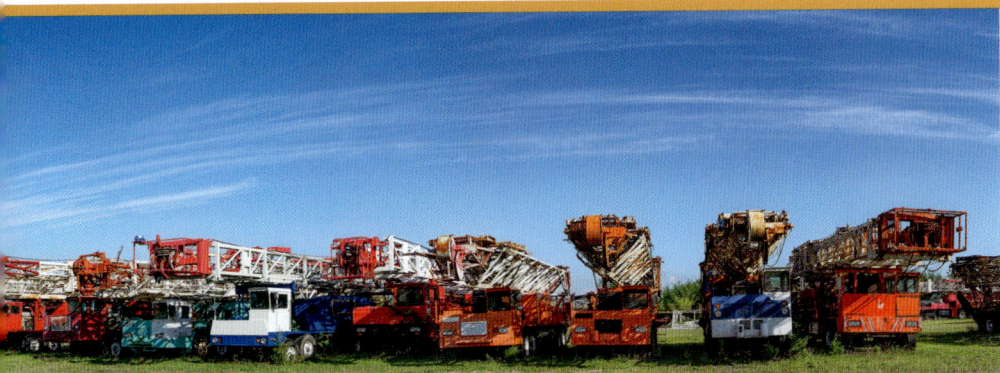

Row of trucks along Route 66, Stroud, Oklahoma

David Skernick

Not all of the things you will find as you travel America's Highway will be in the form of architecture or permanent installations. This row of trucks caught my eye just west of Stroud, Oklahoma. Repeating forms are always good to find. It is an easy composition that usually looks pleasing. The sweeping clouds and the fact that these trucks were both multicolored and had cool ladders attached just added to the worth of the photo opportunity.

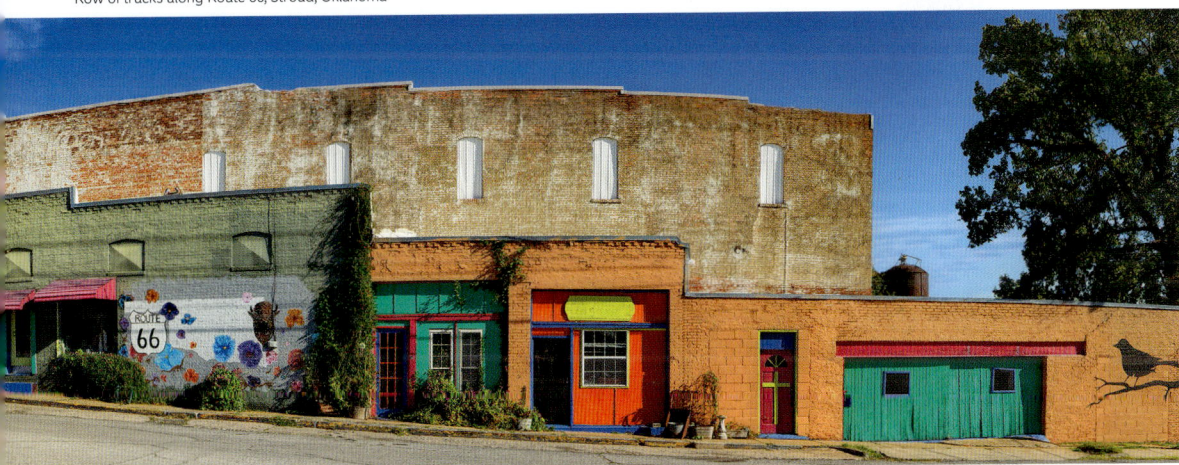

Mural and wall, Bristow, Oklahoma

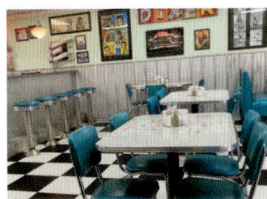

Boomarang Diner

Anne Schlueter

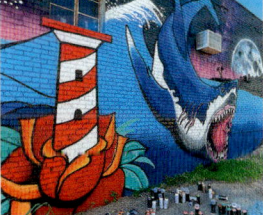

David Skernick Mural in progress *David Skernick*

We stopped for breakfast at the Boomarang Diner in Bristow, Oklahoma—a complete Route 66 experience and terrific food. The building (*above*) was down the street.

Anne shot the interior of the café while we waited for our food. She held her phone crooked to make the photo more interesting. I used my phone to grab a quick shot of

the mural in progress across the street from the Boomarang. We guessed that the painters were out to lunch, but loved that they left their paint cans behind.

94

Sapulpa, Oklahoma

The Rock Creek Bridge was constructed in 1924. It was then part of the Old Ozark Trail. It became part of Route 66 in 1926. Anne included lots of the old bricks to give a feeling of what the old road looked like. I shot the detail on the bridge. There was no explanation as to what the memorial is about or what it commemorates, but I found it interesting and somewhat touching.

You can stay on the old road across most of Oklahoma. Just before Sapulpa, coming from the west, be careful not to turn right on Oklahoma State Highway

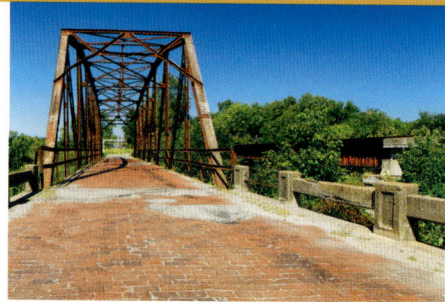

Rock Creek Bridge, Sapulpa, Oklahoma   *Anne Schlueter*

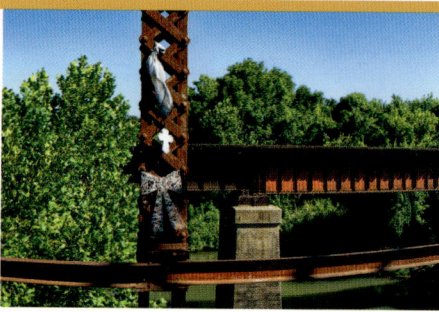

Memorial on bridge, Sapulpa, Oklahoma   *David Skernick*

66. The old road goes straight. The two roads do stay together for a time, but they split here. You will know you are following historical 66 if you see the giant gas pump

on the next page and the Rock Creek Bridge (*above*) off to your left. Watch carefully and follow the signs that say "Historical" Route 66.

Michael Jones, the owner of Gasoline Alley, is one of the people bringing back the history and fun that is Route 66. His new business is full of all kinds of cool 66 memorabilia. He was happy to let me photograph both him and the restroom in his store. His exact words were "You gotta check out my restroom!" How could I not? The restroom pano is made up of thirty-six photos taken in four rows with a 50mm lens. The work that went into this small room is amazing. Yeah—I'll say it—you gotta see it!

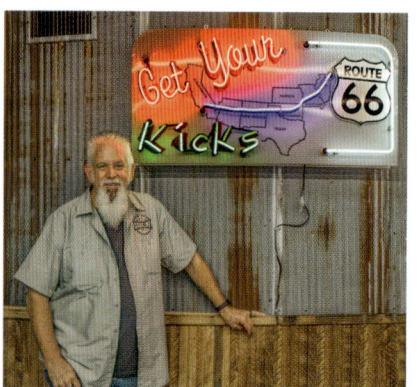

Mike Jones, Gasoline Alley, Sapulpa, Oklahoma *David Skernick*

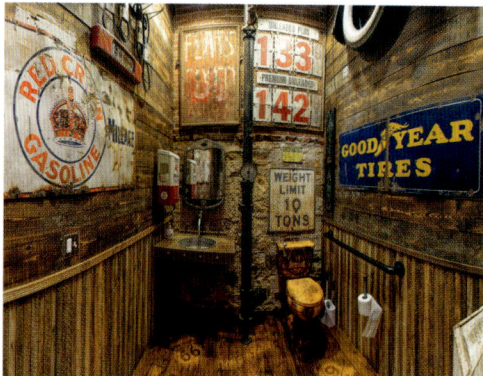

Restroom, Gasoline Alley   *David Skernick*

Mike took the time to write down some of the places he felt I should not miss up the road. That kind of helpfulness is something I have come to expect along the Mother Road. Thanks,

Mike—I found them all! He came out to photograph me and Bob the Truck as I added the new stickers I picked up in his store. He posted the pictures on his social media that night.

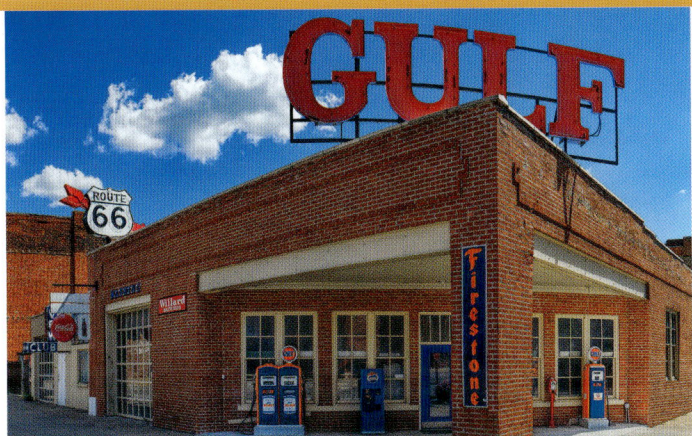

Gulf station, corner of Water and Hobson, Sapulpa, Oklahoma   *David Skernick*

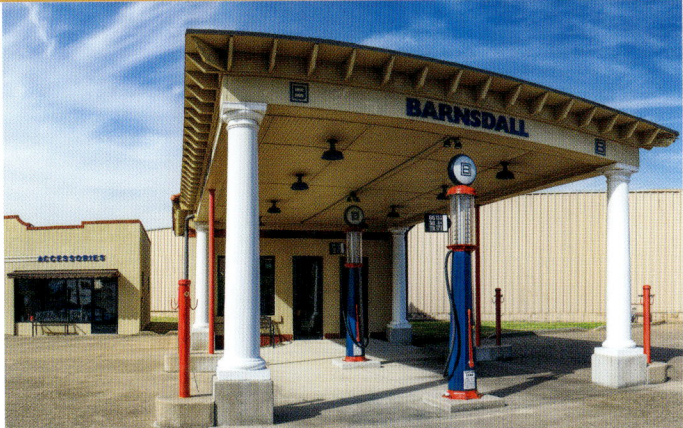

Barnsdall Station, corner of Water and Lee, Sapulpa, Oklahoma   *David Skernick*

This terrific Route 66 Gulf gas station is in Sapulpa, Oklahoma. I spent some time photographing this station carefully because the light and clouds were perfect. You never know what will inspire you to take the time to painstakingly craft a photograph. For me, my phone is for snapshots—nothing wrong with that, but what makes me want to take the time to set up my tripod, choose the best settings and lens, and really take my time to compose a photo is not always obvious. I'm sure you can relate! I found the Barnsdall Station on another trip. You need to look around for these two old stations. They are not on the marked alignment of Route 66.

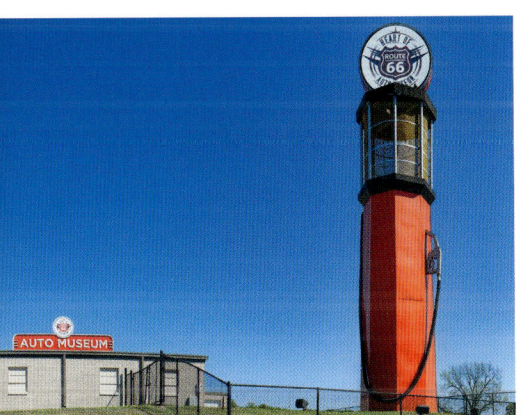

Heart of 66 Auto Museum, Sapulpa, Oklahoma   *David Skernick*

The Heart of Route 66 Auto Museum is worth visiting. Inside you will find a wonderful collection of old cars beautifully displayed and in perfect shape. The owner can answer any questions you might have about the vehicles, or about Route 66. The gas pump at the outside of the museum, which you see here, is 66 feet tall. I had to stand across the street to get it into the shot. Giants are one of the fun and photographically challenging parts of America's Highway. Everyone knows the trick of standing under a subject and looking up to make it appear taller. There is no need to make a 66-foot gas pump look taller! I wanted to show the height, but I did not want a distorted shot, so I backed way up and included the one-story museum to help tell my story and show scale.

Tulsa, Oklahoma

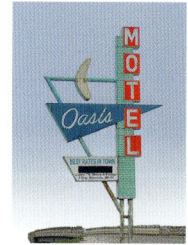

Oasis sign *David Skernick*

Tulsa, Oklahoma, definitely got the Route 66 memo! Coming in from the west, stay on Frankoma Road after Sapulpa. You will take a left turn where it says 116, but then just stay straight. Do not follow 116 a second time. You will not see signs for a while, but if you stay straight, the signs will be all over the place once you enter Tulsa. The road becomes 11th Street (Route 66). You will see lots of murals and other great photo opportunities throughout Tulsa. I used a low angle for the photo on the right to accentuate both the size of the train and the tower. I can't vouch for the food at the Rancho Grande, but the smells were intoxicating. I had to stop for the Desert Hills Motel. I love the simplicity of this shot. I had to wait for a couple of cars to leave. Lucky for me I was there just at 11:00—checkout time. If they had not left, I would have recomposed the shot. I am happy I could get what I wanted by waiting a few minutes.

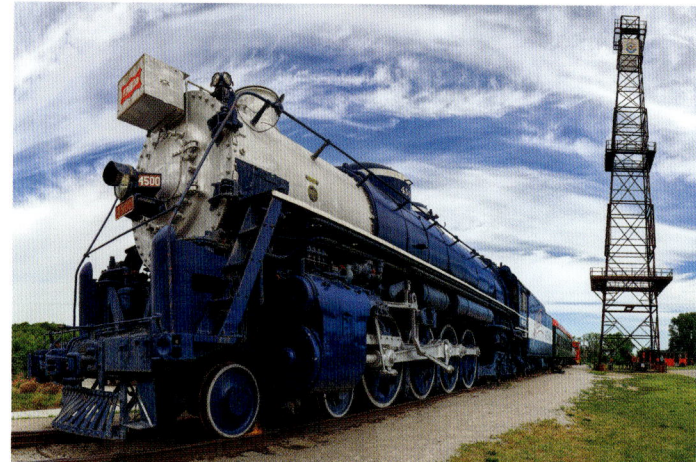

Route 66 Historical Village, Tulsa, Oklahoma　　　*David Skernick*

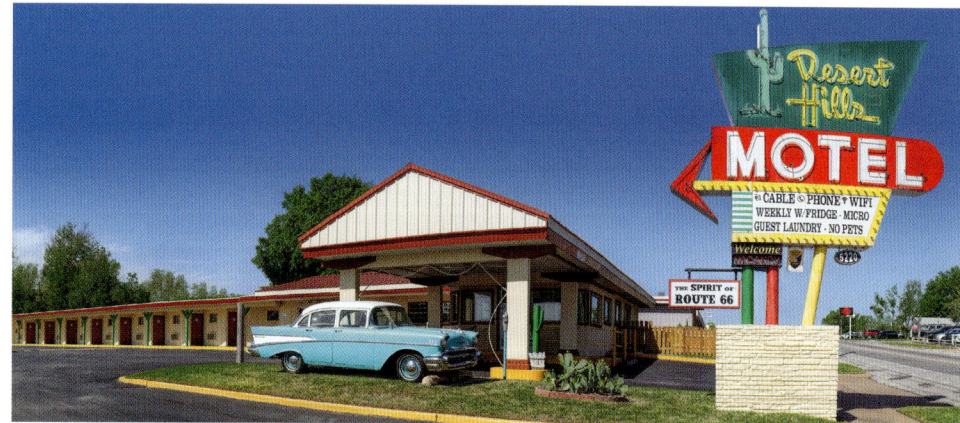

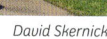

The Desert Hills Motel, Tulsa, Oklahoma　　　*David Skernick*

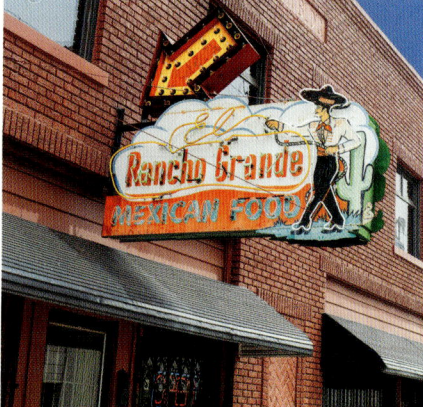

Rancho Grande, Tulsa, Oklahoma　　　*David Skernick*

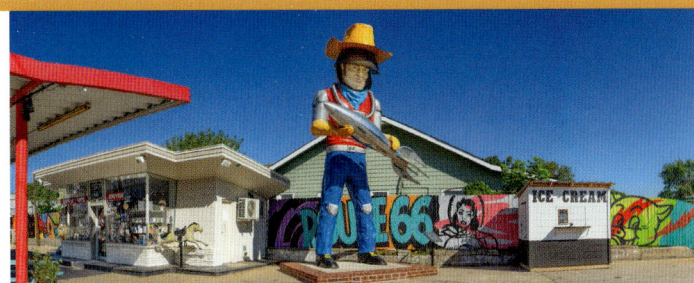

Buck Atoms at Buck Atoms Cosmic Curios, Tulsa, Oklahoma   *David Skernick*

If you are into giants you have to go to Tulsa. It is home to two of the most famous giants on the Mother Road: the Golden Driller and Buck Atoms are worth the traffic! Buck Atoms is a famous Route 66 icon. He disappeared in 1950 and then mysteriously reappeared in May 2018, when legend says his spaceship landed in Tulsa, Oklahoma, at 1347 East 11th Street. I found him there at Buck Atoms Cosmic Curios on 66. Don't miss this fun shop and great photo op! The Spirit Dog Training building is fantastic. I shot from the corner to try and get all of the cool stuff in one shot. Route 66 seems to inspire these types of design and decorations.

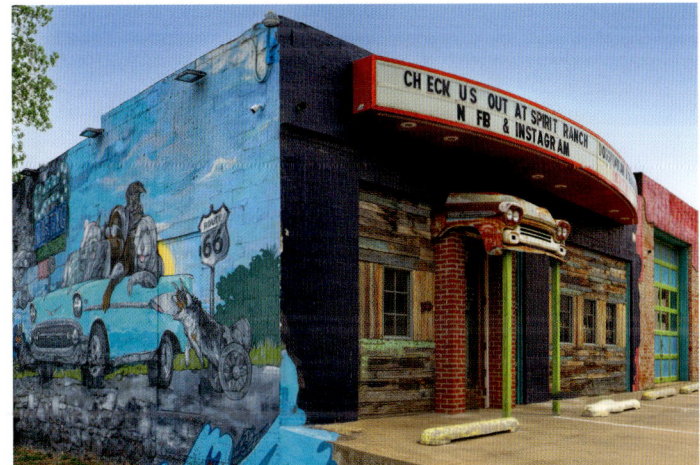

Spirit Dog Training, Tulsa, Oklahoma   *David Skernick*

The Golden Driller is a 76-foot-tall, 43,500-pound statue. He was originally created for Tulsa's 1966 International Petroleum Exposition. It's one of the largest freestanding statues in the United States. He is part of the Route 66 family, even though he's not exactly on 66. Just put 4145 E. 21st Street, Tulsa, into your GPS and you'll find him easily. This time I parked Bob the Truck in front for scale.

The Golden Driller, Tulsa, Oklahoma   *David Skernick*

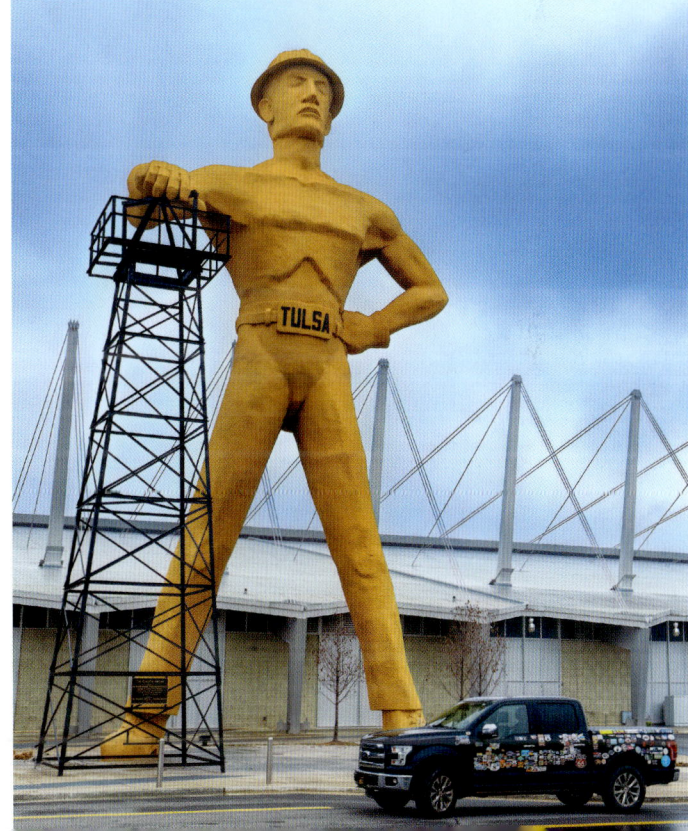

98

The Blue Whale of Catoosa, Oklahoma

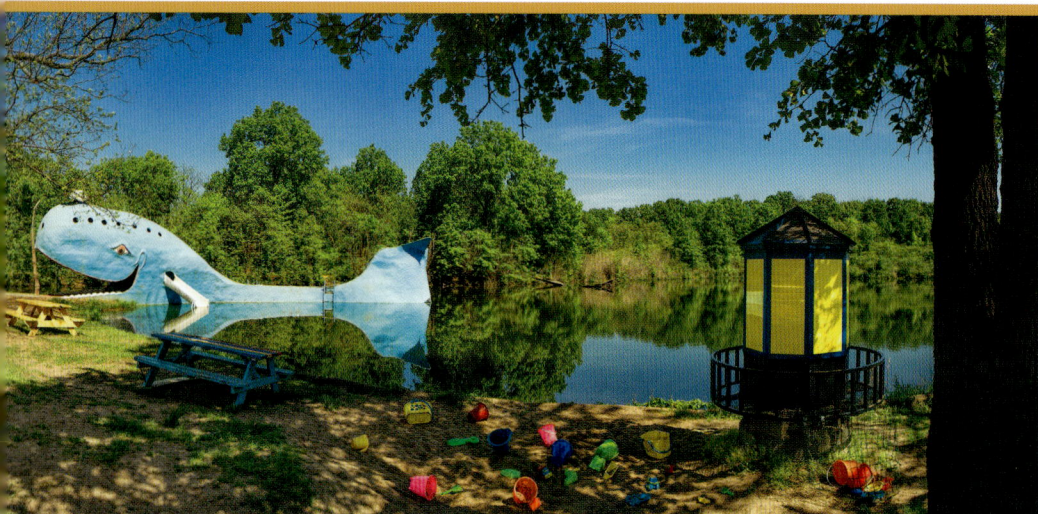

The Blue Whale of Catoosa, Oklahoma

David Skernick

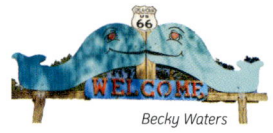

Becky Waters

The Blue Whale of Catoosa was built in the 1970s by Hugh Davis. He made it as a gift for his wife, Zella, who collected whale figurines. Although he built this attraction for just one person, the locals and travelers along Route 66 made it theirs as well. There are lots of fun photos to take here. Take the time to walk around and try different angles. Look for the turtles in the pond too!

Smile!

Anne Schlueter

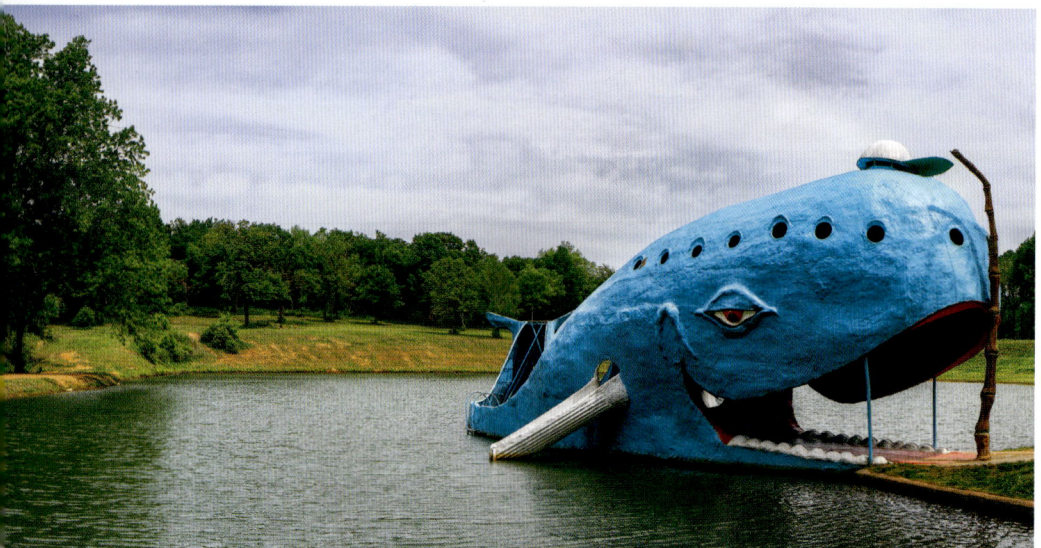

Another day, another angle

David Skernick

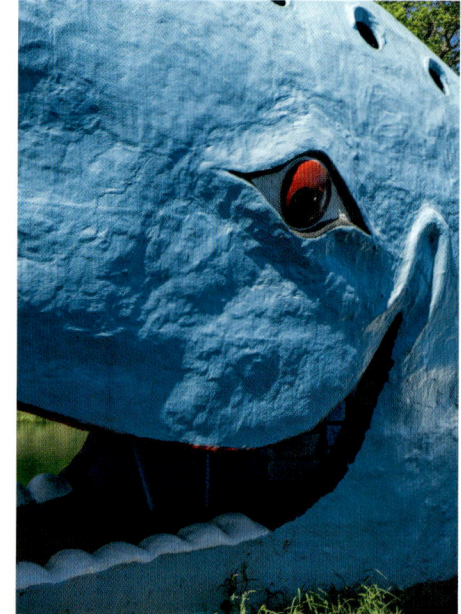

Chelsea and Vinita, Oklahoma

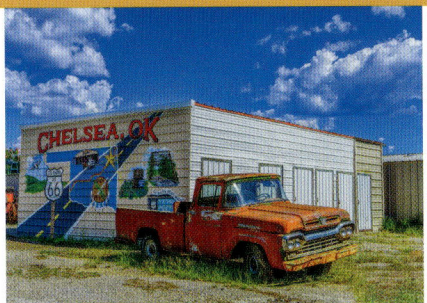
Chelsea, Oklahoma, mural and truck *Becky Waters*

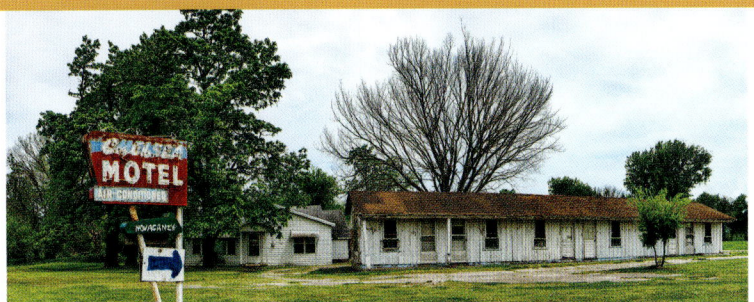
The Chelsea Motel, Chelsea, Oklahoma *David Skernick*

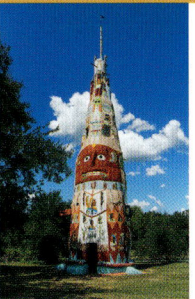
Totem Village *Anne Schlueter*

It may seem obvious, but I'll say it anyway. Look around! See what might go well with your subject the same way you look around the refrigerator to see what might go well with that leftover turkey. The kind of images we create on Route 66 could be called travel or environmental photography. Let's face it—we just like shooting cool stuff, and the Main Street of America is loaded with it. How do we make our shots more than just a facsimile of a thing? One way is to add other things, creating more of a scene or a story.

In Chelsea, the truck on the left, the cloud on the right, and the trees in the middle create stories and frames for our subjects. In Vinita, the door on the wall (*below*) has nothing to do with the mural but somehow makes the shot more interesting. The Muffler Man, "Big Bill" at the Hi-Way Cafe, has his suitcase, so we know he's traveling, and the chief? Okay, he stands alone, which is also a choice.

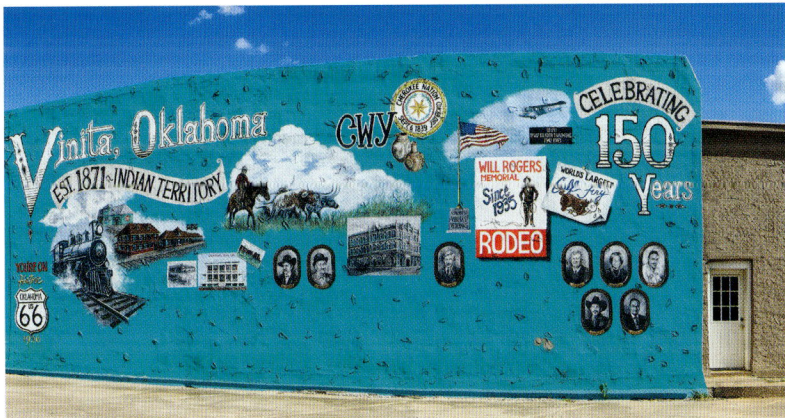
Mural, Vinita, Oklahoma *David Skernick*

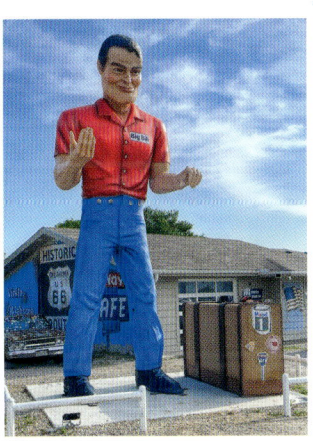
Big Bill *David Skernick*

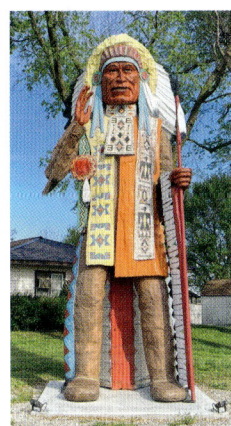
20-foot Chief *David Skernick*

Afton, Oklahoma

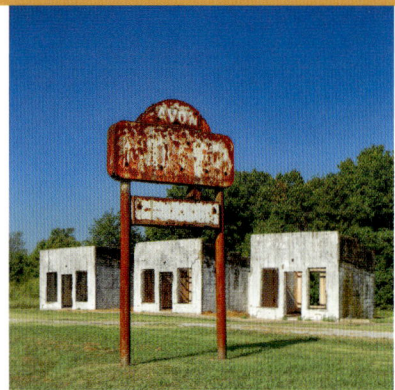

Avon Motel, Afton, Oklahoma   *David Skernick*

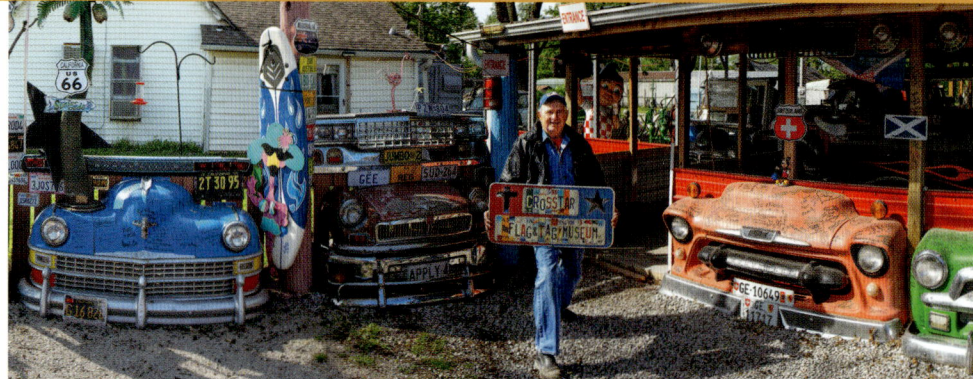

Al Childs and the Cros Star Museum, Afton, Oklahoma   *David Skernick*

There is minimalism and then there is Al Childs. Minimalism is an art form celebrating simple and often-massive forms. As photographers, it is the simple part that we sometimes seek. Think of trying to make a statement with fewer words or more-concise words. It's sort of like that. When I found the old Avon Motel in Afton, Oklahoma, there was almost nothing left. How do you photograph nothing? I tried for the simplest and least cluttered surroundings I could find. In that same little town you will find the Cros Star Museum, owned and operated by Al Childs. In my humble opinion, Al is the king of nonminimalism. You will love him, his dog, and his collections.

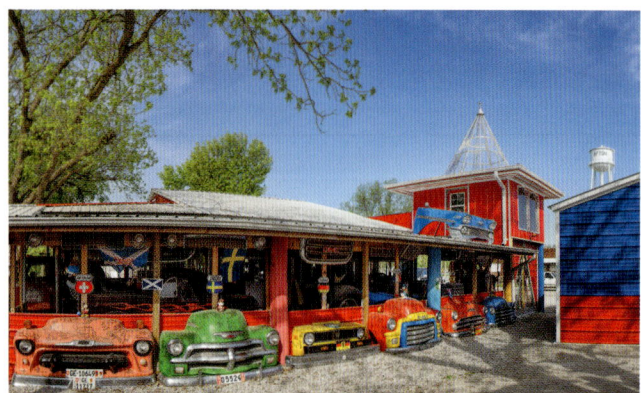

The Cros Star Museum, Afton, Oklahoma   *David Skernick*

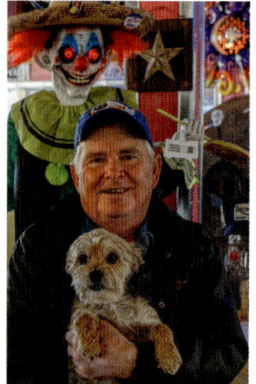

Al and Charlie   *David Skernick*

Al, shown here advertising the museum and posing with his dog, Charlie, and some clown, collects everything. Many things in his museum are made to move, bob, bounce, and even bark. He wants you to touch everything, to really experience and appreciate his finds. He'll follow you around, giving you the story behind each of his fantastic exhibits, and he is happy to have you take as many photos as you like!

Miami and Commerce, Oklahoma

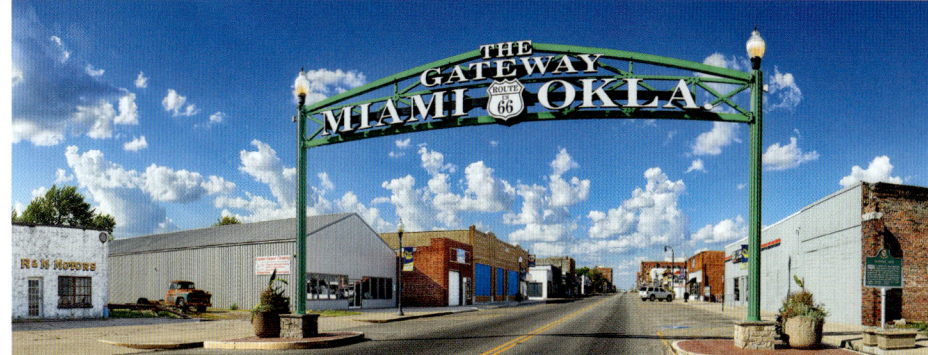

The Gateway, Miami, Oklahoma

David Skernick

The time of day when you come across something you want to photograph may seem out of your control. I often choose to stay overnight somewhere earlier than I planned, or to hang around for a while to be at the right place at the right time. The afternoon light and clouds made the shot to the right in Miami special. That time I was just lucky. Route 66 Cookies in Commerce, Oklahoma, faces due east, and the Conoco station due west. I shot the Conoco station (*below*) one afternoon. I planned to come back some time to shoot the cookie store in the morning. Becky and Anne were with me on another trip. It was afternoon again. It wasn't so much planning as just circumstance. By then, I had my morning shot but wasn't crazy about it. I was happily surprised when Becky captured the cool backlit shot

(*right*) at the "wrong" time. The sunburst combined with the wide-angle distortion to give the photo a fun feel that matches the subject. Anne shot directly into the open shade to get her detail shot without any light flare. You can always fill your frame with shade for clean, even light.

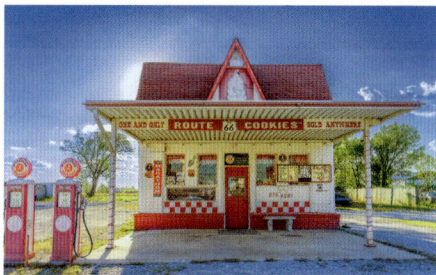

Cookies backlit

Becky Waters

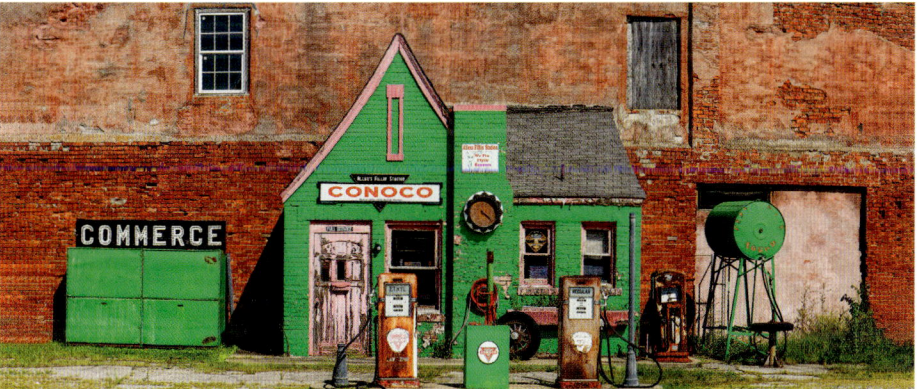

Conoco station, Commerce, Oklahoma

David Skernick

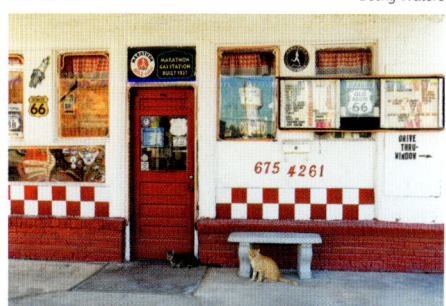

Cats at Cookies

Anne Schlueter

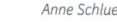

Baxter Springs, Kansas

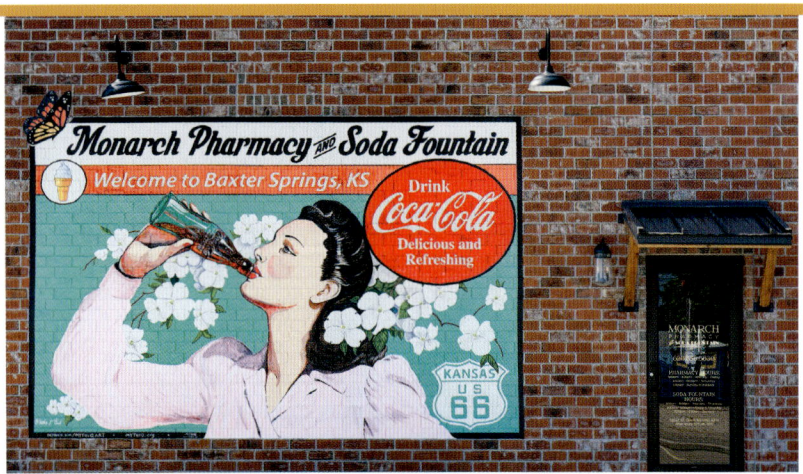

Monarch Pharmacy, Baxter Springs, Kansas

David Skernick

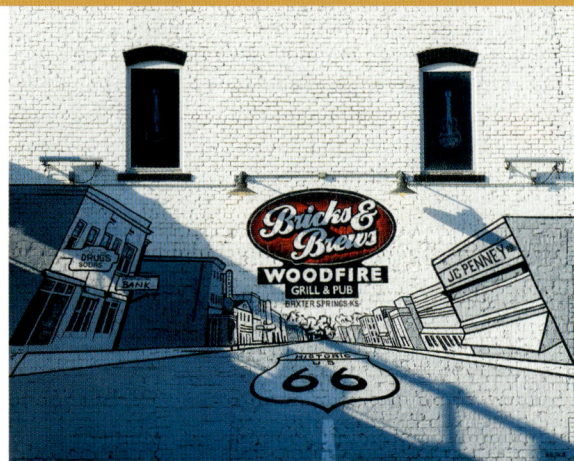

Bricks & Brew, Baxter Springs, Kansas

Anne Schlueter

There are 13.2 miles of Route 66 that run through Kansas. That's about 0.5 percent of the total miles, but try not to skip it. The murals (*above*) in Baxter Springs, Kansas, are worth a look. The Rainbow Curve Bridge (commonly just called the Rainbow Bridge) was built in 1923 over Bush Creek. The sign there says it is the last Marsh arch bridge remaining along Route 66. One time when I was there, Brush Creek was deep enough for me to get a reflection of the bridge. Becky had to find another angle for her shot, since the river was dry when we were there together. The last time I went, there was water again. The real magic happened when the clouds rose in the same shape as the bridge, giving me a perfect repeating form. Try to return to your favorite places when you can. You never know how the seasons, the weather, or your attitude will change. I try not to repeat an old shot, but instead to look for a new way to see an old friend.

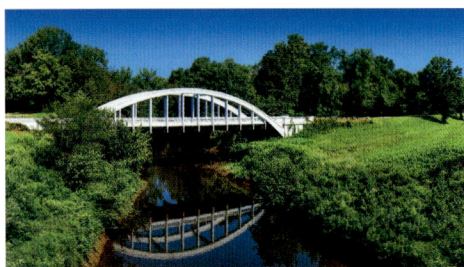

Rainbow Bridge, Baxter Springs, Kansas

David Skernick

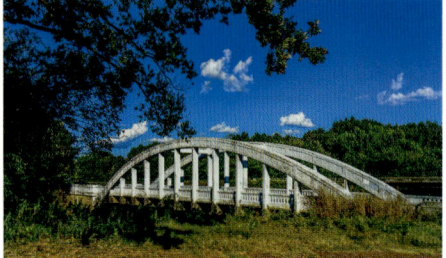

Rainbow Bridge, early fall

Becky Waters

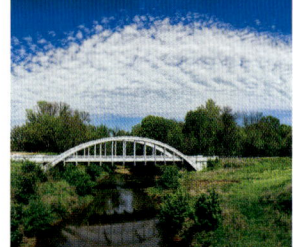

Rainbow Bridge, early spring
David Skernick

Galena, Kansas

Gearhead Curios, in Galena, Kansas, is one of those places where you can spend some serious time with your camera. This book would be the size of a phone book if I included every image I have, or could shoot, along the route, especially in places like this. Aaron Perry (*below*) is proudly posing in the Curio Shop's restroom, which he designed and built. When you are there, make sure you try belt sander racing. It's a blast!

The mural on Main Street (Rt 66) in Galena, Kansas, is a much-simpler location. There are often many ways you can frame your photos, but with only two dimensions, there is a limit. I chose to include the two streetlamps to give the composition some depth. You know I love to include things such as random doors.

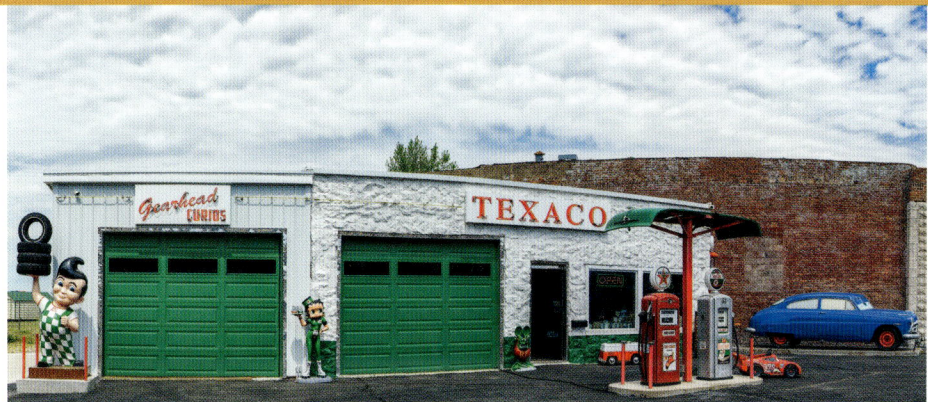

Gearhead Curios, Galena, Kansas   *David Skernick*

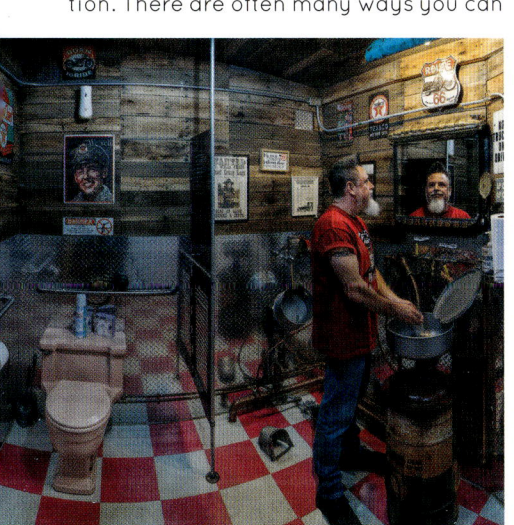

Aaron posing in his amazing restroom in Gearhead Curios   *David Skernick*

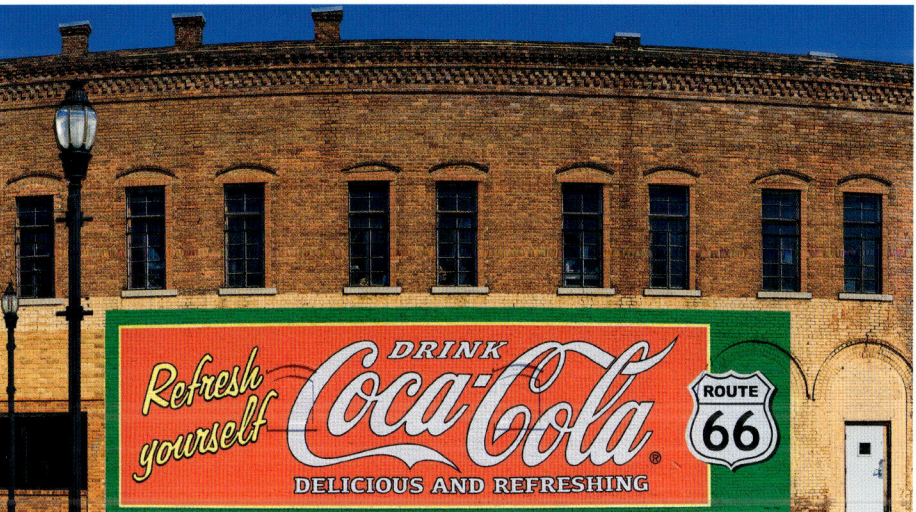

Main Street, Galena, Kansas   *David Skernick*

Where Was That?

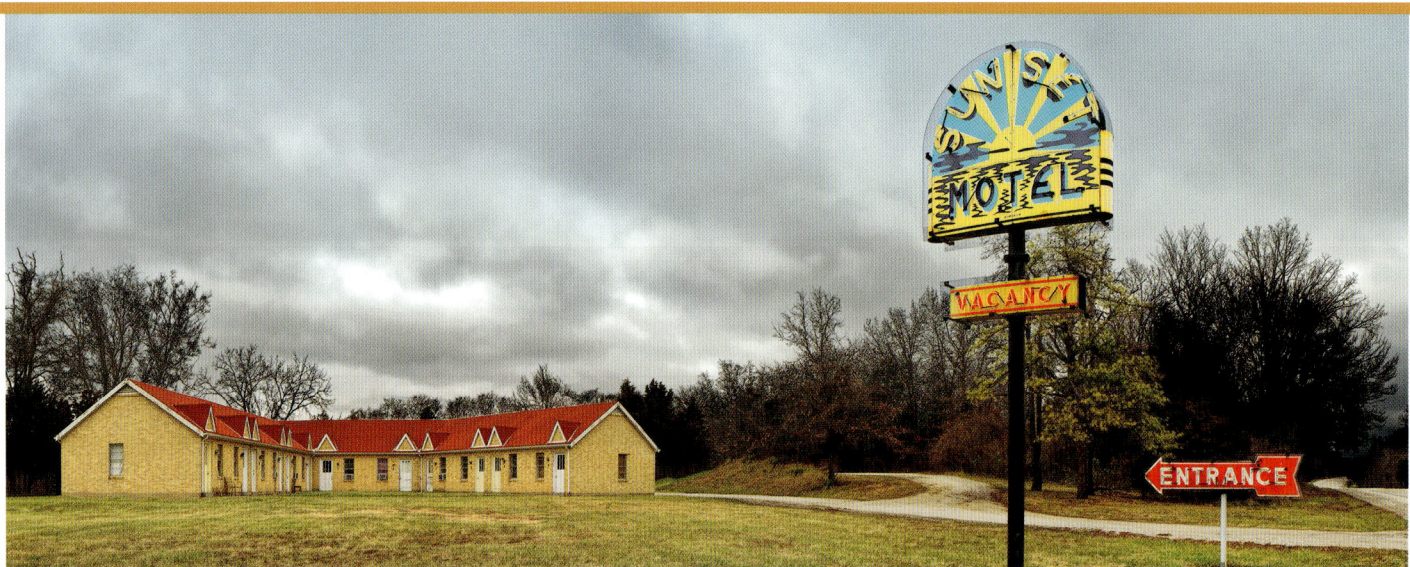

Sunset Motel, Villa Ridge, Missouri

David Skernick

I took this photo years before Schiffer Publishing began publishing my books. All I knew was that I had shot it on Route 66 in Missouri. When I went to add it to this book, I realized that I was not sure exactly where in Missouri I had been. I figured it out recently with the help of generous Route 66 experts on the internet, but I chose to keep it here at the southern end of Missouri, rather than at the northern end, where it belongs, to make this point. This is a good time to talk about keeping track of where you are! If you are shooting with a phone, or one of the newest cameras, you might have a built-in GPS and then will be able to find out exactly where you were when you tripped the shutter. You could simply take a quick phone shot every time you stop for just this purpose. Some of my students do that. Me? I'm an old guy. I'm a note taker.

I keep this thing I call a "score" with me on all trips. It is just one of those small pads of paper, but mine has clips all over it so I can easily flip to whatever page I need. You can see a few of them on the facing page. I write down the state I'm in, every road I take, where I stop for the night, especially good or bad roads, mileage, oil changes, good motels, bad motels, people I meet along the way, and, most importantly, every picture I take. No need for settings; that's what metadata is for. The notepad method gives me plenty of room for extra notes, like "best in PM," or "Used a 5× Neutral Density filter here," or "Amazing cheeseburger across the street." Yes, I keep track of everything. I have a terrible memory and don't want to leave anything important out that I might want to remember or share when showing my photos years (or even months) later.

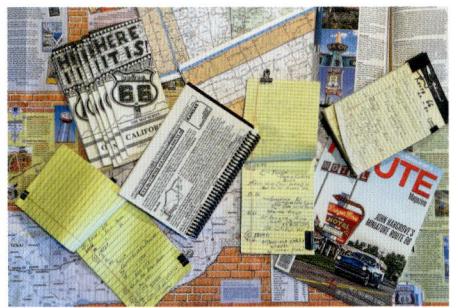

Trip notes — *David Skernick*

When I am working on a book, I typically drive every road I can find and keep my eyes open for photo opportunities. If I am there at the wrong time, I may decide to come back, or I might just skip that shot. Sometimes the photos that I have skipped kind of haunt me until I get back to them on a future trip. I rarely do research in advance. I love to "come around a corner as a photograph is about to happen." Ansel Adams claimed that he had that good fortune. If it worked for him . . . I like to react to what I find, to see it for the first time, to discover it! Route 66 is different. For one thing, it is just one road (more or less), but I wanted to find all the "alignments." For this trip, the more prepared you are, the more likely you will be to see more of the road and find all of the wonderful gifts that Route 66 offers. I hope you are finding that this book is helping you in exactly that way.

Joplin, Missouri

As a photographer, one of the things you want to look for is inconsistencies. Things that don't quite fit together make for interesting compositions. Here the strange combination of the broken sign and the pristine mural work off each other in a way that forces you to look at everything in the photo just a little more carefully.

Welcome to Joplin, Missouri — *David Skernick*

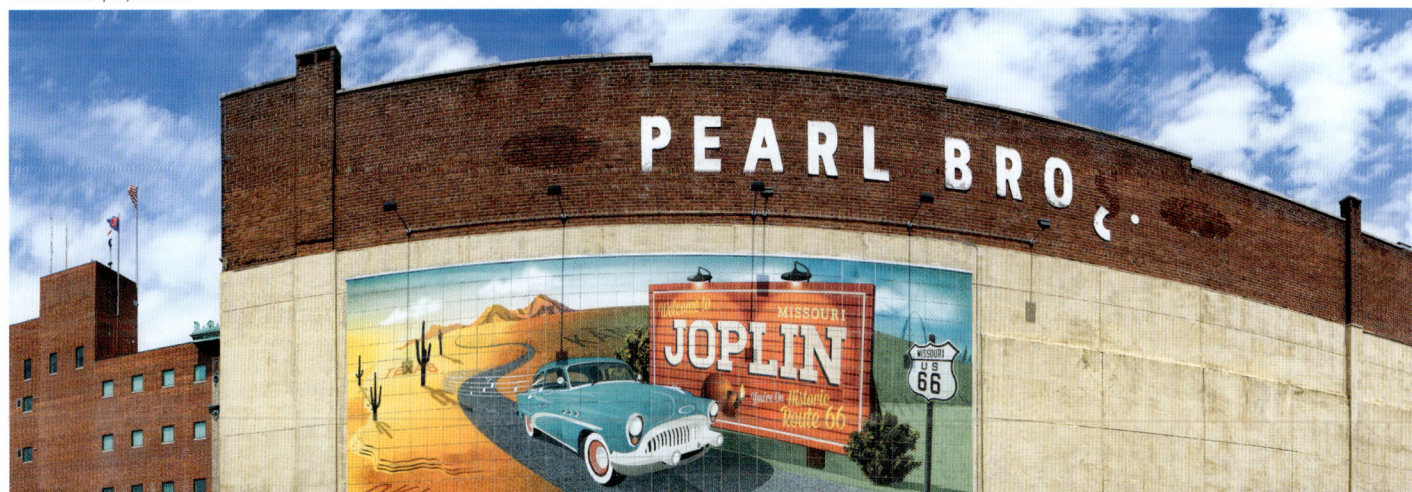

Carthage and Spencer, Missouri

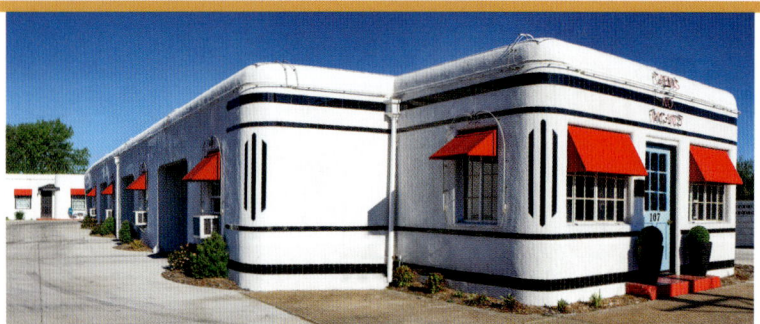

Boots Motor Court, Carthage, Missouri — *David Skernick*

66 Drive-In, Carthage, Missouri — *David Skernick*

Both of these photos were taken from odd angles. That is, I was not "squared" to my subject. Squared means directly in front of and at the center height in relation to the object you are photographing. If you want no distortion at all, you need to be squared to your subject. Okay—but these times, I wanted a little distortion so you could see the complete building on the left and have a sense of fun on the right. Remember, these choices are up to you, but you need to make them consciously so you can have complete control of your image.

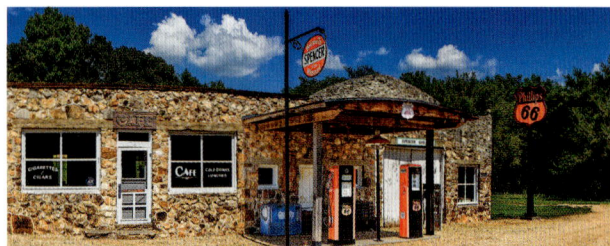

Spencer, Missouri, Cafe and Gas Station — *David Skernick*

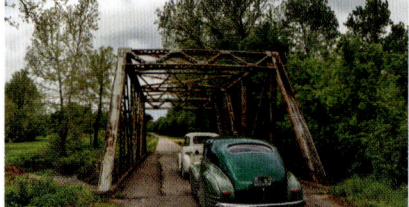

Spencer Bridge — *David Skernick*

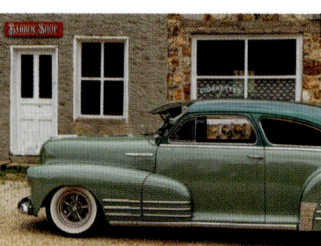

Spencer Barber Shop — *Anne Schlueter*

Spencer, Missouri, can be found on the original 1926 alignment of Route 66. Look for a sign pointing to the right about 6 miles west of Heatonville. Built in the 1930s, it included Spencer Store, Spencer Cafe & Barbershop, and Spencer Garage and Service Station (Phillips 66). Some of the buildings have been renovated.

Opportunity knocks: When I was there a couple of years ago, I had one of those perfect-light days. I got there just when the sun was lighting the building and there were perfect clouds in the sky. Recently, when I returned with a workshop, these nice folks came along in 1948 Chevys! We flagged them down and asked them to pose their cars on the bridge and in front of the buildings. They were happy to help. I emailed the pics that night. Try to take advantage of every lucky break that comes your way, and, of course, always pay it forward. I'll send a book to my new friends with the cool cars as well. Hope they like it!

Gary's Gay Parida, Ash Grove, Missouri

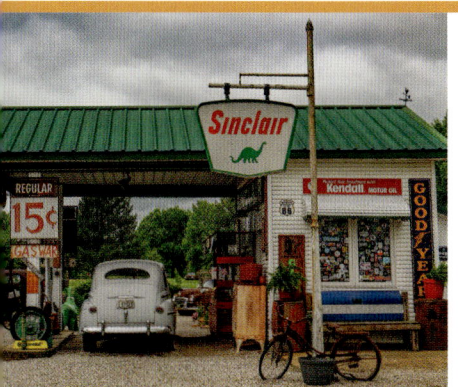

Gay Parita Sinclair, Ash Grove, Missouri   *Anne Schlueter*

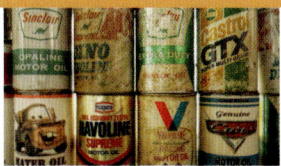

Oil cans   *Becky Waters*

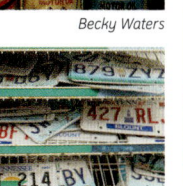

License plates   *Becky Waters*

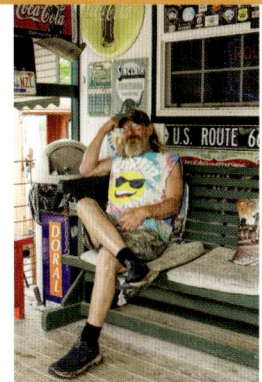

Gary   *Becky Waters*

Many of the sites along Route 66 are about collections. Gary's Gay Parita is one of the most varied. There are cars, toys, and sewing machines, just to name some, and then there is Gary. He has a wealth of memories and facts that he is happy to share. This is a must-stop along our route. It is filled with the kind of eye candy a photographer can play with for hours. Make sure you say hi to Gary for us!

Plano Ghost Town, Missouri

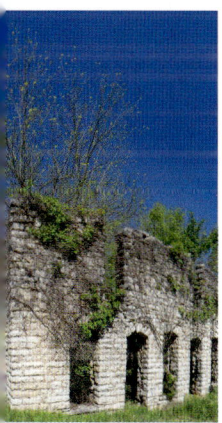

Plano Ghost Town, Missouri
David Skernick

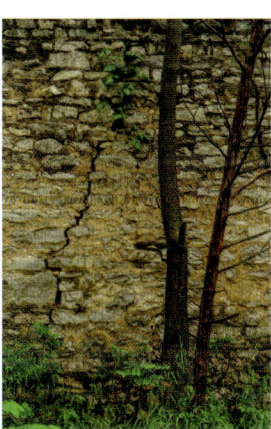

Plano interior   *Becky Waters*

All that is left is this single building, but Plano is a great place to spend some time and take some interesting photos. I went for the whole thing; Becky went inside and Stephanie got fixated on the windows. Each of us found a different story to tell. Note the little extras in each shot. I included the road. I like to do that. I think it gives you a sense of place. It lets you know where you are. Becky found the replication of the tree trunks and the crack in the wall. Which did you see first? When shooting doors, windows, or archways, you need to make sure there is something interesting inside each frame. If you are going to make me look, give me something to see.

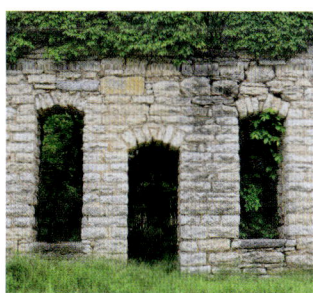

Windows   *Stephanie Billings*

108

The Rockwood Motor Court, Springfield, Missouri

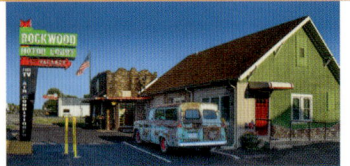

Rockwood Motor Court, Springfield, Missouri
David Skernick

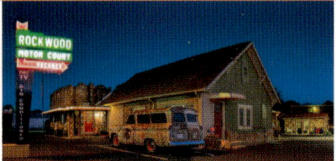

Rockwood Motor Court at night   *David Skernick*

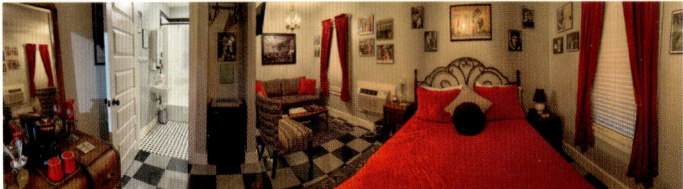

The Movie Room, Rockwood Motor Court   *Anne Schlueter*

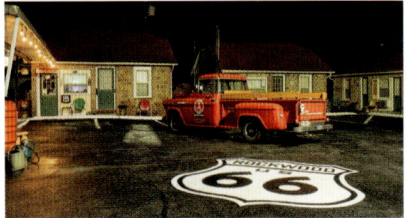

Lulu and the Rockwood Motor Court   *Becky Waters*

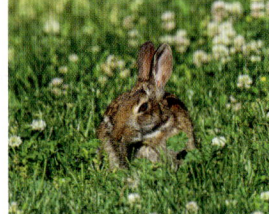

Bunny on the Rockwood property
David Skernick

Whether it is a great room, a beautiful truck, or a bunny rabbit, you always need to take advantage of happenstance. Neither the truck nor the bunny was expected. We just got lucky. Becky got the truck, Anne got the Movie Room, and I took an early walk and found that cute bunny. You can't plan for stuff like that, but you can be ready. Keep your camera handy and your batteries charged.

In Springfield, Missouri, all you need to do is look for College Street. It turns into St. Louis Street north of Route 13. Those roads follow Route 66. They are full of great Mother Road attractions, including several museums, cafés, and tons of murals and signs, as you will see in the coming pages. You will want to spend a few days.

I stay at the Rockwood Motor Court in Springfield, Missouri. It is terrific. Built in 1929, the Rockwood is the oldest operating court on Route 66. Every room is different. If you ask owners Phyllis or Tim, they might give you a tour. Anne stayed in the "Movie Room" and shot this pano with her phone.

As soon as I checked in the first time, I ran out to the front to take a photo in the perfect late-afternoon light. I like this shot. It shows the location and highlights the old car, and, well, you gotta love that flag!

Just after sunset, I took the second photo you see here. I like to get that last little bit of light and color in the sky when I shoot what essentially are night photos. You have to have a plan and to time it just right. Often you will have only one chance per night.

For night photography, I recommend aperture priority ("A" or "AV," depending on your brand of camera). You set the f/stop for the depth of field you want, and the camera will set your shutter speed. If you are using a tripod (and you really should be), set your ISO low (50, 100, or 200) and use a cable release, timer, or exposure delay (Nikon) to get a perfect, sharp image.

Becky found Doug, the owner of that beautiful red truck. He was staying at the motor court while we were there too. He happily moved Lulu the truck to just the right spot for the photo. I found the little bunny hopping around the property one morning. He was perfectly calm and willing to pose for this photo.

Springfield, Missouri

I found the giant chef on the road as I was driving through Springfield. I jumped out of my truck and grabbed the shot with my trusty iPhone. I used to keep a small point-and-shoot camera handy for shots like this, but today's cell phones are better and easier, and you always know where yours is.

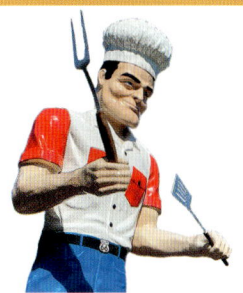

Chef, Springfield, Missouri
David Skernick

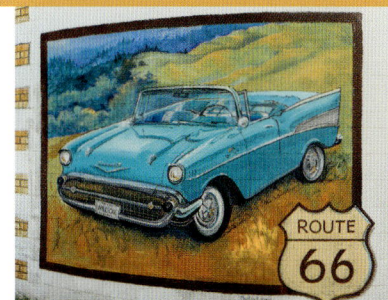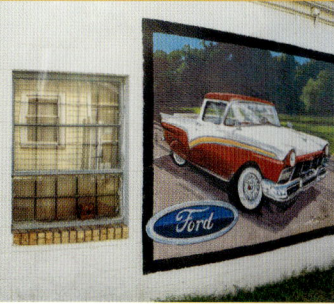

Don's Old Cars and Antiques, Springfield, Missouri   *David Skernick*

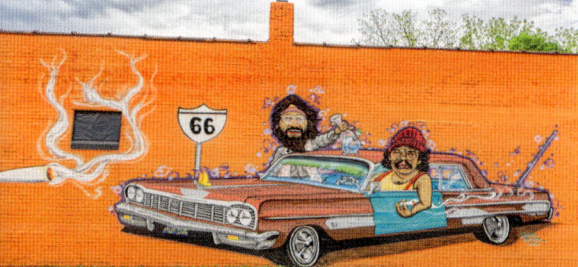

Cheech and Chong on Route 66 in Springfield, Missouri   *Monica Bayless*

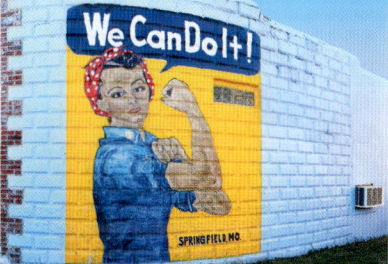

We Can Do It, Springfield, Missouri   *David Skernick*

You have shot a lot of great murals by now. How can you keep making interesting photos? Try a weird angle like Monica did. Use a wide-angle lens for distortion like I did (*above*), or add something of your own (without defacing someone else's art).

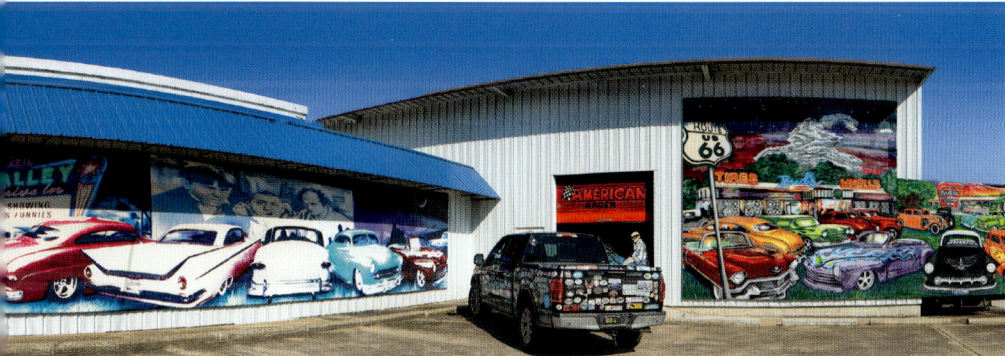

Bud's and Bob the Truck, Springfield, Missouri   *David Skernick*

Cars have naturally played a huge part in Route 66 lore. The film *Cars* (2006) featured a composite of locations along the route, bringing the attention of a new generation to the Mother Road. Bob's Tires in Springfield had yet another spectacular mural on their outside walls depicting vintage parked cars. I couldn't resist adding Bob the Truck to the scene.

Lebanon, Missouri

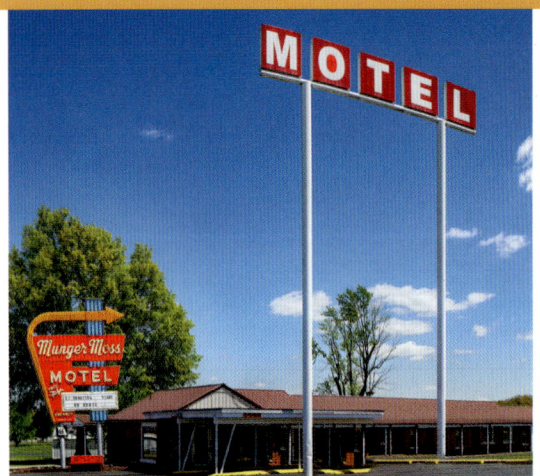

Munger Moss Motel (day), Lebanon, Missouri   *David Skernick*

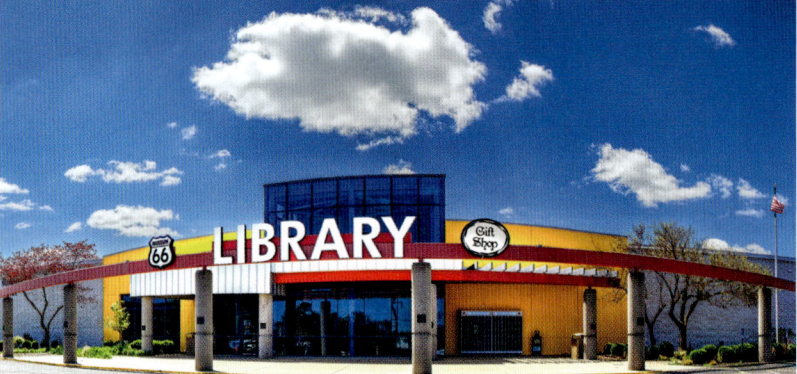

Lebanon Library and 66 Museum, Missouri   *David Skernick*

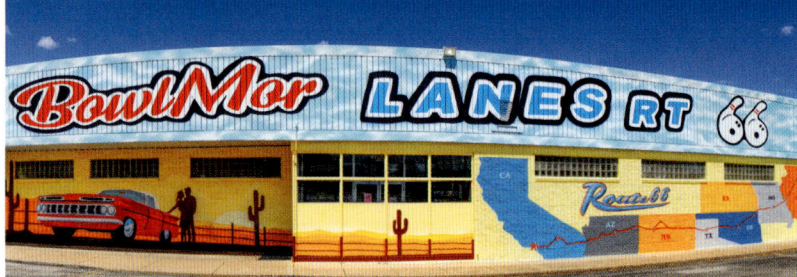

BowlMor, Lanes RT 66, Lebanon, Missouri   *David Skernick*

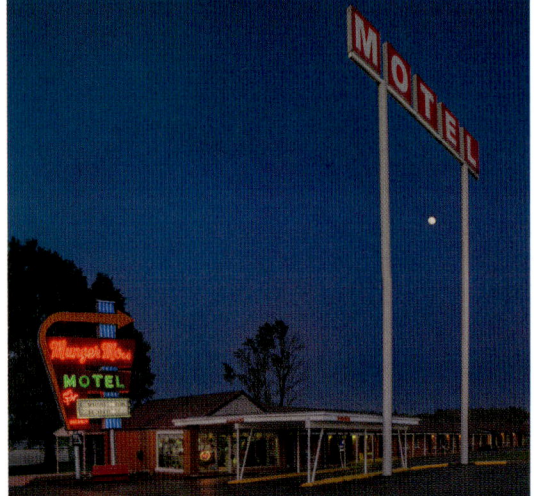

Munger Moss Motel (night), Lebanon, Missouri   *David Skernick*

In Lebanon, Missouri, look for the Munger Moss Motel. In 1946, it was built as an addition to an existing restaurant and gas station. I got there in time to take advantage of the golden-hour light. Golden hour is that beautiful, warm light you get when the sun is low in the sky. You get two chances a day, but the afternoon light was perfect for the library and BowlMar Lanes as well. I stayed overnight to get the night shot I've always wanted. The moon was a happy surprise. If you are looking for a place to spend the night, the Munger Moss Motel has nice rooms and a friendly staff. The prices are right too!

Devil's Elbow, Missouri

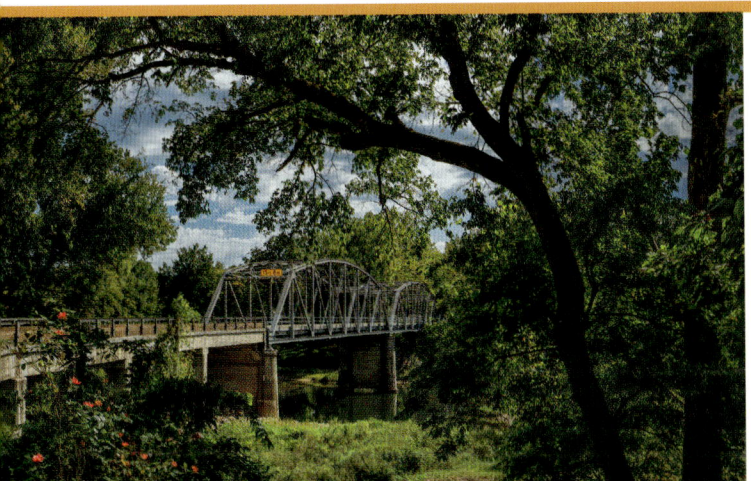

Devil's Elbow Bridge, Missouri

David Skernick

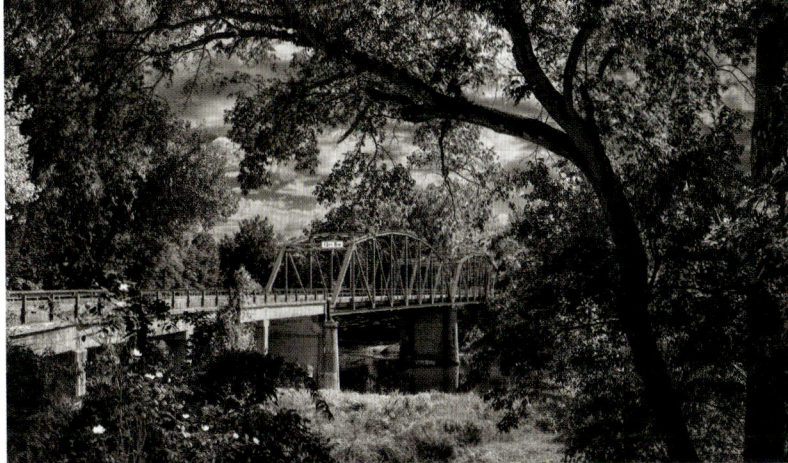

Devil's Elbow Bridge, black and white

David Skernick

Interstate 44 took the place of much of Route 66 in this area, but if you stay on the frontage roads, you will find remnants of the old road. There are buildings, signs, and businesses along the way. Watch the signs for the Devil's Elbow turnoff, and you will find one of those old alignment loops that will lead you onto Teardrop Road and to this terrific bridge (*above*). Built in 1923, the Devil's Elbow Bridge carried the original Route 66 across the Big Piney River. There is a new bridge built in 1943 along the new alignment of the route that bypassed this bridge completely. Used only by local traffic, this bridge was eventually condemned for lack of upkeep. It was restored in 2013 by Route 66 activists. Yes, there are Route 66 activists. A big shout-out to them!

There used to be a great BBQ place called the Elbow Inn. I took my photos of the bridge from the edge of the old parking lot. The building is still there. I hope someone buys it and brings back the old café. If you are there and it has been renovated, please let me know! Maybe we can meet for some baby-back ribs!

You will want to spend some time here. Walk around and see where the lines lead, and what you can include with the bridge to tell the story you want to tell. I chose an angle on the far side, where I could take advantage of some big trees to frame my shot. The flowers gave my composition the balance I wanted. When I processed this photo, I couldn't decide between black and white or color. Which do you like better? I made the black and white super contrasty to give the scene more depth and to make it look more congested.

Cuba, Missouri

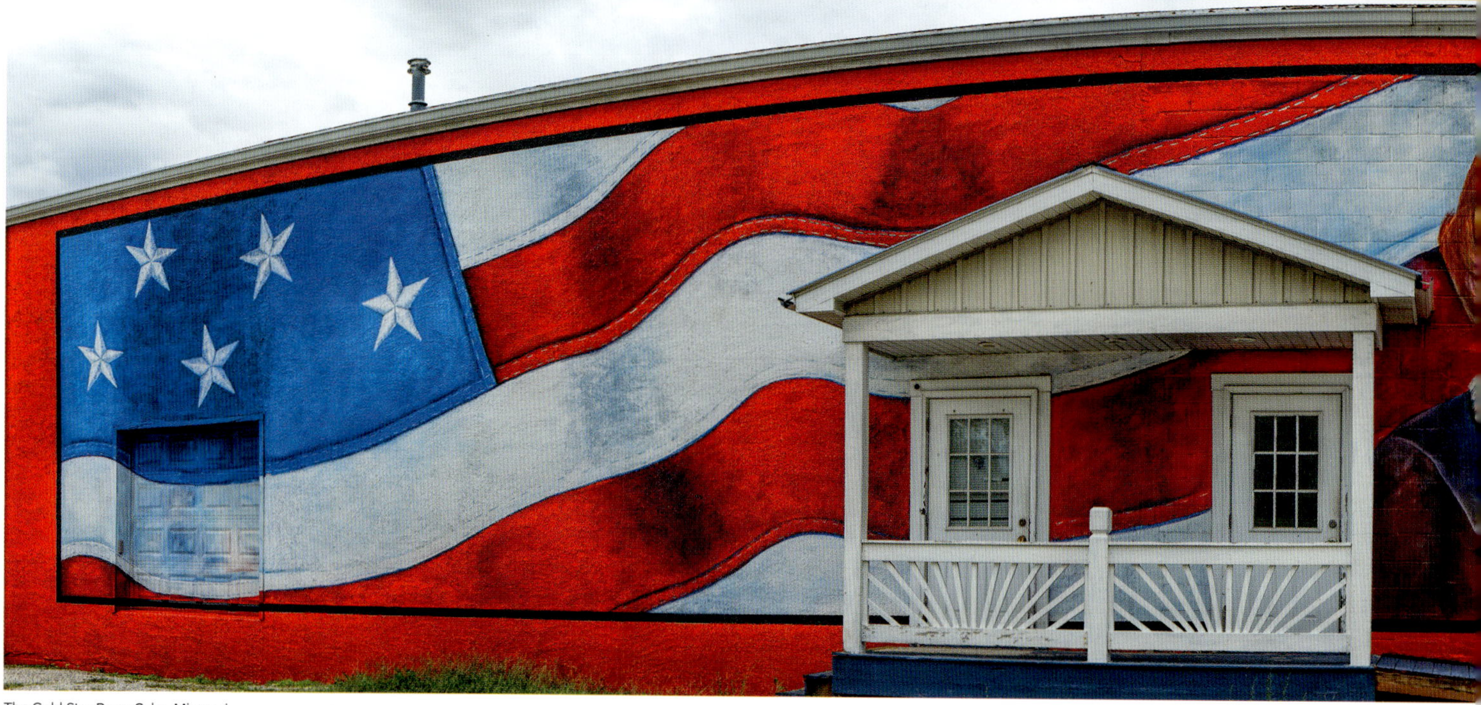

The Gold Star Boys, Cuba, Missouri

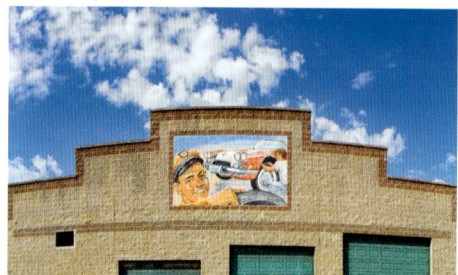

Garage mural, Cuba, Missouri   *David Skernick*

Cuba, Missouri, is known as "Mural City." Last I heard, there are fourteen outside murals. As always, think carefully about what you want to include and exclude along with your mural. I loved the porch above and therefore chose to include the entire wall. There were cars and parking spaces in front of the doors on the left. I chose not to include those and was happy to simply cut off the doors. I thought the newspaper building on the right added to the story, so I shot from across the street to include all of it. Note: The building is no longer owned by the newspaper.

Murals are fairly easy to photograph. You can use your camera or phone to get a pano, or crop to create one in postprocessing. Watch your depth of field with a long mural like the one above. I used f/11 to get it all sharp and clear.

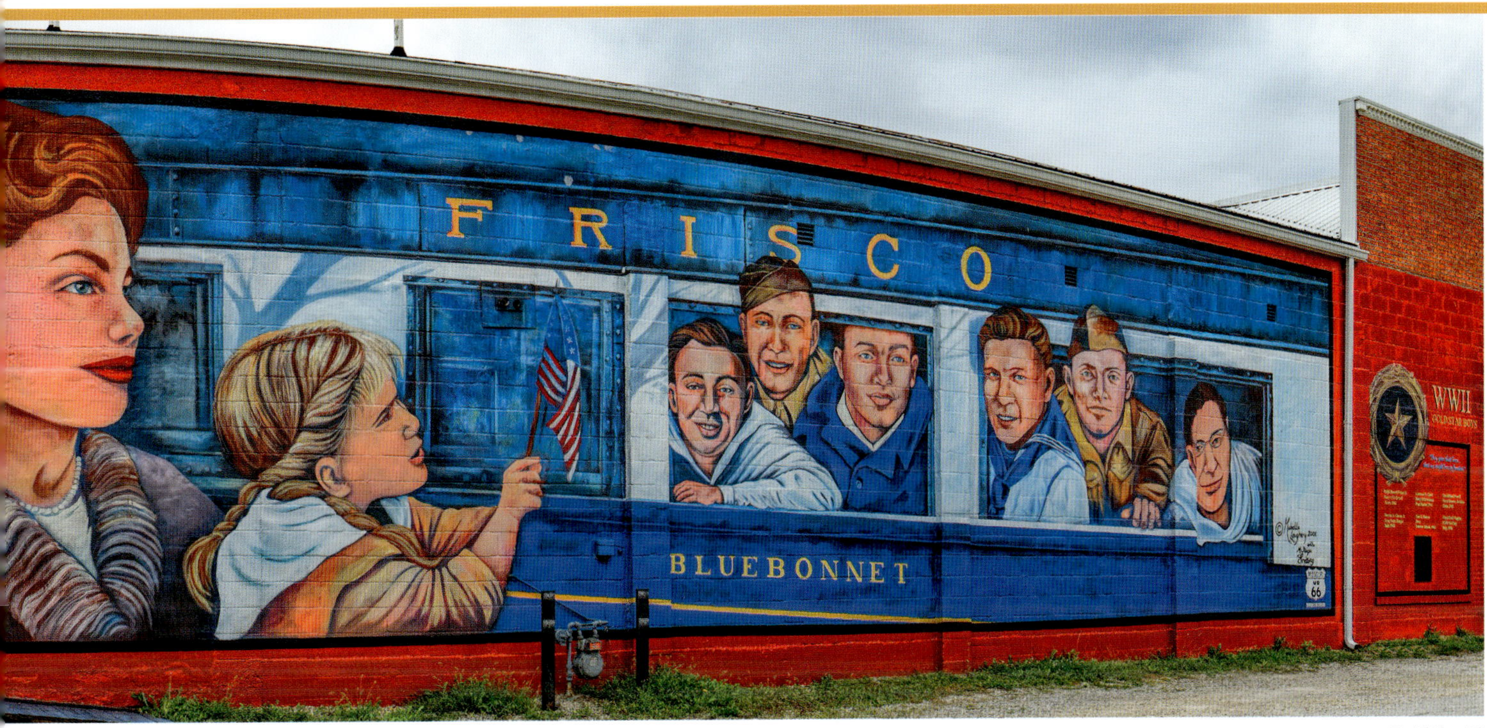

David Skernick

The Blue Bonnet Train (*above*) was the train that took local boys to fight in World War II. The mural titled *The Gold Star Boys* is on Washington Street, just off Route 66.

Bette Davis Visits Cuba, on the Cuba Free Press building, tells the story of a local photographer who was almost killed by the actress's husband after he grabbed a picture without permission in 1948, when the couple passed through Cuba.

I know nothing specific about the mural on the left. I think it speaks to all the service stations that sprung up along America's Highway. The garage doors support the story. Always try to include elements that support your statement, and avoid those that do not.

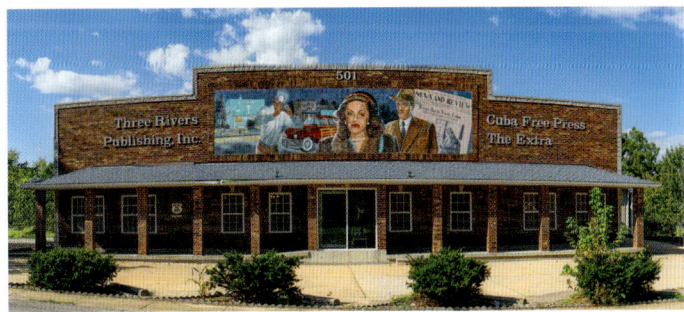

Bette Davis Visits Cuba, Missouri

David Skernick

Cuba, Missouri

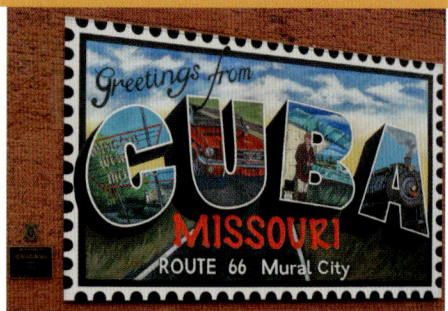

Becky Waters

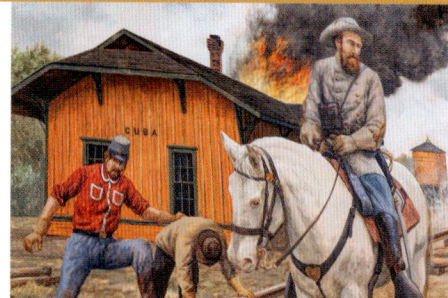

Monica Bayless

In Cuba, Missouri, because there were so many murals, I challenged my students to try an exercise. The game was to look at a mural as if it were a real scene happening in front of you, then photograph it as you would a real occurrence, picking out only what seems the most salient, or what supports the story you want to tell. We all tried. Looks like Anne tried the hardest! Those are all her photos on the opposite page. Wanna play?

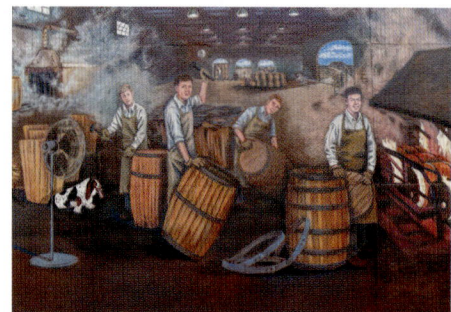

Stephanie Billings

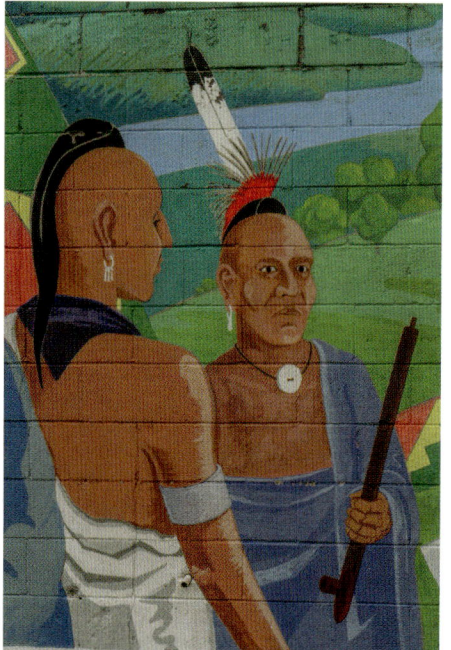

Becky Waters

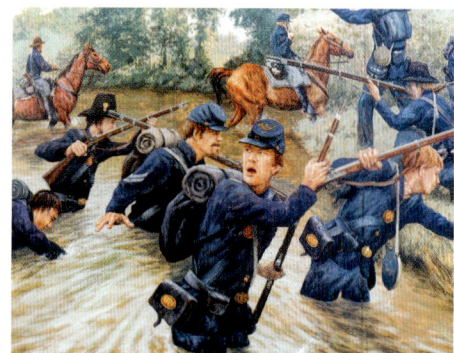

David Skernick

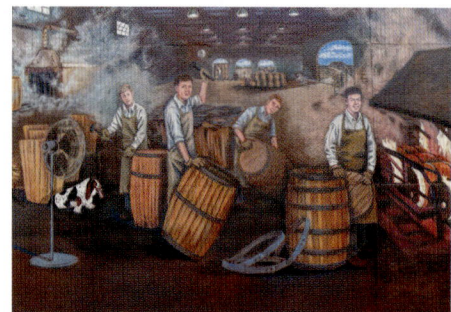

Monica Bayless

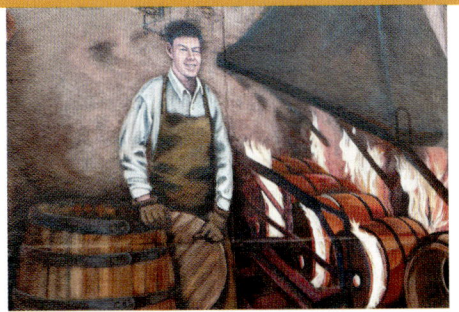
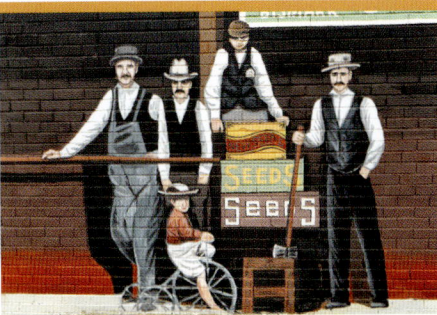
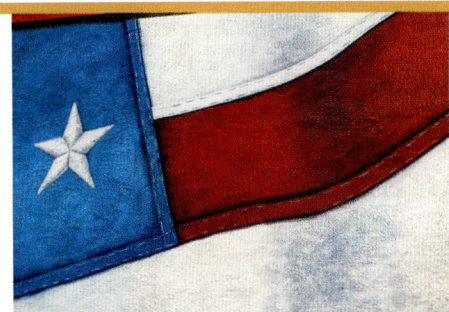
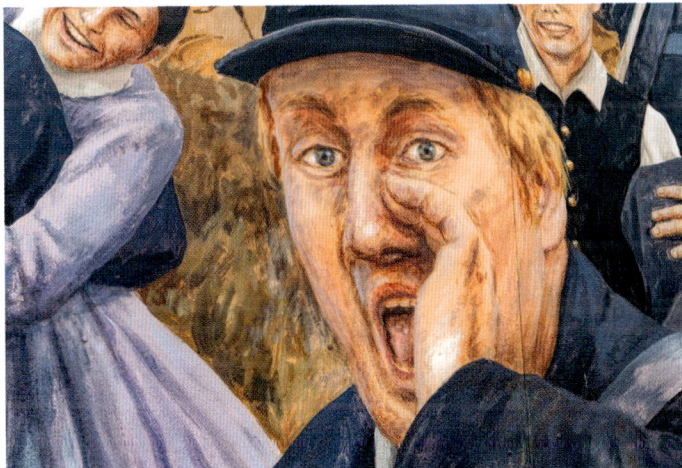
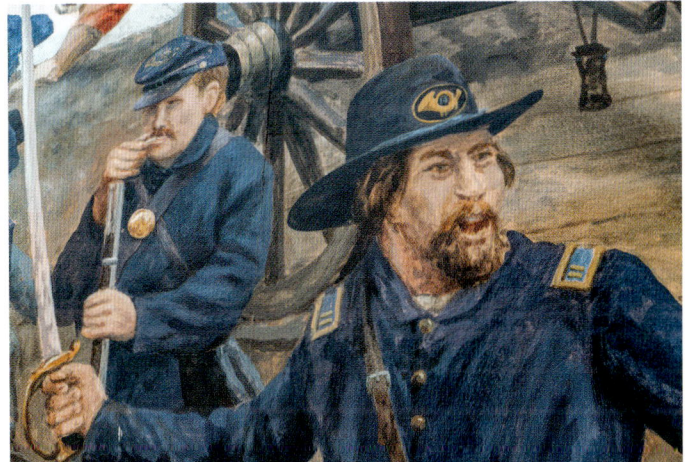

All photos this page by Anne Schlueter

Murals shown on both pages:

Greetings from Cuba

Meeting in Missouri

Gold Star Boys

Battle of the Huzzah

Confederates Come to Cuba

A Day in the Cooperage

Battle at Pilot Knob

Prosperity Corner

Rescue at Leasburg

Cuba, Missouri

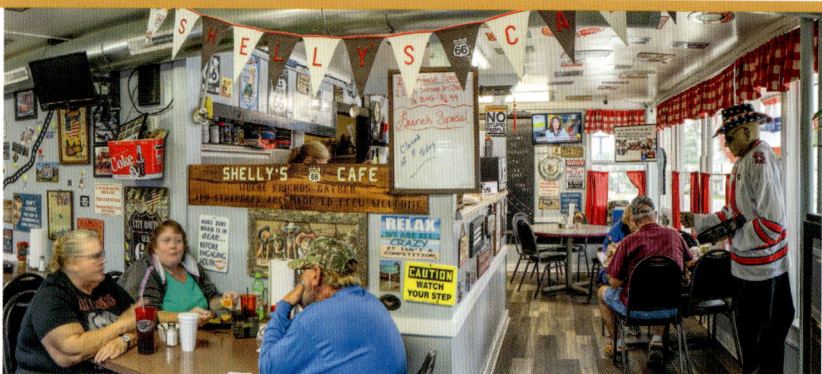

Shelly's Route 66 Cafe interior, Cuba, Missouri

David Skernick

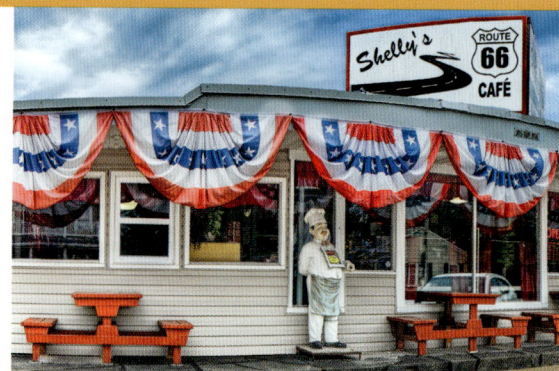

Shelly's Route 66 Cafe exterior, Cuba, Missouri

David Skernick

While in town, check out Shelly's Route 66 Cafe. I had a terrific breakfast there. They were happy to have me photograph inside as well as outside. There's nothing you can do about reflections in glass unless you come back at night. Try to find an angle with reflections you can live with or, better yet, help tell your story. For the interior, I used my tripod and chose an angle where the light from outside would not look too white when I exposed for the interior. I also asked if anyone would mind being in the photo.

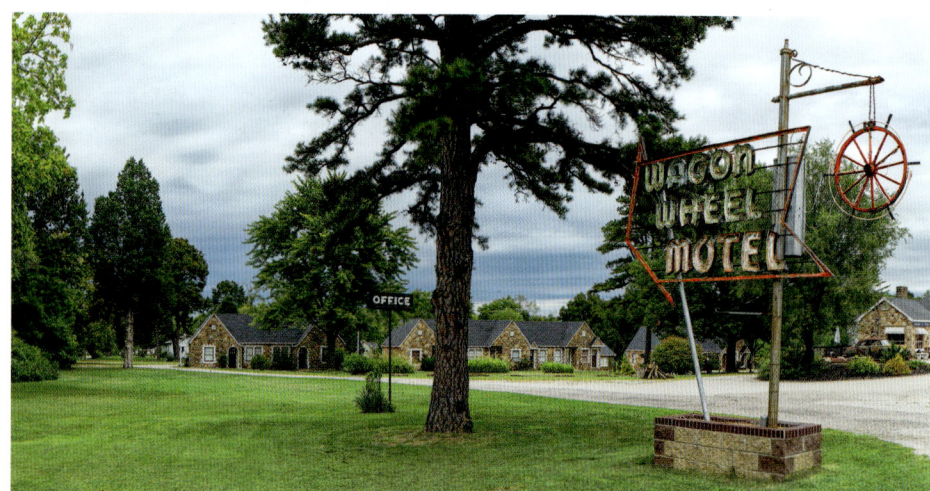

Wagon Wheel Motel, Cuba, Missouri

David Skernick

The Wagon Wheel Motel is the longest continuously operating motel on Route 66. It's a great place to stay if you want to spend time in Cuba. The sign was not turned on when I was there. I "turned it on" in postprocessing, using a curves layer, a hue/saturation layer, and a paintbrush. I was careful to use the actual color of the lights. Is that cheating? I believe that post is part of our art now, but it's up to you how far to go. I find that I will go further and make more-radical changes with subjects such as Route 66 and carnivals than I might for landscapes and wildlife. Make of that what you will. I think as long as you use only your own content, it's still your own art.

Weir on 66, Cuba, Missouri

Patrick Weir, owner of Weir on 66, came out to see what I was up to when he spotted me photographing his Halloween decorations and restaurant. They were closed at the time, but Patrick invited me in and posed behind the bar for me. I never quite get used to how generous and friendly the people are whom I meet along America's Highway. I find nice folks in most of my travels, but there is something about meeting on 66 that makes you feel like you have made a friend for life. I have gone back to places years later and have been remembered and welcomed back. Those on the route are also generally used to people taking pictures and almost never have a problem with it. Carnivals are like that too. That's one of the reasons why I think of the Mother Road as a 2,448-mile-long carnival! I came back later for a Leroy Burger. You gotta have one, or pretty much anything on the menu, to find out why I stop to visit Patrick every time I'm in town!

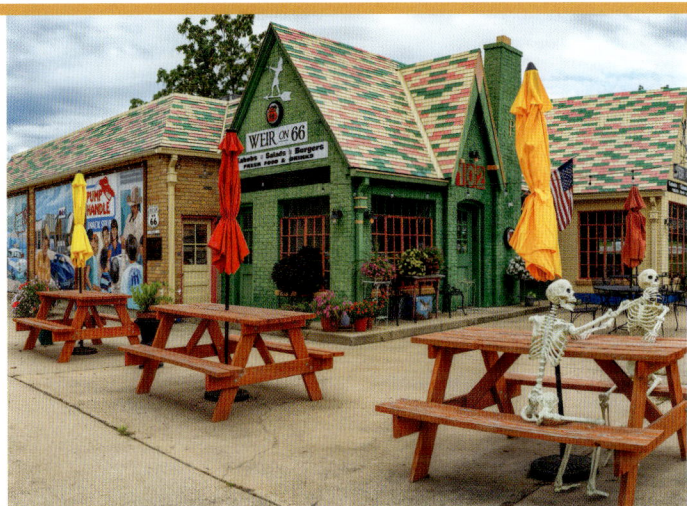

Weir on 66, Cuba, Missouri   *David Skernick*

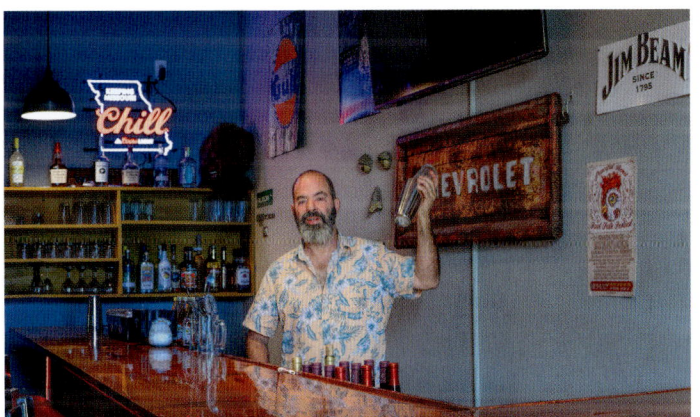

Patrick Weir, Cuba, Missouri   *David Skernick*

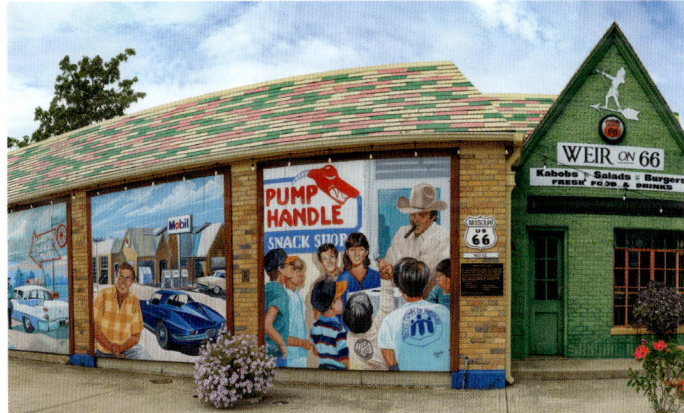

Home of the Leroy Burger, Cuba, Missouri   *David Skernick*

118

Bourbon, Wild Animal Adventure Park, Stanton, and Meramec Caverns, Missouri

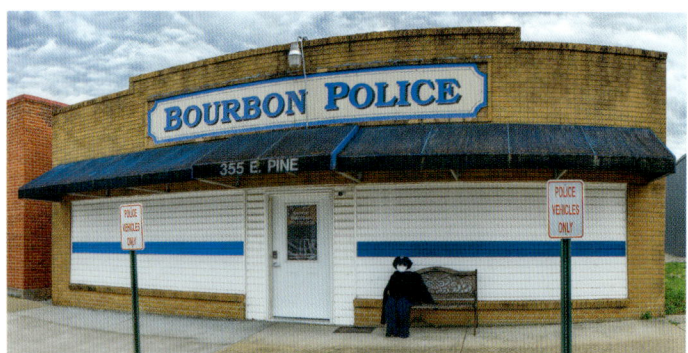

Police station, Bourbon, Missouri

David Skernick

It is no secret that I prefer small towns. Bourbon, Missouri, is a nice place to shoot some fun architecture and Halloween decorations. No traffic, no lights. The small zoo in Stanton is a great stop, especially if you have kids. The staff is friendly, well informed, and helpful. They offer feedings for many of the smaller animals and have a petting zoo as well. Photography here is a challenge. Safety rules have insisted on double fencing. I was too short to get above some of the retaining fences. Use your fastest f/stop (widest opening) and zoom in tight, and you might get lucky like I did a few times. For the ostrich, I used the fences to make the composition more interesting.

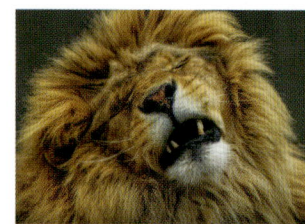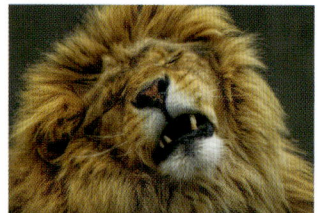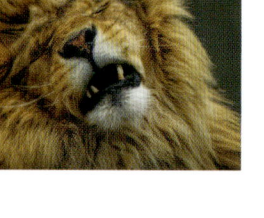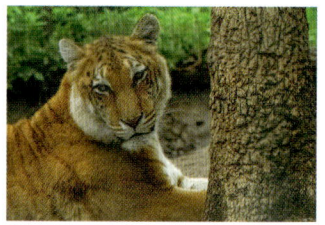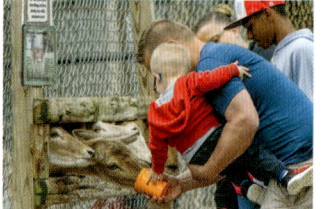

Wild Animal Adventure Park, Stanton, Missouri

David Skernick

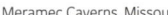

Meramec Caverns, Missouri

David Skernick

In 1720, French explorer Philippe Renault followed legends he had heard from the Osage Indians to find the largest cave west of the Mississippi. He was especially interested in the claim that the walls of the cave were "veins of glittering yellow metal." What he found was saltpeter rather than gold. Since the mineral was used in the creation of gunpowder, "Saltpeter Cave" was mined heavily for 144 years.

Now called Meramec Caverns, the golden walls attract visitors from all over the world. It may be the biggest Route 66 attraction. At a constant 60 degrees Fahrenheit, the cave is a pleasant place to take some photos in any season. Bring a tripod to do your best work, or just take your phone and enjoy the tour.

Pacific, Wildwood, and St. Louis, Missouri

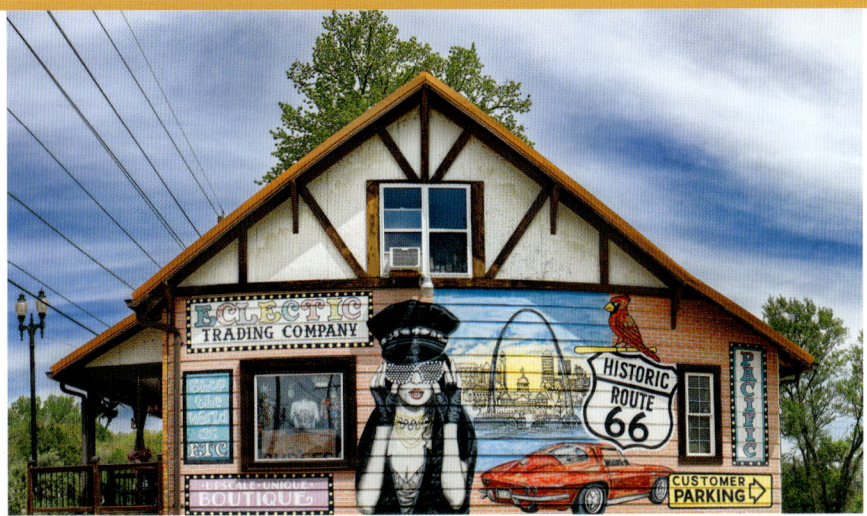

The Eclectic Trading Company, Pacific, Missouri

David Skernick

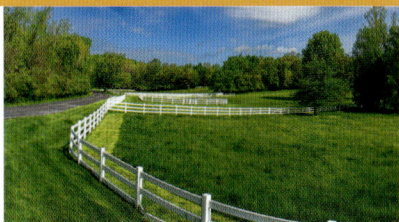

Bassett Road, Wildwood, Missouri   David Skernick

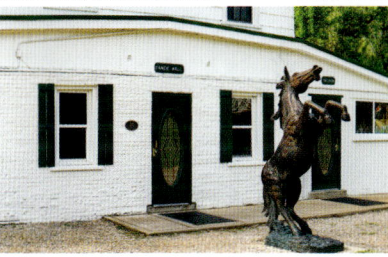

Stovall's Grove, Missouri   David Skernick

South of St. Louis, you have two alignment choices. Stay on the frontage roads alongside Interstate 44, and you will go through a couple of nice little towns, including Pacific. I found this mural there and had to stop. This time I left the power lines. I thought they added to the emotion of the artwork. The other option is to go up State Route 100 East. Here you will travel through some ranch country with a few nice photo opportunities. Stovall's Grove's "A Country Western Honky-Tonk" has been there since 1935.

I drove through St. Louis knowing that there were some Route 66 opportunities to look for. I found the arch and got up close with a wide-angle lens to make an interesting composition without tourists in the way.

I also found Ted Drewes Frozen Custard. That was worth the time I spent navigating through the city! They were celebrating their ninety-fifth anniversary. I got to meet Fredbird, the St. Louis Cardinals mascot! I had coffee ice cream with toffee chips. They call it "concrete." It's a shake so thick they serve it upside down. Another great reason to drive along America's Highway!

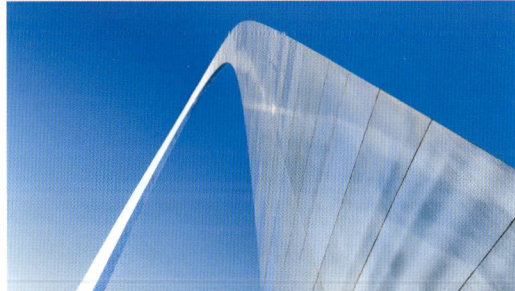

St. Louis Arch, Missouri   David Skernick

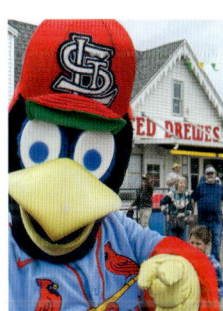

Fredbird   David Skernick

120

Barns of Missouri Along Route 66

I love barns. There it is. You got it in writing. I admit it. They have tons of personality, they are all different, and they are just fun to photograph. Much of Route 66 takes you through farmland, and that means barns! Here are some barns in Missouri. When you come across a subject, such as a barn, that gets your attention, look around for what you can add to the composition. They give awards to supporting actors and actresses for good reason. They make the story better and help the stars do their best work. What can you find to support the star of your photo? Look for repeating forms, frames, and balancing elements, or anything else that might further the story you want to tell.

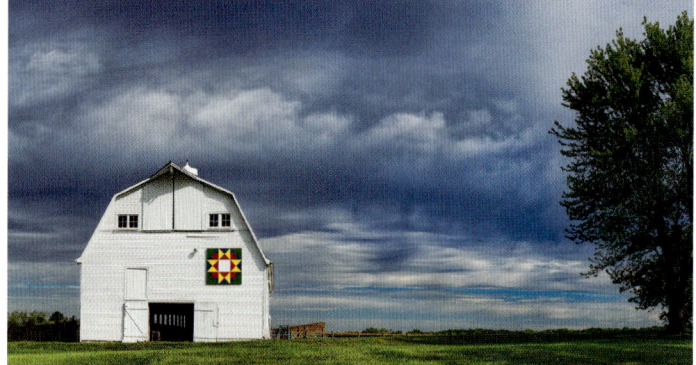

Barn on Indian Prairie Road, Missouri

David Skernick

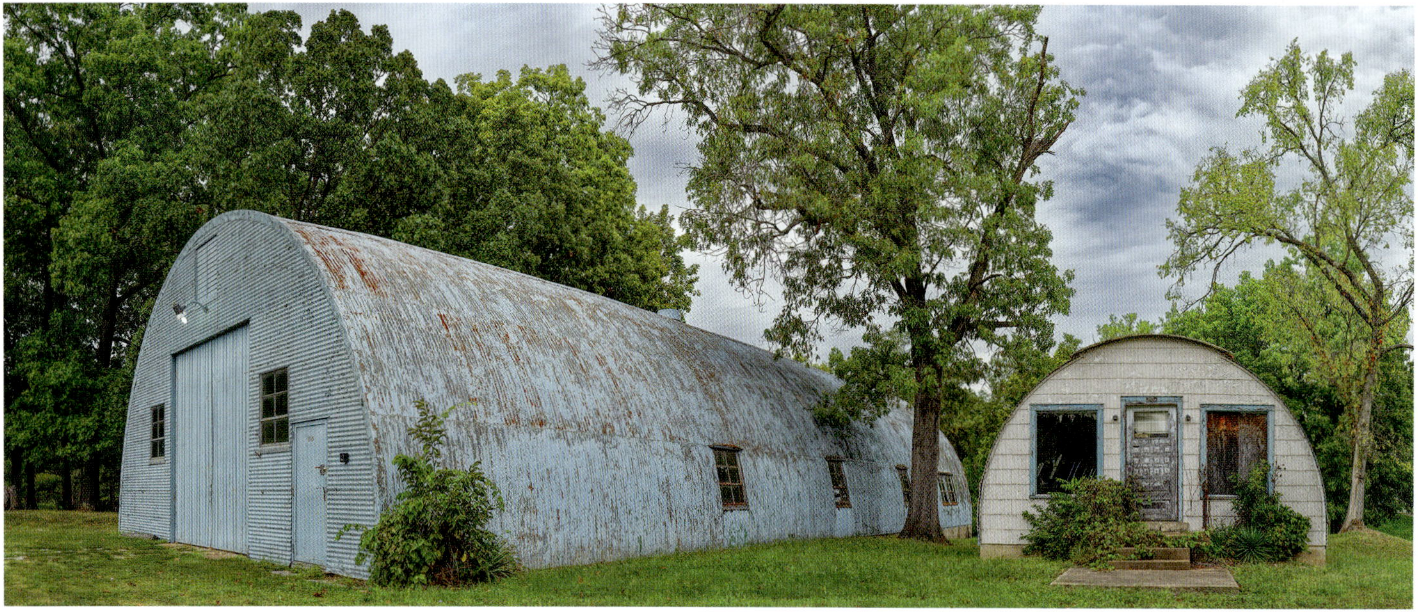

Barns near Villa Ridge, Missouri

David Skernick

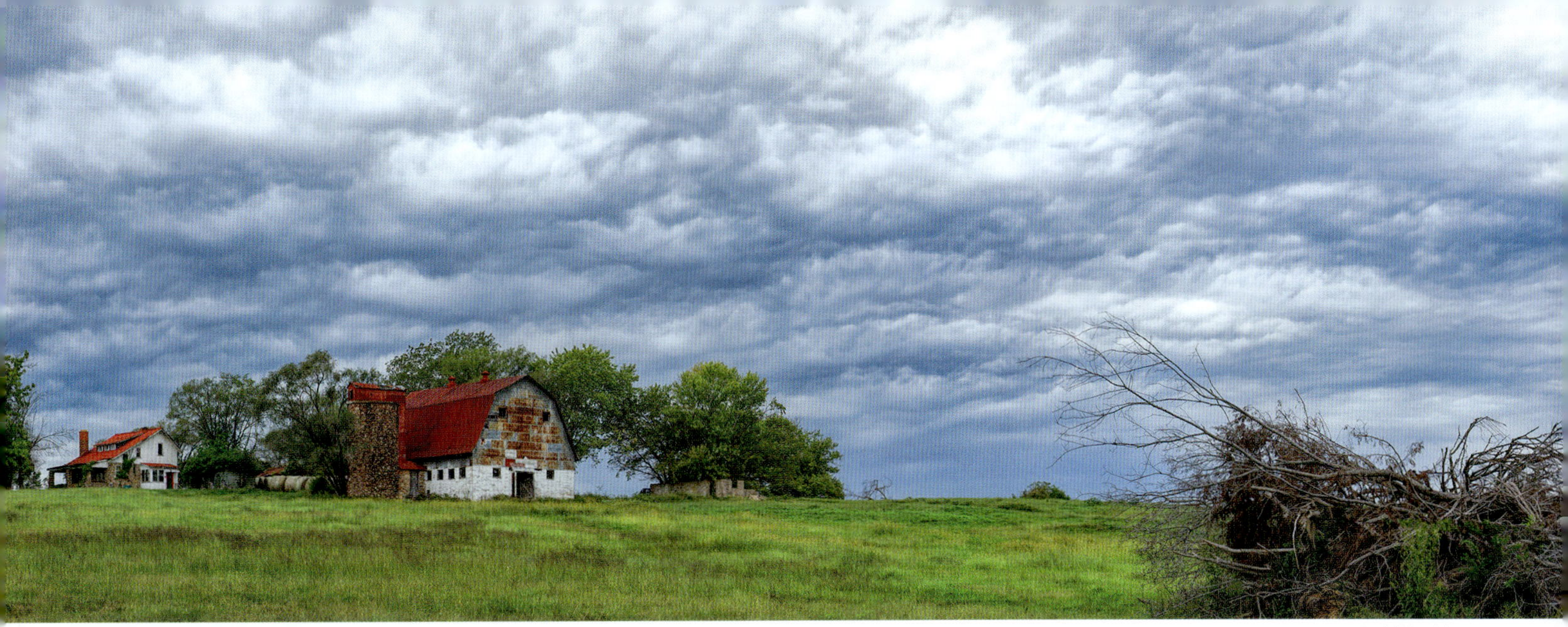

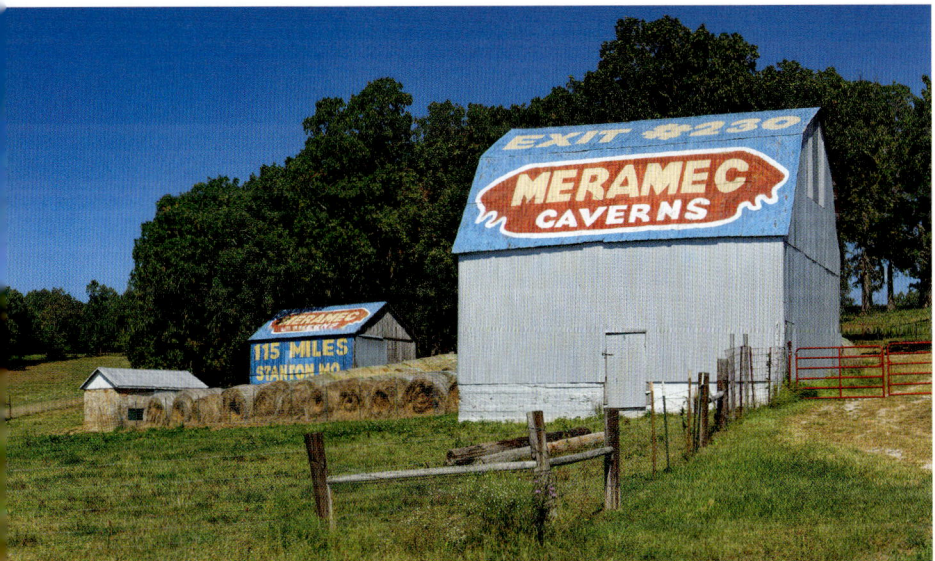

Barn near Bourbon, Missouri

David Skernick

Meramec Caverns barns, Phillipsburg, Missouri

David Skernick

I found these barns near Phillipsburg. Beginning in the 1930s, there were more than four hundred barns advertising the famous Meramec Caverns in fourteen states. There are fewer than fifty remaining. I have found four surviving Meramec Caverns barns that still exist along Route 66. I chose to photograph two. You will find the second in Illinois. The others just didn't do it for me. The trees form a simple background here, and the fence on the left is a nice leading line. The hay rolls were a gift. Often I find that my photos are improved by a lucky break such as hay rolls, great clouds, or a cow standing in the perfect spot. In this shot the lack of clouds was lucky too. Clouds may have distracted from the barns and their message. This sky is a simple negative space. I tell all my students that I believe great nature photography is 90 percent luck, 90 percent skill, and 40 percent equipment.

122

Mount Olive, Litchfield, and Palmyra, Illinois

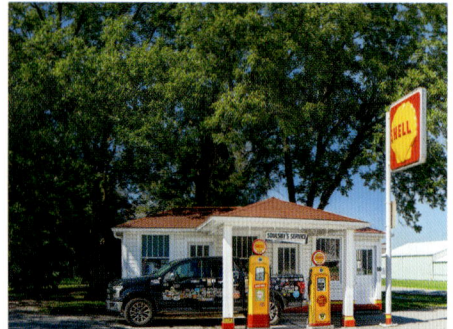

Soulsby's Service Station, Mount Olive, Illinois *David Skernick*

Soulsby's Shell Station in Mount Olive, Illinois, opened in 1926. Imagine the vehicles that filled up there one hundred years ago! Cars and trucks were smaller when this gas station was first in use. I wanted to show the small size of the station and tiny museum. Pulling Bob the Truck up to the pumps was a good start. A Ford F-150 would probably look as big as a freight train to a guy driving a 1926 Packard. It was a tight fit! Tall trees surround the property. I'm always looking around to see what I can use to tell my story. I could have used the trees just to frame my subject, but here was an opportunity to do that and make the station appear smaller as well. The bigger the trees, the smaller the building will look in comparison. By not showing the tops of the trees, they "feel" even taller. When you cut something off, it will almost always appear bigger, because your imagination completes the scene.

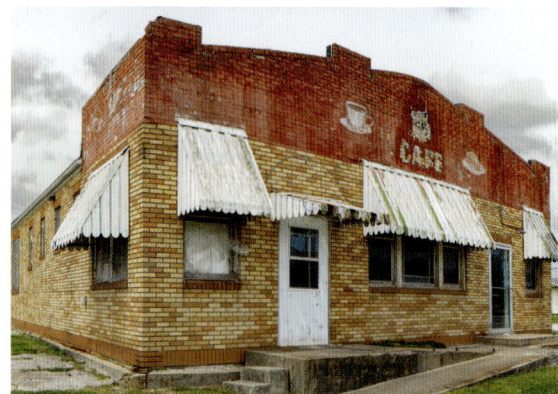

Old Route 66 Cafe, Litchfield, Illinois *David Skernick*

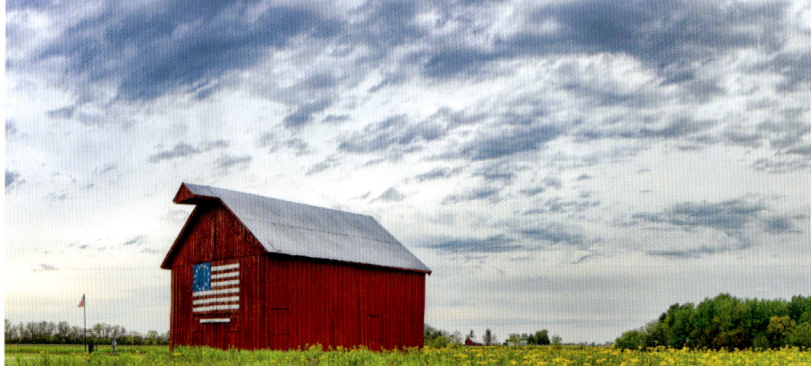

Betsy Ross flag barn, Palmyra, Illinois *David Skernick*

I photographed these two buildings (*above*) from the corners to show depth. I chose very little sky for the old café on the left. I wanted it to look a little more "falling down." Did it work? Does it look just a little more pitiful? I shot it along the 1930–40 alignment, so we know it's been there a long time. It is always up to you to find a way to accentuate what you find. I wanted the Betsy Ross flag barn to look small and almost vulnerable. I gave it lots of space and included tons of the threatening clouds I had that day.

Coming up from Missouri, you have two choices. You can sort of hug Interstate 55 and find Route 66 segments and towns, or you can head over to Illinois State Highway 4, which is another alignment of Route 66. I suggest you spend time on both.

Docs, Girard, Illinois

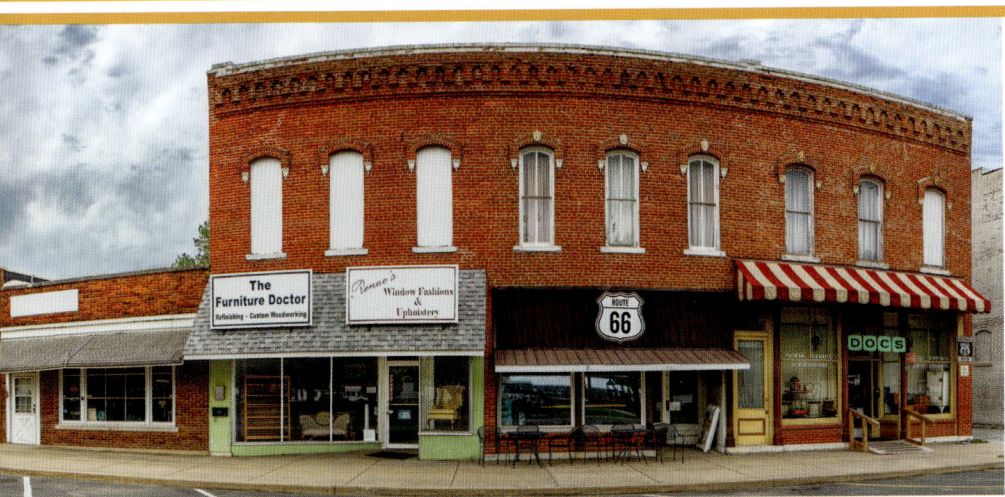

Town Square, Girard, Illinois

David Skernick

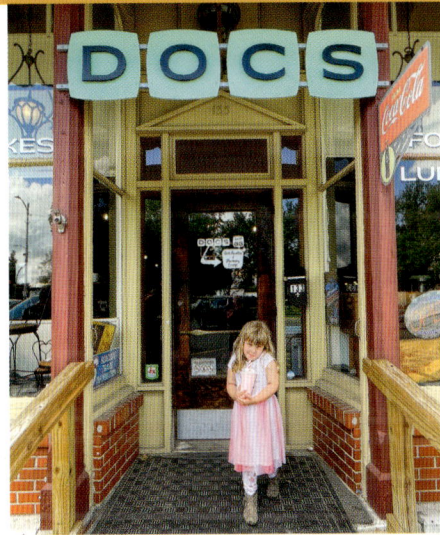

Chay

David Skernick

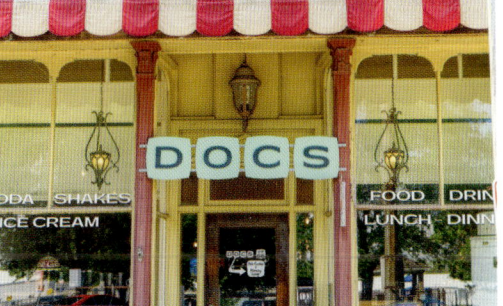

◄ *Docs, Girard, Illinois*
Becky Waters

We were eating lunch at Docs when Susan looked up at some folks walking out and said, "Aww, look, her milkshake matches her dress." I was up like a shot, phone in hand. I stopped four-year-old Chay and her dad just outside the door and asked if I could take a picture for this book. Dad said yes, and Chay, at first shy, let me lead her back to the storefront. The pose was all Chay. Thanks, Susan; thanks, Chay!

124

Sugar Creek Covered Bridge, Illinois

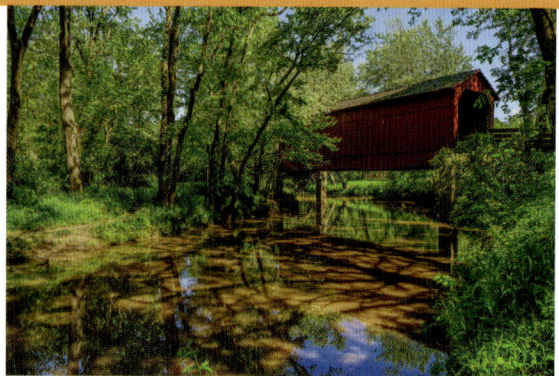

Sugar Creek and bridge, Illinois

Becky Waters

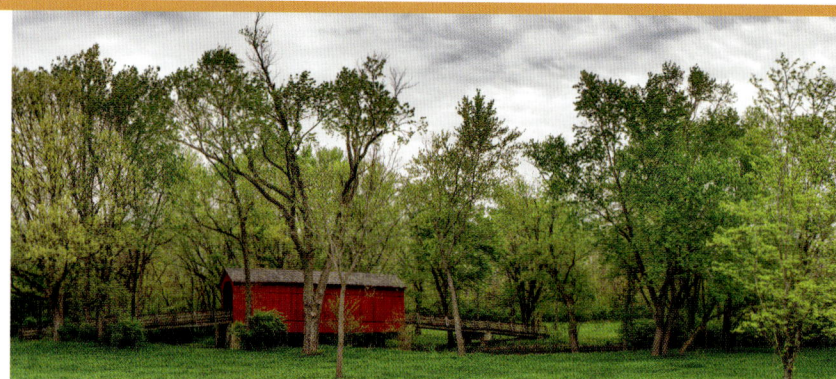

Sugar Creek Covered Bridge from Covered Bridge Road, Illinois

David Skernick

The Sugar Creek Covered Bridge is just southeast of Chatham, Illinois. Originally built in either 1827 or 1880 (sources disagree), it is found squarely between the two Route 66 alignments in southern Illinois. Whether you are on Illinois Highway 4 or following the frontage roads of Interstate 55, keep an eye out for a small brown sign that will lead you to the Sugar Creek Covered Bridge.

As you can see, we shot from many angles. Susan took advantage of some other folks being there and asked them to walk through holding hands. She then turned her photo to black and white in postprocessing so they would stand out from the bridge. The color red will attract your eye. In black and white, the couple gets more attention.

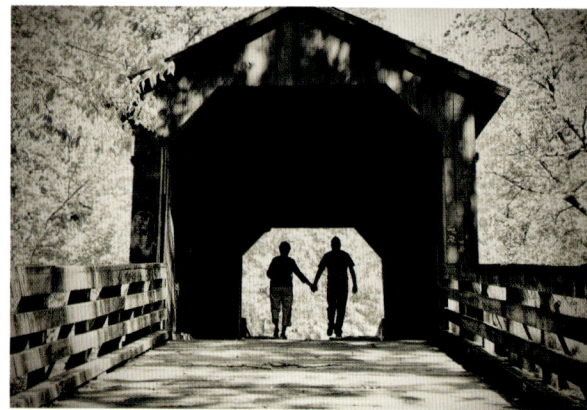

Couple from Denver

Susan Vizuary

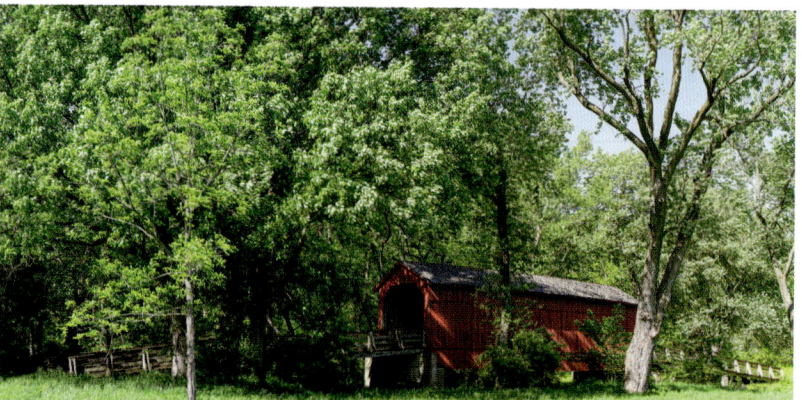

Bridge from the field

David Skernick

There is a section of historic Route 66 brick road in Auburn, Illinois. Becky shot from the middle of the road and chose a low angle. No need to get cute. The perfect light and clouds made it great.

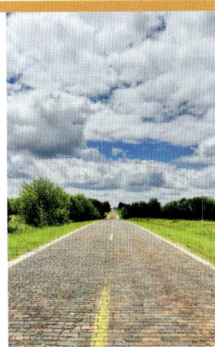

Route 66, Illinois   *Becky Waters*

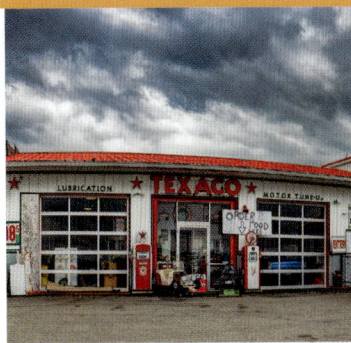

Motorheads Bar & Grill Museum, Springfield, Illinois   *David Skernick*

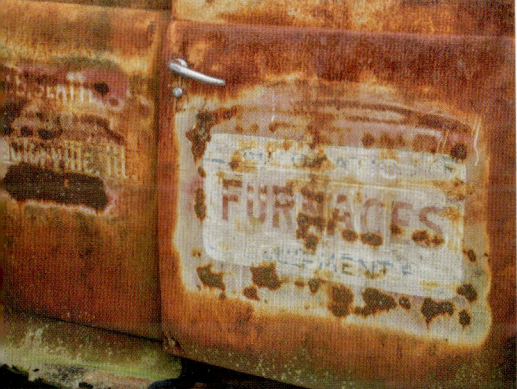

Rusted door, Motorheads   *Susan Vizuary*

As you enter Springfield, Illinois, from the south look for the huge Route 66 sign at Motorheads Bar & Grill and Museum. Okay, I'll say it—you can't miss it! This place, on top of having great food and spirits, is surrounded by pure eye candy for photographers. We wanted to spend the day but had only a couple of hours. Short telephoto lenses are great for cherry-picking your shots. By the way, that sign stands on 60-foot poles and is slightly bigger than the one in Elk City, Oklahoma, at the National Route 66 Museum.

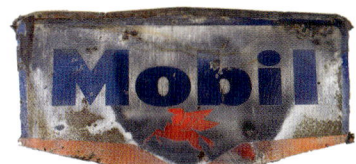

Old Mobil sign, Motorheads   *Stephanie Billings*

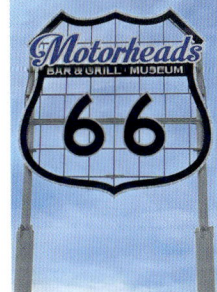

Giant sign   *David Skernick*

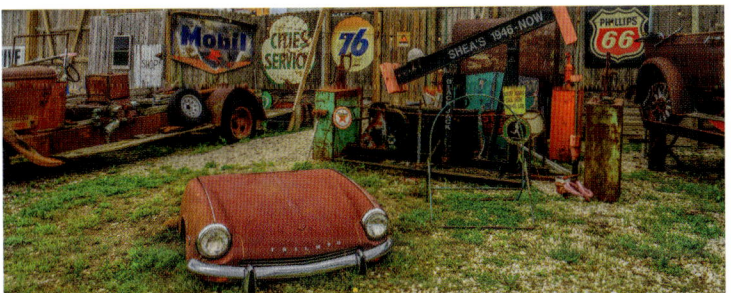

Triumph   *Becky Waters*

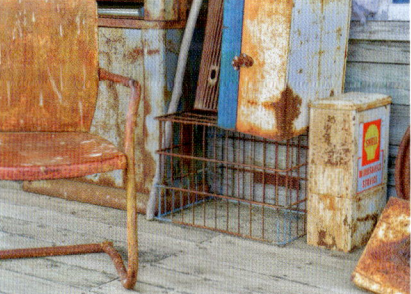

Eye candy   *Susan Vizuary*

126

Cozy Dogs Drive-In, Springfield, Illinois

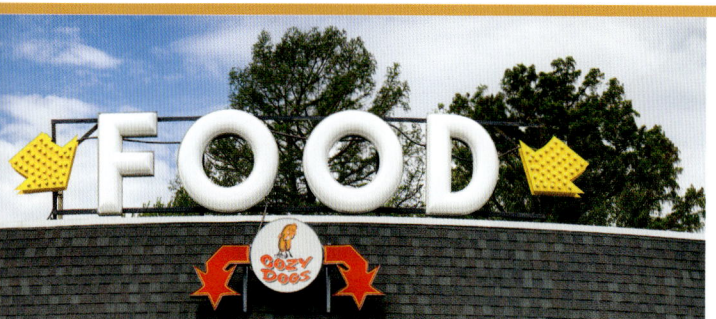

Cozy Dogs Drive-In, Springfield, Illinois

David Skernick

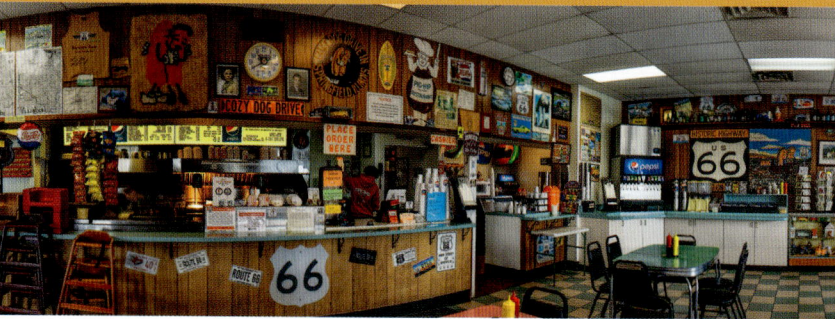

Cozy Dogs Drive-In interior, Springfield, Illinois

David Skernick

Drive-in sign

Becky Waters

There are cafés and restaurants and there are legends. The Cozy Dogs Drive-In in Springfield, Illinois, qualifies as a true legend. Ed Waldmire opened the drive-in in 1949. He said he dreamed up the cozy dog as he served in World War II. The cozy dog is what we usually call a corn dog, but I gotta say, this one is special. If you know my books, you might be aware that one is titled *American Carnival*. I know corn dogs. Maybe it's just the ambiance. In any case, you need to put this one on your list for a "must visit hungry." All the food is good, the staff is great, and the stuff on the walls is wonderful, but the cozy dogs are the best! Come in for a dog and you will be sure to leave with a smile, a happy tummy, and a great memory.

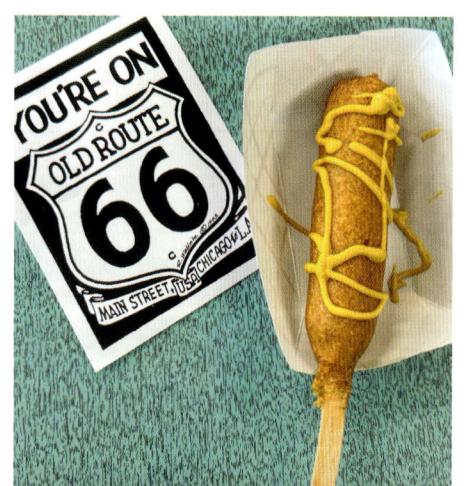

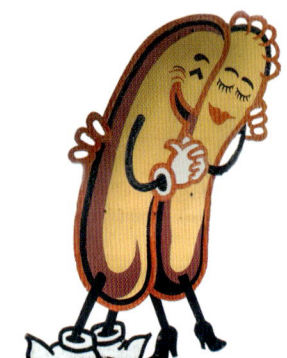

Cozy dogs

Anne Schlueter

◀ Cozy dog
Becky Waters

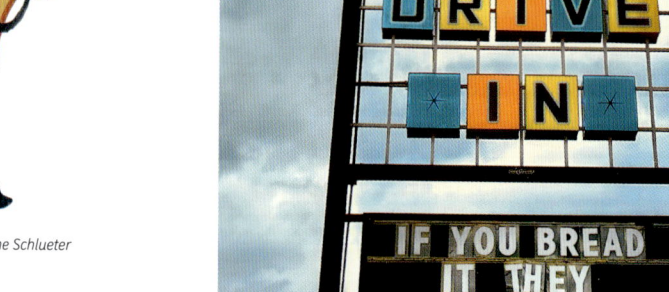

127

Springfield and Williamsville, Illinois

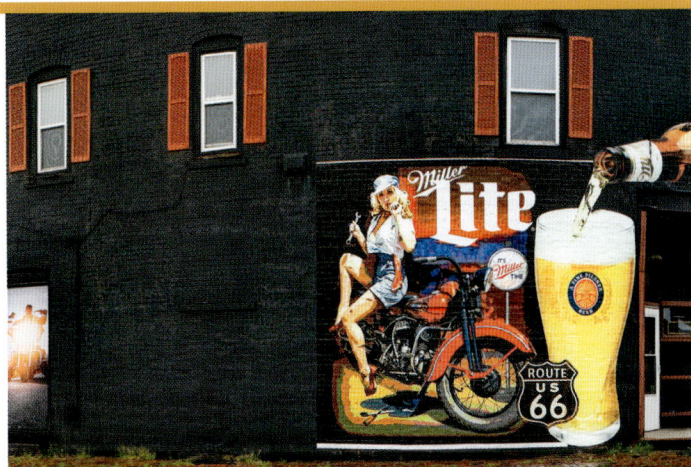

Jackson's Handlebar, Springfield, Illinois

David Skernick

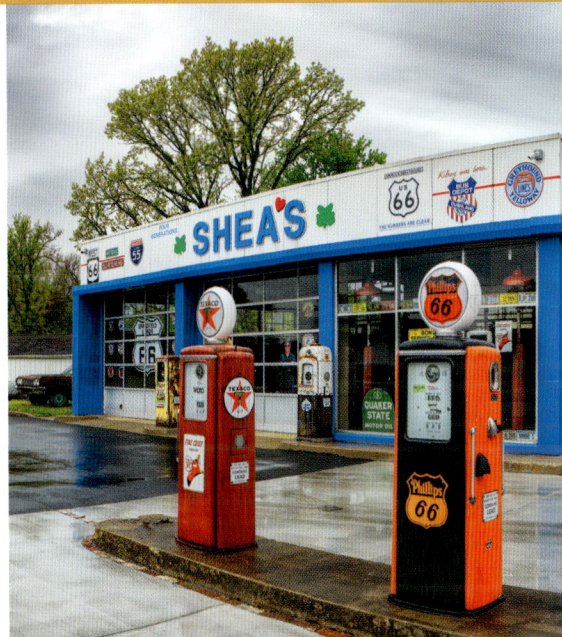

Shea's Station, Springfield, Illinois

David Skernick

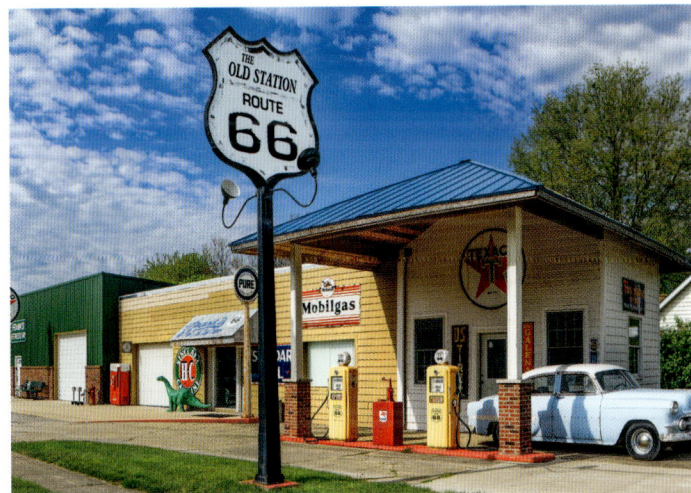

The Old Station, Williamsville, Illinois

David Skernick

On Peoria Street, at the north end of Springfield, you will again be in the middle of a city that transforms into the Mother Road. The state fairgrounds are there and have an exhibit called the "Route 66 Experience." It is up all year long. There are several other sites, including a tiny gas station and a few signs. I spent some time with Randy, the owner of Shea's Station, and with the sign on Jackson's Handlebar, because I found them more interesting in the rain that day. By the time I got to the Old Station in Williamsville, the rain had stopped and I had one of those beautiful skies you get after a storm. Weather will help determine what and how you photograph. That is one of the reasons I like to return to an area over and over. I look forward to my next visit.

Lincoln, Illinois

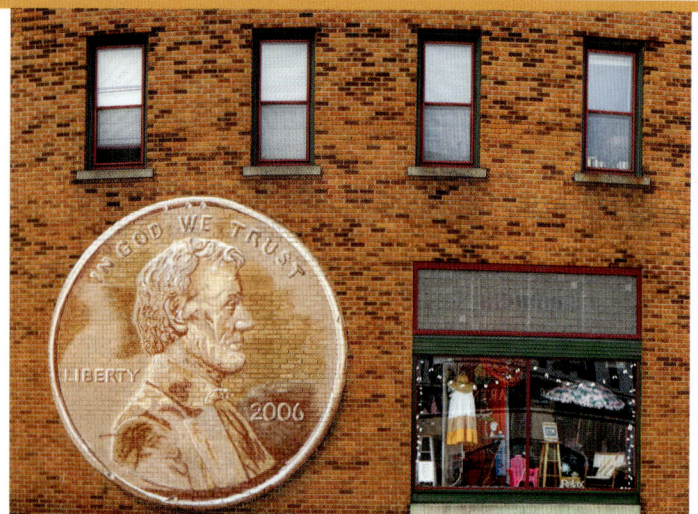

Penny mural, Lincoln, Illinois

David Skernick

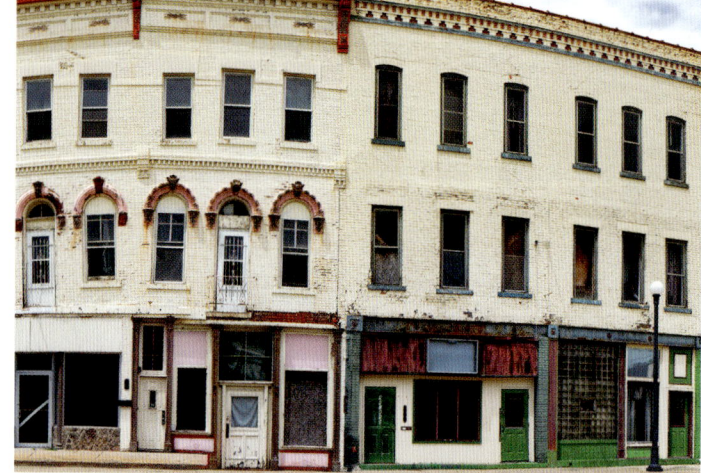

Windows and doors, Lincoln, Illinois

David Skernick

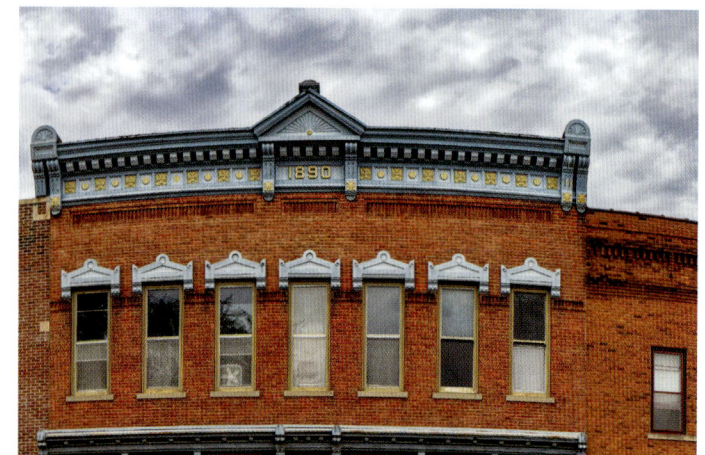

Box fan, Lincoln, Illinois

David Skernick

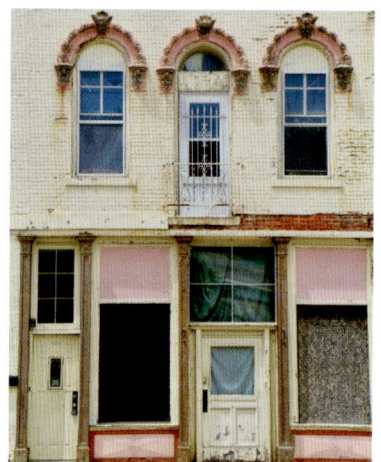

Windows, Lincoln, Illinois

Susan Vizuary

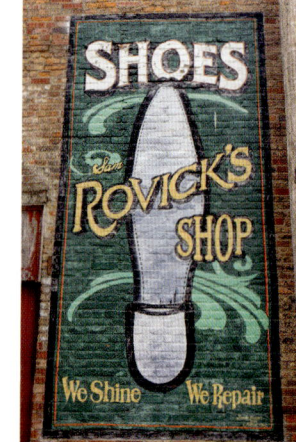

Shoes, Lincoln, Illinois   *Stephanie Billings*

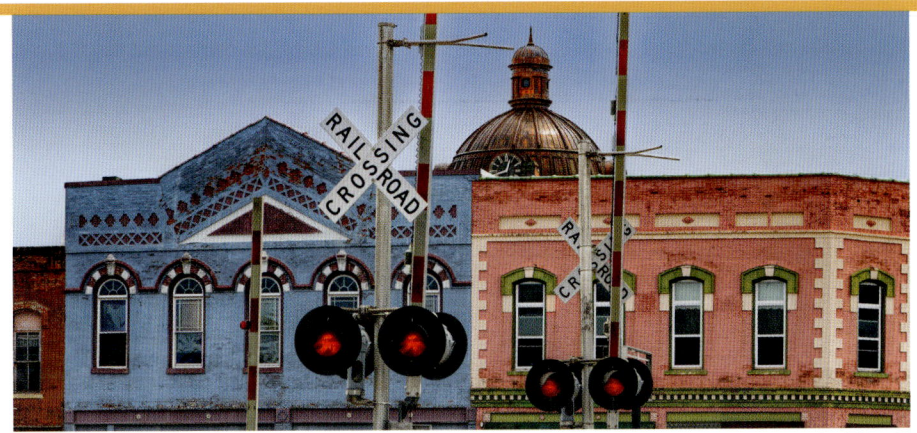

Railroad and downtown, Lincoln, Illinois

David Skernick

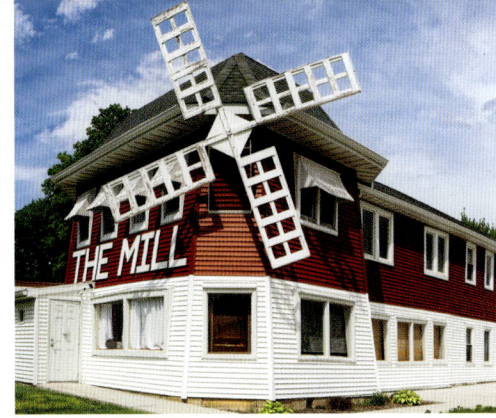

The Mill, Lincoln, Illinois

David Skernick

There are several alignments of America's Highway crisscrossing the small town of Lincoln, Illinois. Each is worth checking out. The architecture downtown caught my eye for its patterns and character. When you find something that captivates you, give in! I tried my best to capture what I saw as controlled chaos. There seemed to be movement in the stillness and order in the jumble of windows, doors, murals, tracks, and walls. Look how differently Susan and I shot the same wall of windows and doors (*left*). I was struck by how much there was, and created a huge double panorama, while Susan looked for a more concise statement. Both are valid. Which do you prefer, or what would you have done differently? The Mill (*above right*) was a famous Route 66 restaurant and is now a museum.

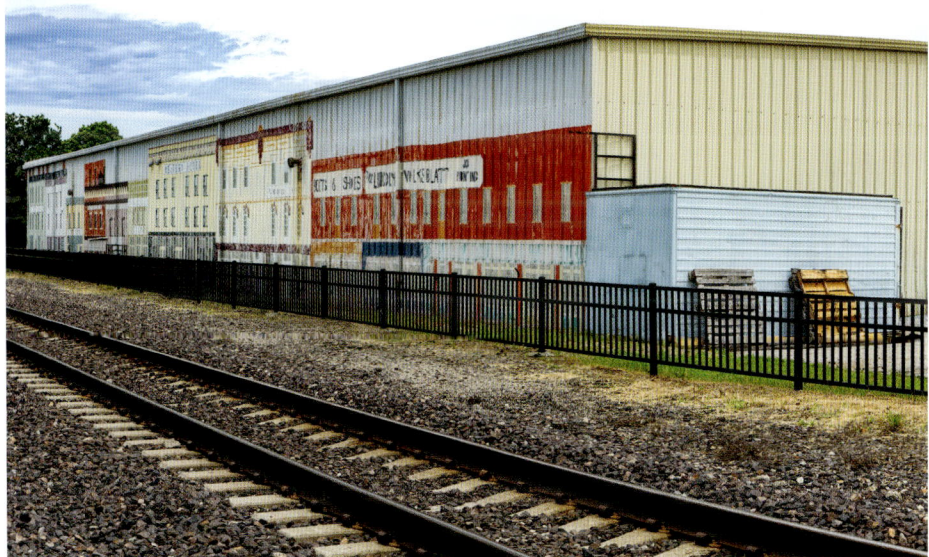

The Other Side of the Tracks, Lincoln, Illinois

David Skernick

American Giants Museum, Atlanta, Illinois

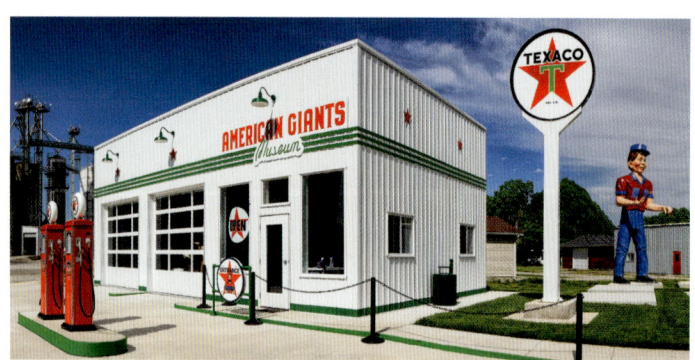

The American Giants Museum, Atlanta, Illinois

David Skernick

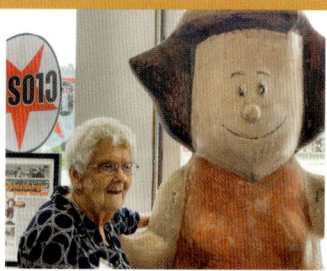

Darlene   *David Skernick*

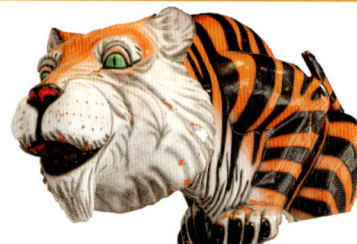

Exon tiger   *Anne Schlueter*

Darlene (*left*) is a volunteer at the museum. She has a wealth of information and is full of great stories. I'm grateful to Bill Thomas, the owner of the museum, for introducing me to the Route 66 Centennial Commission.

A small museum filled with super huge giants . . . absolutely do not miss this one. The best light for the outside is in the afternoon. Look how every line stands out. I understand that there will be many more giants by the time of the Route 66 Centennial in 2026. Look for me—I will be coming to visit the new personalities! When photographing inside, watch out for the big windows. The difference between the bright outside light and the interior (though well lit) can be enough either to put your inside subject into deep shadow or to give you blinding highlights in your background. Try harder than usual to fill your frame with your subject. You can use the walls as backgrounds as Stephanie did for her leg photo.

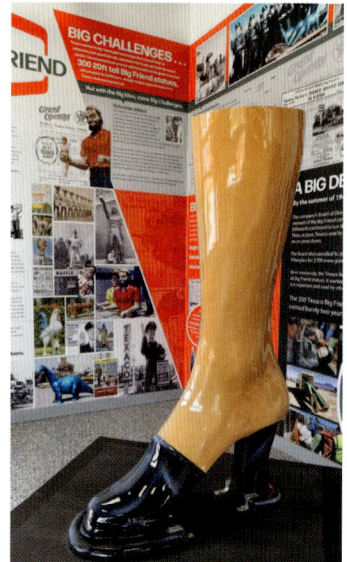

Giant leg   *Stephanie Billings*

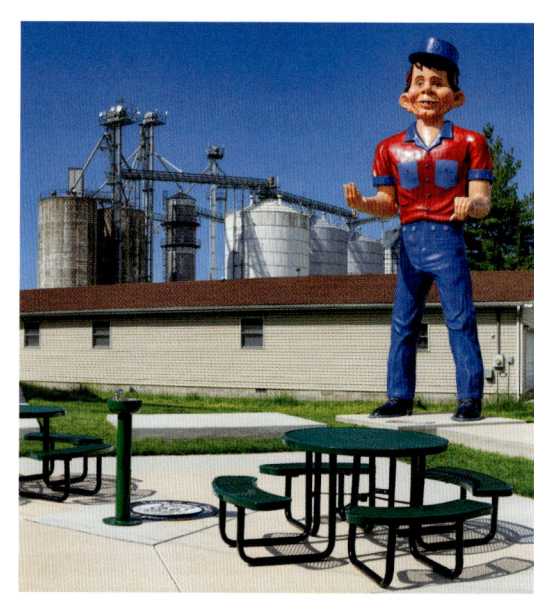

Snerd at the American Giants Museum, Atlanta, Illinois   *David Skernick*

Atlanta, Illinois

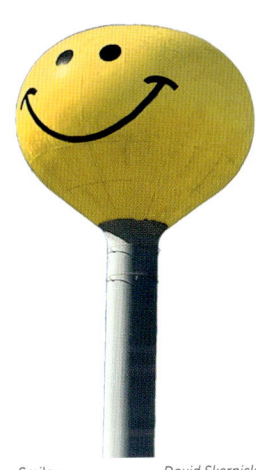

Smiley   *David Skernick*

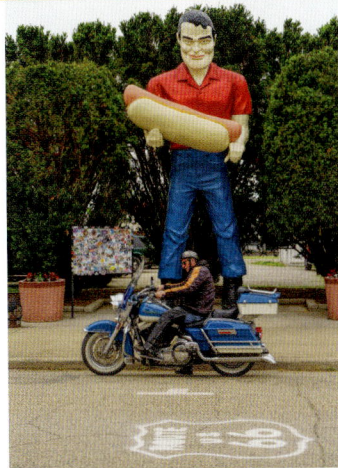

Tall Paul and Harley rider, Atlanta, Illinois
Becky Waters

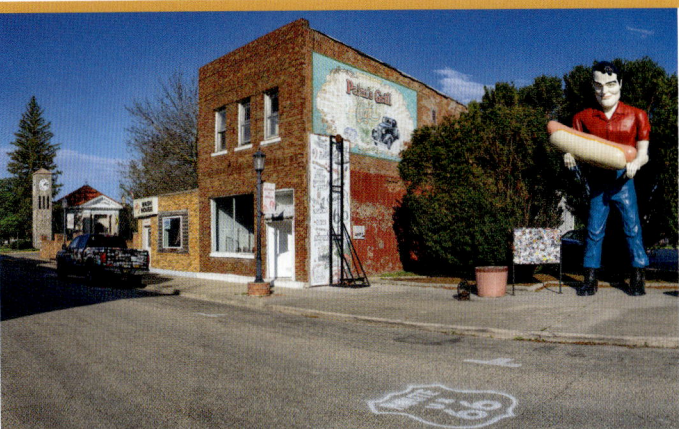

Tall Paul, Atlanta, Illinois   *David Skernick*

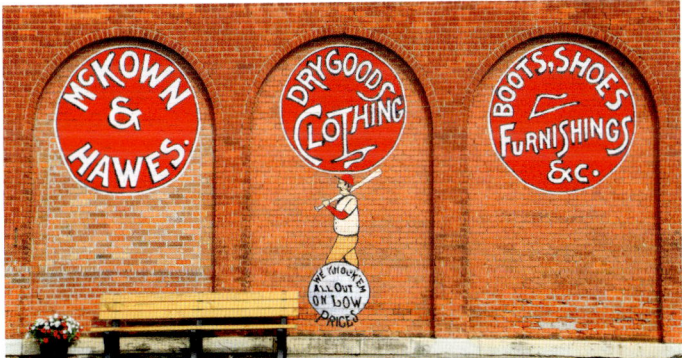

McKown & Hawes, Atlanta, Illinois   *Susan Vizuary*

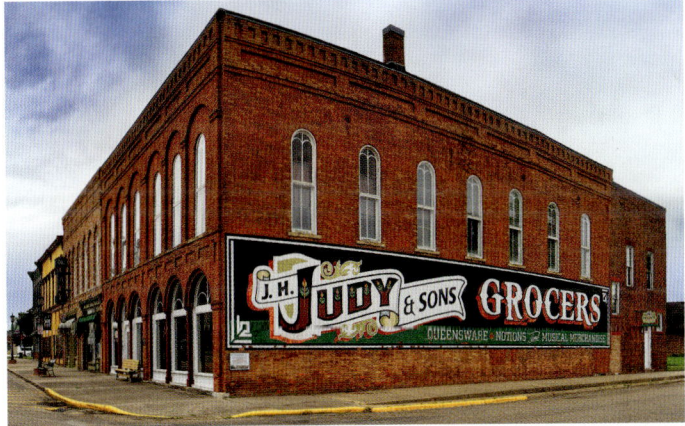

J. H. Judy & Sons Grocers, Atlanta, Illinois   *David Skernick*

Be sure to explore all of Atlanta, Illinois. Aside from a superb collection of giants, there is wonderful architecture, terrific little shops, good food, and nice people. There is an area on the far side of town (a few blocks over) with some older buildings and barns. I like to stay in Atlanta. It is a quiet town with a perfect location to use as a home base for exploring Route 66 in Illinois.

McLean and Chenoa, Illinois

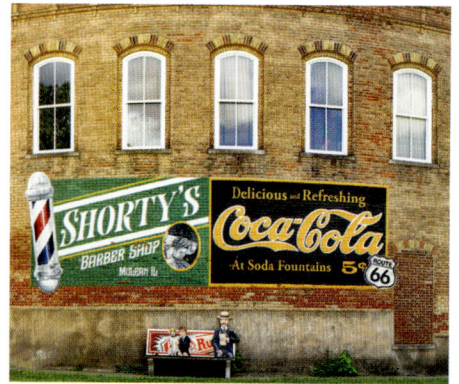

McLean, Illinois   *David Skernick*

Heading north on Route 66 after Atlanta, you will come to the small town of McLean. I found some pretty farm roads and this terrific wall there. Even the smallest towns have a big Route 66 tradition. Look carefully and see if you can find little gems that are not in this or any other book. We all are collectors on Route 66. Some collect cars or giants or signs. We collect photos.

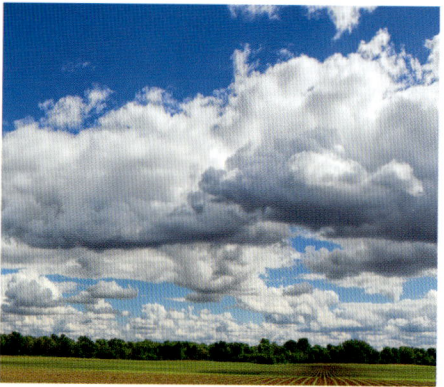

Farm near McLean, Illinois   *David Skernick*

An old service station, a vintage car, and a reflection. It was that reflection that got my attention, so I made that my subject. The car and building are only partially seen. The reflection is given importance by being complete, even though it takes up less space. This is one of those times when I titled my shot before choosing my composition. *Storm Cloud Reflection* meant the car and building needed to be only supporting elements.

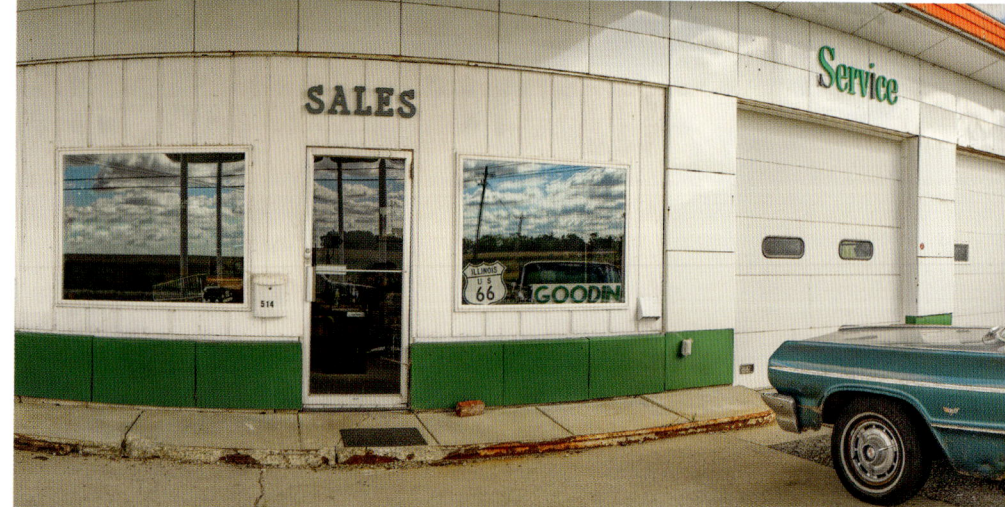

Storm clouds reflection, Chenoa, Illinois   *David Skernick*

Pontiac, Illinois

Hiding inside Pontiac, Illinois, like a pearl inside an oyster, is a small Route 66 paradise. Fantastic murals, interesting museums, and a rich history all are waiting for you. As with most Illinois towns, there are several alignments. Each has its own happy surprises. We spent our time near and around the courthouse and enjoyed hours of photography bliss.

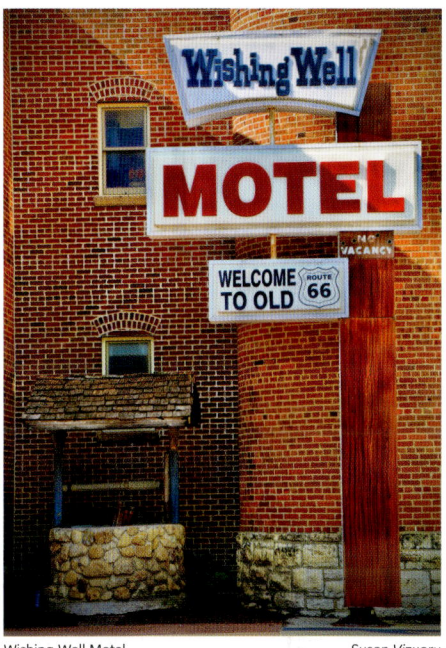

Wishing Well Motel   *Susan Vizuary*

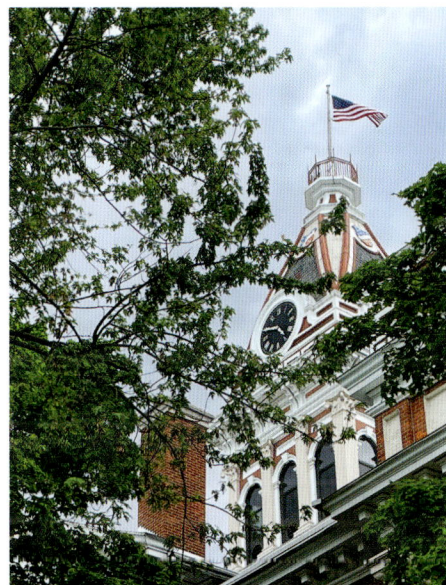

Courthouse, Pontiac, Illinois   *David Skernick*

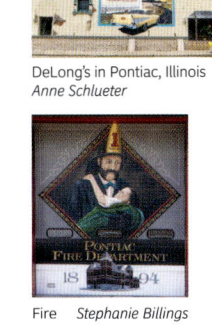

DeLong's in Pontiac, Illinois
Anne Schlueter

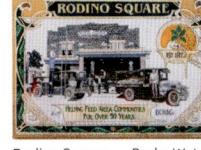

Rodino Square   *Becky Waters*

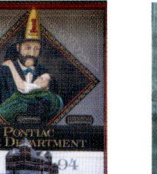

Fire   *Stephanie Billings*

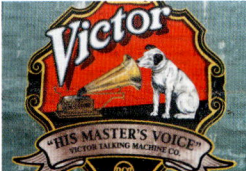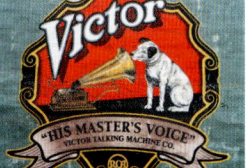

The Master's Voice   *Becky Waters*

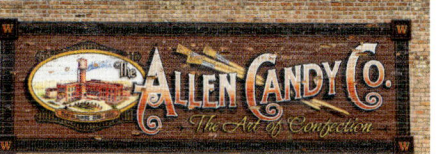

Allen Candy Co., Pontiac, Illinois   *Anne Schlueter*

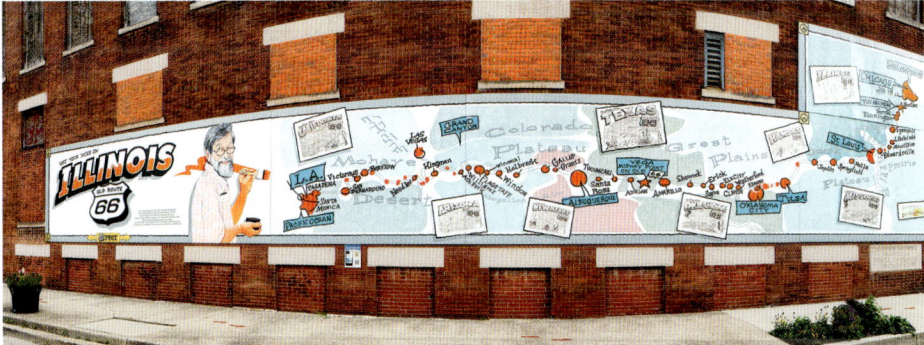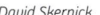

Waldmire Memorial, Pontiac, Illinois   *David Skernick*

Pontiac, Illinois

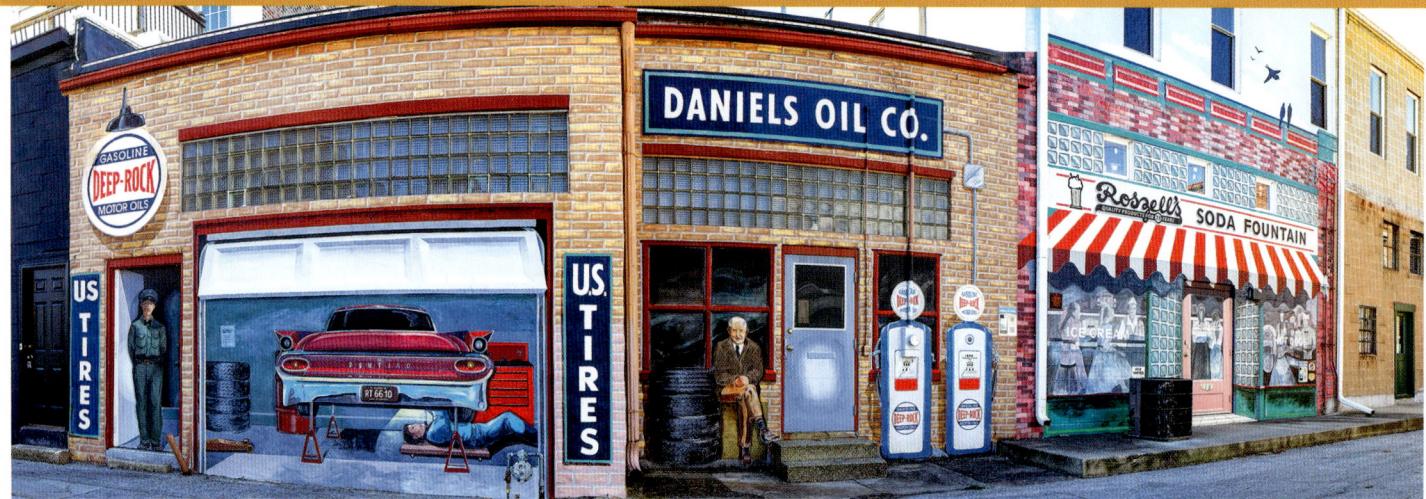

Daniels Oil, Pontiac, Illinois

David Skernick

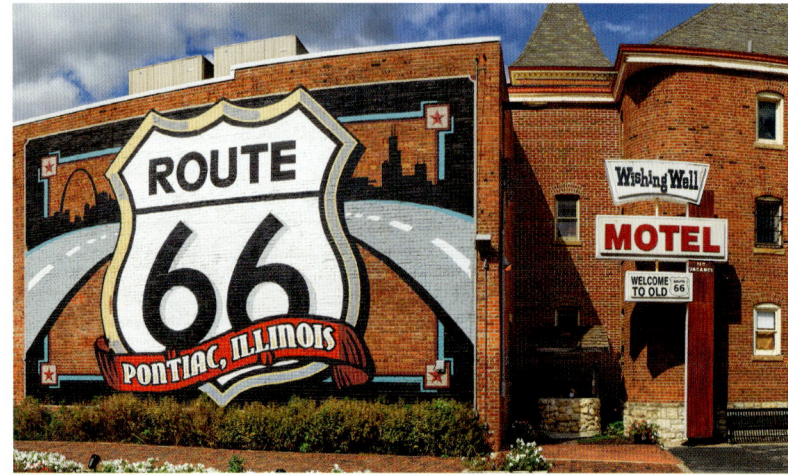

Wishing Well Motel, Pontiac, Illinois

David Skernick

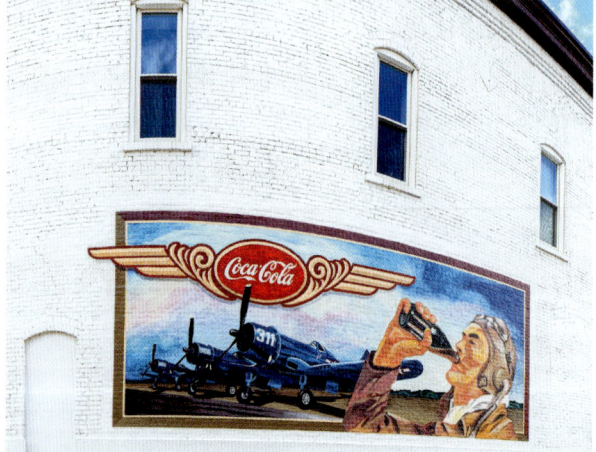

Drink Coca-Cola by Sonny Franks, Pontiac, Illinois

David Skernick

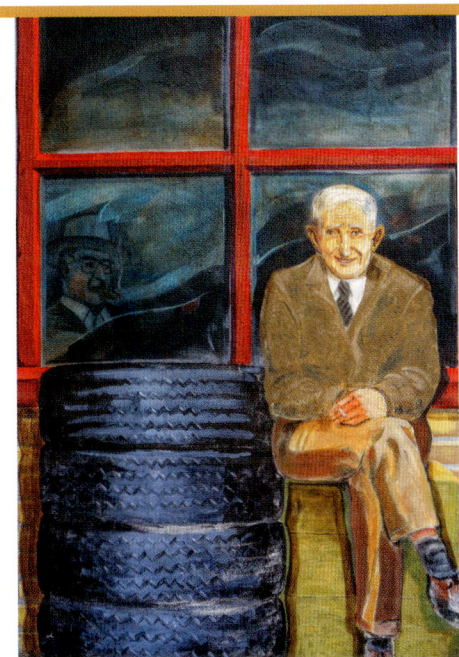

Daniels · *Becky Waters*

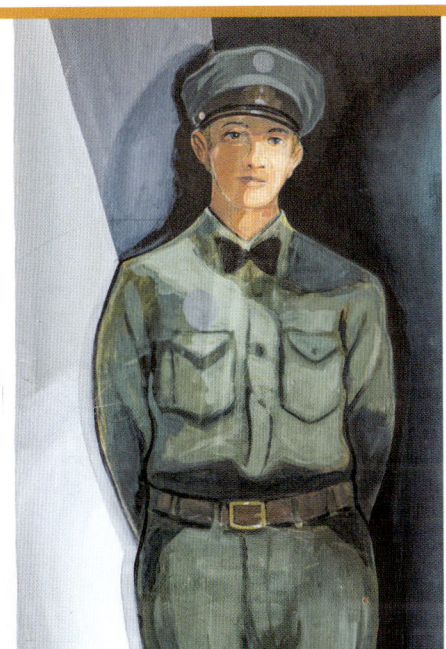

Attendant · *Anne Schlueter*

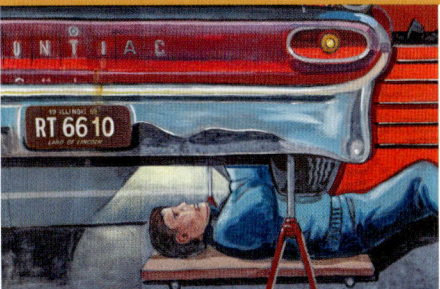

Mechanic · *Anne Schlueter*

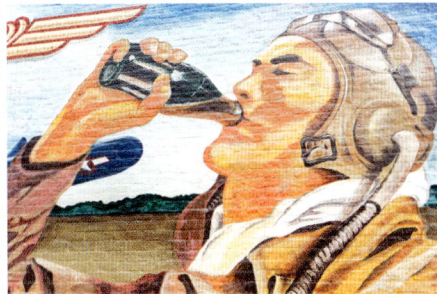

Pilot · *Anne Schlueter*

Even or consistent light is important when you are photographing any mural. If a large portion of your subject is in shadow or has too much glaring light on it, you might have to give it up or come back another time. You could try a neutral-density filter or do things in postprocessing to even up the light, but on a flat subject such as a wall, it can be impossible to make it look just right. Full shade is fine (actually great!). I am not suggesting that you shoot only in full sun. The Coca-Cola

advertisement (*left*) was photographed in open shade. That is flat, or continuous, shade, which you will find on the opposite side of the building from the sunny side. I included a little sky at the top of that shot but had to darken it quite a bit in postprocessing.

For the Wishing Well Motel sign and adjoining mural, I had the sun at my back. The pretty light on the wall and pretty sky came together nicely. I was happy to be able to show the interesting roofline. I had

to come back in the morning to get the entire Daniels Oil mural. It was behind me as I shot the sunny wall, and when I turned around, there was just too much glare from behind the wall to get the shot. The next morning was overcast! That is a gift for murals, since it provides constant, even light.

During a workshop, we visited Pontiac and were lucky to have a partly sunny day. Anne and Becky waited for the sun to hide behind clouds to get the detail shots (*above*) in the even light of shade.

Odell and Dwight, Illinois

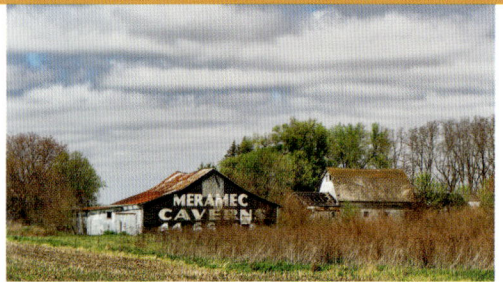

Meramec Caverns barn, Odell, Illinois
David Skernick

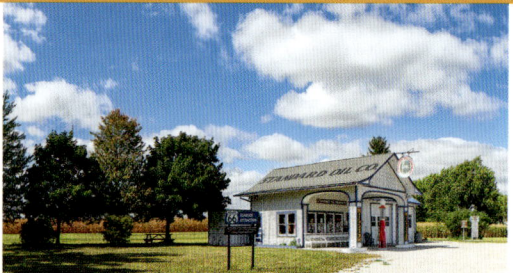

Standard Oil gasoline station, Odell, Illinois
David Skernick

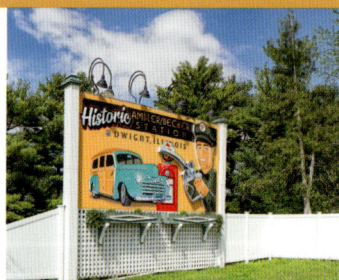

Ambler Becker Station sign, Dwight, Illinois
David Skernick

Check out our second Meramec Caverns barn (*upper left*). It is well off the road but still creates an effective advertisement. Notice that your eye went right to it, even though it is small in the frame. It becomes the subject of the image even when small, since it has writing and is the only thing that is different. That always works. Imagine a photo of a box of red apples with only one green apple. Even though red almost always gets your attention, the green one, because it is the only green one, will become the subject of the shot. In two of the above images, I also sought to show their surroundings and give you a feel for how secluded they both are. The sign (*above right*) is relatively small, but with the frame of the fence and the size in the photo, it appears bigger. The large gas station appears small because it's far away and surrounded by big trees and clouds. Size is under your control!

The Shop, Gardiner, Illinois

The Shop in Gardiner (*right and following*) is another "can't miss" attraction, I wanted to share how this amazing store looks so small from the outside and felt large on the inside. Bob and the tree gave scale to the outside, and I used panoramas inside to evoke more space. A wide-angle lens would do roughly the same thing.

The Shop, exterior, Gardiner, Illinois ▶
David Skernick

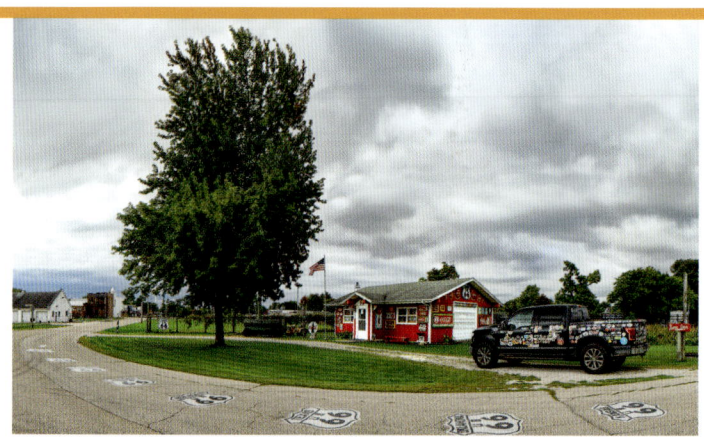

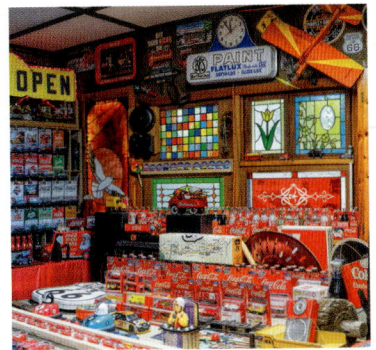

The Shop, interior, Gardiner, Illinois *David Skernick*

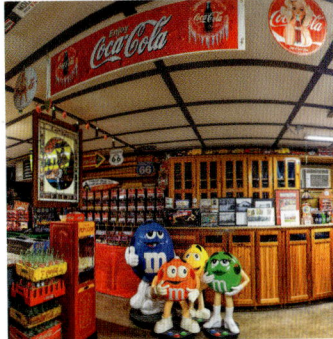

The M&M Guys in the Shop *David Skernick*

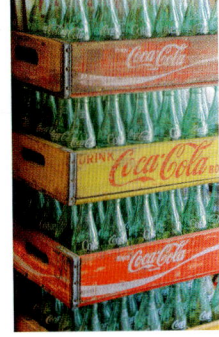

Coke bottles, the Shop
Susan Vizvary

Now that we have the size thing handled, let's talk about what you will find here. Tom Perkins loves Coca-Cola. We have seen many different collections on our ride along Route 66. This one is incredible. In a tiny space, Tom has assembled everything Coke. Whether you like Coke or not, you have to come meet Tom and see his collection.

The Polk-A-Dot Drive Inn, Braidwood, Illinois

Shoot what you can, when you can. The Polk-A-Dot Drive Inn in Braidwood, Illinois, is a cool burger joint with great food and fantastic visuals. It was so crowded when we were there that we were forced to shoot just these small areas to avoid cars and people in our shots. That is okay. It was those figures that got our attention as we were driving by. That and the smell of those heavenly cheeseburgers.

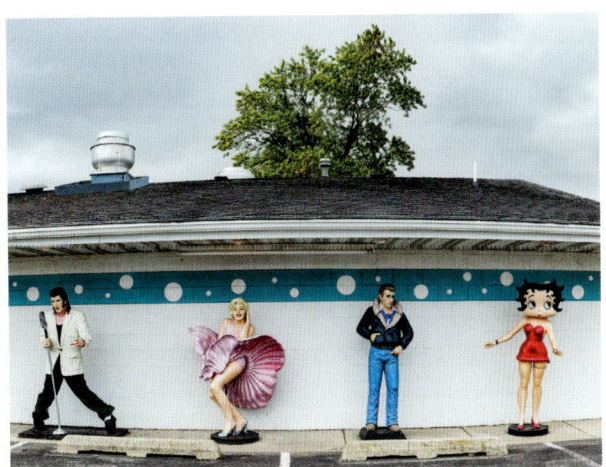

Polk-A-Dot Drive Inn, Braidwood, Illinois *David Skernick*

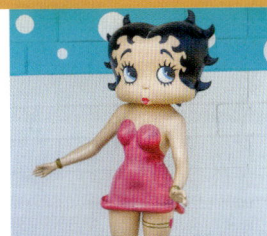

Betty Boop *Becky Waters*

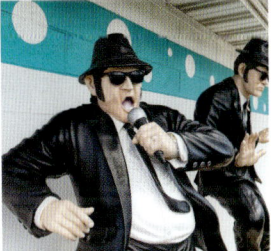

The Blues Brothers *Anne Schlueter*

138

Wilmington, Illinois

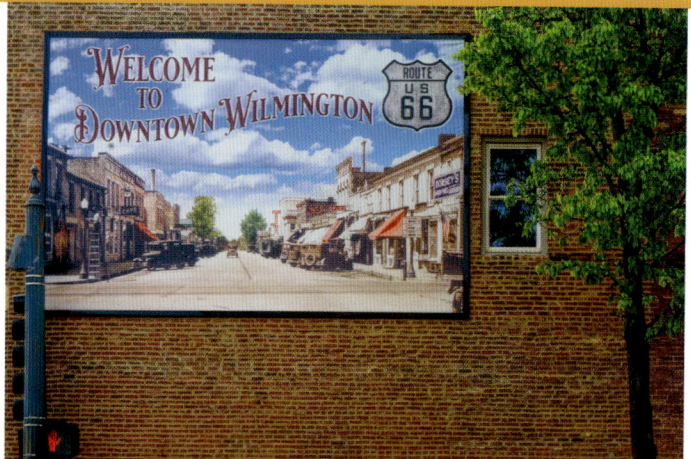

Welcome to downtown Wilmington, Illinois

Becky Waters

This photo says it all. Welcome to downtown Wilmington, and definitely stop! Here you will find another friendly little town along America's Highway. Wilmington is filled with antique shops, murals, and all kinds of surprises and good photo opportunities, as well as good food and places to stay. Watch for glare and your own reflections in the glass windows. Ask permission when you can for outside, and always for inside pictures. Use your phone when a tripod and "big" camera make you feel like a bull in a china shop. Some of these actually are china shops!

124 Water Street, Wilmington Illinois

David Skernick

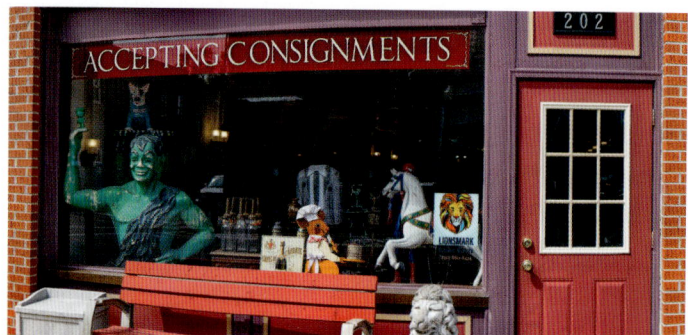

Lionmark, Water Street, Wilmington, Illinois

David Skernick

Take your time and enjoy the slow pace. You are headed for extremely crowded areas and massive traffic as you approach the eastern terminus of Route 66 in Chicago. Stop in Wilmington for a quiet walk and maybe some ice cream.

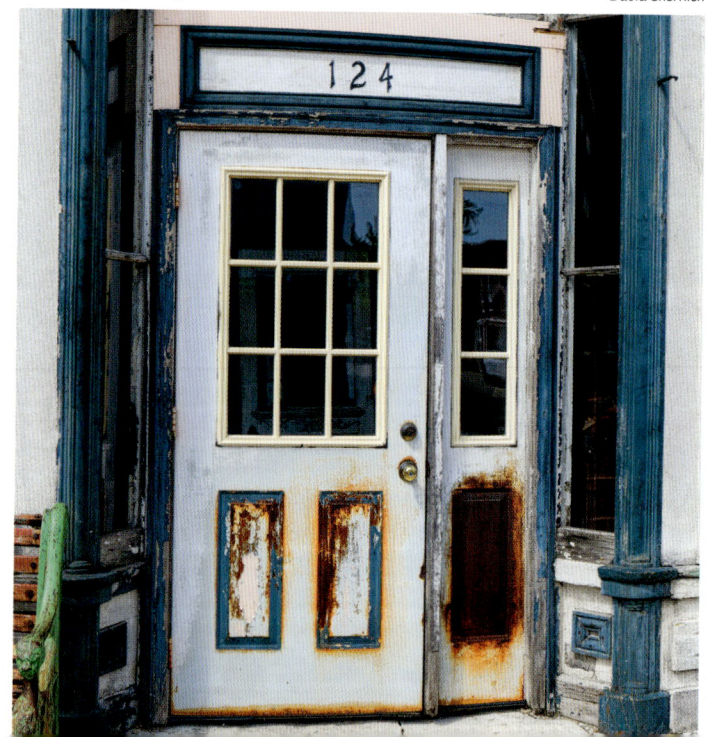

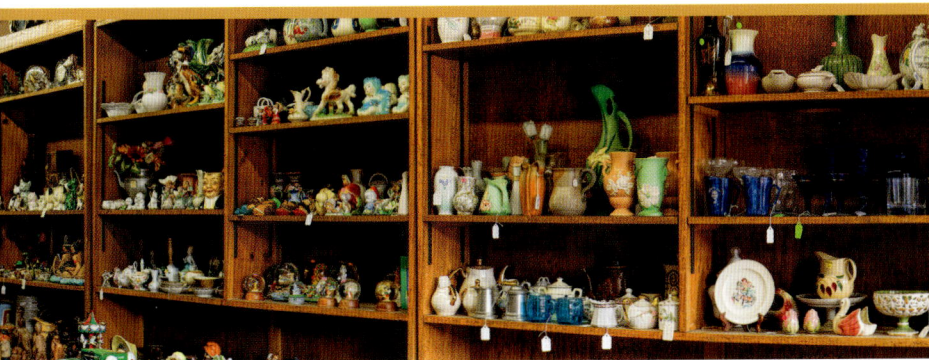

Rick's Relics, Wilmington, Illinois

David Skernick

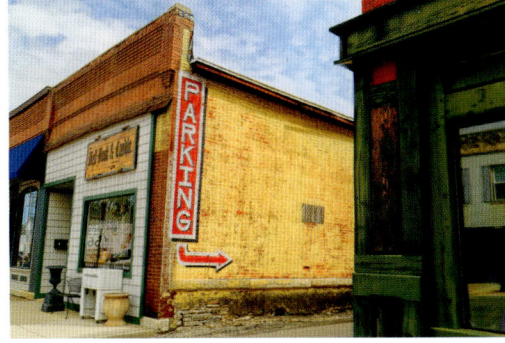

Parking, Wilmington, Illinois

Susan Vizuary

While I was in Wilmington, just after I got the shot below of the Gemini Giant, a tour bus showed up and forty people poured out to see one of the last Muffler Men. They were from France! It is about 4,250 miles from Paris, France, to the Gemini Giant on Route 66 in Wilmington, Illinois! Just saying—people come from all over the world to travel the Main Street of America. I have personally met folks from China, France, Slovakia, Finland, Germany, Argentina, Sweden, Japan, and England, just to name a few. There is something very special and a little magic about this road, but you have discovered that for yourself by now. I just wanted to acknowledge it (again) here.

By the publishing of this book, the Gemini Giant will be in his new home in Wilmington Park. The reason he was moved is a long story, and I'm not sure I have all the facts. I am just glad that Wilmington will get to keep him. Things change on the route all the time. It's why so many of us will continue to drive it over and over again. You are always welcome back on Route 66!

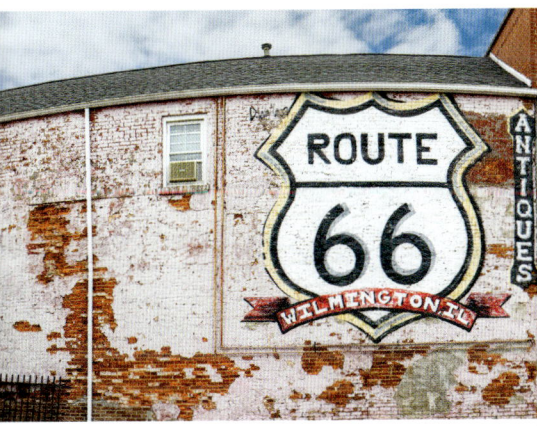

Mural, Wilmington, Illinois

David Skernick

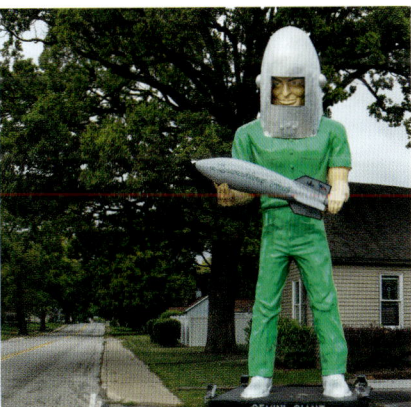

Gemini Man, Wilmington, Illinois

David Skernick

Joliet, Illinois

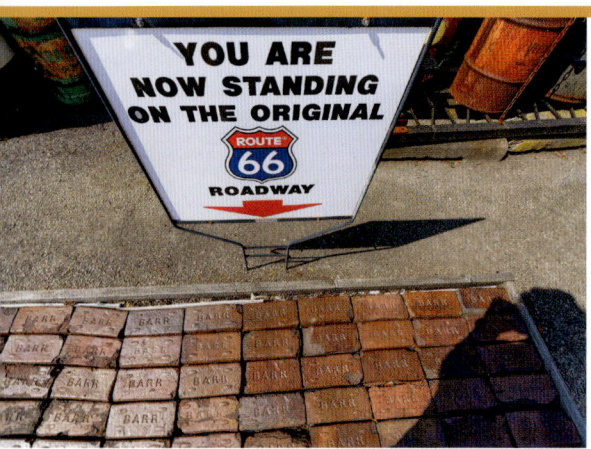

Dicks on 66, Joliet, Illinois

David Skernick

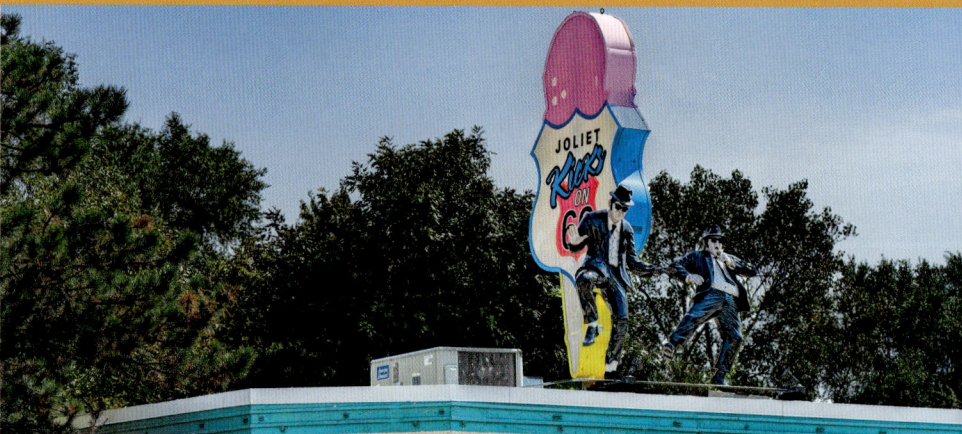

Rich and Creamy Ice Cream, Joliet, Illinois

David Skernick

We are now only 50 miles or so from Chicago and the end of our journey. Joliet, Illinois, is known for many things: the old Joliet Prison, the Rialto Theater, the Joliet Area Historical Museum, and the Chicagoland Speedway. It is also the home of Jake and Elwood Blues, the Blues Brothers. The 1980 film titled *Blues Brothers* gave Joliet a new claim to fame, and just like that, the Blues Brothers became part of Route 66 lore.

You can see the old and the new (*above*). At Dicks on 66, I stood on the original bricks of the road itself. I shot with my phone and included my shadow because I was there! It is a true tourist shot, and there is nothing wrong with that. The other shots I took with my phone of Dicks on 66 were not sharp enough to be used in this book. Use your phone but treat it like a camera. By that, I mean hold it steady and compose your photos carefully. I did not do it that morning. I usually try, but maybe I was tired, or excited to be almost finished, or both. I took more time with the Rich and Creamy sign. I took it from across the street with a long lens. I wanted only the sign. The shop looked great, but it was

closed for the season when I was there, and I didn't like the lonely feel of a place that must be so alive when it is open.

After Joliet, I drove the rest of the way into Chicago. It was tricky to stay on Route 66, but I carefully navigated the crowded streets as I looked forward to what I hoped would be an incredible photo opportunity at the end of the line. I felt a little lonely for my friends and sorry that we wouldn't be together to see this last great scene, but I thought if it was great, I could bring them another time.

Finally, I reached the end on East Adams Street in Chicago. I had to park illegally and jump out of Bob the Truck quickly to grab the shot on the right with my mirrorless camera. I brought that camera because I thought there might be crowds, and I wanted a smaller camera than my DSLR so I could be less obvious.

Okay, no crowds, just one little sign, but it's worth going all the way to Chicago. It is a fantastic city with wonderful people and amazing architecture, museums, and sports. Who am I kidding? I would drive there just for the deep-dish pizza!

Chicago, Illinois

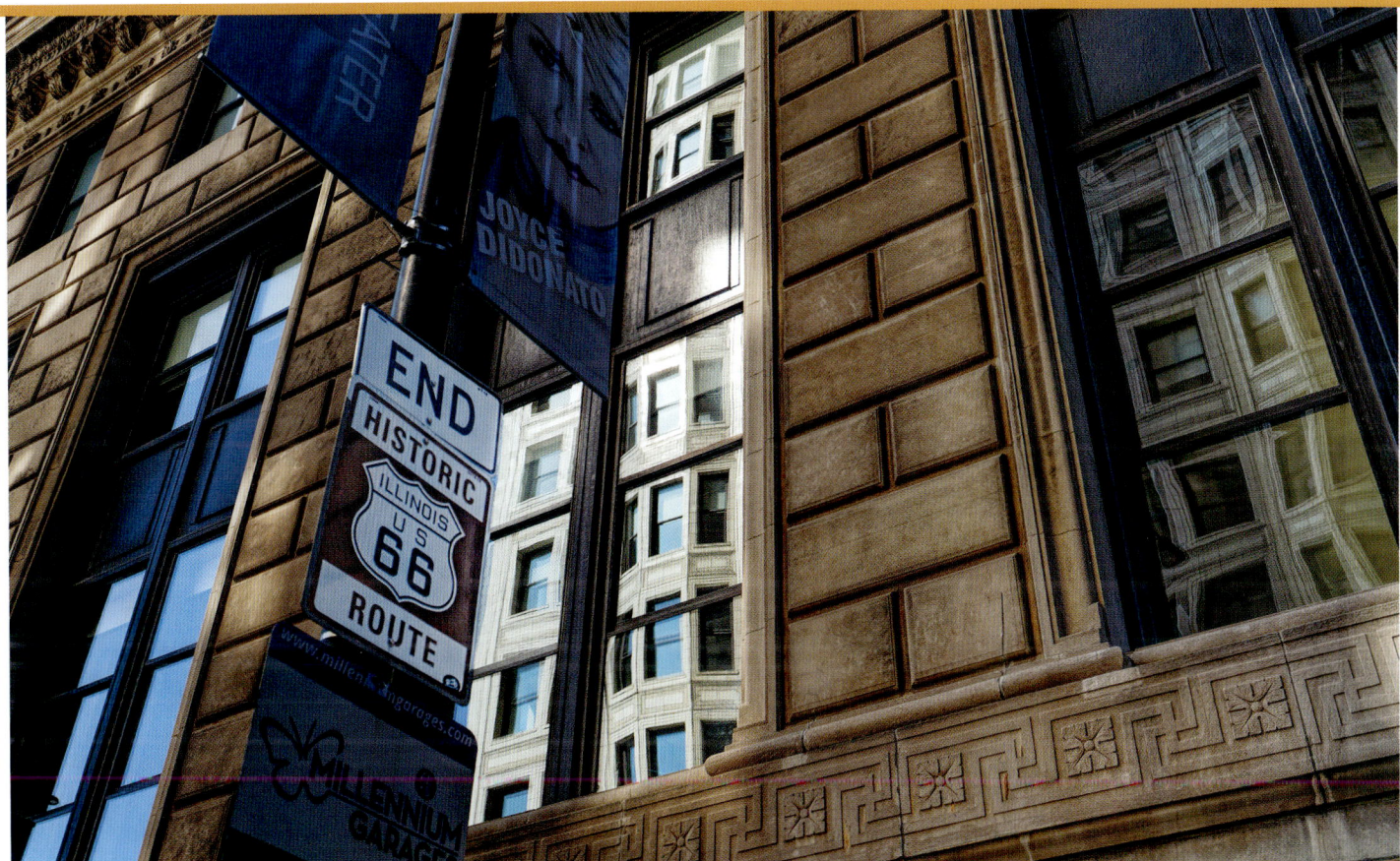

Eastern terminus of Route 66, East Adams Street, Chicago, Illinois

David Skernick

This is the eastern terminus of Route 66. Kind of a letdown, but then it was never about getting there, but about the journey itself. I drove the entire 2,448 miles—many of them several times. I traveled extra miles to follow many of the older alignments. I and my students took hundreds of photos. We ate fantastic food, saw countless new things, and made many, many new friends. I don't want it to end. Even now I'm planning my next trip.

Bob the Truck on Route 66

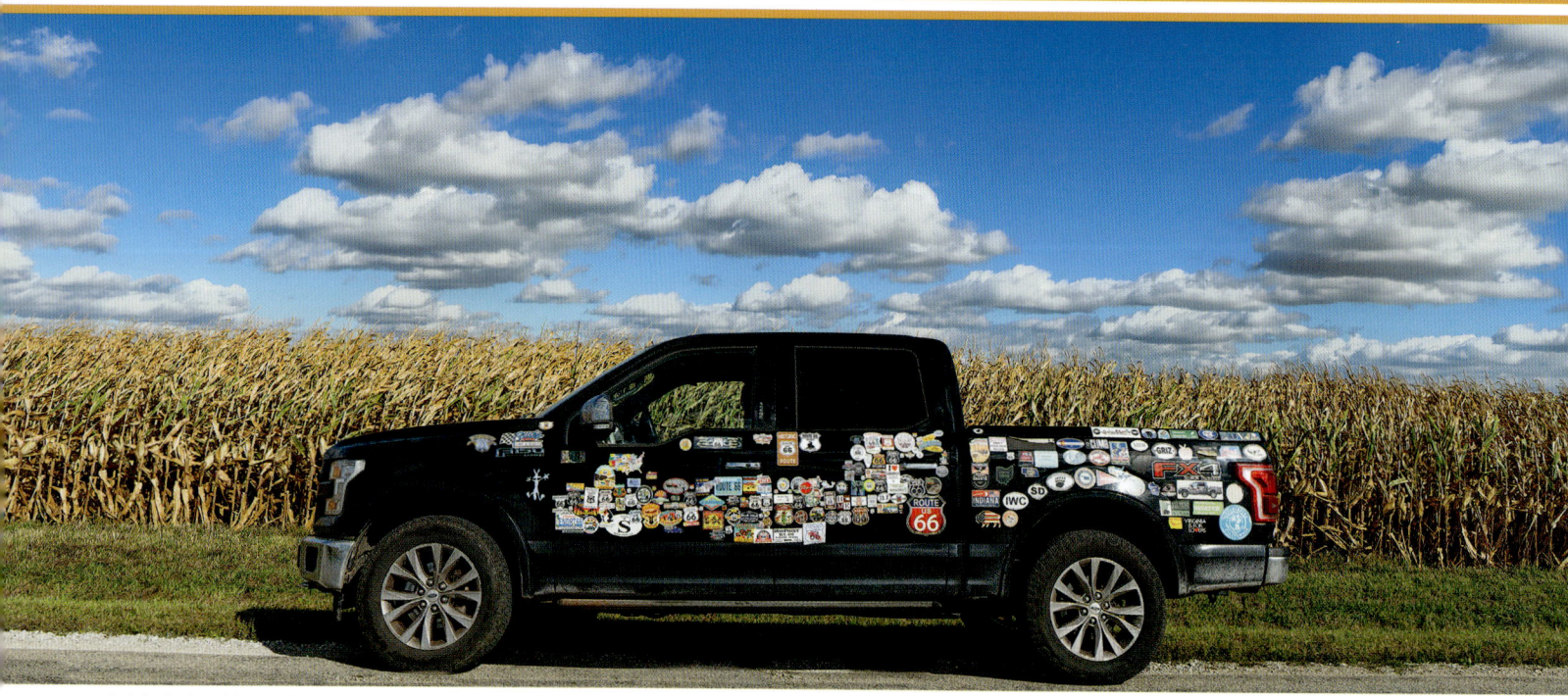

Bob the Truck and the completed sticker map, Route 66, Illinois

David Skernick

Although my faithful truck, Bob 4, has Route 66 stickers interspersed with others on all three sides, I created the map of the Mother Road, in stickers, on the two doors facing. They are in order by state and follow the general shape of the route. When I decided to do this, I had no idea how excited the folks I met along the way would be to see, photograph, and contribute to this project. Everywhere I went on Route 66, people came outside to watch the stickers go on. They took pictures of me and the truck to share on social media.

By the end of my tour, I found shopkeepers waiting for me. They had heard that there was a guy heading north making a sticker map on his truck. One woman called me a legend. Funny that this would be my legacy on Route 66.

I will bring a copy of this book to each of those shop owners and museum docents and hope they see how much I love and respect them, and their special road.

Acknowledgements

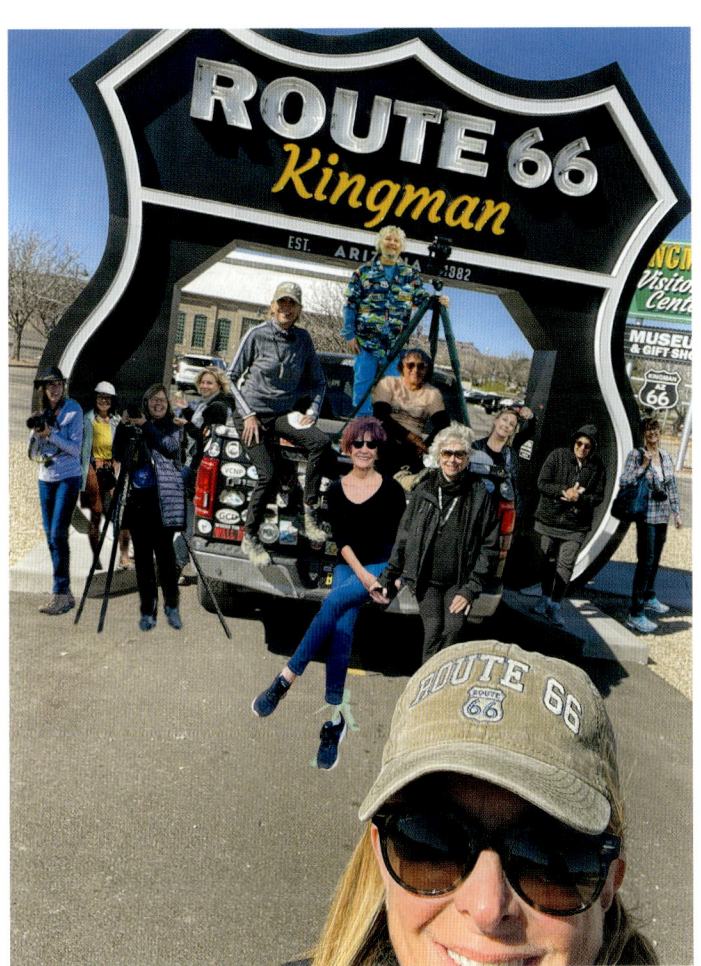

I am so incredibly grateful to this group of photographers. They call themselves my students, but I have learned more from them than I ever learned in school, or on my own. To teach is to learn, but to teach those with talent is that times a billion. Thanks to these fantastic women and to my wife, Ria, and friend Brian, this book is what it is. I hope all who read it get as much out of it as I did creating it.

Full disclosure: This group was not in one location at any given time. The original shot was a selfie group shot of myself and four others. It was taken by Susan Vizvary. I Photoshopped the others into the shot with photos taken on various other Route 66 workshops.

David Skernick, 2025

Photos by *(left to right)*:
Kathi Mangel
Becky Waters
Anne Schlueter
Jackie Rosenthal
Judy Nussenblatt
Carol Zulman
David Skernick
Stephanie Billings
Gayle Pepper
Diane Waldron
Barbara Balik
Monica Bayless
Susan Vizvary

Appendix

	Image Name	Camera Type	Focal Length	F/Stop	Shutter Speed	ISO	Pano Image Count	Pano Levels
001	Title Page Background	Nikon D850	85mm	f/11	1/200	64	8	1
002	Group Shot	iPhone 12 Pro	2.7	f/2.2	1/800	25	n/a	n/a
003	Illustration – Contents	no data						
004	1966 Camaro	Canon EOS	24mm	f/1.6	1/80	100	n/a	n/a
005	Route 66 California	Nikon D850	50mm	f/14	1/80	64	9	1
006	Santa Monica Pier	Sony A7R2	26mm	f/13	1/60	50		
007	End of Trail	cell phone	no data					n/a
008	Alt. West Terminus	Nikon D500	210mm	f/10	1/1600	400	n/a	n/a
009	Chicken Boy	iPhone 8	4.0mm	f/1.8	1/2700	20	n/a	n/a
010	Bridge Detail	iPhone 12	4.2mm	f/1.6	1/1000	32	n/a	n/a
011	Colorado Street Bridge	Canon 6D	24mm	f/8	1/400	100	n/a	n/a
012	Colorado Street Bridge	Canon 6D	35mm	f/8	1/40	100	n/a	n/a
013	Bridge Detail	Canon 6D	24mm	f/8	1/25	100	n/a	n/a
014	Magic Lamp Inn	iPhone 12	4.2mm	f/1.6	1/3000	32	n/a	n/a
015	Wigwam Detail	Canon 5D	70mm	f/10	1/250	100	n/a	n/a
016	Wigwam Pano	Sony A7R2	55mm	f/13	1/200	100	18	2
017	Wigwam Interior	cell phone	no data				phone	pano
018	Museum Mural	Nikon D850	85mm	f/9.0	1/320	64	9	1
019	Cross Eyed Cow	Nikon D850	85mm	f/10	1/60	64	9	1
020	Bottle Ranch	Nikon D850	85mm	f/11	1/200	200	16	1
021	Bottle Tree	Nikon D300S	105mm	f/8	1/1000	400	n/a	n/a
022	Bottles	Nikon D300S	135mm	f/8	1/90	200	n/a	n/a
023	Bagdad Cafe	Nikon D850	35mm	f/11	1/3	64	14	2
024	Roy's Cafe	Sony A7R4	55mm	f/11	1/8	200	n/a	n/a
025	Roy's Motel	Nikon D810	85mm	f/11	1/25	64	14	2
026	Roy's Motel Night	Sony A7R4	35mm	f/12	4"	100	n/a	n/a
027	66 Motel Sign	Nikon D850	85mm	f/11	1/200	64	8	1
028	Route 66 Pizza	Nikon D850	50mm	f/10	1/160	64	6	1
029	Sage Detail	Nikon D850	50mm	f/16	1/160	64	5	1
030	Deco Foodservices	Nikon D850	50mm	f/11	1/250	64	7	1
031	Garage Mural	Nikon D850	50mm	f/11	1/250	64	n/a	n/a
032	Museum Mural	iPhone 12	4.2mm	f/16	1/2800	32	n/a	n/a
033	Snowy Egrets	Nikon D500	320mm	f/6.7	1/3200	8000	n/a	n/a
034	Egrets in Flight	Nikon D500	500mm	f/5.6	1/3200	2200	n/a	n/a
035	Blackbird	Nikon D500	500mm	f/5.6	1/3200	900	n/a	n/a
036	BNSF Train	Nikon D750	50mm	f/11	1/100	100	24	2
037	Oklahoma Train	Nikon D600	35mm	f/11	1/200	100	8	1
038	Oatman Hotel	Nikon D300	80mm	f/4.8	1/1000	100	n/a	n/a
039	Singing Cowboy	Nikon D800	50mm	f/6.3	1/160	25600	n/a	n/a
040	Cash Wall	Canon 5D	100nn	f/4	1/15	400	n/a	n/a
041	Oatman Burros	Canon 5D	270mm	f/7.1	1/2000	640	n/a	n/a
042	Oatman Burros 2	Nikon D500	230mm	f/8	1/1000	400	n/a	n/a
043	Sitgreaves Pass.	Nikon D810	50mm	f/10	1/100	64	18	2
044	Teddy Bear Cholla	Nikon D810	50mm	f/11	1/100	64	16	2
045	Route 66, Arizona	Canon 5D	32mm	f/10	1/400	160	n/a	n/a
046	Rt. 66 Pop Bottles	Canon 7D	46mm	f/10	1/20	16000	n/a	n/a
047	Classic Car	Canon 5D	70mm	f/11	1/160	100	n/a	n/a
048	Cool Springs Portrait	Canon 5D	95mm	f/10	1/60	100	n/a	n/a
049	Shop Owner	Canon 7D	50mm	f/8	1/125	16000	n/a	n/a
050	Rickety Cricket	Canon 5D	18mm	f/11	1/6	100	n/a	n/a
051	Rickety Cricket 2	Canon 5D	20mm	f/11	1/15	100	n/a	n/a
052	Kingman Club	Canon 5D	50mm	f/11	1/2	100	n/a	n/a
053	Primp My Pet	Nikon D850	85mm	f/11	1/200	64	7	1
054	Mr. D's	Nikon D850	135mm	f/8	1/20	64	8	1
055	Motel Route 66	Canon 5D	35mm	f/8	1/160	100	n/a	n/a
056	Motel Route 66 2	Canon 7D	200mm	f/11	1/2000	400	n/a	n/a
057	Giganticus Headicus	Nikon D810	35mm	f/11	1/25	64	9	1
058	Close-up	Canon 5D	100mm	f/8	1/2000	400	n/a	n/a
059	Close-up 2	Canon 5D	100mm	f/5.6	1/2500	400	n/a	n/a
060	Old Truck	Canon 5D	18mm	f/13	1/250	200	n/a	n/a
061	Dudley meets G. H.	iPhone	4.2mm	f/1.6	1/3000	32	n/a	n/a
062	66 East of Kingman	Nikon D810	35mm	f/11	1/26	64	6	1
063	66 E of Kingman 2	Nikon D850	85mm	f/13	1/100	64	26	2
064	BNSF Railroad	Nikon D810	135mm	f/9	1/160	125	10	1
065	Hackberry Store	Nikon D810	50mm	f/10	1/200	64	8	1
066	Hackberry Wall	Canon 5D	24mm	f/11	1/255	200	n/a	n/a
067	Hackberry Car	Canon 5D	24mm	f/11	1/400	200	n/a	n/a
068	Hackberry Outhouse	Canon 5D	45mm	f/8	1/125	100	n/a	n/a
069	Frozen Bottles	Canon 5D	105mm	f/11	1/10	100	n/a	n/a
070	Hackberry Interior 1	Canon 5D	15mm	f/8	1/2	100	n/a	n/a
071	Hackberry Int 2	Canon 5D	65mm	f/16	1/6	250	n/a	n/a
072	Hackberry Int 3	Nikon D800	28mm	f/8	1/4	100	n/a	n/a
073	Whoop Ass	Canon 7D	55mm	f/13	1/60	250	n/a	n/a
074	License Plates	Canon 5D	105mm	f/4	1/8	400	n/a	n/a
075	Lion	Nikon D500	500mm	f/5.6	1/2000	1250	n/a	n/a
076	Llama	Nikon D500	480mm	f/5.6	1/2000	400	n/a	n/a
077	Tiger	Nikon D500	500mm	f/5.6	1/2000	800	n/a	n/a
078	Capybara	Nikon D500	500mm	f/5.6	1/2000	1000	n/a	n/a
079	Tiger	Nikon D500	500mm	f/5.6	1/2000	1250	n/a	n/a
080	Black Leopard	Nikon D500	450mm	f/5.6	1/2000	1100	n/a	n/a
081	Frontier Motel	Nikon D850	50mm	f/9	1/200	64	6	1
082	Giant Dinosaur	Nikon D850	135mm	f/10	1/160	64	8	1
083	Motel Interior	Nikon D600	35mm	f/11	1/6	100	13	1
084	Motel Sign	Canon 5D	40mm	f/5.6	1/10	100	n/a	n/a
085	Seligman Grocery	Nikon D850	85mm	f/11	1/250	64	8	1
086	Clayton	Canon 7D	70mm	f/4.5	1/125	1250	n/a	n/a
087	Snow Cap Staff	iPhone 12	4.2mm	f/1.6	1/125	80	Phone	Pano
088	Supal Motel	Nikon D850	85mm	f/8	1/6	64	4	1
089	Sundries Truck	Canon 5D	63mm	f/11	1/160	100	n/a	n/a
090	Seligman Gift Shop	Canon 5D	24mm	f/11	1/15	100	n/a	n/a
091	Flag Mural	Canon 5D	35mm	f/8	1/800	200	n/a	n/a
092	VW Bus	Canon 5D	60mm	f/10	1/320	100	n/a	n/a
093	Burger Sign	Nikon D850	135mm	f/8	1/125	160	n/a	n/a
094	Wall Detail	Canon 7D	40mm	f/11	1/160	100	n/a	n/a
095	Truck	Canon 5D	55mm	f/11	1/160	100	n/a	n/a
096	Signs, Seligman	Canon 5D	60mm	f/10	1/100	100	n/a	n/a
097	Main Street	Sony A7R4	40mm	f/9	1/160	200	n/a	n/a
098	Roadkill Cafe	Canon 7D	80mm	f/8	1/250	200	n/a	n/a
099	Motel, Seligman	Canon 7D	55mm	f/13	1/250	400	n/a	n/a
100	Grandma Betty	iPhone 12	4.2mm	F1.6	1/60	200	n/a	n/a
101	House, Seligman	Canon 5D	32mm	f/11	1/45	100	n/a	n/a
102	Garage	Canon 5D	105mm	f/5.6	1/1600	400	n/a	n/a
103	Old Post Office	Nikon D850	85mm	f/11	1/125	64	6	1
104	Blue Moon Eclipse	Nikon D810	135mm	f/7.1	1/125	1600	n/a	n/a
105	Copper Cart	Nikon D850	85mm	f/11	1/160	64	18	2
106	Looking West	Nikon D850	135mm	f/8	1/125	160	7	1
107	Looking East	Nikon D850	135mm	f/11	1/8	64	6	1
108	Curious Colt	Nikon D500	360mm	f/7.1	1/2000	2200	n/a	n/a
109	Wild Horses	Nikon D500	450mm	f/5.6	1/2500	360	n/a	n/a

#	Title	Camera	Focal	Aperture	Shutter	ISO		
110	58 Chevy	Canon 5D	58mm	f/7.1	1/800	400	n/a	n/a
111	Train Crossing	Canon 5D	32mm	f/11	1/500	800	n/a	n/a
112	Train Car	Canon 5D	60mm	f/2.4	1/640	160	n/a	n/a
113	Addicted to Rt 66	Nikon D850	50mm	f/10	1/320	64	21	3
114	Chris	Canon 5D	18mm	f/8	1/10	640	n/a	n/a
115	Interior and Elvis	Nikon D850	50mm	f/13	1/5	64	7	1
116	Miniature Cars	Canon 5D	229mm	f/11	1/2	100	n/a	n/a
117	Pete's Gas Station	Sony A7R4	28mm	f/14	1/60	200	n/a	n/a
118	Signs	Canon 5D	70mm	f/7.1	1/2000	400	n/a	n/a
119	Turquoise Tepee	Canon 5D	58mm	f/5.6	1/3200	400	n/a	n/a
120	Cafe 66	Nikon D850	50mm	f/11	1/200	64	8	1
121	Motor Hotel	Canon 5D	24mm	f/8	1/180	100	n/a	n/a
122	Pipe Creek	Nikon D810	50mm	f/13	1/160	64	10	4
123	Desert View	Nikon D750	50mm	f/11	1/250	200	11	1
124	Yavapai Point	Nikon D750	85mm	f/8	1/400	200	8	1
125	Near Mather Point	Nikon D750	50mm	f/8	1/200	100	16	2
126	Miz Zips	Nikon D850	50mm	f/13	1/250	64	n/a	n/a
127	Let's Eat	Nikon D850	50mm	f/13	1/250	64	n/a	n/a
128	Whispering Winds	Nikon D850	50mm	f/11	1/250	64	5	1
129	WW Sign	Nikon D850	50mm	f/11	1/250	64	n/a	n/a
130	66 Motel	Nikon D850	50mm	f/9.0	1/320	64	n/a	n/a
131	Hotel Monte Vista	Nikon D850	135mm	f/11	1/125	64	6	1
132	Mural, Flagstaff	Sony A7R4	90mm	f/8	1/250	400	n/a	n/a
133	Salsa Brava	Nikon D850	50mm	f/9.0	1/125	64	n/a	n/a
134	Ganado, AZ	Nikon D850	50mm	f/13	1/125	64	14	2
135	Geronimo, AZ	Nikon D850	50mm	f/13	1/160	64	4	1
136	Kadampa Temple	iPhone 12	4.2mm	f/1.6	1/2000	32	n/a	n/a
137	Motel Sign	Nikon D810	85mm	f/9	1/500	100	10	1
138	Indian Center	Nikon D850	50mm	f/14	1/160	64	9	1
139	Twin Arrows	Nikon D810	35mm	f/8	1/400	64	5	1
140	Trading Post	Sony A7R3	28mm	f/11	1/160	200	n/a	n/a
141	Single Arrow	Canon 5D	100mm	f/8	1/2000	400	n/a	n/a
142	Route 66, Winslow	Sony A7R2	16mm	f/8	1/250	100	n/a	n/a
143	. . . on the Corner	Sony A7R2	20mm	f/11	1/60	160	n/a	n/a
144	Earl's Motor Court	Nikon D850	50mm	f/14	1/160	64	16	2
145	Giant Jackrabbit	iPhone 12	4.2mm	f/1.6	1/8400	50	n/a	n/a
146	Jackrabbit Sign	Sony A7R3	40mm	f/13	1/60	200	n/a	n/a
147	Wigwam at Night	Sony A7R3	35mm	f/16	4"	100	n/a	n/a
148	Holbrook Inn	Sony A7R3	35mm	f/11	1/200	400	n/a	n/a
149	Wigwam Motel	Nikon D850	50mm	f/9	1/400	64	10	1
150	Motel 66	iPhone 12	4.2mm	f/1.6	1/30	640	n/a	n/a
151	Blue Mesa Trail	Nikon D850	50mm	f/14	1/60	64	26	2
152	Top of the Trail	Nikon D850	50mm	f/14	1/100	64	13	1
153	The Tepees	Nikon D850	50mm	f/11	1/125	64	12	1
154	Tepees BW	Nikon D850	50mm	f/11	1/125	64	12	1
155	Painted Desert	Nikon D850	50mm	f/9.0	1/160	64	28	2
156	Whiting Brothers	Nikon D750	85mm	f/11	1/140	100	20	2
157	W.B. Motel Sign	Nikon D850	135mm	f/5.0	1/500	64	n/a	n/a
158	Whiting Bros. Station	Nikon D850	85mm	f/11	1/125	64	16	2
159	W.B. Sign	Sony A7R4	24mm	f/8	1/800	160	n/a	n/a
160	Whiting Bros. Sign	Sony A7R2	29mm	f/8	1/800	160	n/a	n/a
161	Back of the Sign	Sony A7R2	34mm	f/8	1/320	160	n/a	n/a
162	Blue Source Sign	iPhone 12	4.2mm	f/1.6	1/8400	32	n/a	n/a
163	Route 66 Diner	Nikon D850	50mm	f/6.3	1/500	64	n/a	n/a
164	Hotel El Rancho	iPhone 12	4.2mm	f/1.6	1/1400	32	n/a	n/a
165	El Rancho Sign	iPhone 12	4.2mm	f/1.6	1/2500	32	n/a	n/a
166	Indian Market	Nikon D750	50mm	f/11	1/200	100	8	1
167	Allen's Garage	Nikon D850	50mm	f/10	1/250	64	8	1
168	3 Horses	Nikon D500	320mm	f/9.0	1/3200	1000	n/a	n/a
169	St. Joseph's Church	Nikon D850	50mm	f/11	1/250	64	9	1
170	Paths 01 Mural	Sony A7R2	28mm	f/20	1/15	100	n/a	n/a
171	El Don Motel Sign	Nikon D850	50mm	f/5.6	1/1000	64	n/a	n/a
172	Route 66 Sign	Nikon D850	135mm	f/10	1/60	64	n/a	n/a
173	Dog House	Sony A7R2	55mm	f/8	1/640	160	n/a	n/a
174	Lindy's Diner	Nikon D850	24mm	f/8	1/320	100	n/a	n/a
175	Zia Motor Lodge	Sony A7R2	34mm	f/8	1/640	160	n/a	n/a
176	Garcia's Kitchen	Nikon D850	50mm	f/5.6	1/500	64	2	1
177	Tewa Lodge Sign	iPhone 12	4.2mm	f/1.6	1/5800	32	n/a	n/a
178	Paul Bunyon	iPhone 12	4.2mm	f/1.6	1/3200	32	n/a	n/a
179	Westward Ho Motel	Nikon D850	85mm	f/10	1/100	64	n/a	n/a
180	Kimo Theater	Sony A7R2	55mm	f/20	1/50	100	n/a	n/a
181	Kimo Windows	Sony A7R4	70mm	f/16	1/100	80	n/a	n/a
182	DeAnza Motor Lodge	Sony A7R2	28mm	f/20	1/81	100	n/a	n/a
183	Tinkertown Wedding	Canon 5D	100mm	f/4.5	1.6"	100	n/a	n/a
184	Tinkertown Barker	Sony A7R2	85mm	f/9.0	2.5"	100	n/a	n/a
185	Tinkertown Clowns	Sony A7R2	85mm	f/20	6"	100	n/a	n/a
186	Tinkertown Gypsy	Sony A7R3	24mm	f/5.6	1/100	1000	n/a	n/a
187	Tinkertown Bottles	Nikon D7100	55mm	f/13	1/15	125	n/a	n/a
188	Tinkertown Drum	Nikon D850	62mm	f/11	2"	100	n/a	n/a
189	Tinkertown Cowboy	Canon 5D	100mm	f/4.0	2"	100	n/a	n/a
190	Tinkertown Tickets	Sony A7R2	85mm	f/20	6"	100	n/a	n/a
191	Tinkertown Cows	Canon 5D	100mm	f/4.5	2"	100	n/a	n/a
192	Tinkertown Treats	Sony A7R2	85mm	f/8	1"	100	n/a	n/a
193	Tinkertown Circus	Sony A7R2	85mm	f/10	1/6	100	n/a	n/a
194	Tinkertown Pioneer	Sony A7R3	50mm	f/11	1"	100	n/a	n/a
195	Tinkertown Speaker	Nikon D850	55mm	f/8	1/4	100	n/a	n/a
196	Tinkertown Painting	Sony A7R3	34mm	f/11	1/2	100	n/a	n/a
197	Tinkertown Porch	Nikon D7100	24mm	f/11	1.6"	100	n/a	n/a
198	Tinkertown Wagon	Nikon D850	50mm	f/5.6	1/8	100	n/a	n/a
199	Indian Curios	Nikon D850	50mm	f/13	1/125	64	8	1
200	Rt 66 Train Car	iPhone 14	6.9mm	f/1.8	1/5300	80	n/a	n/a
201	Standard Oil Man	Nikon D7100	40mm	f/5.6	1/640	125	n/a	n/a
202	Black Cat	Nikon D850	48mm	f/13	1/3	250	n/a	n/a
203	Fireworks World Int	Nikon D850	50mm	f/13	1/6	64	12	1
204	Fireworks World Ext	Nikon D850	50mm	f/10	1/320	64	3	1
205	Sunset Motel Sign	Nikon D850	85mm	f/1.8	1/640	64	n/a	n/a
206	Comet II Restaurant	Nikon D850	50mm	f/13	1/160	64	11	1
207	Comet Rest at Night	iPhone 12	4.2mm	f/1.6	1/120	1600	phone	pano
208	Jonny at Comet II	iPhone 12	4.2mm	f/1.6	1/60	160	n/a	n/a
209	Comet II Sign	Nikon D850	50mm	f/10	1/250	64	6	1
210	Pie Man	Nikon D7100	26mm	f/5.6	1/13	200	n/a	n/a
211	La Mesa Motel	Nikon D850	45mm	f/88	1/5	200	n/a	n/a
212	La Mesa Motel Sign	Nikon D850	50mm	f/11	1/200	640	n/a	n/a
213	Old Gas Station	Nikon D7100	18mm	f/11	1/320	200	n/a	n/a
214	Closed Restaurant	Nikon D850	50mm	f/9.0	1/160	64	6	1
215	Sun 'n Sand Sign	iPhone 12	4.2mm	f/1.6	1/6900	32	n/a	n/a
216	Rio Pecos Ranch	Nikon D850	50mm	f/7.1	1/250	200	n/a	n/a
217	Blue Lake Park	Nikon D850	35mm	f/11	1/200	64	6	1
218	Blue Hole	Nikon D850	35mm	f/16	1/60	64	18	2
219	Rt 66 Museum Big Boy	Nikon D850	50mm	f/13	3"	64	5	1
220	Route 66 Museum	Nikon D850	135mm	f/16	4"	64	8	1
221	Museum – Used Cars	Canon 5D	15mm	f/8	1/20	100	n/a	n/a
222	The Santa Rosa Kid	Sony A7R3	42mm	f/10	1/15	160	n/a	n/a
223	Chevy Grill	Sony A7R3	24mm	f/11	1/30	640	n/a	n/a
224	1948 Buick	Nikon D850	55mm	f/2.8	1/30	100	n/a	n/a
225	Buick Hood	Nikon D850	24mm	f/10	1/8	100	n/a	n/a

#	Title	Camera	Focal	Aperture	Shutter	ISO		
226	Reflection Design	Sony A7R3	70mm	f/10	1/5	160	n/a	n/a
227	Parking Light	Sony A7R3	42mm	f/11	1/15	640	n/a	n/a
228	Outside Display	Nikon D850	24mm	f/11	1/800	100	n/a	n/a
229	Fender Reflection	Nikon D7100	135mm	f/5.6	1/6	100	n/a	n/a
230	VW Rust	Canon 5D	24mm	f/11	1/5	100	n/a	n/a
231	Mercury Monterey	Nikon D850	45mm	f/14	1/4	160	n/a	n/a
232	Flames	Canon 5D	55mm	f/8	1/15	100	n/a	n/a
233	Buick Century	Canon 5D	35mm	f/10	1/8	100	n/a	n/a
234	Chevrolet 3100	Nikon D7100	28mm	f/8	1/3	100	n/a	n/a
235	St. Rose of Lima	Sony A7R3	30mm	f/13	1/60	125	n/a	n/a
236	St. Rose of Lima Door	Nikon D850	50mm	f/11	1/160	64	n/a	n/a
237	St. Rose of Lima Grave	Sony A7R3	70mm	f/11	1/1000	320	n/a	n/a
238	Puerto de Luna Church	Nikon D850	50mm	f/11	1/200	64	21	3
239	Cuervo House	Nikon D850	85mm	f/13	1/50	64	6	1
240	Cuervo Church	Sony A7R3	35mm	f/22	1/125	250	n/a	n/a
241	Cuervo House 2	Sony A7R3	35mm	f/11	1/125	100	n/a	n/a
242	Cuervo Car	Sony A7R3	35mm	f/10	1/125	320	n/a	n/a
243	Blue Swallow Motel	Nikon D810	35mm	f/11	1/4	100	6	1
244	Courtyard	Nikon D810	35mm	f/11	1/4	100	6	1
245	Porch	Canon 7D	45mm	f/11	1/200	100	n/a	n/a
246	Motel Rooms	Sony A7R4	28mm	f/14	1/2	100	n/a	n/a
247	Neon Sign	Sony A7R4	85mm	f/7.1	1/30	100	n/a	n/a
248	Tepee Curios	Nikon D810	35mm	f/11	1/2	100	8	1
249	Tepee Sign	Canon 5D	20mm	f/11	1/8	100	n/a	n/a
250	Texaco Station	Canon 5D	28mm	f/11	1/140	100	n/a	n/a
251	Garage Wall	Canon 7D	31mm	f/11	1/50	200	n/a	n/a
252	Garage	Canon 7D	18mm	f/11	1/60	640	n/a	n/a
253	Esso Station	Nikon D810	35mm	f/11	1/320	100	7	1
254	Polly Gas	Nikon D810	85mm	f/11	1/400	100	8	1
255	Texaco Towing	Canon 7D	28mm	f/5.6	1/2500	200	n/a	n/a
256	Tow Truck	Nikon D700	35mm	f/11	1/160	200	7	1
257	Hood Ornament	Canon 5D	155mm	f/8	1/250	100	n/a	n/a
258	Odeon Theater	Nikon D810	35mm	f/11	1/400	100	7	1
259	Motel Safari	Nikon D750	50mm	f/10	2"	100	12	2
260	Paradise Sign	Canon 5D	105mm	f/11	1/250	100	n/a	n/a
261	Paradise Motel	Nikon D850	135mm	f/11	1/200	100	22	2
262	La Cita 2022	Nikon D850	50mm	f/11	1/80	64	9	1
263	La Cita 2016	Sony A7R3	20mm	f/11	1/60	160	n/a	n/a
264	Deli	Nikon D810	35mm	f/11	1/800	100	12	2
265	Del's Sign	Canon 5D	26mm	f/11	1/160	100	n/a	n/a
266	Ranch House	Sony A7R3	30mm	f/16	1/160	100	n/a	n/a
267	Paradise Cafe	Nikon D810	85mm	f/11	1/100	100	12	1
268	American Badger	Nikon D500	500mm	f/7.1	1/1000	220	n/a	n/a
269	Desert Cottontail	Nikon D500	370mm	f/7.1	1/1600	1100	n/a	n/a
270	Ute Lake Grasses	Nikon D810	35mm	f/11	1/100	100	8	1
271	Mountain Bluebird	Nikon D500	500mm	f/8	1/2000	320	n/a	n/a
272	Sunset, Ute Lake	Nikon D810	35mm	f/11	1/20	100	7	1
273	Bob 4 at Midpoint	Nikon D850	85mm	F139	1/160	64	8	1
274	Bent Door Station	Nikon D850	85mm	f/13	1/30	64	9	1
275	GMC Truck	Nikon D810	85mm	f/13	1/150	100	7	1
276	Rooster's, Vega	Nikon D850	85mm	f/11	1/160	64	8	1
277	Big Texan	Nikon D850	50mm	f/11	1/200	64	6	1
278	Slug Bug and Wall	iPhone 12	4.2mm	f/1.6	1/2800	32	n/a	n/a
279	Cadillac Ranch 2	Nikon D810	35mm	f/10	1/250	100	5	1
280	Slug Bug Window	iPhone 12	4.2mm	f/1.6	1/950	32	n/a	n/a
281	Slug Bug Kids	Nikon D850	50mm	f/13	1/125	64	5	1
282	Cowboy	Sony A7R3	24mm	f/14	1/160	200	n/a	n/a
283	6th and Virginia	Nikon D850	50mm	f/10	1/200	64	6	1
284	6th Street Massacre	Nikon D850	50mm	f/14	1/50	64	7	1
285	Hide and Seek Ext	Nikon D850	50mm	f/13	1/15	64	5	1
286	Hide and Seek Int	Nikon D850	50mm	f/13	1.6"	64	3	1
287	Pork and Torque	Nikon D850	50mm	f/13	1/160	64	6	1
288	Dmngo Arte	Nikon D850	50mm	f/11	1/50	64	6	1
289	Dmngo Unmasked	Nikon D850	50mm	f/11	1/50	64	6	1
290	Britten USA	Nikon D850	85mm	f/10	1/200	64	9	1
291	Grain Storage	Nikon D850	85mm	f/11	1/100	64	5	1
292	Robinson Grain Co	Nikon D850	50mm	f/13	1/160	64	14	2
293	Groom News	Nikon D850	85mm	f/10	1/200	64	6	1
294	1st Phillips 66 in Texas	Nikon D850	50mm	f/10	1/125	64	5	1
295	Horse and Colt	Nikon D500	340mm	f/9.0	1/3200	7200	n/a	n/a
296	U Drop Inn	Nikon D850	50mm	f/13	1/250	64	22	2
297	U Drop and Moon	Nikon D850	50mm	f/16	1/2	64	10	2
298	U Drop at Night	Nikon D850	35mm	f/13	1/3	64	15	3
299	Shamrock Mural	Nikon D850	50mm	f/8	1/80	64	10	1
300	Magnolia Gas Station	Nikon D850	85mm	f/11	1/150	64	7	1
301	Tower Plaza Mural	Nikon D850	85mm	f/10	1/60	64	9	1
302	Tye Thompson	Nikon D500	135mm	f/2.2	1/400	100	n/a	n/a
303	Tye's Last	iPhone 12	4.2mm	f/1.6	1/950	32	n/a	n/a
304	Artist Village	Nikon D850	85mm	f/11	1/50	64	8	1
305	Dumpster Art	iPhone 12	4.2mm	f/2.4	1/950	32	n/a	n/a
306	Tye's House	iPhone 12	4.2mm	f/1.6	1/1000	32	n/a	n/a
307	Meals on Wheels	iPhone 12	4.2mm	f/1.6	1/1500	32	n/a	n/a
308	Water Bottling Co	Nikon D850	85mm	f/11	1/15	64	7	1
309	City Meat Market	Nikon D850	50mm	f/11	1/400	64	18	2
310	Harley	Nikon D850	35mm	f/11	3"	64	18	2
311	Roger Miller Mural	Nikon D850	85mm	f/11	1/30	64	9	1
312	West Winds Motel	Nikon D850	85mm	f/10	1/100	64	7	1
313	66 Lounge Mural	iPhone 12	1.6mm	f/2.4	1/1000	25	n/a	n/a
314	Western Motel Sign	iPhone 12	4.2mm	f/1.6	1/6400	32	n/a	n/a
315	Mother and Calf	Nikon D500	500mm	f/7.1	1/4000	9000	n/a	n/a
316	Old Gas Station	Nikon D850	35mm	f/9.0	1/1250	64	7	1
317	Granary, Sayre	Nikon D850	85mm	f/13	1/250	64	6	1
318	National Rt 66 Museum	Nikon D810	85mm	f/13	1/250	100	18	2
319	Old Town Museum	Nikon D810	85mm	f/11	1/500	100	6	2
320	Dudley	iPhone 12	1.6mm	f/2.4	1/700	25	n/a	n/a
321	Big Rt 66 Sign	Nikon D850	35mm	f/5.6	1/1000	64	n/a	n/a
322	Big Rt 66 Sign 2	Nikon D850	35mm	f/5.6	1/1000	64	n/a	n/a
323	Bison	Nikon D500	450mm	f/6.3	1/3200	2500	n/a	n/a
324	Tree at Clinton Lake	Nikon D850	50mm	f/10	1/100	64	7	1
325	Bison Calf	Nikon D500	500mm	f/8	1/1600	900	n/a	n/a
326	Red-Winged Blackbird	Nikon D500	500mm	f/8	1/3200	2800	n/a	n/a
327	Long Horned Cattle	Nikon D500	260mm	f/8	1/2000	2800	n/a	n/a
328	Ibis	Nikon D500	500mm	f/7.1	1/1600	560	n/a	n/a
329	Clinton Mural	Nikon D850	85mm	f/10	1/20	64	7	1
330	Belter's Auto Salvage	Nikon D810	85mm	f/11	1/320	100	18	2
331	The Clancy Hotel	iPhone 12	1.6mm	f/2.4	1/1200	50	n/a	n/a
332	McLain Rogers Park	Nikon D850	50mm	f/13	1/80	64	9	1
333	Rt 66 Museum Clinton	iPhone 12	4.2mm	f/1.6	1/3600	32	phone	pano
334	Cherokee Trading Post	iPhone 12	4.2mm	f/2.4	1/2400	24	phone	pano
335	312 Lucille's Gas Station	Nikon D850	50mm	f/13	1/60	64	8	2
336	Canadian River Bridge	Nikon D850	50mm	f/13	1/60	64	11	1
337	John Cerney Murals (3)	iPhone 12	4.2mm	f/1.6	1/1600	32	n/a	n/a
338	Historical El Reno	Nikon D850	85mm	f/10	1/20	64	10	1
339	Squawk-N-Skoot	Nikon D850	85mm	f/10	1/25	64	7	1

#	Name	Camera	Focal	Aperture	Shutter	ISO		
340	El Reno Bowl	Nikon D850	50mm	f/13	1/80	64	10	1
341	Edward at Roberts	iPhone 12	4.2mm	f/1.6	1/60	64	n/a	n/a
342	Yukon's Best Flour	Nikon D850	50mm	f/10	1/320	64	12	2
343	Summer of 66 Mural	Nikon D850	85mm	f/11	1/50	64	14	1
344	Bridge over Overholser	Nikon D850	50mm	f/11	1/100	64	12	2
345	Tom's Barbershop	Nikon D850	50mm	f/13	1/80	64	20	2
346	The Round Barn	Nikon D850	50mm	f/11	1/125	64	8	1
347a	Pops on 66 Day	Nikon D850	35mm	f/11	1/250	100	n/a	n/a
347b	Pops on 66 Night	Nikon D850	35mm	f/11	3"	100	n/a	n/a
348	Barf!	iPhone SE	4.0mm	f/1.8	1/60	100	n/a	n/a
349	Pop's iPhone Pano	iPhone 12	4.2mm	f/1.6	1/1600	32	phone	pano
350	Welcome to Luther	Nikon D850	85mm	f/11	1/160	64	6	1
351	Seaba Station	Nikon D850	50mm	f/11	1/125	64	4	1
352	Lincoln County Mural 1	Nikon D850	50mm	f/10	1/20	64	5	1
353	Lincoln County Mural 2	Nikon D850	50mm	f/10	1/20	64	4	1
354	1930 Philips 66 Station	Nikon D850	85mm	f/8	1/500	64	9	3
355	Lincoln Motel Sign	iPhone 12	1.6mm	f/1.6	1/100	1600	n/a	n/a
356	Lincoln Motel Rooms	Nikon D850	50mm	f/9.0	1/160	64	6	1
357	Parking Lot Signs	Sony A7R3	24mm	f/16	1/160	200	n/a	n/a
358	101 Foot Bowling Lane	Nikon D850	50mm	f/13	1.6"	64	24	2
359	Trucks near Stroud	Nikon D850	50mm	f/11	1/200	64	11	1
360	Mural, Bristow	Nikon D850	50mm	f/11	1/160	64	8	1
361	Boomarang Cafe	iPhone SE	4.0mm	f/1.8	1/60	64	n/a	n/a
362	Mural in Progress	iPhone 12	4.2mm	f/1.6	1/640	32	n/a	n/a
363	Rock Creek Bridge	Nikon D850	24mm	f/11	1/60	80	n/a	n/a
364	Bridge Memorial	Nikon D850	50mm	f/11	1/100	64	5	1
365	Mike Jones	Nikon D850	50mm	f/8	1/13	64	3	1
366	Restroom	Nikon D850	50mm	f/11	1.6"	64	36	4
367	Gulf Station	Nikon D850	50mm	f/11	1/200	64	6	1
368	Barnsdall Station	Nikon D850	50mm	f/13	1/100	64	14	2
369	Auto Museum	Nikon D850	50mm	f/11	1/125	64	7	1
370	Oasis Motel Tulsa	iPhone 12	4.2mm	f/2.4	1/2400	32	n/a	n/a
371	Historical Village	Nikon D850	50mm	f/13	1/80	64	18	2
372	Desert Hills Motel	Nikon D850	50mm	f/13	1/160	64	8	1
373	Rancho Grande	Nikon D850	50mm	f/11	1/40	64	4	1
374	Buck Atoms	Nikon D850	50mm	f/11	1/250	64	10	1
375	Spirit Ranch	Nikon D850	50mm	f/13	1/100	64	5	1
376	Golden Driller	Nikon D850	50mm	f/10	1/40	64	2	1
377	Blue Whale	Nikon D850	35mm	f/11	1/160	64	10	1
378	Blue Whale Sign	Sony A7R3	100mm	f/8	1/250	100	n/a	n/a
379	Another Angle	Nikon D850	50mm	f/10	1/250	64	6	1
380	Smile!	Nikon D850	58mm	f/11	1/30	80	n/a	n/a
381	Chelsea Mural	Sony A7R3	28mm	f/13	1/60	100	n/a	n/a
382	Chelsea Motel	Nikon D850	50mm	f/10	1/160	64	7	1
383	Totem Village	Nikon D850	29mm	f/11	1/800	500	n/a	n/a
384	Mural, Venita	Nikon D850	50mm	f/11	1/125	64	5	1
385	Big Bill	iPhone 12	4.2mm	f/1.6	1/3900	32	n/a	n/a
386	Chief	iPhone 12	4.2mm	f/2.4	1/2200	32	n/a	n/a
387	Avon Motel	Nikon D850	50mm	f/10	1/250	64	4	1
388	Cross Star Museum, Al	Nikon D850	50mm	f/10	1/160	64	8	1
389	Cross Star Museum	Nikon D850	50mm	f/13	1/100	64	16	2
390	Al Charlie, some clown	Nikon D850	50mm	f/8	1/40	800	n/a	n/a
391	Gateway, Miami	Nikon D850	50mm	f/11	1/160	64	8	1
392	Conoco Station	Nikon D850	85mm	f/10	1/180	64	7	1
393	Cookies Backlit	Sony A7R3	20mm	f/13	1/500	100	n/a	n/a
394	Cats at Cookies	Nikon D850	48mm	f/14	1/6	100	n/a	n/a
395	Monarch Pharmacy	Nikon D850	85mm	f/11	1/160	100	n/a	n/a
396	Bricks & Brew	Nikon D850	70mm	f/11	1/160	100	n/a	n/a
397	Rainbow Bridge	Nikon D850	50mm	f/10	1/400	64	8	1
398	Bridge in Fall	Sony A7R3	28mm	f/13	1/360	100	n/a	n/a
399	Bridge in Spring	Nikon D850	50mm	f/11	1/160	64	16	2
400	Gearhead Curios	Nikon D850	50mm	f/11	1/250	64	6	1
401	Gearhead Restroom	Nikon D850	50mm	f/14	2.5"	64	24	3
402	Main Street	Nikon D850	85mm	f/11	1/200	64	6	1
403	Sunset Motel	Nikon D600	35mm	f/11	1/50	100	9	1
404	Trip Notes	iPhone 12	4.2mm	f/1.6	1/120	125	n/a	n/a
405	Welcome to Joplin	Nikon D850	50mm	f/10	1/250	64	7	1
406	Boots Motor Court	Nikon D850	50mm	f/13	1/160	64	7	1
407	66 Drive-In	Nikon D850	50mm	f/13	1/125	64	7	1
408	Spencer Missouri	Nikon D810	50mm	f/11	1/320	64	7	1
409	Spencer Bridge	Nikon D850	50mm	f/13	1/125	64	6	1
410	Spencer Shop	Nikon D850	70mm	f/10	1/250	320	n/a	n/a
411	Gay Parita	Nikon D850	42mm	f/8	1/2500	200	n/a	n/a
412	Oil Cans	Sony 7RM4	33mm	f/2.8	1/125	640	n/a	n/a
413	License Plates	Sony 7RM4	37mm	f/4.5	1/200	125	n/a	n/a
414	Gary	Sony 7RM4	33mm	f/13	1/250	64	n/a	n/a
415	Plano Ghost Town	Nikon D850	50mm	f/13	1/100	64	21	3
416	Windows	Canon R5	24mm	f/11	1/30	100	n/a	n/a
417	Archway	Sony 7RM4	43mm	f/11	1/6	100	n/a	n/a
418	Rockwood Afternoon	Nikon D850	50mm	f/11	1/250	64	6	1
419	Rockwood at Night	Nikon D850	50mm	f/13	4"	64	7	1
420	The Movie Room	iPhone 14	6mm	f/1.8	1/120	1200	phone	pano
421	Lulu, the Rockwood	Sony 7RM4	32mm	f/9.5	4"	100	n/a	n/a
422	Bunny	Nikon D500	500mm	f/7.1	1/3200	100	n/a	n/a
423	Chef, Springfield	iPhone 12	4.2mm	f/1.6	1/1200	800	n/a	n/a
424	Don's Old Cars	Nikon D850	50mm	f/11	1/80	64	6	1
425	Cheech and Chong	Canon 5D	28mm	f/8	1/320	500	n/a	n/a
426	We Can Do It	Nikon D850	50mm	f/11	1/15	64	14	2
427	Bud's and Bob	Nikon D850	50mm	f/11	1/200	64	10	1
428	Munger Moss Day	Nikon D850	50mm	f/10	1/125	64	4	1
429	Lebanon Library	Nikon D850	50mm	f/13	1/250	64	8	1
430	Munger Moss Night	Nikon D850	50mm	f/11	1/6	64	12	2
431	BowlMor Lanes	Nikon D850	50mm	f/13	1/125	64	9	1
432	Devil's Elbow Color	Nikon D850	50mm	f/14	1/100	64	7	1
433	Devil's Elbow BW	Nikon D850	50mm	f/14	1/100	64	7	1
434	Gold Star Boys	Nikon D850	50mm	f/11	1/100	64	8	1
435	Garage Mural	Nikon D850	50mm	f/10	1/160	64	7	1
436	Bette Davis	Nikon D850	50mm	f/11	1/160	64	7	1
437	Greetings From Cuba	Sony 7RM4	24mm	f/13	1/200	200	n/a	n/a
438	Gold Star Boys 1	Canon 5D	88mm	f/11	1/80	400	n/a	n/a
439	Meeting in Missouri	Sony 7RM4	67mm	f/13	1/200	200	n/a	n/a
440	Battle of the Huzzah	Nikon D850	50mm	f/8	1/25	64	n/a	n/a
441	Confederates in Cuba	Canon 5D	73mm	f/8	1/320	400	n/a	n/a
442	Day at Cooperage 1	Canon R5	35mm	f/8	1/40	100	n/a	n/a
443	Day at Cooperage 2	Nikon D850	48mm	f/8	1/100	100	n/a	n/a
444	Gold Star Boys 2	Nikon D850	62mm	f/6.3	1/320	100	n/a	n/a
445	Rescue at Leasburg	Nikon D850	52mm	f/8	1/200	100	n/a	n/a
446	Prosperity Corner	Nikon D850	24mm	f/8	1/125	100	n/a	n/a
447	Battle of Pilot Knob	Nikon D850	62mm	f/8	1/200	100	n/a	n/a
448	Shelly's 66 Interior	Nikon D850	50mm	f/13	1/8	64	8	1
449	Shelly's 66 Exterior	Nikon D850	50mm	f/13	1/160	64	6	1
450	Wagon Wheel Motel	Nikon D850	50mm	f/13	1/50	64	9	1
451	Weir on 66	Nikon D850	50mm	f/13	1/80	64	5	1
452	Patrick Weir	Nikon D850	50mm	f/11	1/6	64	4	1
453	Home of the Leroy	Nikon D850	50mm	f/11	1/200	64	6	1
454	Police Station	Nikon D850	50mm	f/11	1/15	64	6	1

#	Title	Camera	Focal	Aperture	Shutter	ISO		
455	Ostrich	Nikon D500	500mm	f/5.6	1/2500	4500	n/a	n/a
456	Lion	Nikon D500	440mm	f/5.6	1/2500	2000	n/a	n/a
457	Tiger	Nikon D500	495mm	f/7.1	1/2500	14400	n/a	n/a
458	Feeding the Deer	Nikon D500	300mm	f/5.6	1/3200	10000	n/a	n/a
459	Meramec Cavern	Nikon D700	82mm	f/13	1.3"	200	n/a	n/a
460	Electric Trading Co	Nikon D850	50mm	f./9.0	1/160	64	5	1
461	Stovall's Grove, 1935	Nikon D850	85mm	f/11	1/30	64	7	1
462	Bassett Road	Nikon D850	85mm	f/13	1/160	64	6	1
463	Saint Louis Arch	Nikon D700	18mm	f/16	1/8	100	n/a	n/a
464	Fredbird	iPhone 12	4.2mm	f/1.6	1/1900	32	n/a	n/a
465	Indian Prairie Rd	Nikon D850	85mm	f/10	1/250	64	16	2
466	Villa Ridge	Nikon D850	85mm	f/11	1/60	64	22	2
467	Barn near Bourbon	Nikon D850	85mm	f/10	1/20	64	8	1
468	Meramec Barns	Nikon D850	85mm	f/11	1/160	64	8	1
469	Soulsby's Station	Nikon D850	50mm	f/11	1/180	64	5	1
470	Old 66 Cafe	Nikon D850	50mm	f/11	1/125	64	6	1
471	Betsy Ross Flag Barn	Nikon D850	50mm	f/13	1/25	64	5	1
472	Town Square, Girard	Nikon D850	50mm	f/11	1/40	64	7	1
473	DOCS	Sony 7RM4	70mm	f/9.5	1/90	100	n/a	n/a
474	Chay	iPhone 12	1.6mm	f/2.4	1/125	25	n/a	n/a
475	Low Angle	Sony 7RM4	24mm	f/5.6	1/250	100	n/a	n/a
476	Sugar Creek Covered Bridge	Nikon D850	50mm	f/10	1/50	64	8	1
477	Couple from Denver	Canon 5D	73mm	f/13	1/13	100	n/a	n/a
478	Bridge from Field	Nikon D850	85mm	f/11	1/30	64	7	1
479	Brick Route 66	iPhone 14	2.2mm	f/1.6	1/25	1000	n/a	n/a
480	Motorheads, Museum	Nikon D850	50mm	f/11	1/100	64	8	1
481	Rusted Door	Canon 5D	85mm	f/14	1/25	100	n/a	n/a
482	Mobil Sign	Canon R5	35mm	f/11	1/60	100	n/a	n/a
483	Motorheads 66 Sign	iPhone 12	1.6mm	f/2.4	1/2000	25	n/a	n/a
484	Triumph	Sony 4RM4	24mm	f/11	1/90	100	n/a	n/a
485	Eye Candy	Canon 5D	73mm	f/11	1/6	100	n/a	n/a
486	Cozy Dog	iPhone 14	2.2mm	f/1.6	1/25	1000	n/a	n/a
487	Drive-In	Nikon D850	50mm	f/10	1/160	64	5	1
488	Drive-In Sign	iPhone 13	4.2mm	f/2.2	1/2000	35	n/a	n/a
489	Cozy Dogs	iPhone 14	2.2mm	f/2.2	1/120	50	n/a	n/a
490	Cozy Dog Interior	Nikon D850	50mm	f/13	1/2	64	24	2
491	Jackson's Handlebar	Nikon D850	50mm	f/11	1/8	64	5	1
492	Shea's Station	Nikon D850	50mm	f/11	1/40	64	8	2
493	The Old Station	Nikon D850	50mm	f/13	1/200	64	5	1
494	Penny Mural	Nikon D850	85mm	f/9.0	1/30	64	4	1
495	Windows and Doors	Nikon D850	85mm	f/13	1/100	64	14	2
496	Box Fan	Nikon D850	85mm	f/9.0	1/200	64	5	1
497	Windows	Canon 5D	84mm	f/8	1/250	100	n/a	n/a
498	Shoes	Canon R5	42mm	f/8	1/160	400	n/a	n/a
499	Downtown Lincoln	Nikon D850	85mm	f/10	1/80	64	5	1
500	The Mill	Nikon D850	50mm	f/13	1/200	64	5	1
501	Other Side of Tracks	Nikon D850	85mm	f/13	1/80	64	5	1
502	Giants Museum	Nikon D850	50mm	f/13	1/250	64	9	1
503	Darlene	iPhone 12	4.2mm	f/1.6	1/120	50	n/a	n/a
504	Exon Tiger	Nikon D850	70mm	f/11	1/4	100	n/a	n/a
505	Leg	Canon R5	28mm	f/13	1/20	640	n/a	n/a
506	Snerd	Nikon D850	50mm	f/13	1/160	64	3	1
507	Smiley Face	iPhone 12	4.2mm	f/2.2	1/800	35	n/a	n/a
508	Tall Paul and Harley	Sony 7RM4	50mm	f/11	1/45	100	n/a	n/a
509	Tall Paul, Atlanta	Nikon D850	50mm	f/11	1/200	64	14	2
510	McKown & Hawes	Canon 5D	80mm	f/11	1/160	100	n/a	n/a
511	Judy & Sons Grocers	Nikon D850	50mm	f/11	1/60	64	5	1
512	McLean, Illinois	Nikon D850	50mm	f/11	1/50	64	4	1
513	Farm Near McLean	Nikon D850	50mm	f/11	1/250	64	7	1
514	Storm Reflection	Nikon D850	135mm	f/16	1/100	64	7	1
515	Pontiac Courthouse	iPhone 12	4.2mm	f/1.6	1/1150	32	n/a	n/a
516	The Master's Voice	Sony 7RM4	48mm	f/13	1/30	100	n/a	n/a
517	DeLong's, Pontiac	Nikon D850	38mm	f/11	1/30	100	n/a	n/a
518	Fire	Canon R5	43mm	f/11	1/30	100	n/a	n/a
519	Rodino Square	Sony 7RM4	24mm	f/11	1/125	100	n/a	n/a
520	Allen Candy	Nikon D850	62mm	f/11	1/20	100	n/a	n/a
521	Wishing Well Sign	Canon 5D	105mm	f/11	1/40	100	n/a	n/a
522	Waldmire Memorial	Nikon D850	50mm	f/11	1/25	64	10	1
523	Daniel's Oil Mural	Nikon D850	50mm	f/11	1/20	64	8	1
524	Wishing Well Motel	Nikon D850	50mm	f/13	1/200	64	6	1
525	Drink Coca-Cola	Nikon D850	50mm	f/11	1/20	64	12	2
526	Daniels	Sony 7RM4	34mm	f/6.7	1/125	100	n/a	n/a
527	Mechanic	Nikon D850	62mm	f/11	1/50	100	n/a	n/a
528	Pilot	Nikon D850	36mm	f/11	1/15	100	n/a	n/a
529	Attendant	Nikon D850	70mm	f/11	1/15	100	n/a	n/a
530	Meramec Barn	Nikon D850	50mm	f/13	1/125	64	8	1
531	Standard Oil	Nikon D850	50mm	f/11	1/125	64	22	2
532	Billboard, Dwight	Nikon D850	50mm	f/9.0	1/250	64	5	1
533	The Shop	Nikon D850	54mm	f/11	1/100	64	18	2
534	The Shop Interior	Nikon D850	50mm	f/13	1/2	64	5	1
535	M&M Guys	Nikon D850	50mm	f/11	1/3	64	21	3
536	Coke Bottles	Canon 5D	82mm	f/11	1/2	100	n/a	n/a
537	Polk-A-Dot Drive In	Nikon D850	50mm	f/8	1/80	64	5	1
538	Betty Boop	Sony 7RM4	67mm	f/6.7	1/200	125	n/a	n/a
539	The Blues Brothers	Nikon D850	32mm	f/13	1/80	160	n/a	n/a
540	Welcome to Downtown	Sony 7RM4	69mm	f/11	1/125	125	n/a	n/a
541	Lionmark, Water St.	Nikon D850	85mm	f/10	1/80	64	6	1
542	124 Water Street	Nikon D850	85mm	f/11	1/80	64	8	2
543	Rick's Relics	Nikon D850	85mm	f/16	1.3"	64	7	1
544	Parking, Wilmington	Canon 5D	32mm	f/11	1/125	100	n/a	n/a
545	Mural, Wilmington	Nikon D850	50mm	f/8	1/60	64	4	1
546	Gemini Giant	Nikon D850	50mm	f/13	1/60	64	4	1
547	Dicks on 66	Sony 7RM2	16mm	f/11	1/800	100	n/a	n/a
548	The Blues Brothers	Sony A7R2	135mm	f/7.1	1/800	100	n/a	n/a
549	Eastern Terminus	Sony A7R2	35mm	f/8	1/200	100	n/a	n/a
550	Finished Map on Bob	Nikon D850	50mm	f/11	1/250	64	7	1